D0432257

THE SMITHSONIAN
150 YEARS OF ADVENTURE, DISCOVERY, AND WONDER

JAMES CONAWAY

SMITHSONIAN BOOKS Washington, D.C.

ALFRED A. KNOPF New York

1995

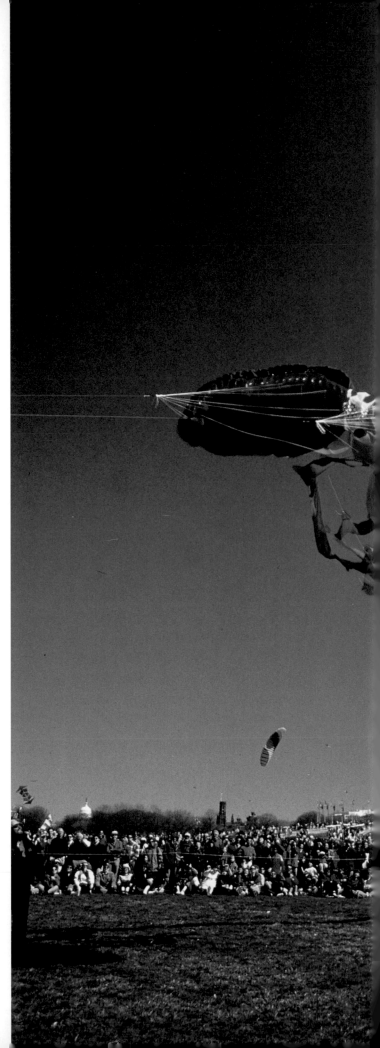

THIS IS A BORZOI BOOK
PUBLISHED BY ALFRED A. KNOPF, INC.

ALSO PUBLISHED BY SMITHSONIAN BOOKS

©1995 Smithsonian Institution

Library of Congress Cataloging-in-Publication Data

Conaway, James.
The Smithsonian : 150 years of adventure, discovery, and wonder / by James Conaway.
--1st ed.
p.   cm.
Includes index.
ISBN 0-679-44175-1 (hardcover)
1. Smithsonian Institution--History.   I. Title.
O11.S8C66   1995
069'.09753--dc20   95-17667   CIP

Manufactured in the United States of America

First Editon

02   01   00   99   98   97   96   95

5   4   3   2   1

Editor's note: To include some of the Smithsonian's people—for they are among the great treasures of the Institution—the Editors have included special staff-written "side-bars," distinguished by a tint. In addition, the author has included "Profiles" of specially noteworthy Smithsonian people or undertakings at the end of each chapter.

Illustrations pages 1-9: From the Smithsonian: (page 1) an *Allosaurus* skull found in 1858 in Canyon City, Colorado; (page 2) a Panamanian glass frog, Smithsonian Tropical Research Institute; (page 3) a sculpture of Aizen Myo-o (Ragaraja), a Japanese Buddhist deity, dated 1293; (page 4) a cross section of a nautilus shell; (page 5) *Eye of a Lady*, by an unidentified artist, circa 1800; (right) an entry in the 1993 Smithsonian kite festival; (opposite) a Pony Express commemorative stamp; (page 8) an 1858 sewing-machine patent model designed by David W. Clark, of Bridgeport, Connecticut; and (page 9) the spacesuit worn by astronaut David R. Scott, commander of the July 1971 Apollo 15 lunar mission.

CONTENTS

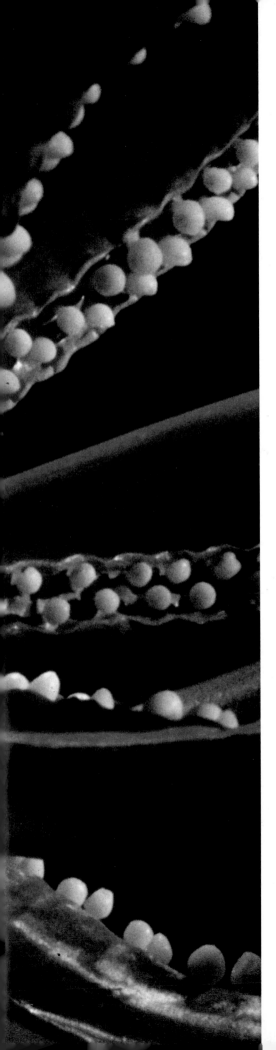

INTRODUCTION

Whether they arrive by air or by road, few visitors to Washington, D.C., can long avoid the expanse of green that extends from the Capitol to the Lincoln Memorial. There is nothing quite like it in any other city; it dwarfs the Champs Élysées, and surpasses the monumental intent of Roman architects not in size alone, but in the majesty of open space and the character of the buildings sharing it.

Some are heroic, others fanciful, a few even discreet. All contain some aspect of the largest museum complex on Earth, an audacious array of empirical and intellectual endeavors known as the Smithsonian Institution. It is this collective vessel for knowledge and human experience, not Congress, nor the federal agencies, nor even the memorials to former Presidents of the United States, that makes Washington, D.C., unique and of such ongoing historical relevance.

That these museums are free to all is just one of the paradoxes of the Smithsonian's extraordinary, often strange story. It is told here in its entirety for the first time by an admitted partisan, neither a scholar nor a member of the Smithsonian empire but a visitor much like any other. It is a story of immense importance, whoever tells it, as much for the nation as for human inquiry.

National Museum of Natural History cephalopod specialist Clyde Roper helped develop this life-size (35-foot) model of the elusive giant squid (*Architeuthis*), which resides today at the Santa Barbara Museum of Natural History.

I first came to the Mall not as a high-school senior in the spring of adolescence but as an adult with a wife and children of my own, recently moved to Washington, all of us

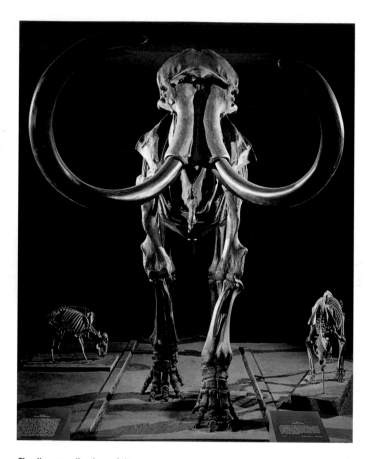

The diverse collections of the Smithsonian range from the National Museum of Natural History's woolly mammoth skeleton to the National Portrait Gallery's portrait of George Washington by Rembrandt Peale to orchids from the National Orchid Collection.

struck by the diversity of the Smithsonian and its apparently limitless ambitions. For close to a year we came back weekly in an attempt to comprehend this challenging and entertaining, if daunting, place.

Wandering one afternoon in the Arts and Industries Building adjacent to the Castle—the airy in the shadow of the outrageous—amid steam engines and stuffed animals, I began to wonder about the impulse behind such a polyglot collection. These remnants of the 1876 Centennial celebration in Philadelphia indicated an earlier, industrial vision of America. Had they come to a Darwinian dead end, museologically speaking, or did they represent some crucial stage in the Smithsonian's long, often cantankerous evolution? It happened to be the latter.

IN THE 19TH CENTURY, THE SCULPTOR HORATIO Greenough wrote of the Smithsonian's "Castle" on the Mall, "the models whence it has been imitated are both 'rich and rare'—the connoisseurs may well 'wonder how the devil it got *there*.'" Not long ago, charged with the task of writing about the history and scope of the Smithsonian for its 150th anniversary, I set out to discover something of these origins myself. The landscape proved to be as complex as it was colorful, the expanding view as broad as the imagination. I learned that the Institution did not amass useless artifacts, but collected objects deemed of inestimable value to the development of the mind and the American consciousness; it was not a government agency, but it did depend upon public funds ($371 million annually would be considered a lot of money anywhere but in Washington).

It had in its possession roughly 140 million objects, a fact with all the apparent practicality of a star count. The four million butterflies and moths, however, seemed a bit more approachable. They were kept on the upper floors of the National Museum of Natural History in inglorious metal cases, the sort that also contained raccoon skulls of every possible variation, fruit bats, dung beetles, and millions more well-preserved tenants, all resonating within the dome of creation. Species now extinct as well as those still developing wait there in taxonomic distinction for instructing and, yes, inspiring future generations.

My inquiries eventually took me far from Washington: 120 feet up a saber tree in a Panamanian rain forest, with my daughter, Susanna, and a young biologist in pursuit of epiphytes; I can still smell salt air blowing across Carrie Bow Cay, in Belize, and see two scientists emerging from the Caribbean in scuba gear; how remarkable the good humor of the physicist in Cambridge, Massachusetts, tracking asteroids that might collide with Earth; how dry the prevarications of the English archivist in the castle in Northumberland, discomforted by my questions about James Smithson's illegitimacy.

At some point, I began to think of the Smithsonian as a university in the purest sense. It might not matriculate students, but it sought to make everything comprehensible. *Whistler's Mother*—and the portrait of the artist's father—shared the Smithsonian firmament with moon rocks, but also with the deductions of an anthropologist attuned to the needs of paleolithic humans, with the recorded habits of the staghorn fern, with the tale told by a Passe Païpaï storyteller on the Mall one fine morning in July.

The Smithsonian may own, among other priceless commodities, the Fort McHenry flag, the Wright brothers' *Flyer*, the First Ladies' gowns, and the world's largest deep-blue diamond. The Smithsonian's collection of flying machines may constitute the world's fourth largest air force. But these are the proverbial tip of an iceberg made up of hundreds of thousands of studies in tandem with thousands of programs in hundreds of far-flung offices and encampments controlled from a mere 18 bureaus of the one, over-arching Smithsonian sun.

People, not objects, determined the Institution's course, and provided the greater interest. The Smithsonian now has 6,500 employees, but it was conceived of in the mind of a single scientist—one stricken with romantic idealism—and nurtured for a century and a half by those more attuned to truth than to the crafts of bureaucracy. It is their stories that prevail.

The Smithsonian's immeasurable resources render it more than a museum, and Washington, D.C., more than a political and touristic destination. The Institution may encompass science, history, art, and technology, but it is imbued with national significance beyond the import of its collections, and—just as importantly—with the power of individual perception.

I BRIGHT LAMPS, BOLD ADVENTURE: 1846–1878

On a muggy September morning in 1846, an unlikely collection of men came together in a vast field on the edge of Washington, District of Columbia. Included were the President, Vice President, and Chief Justice of the United States and other dignitaries, all performing an undignified task: choosing a plot for a structure as yet unplanned in the neighborhood of an open sewer.

The Capitol stood

In John Gast's portrayal of America's westward movement, bison herds and Indians retreat as a radiant Manifest Destiny—stringing telegraph wire in her wake—leads homesteaders and other settlers, wagons and railroads across the Great Plains.

Argillite carvings (circa 1841) of sea captains by the Haida Indians of Queen Charlotte Islands, British Columbia, stand before a model of the *Vincennes*, the flagship for the U.S. Exploring Expedition of 1838–42. The dissemination of new information on whaling and sealing grounds proved a boon to New England's whaling industry, shown here in action in an 1835 sketch by Cornelius B. Hulsart.

out starkly to the east, incongruous above the tattered line of shops and houses extending along the northern edge of what would become the Mall. Washington was still a backwater, a city built where one should not have stood, with a low, watery periphery and narrow, often squalid streets. Envisioning grand architecture in this malodorous commons required imagination.

The plot being sought that September morning was to support an institution to be founded in Washington dedicated to a vague directive—"the increase & diffusion of knowledge"—and the search represented the end of long, rancorous debate in Congress. The President, James Knox Polk, a Democrat and a believer in Manifest Destiny, later wrote in his diary that he had passed "nearly an hour with them on foot in examining the grounds." The outing, however, concluded without any decision's being made.

Polk went back to the White House. As the 11th President, he had other things on his mind, among them a border dispute with Great Britain in Oregon and a war with Mexico, also over territory. The expeditions of John C. Frémont had opened up the land west of the Mississippi River to dreams of acquisition; Polk was in the process of adding more territory to the United States than any

President since Thomas Jefferson, and territorial expansion had acquired an almost religious intensity.

America was still malleable in the fall of 1846, about to enter the Industrial Revolution but predominantly rural, underpopulated (there were fewer than 21 million Americans), and vast. A radical new mode of transportation, the railway train, was compressing time and landscape, but there were only 9,000 miles of track in the United States, and immigrants were streaming west by more conventional means, the covered wagon.

Most Americans had no contact whatsoever with the federal government except through the postal service. Science, the passion of the distant, deceased Englishman who had so mysteriously endowed the institution destined to rise in the Capitol's front yard, was in its infancy, the study of matter and energy not yet even referred to as "physics."

That September morning's activity, the shadowy institution, like the words, "the increase & diffusion of knowledge," may have seemed abstract to Polk, unrelated to the young country's character and its prospects. But, beyond the imaginings of anyone, the nascent institution would prove invaluable in defining what was—and what would become—truly and lastingly American.

A GIFT

"He who has profound knowledge often sees a lot where others see nothing."
—JAMES SMITHSON

A letter written in 1806 by an obscure scientist to one of renown foreshadows what 40 years hence was to become a unique creation: "It seems to me, Sir, that the man of genius who through important discoveries expands the scope of the human mind is entitled to something beyond a mere and fruitless admiration.... The works of scientists being for all nations, they themselves should be looked upon as citizens of mankind."

This "citizen of mankind" was James Smithson, a product of upper-class England, but one who was bereft of social standing, an *amateur* in the true sense of the word and a somewhat sad, shadowy figure as well. Smithson was addressing the naturalist Georges Cuvier, who was known as the founder of comparative anatomy, and, after his signature, Smithson wrote, tellingly, "English Lord."

He was nothing of the sort. A bastard whose ambitious and, by today's standards, licentious father had married into aristocracy, Smithson had inherited his money through the family of his mother, a widow and reputedly a direct descendant of Henry VII. But no recognition from either side had accrued to her illegitimate son, who keenly felt this rejection.

In his early forties at the time he wrote to Cuvier, Smithson had financed his scientific career with his inheritance. His view of his own origins and obligations was just one ambiguity in a life alternately dedicated and frivolous (Smithson became a compulsive gambler in later

life), aristocratic and egalitarian, narrow and of enormous consequence to the world.

Today the search for the man is less than satisfying, always interesting. Although he spent many years on the European continent, the wellspring of the Enlightenment, it was England that shaped him. His father's family was rooted in north Yorkshire; the ancestral home is gone, but the little church at Stanwick, rebuilt often since the seventh century, contains the vault, illuminated by light filtering through Tudor windows, where James Smithson's great-grandfather was buried. Ancient sandstone effigies on the broad sills have eroded with time, but the sounds of wind whistling past the stone battlements, like the sight of sheep in the meadow, can't differ much from the scene in 1740.

That year, Hugh Smithson, who was to become James Smithson's father, married the daughter of the Earl of Northumberland, and, after the earl's death, acquired considerable wealth and property, including the elemental but beautiful Alnwick Castle in Northumberland and Northumberland House, in London, the residence painted by Canaletto in 1752. Hugh Smithson established himself as a man of taste, with political abilities and at least a curiosity for science: Syon House, another of his inherited estates, up the Thames from London, became a noted botanical garden like those nearby at Kew.

In the summers, Hugh Smithson conducted experiments at Alnwick, where old retorts were later found in what was known informally as "the Chemistry Tower." His portrait in the main hall, like the one of him by Gainsborough at Syon, depicts the imperious attitude of a man of the world, in silver cloak and red sash. Periodically left alone by his wife, one of the queen's attendants, and suffering from gout, Hugh often took the mineral cures at Bath, where society people were thrown together. There, in 1764, Hugh Smithson impreg-

nated Elizabeth Hungerford Keate Macie, who was directly descended from the Hungerfords of Studley.

Mrs. Macie was the great-grandniece of Charles, Duke of Somerset, and a cousin of Hugh's wife. In 1765, she gave birth to James Smithson in Paris, where women of means in similar circumstances often retired. Her son was only one of several illegitimate children of the prolific Hugh Smithson, who, after ingratiating himself to King George III, was awarded by Parliament the name of Percy and the first dukedom of Northumberland, neither of which would benefit his illegitimate son.

James Smithson was naturalized at age nine, but, because he was born under the bar sinister, he was precluded from entering the army, the church, the civil service, or politics. There is no indication that young James Lewis Macie, as Smithson was known in his youth, ever saw the Duke of Northumberland or gained entrance to Northumberland House, Syon, or Alnwick Castle. Instead, he became the beneficiary of money inherited by his mother from the Studleys.

The young man attended Pembroke College, Oxford, where he studied chemistry and mineralogy, and, at the age of 19, traveled to Scotland on a geological expedition with French scientist M. Faujas de St. Fond. Dressed in mortarboard and gown in an anonymous portrait painted in 1786, his final year at Pembroke, Smithson appears a frail young man; today, near window boxes of flowering lobelia, his profile graces a plaque in the college's front quad, installed on the Smithsonian's 50th anniversary.

SMITHSON JOINED THE ROYAL SOCIETY OF LONDON for Improving Natural Knowledge in 1787. Its youngest member, he was championed by Henry Cavendish, the definer of the chemical makeup of air and water. Three years later, he presented his first scientific paper, on the subject of tabasheer, a substance found in bamboo; the

This portrait of a youthful James Smithson was painted in 1786, the year he graduated from Pembroke College, Oxford. The illegitimate son of Sir Hugh Smithson, 1st Duke of Northumberland, James never saw his father. Above, weapons from the collections of Alnwick Castle, the ancestral home to which Smithson never gained entrance.

paper was one of some 200 he would write, at least 27 of which were published.

At a time when chemistry and mineralogy were new-blown and geology barely existed, Smithson's contributions to science involved a natural curiosity. He was the first to make the distinction between the native carbonate and silicate of zinc in what was then classified as one mineral, "calamine." The carbonate is now known as smithsonite.

Apparently uninterested in theory, Smithson experimented painstakingly with a broad range of natural substances and with plant species ranging from daisies to artichokes, often using a portable laboratory. His method was modern in the sense that he understood the law of definite proportions—that compounds always contain proportionately the same elements—before the atomic theory had been proposed.

Smithson once captured for analysis a tear running down a woman's cheek. Unfortunately, the particulars of that tantalizing event are unknown.

He opposed monarchy on principle, and wrote from Paris, in 1792, three years after the fall of the Bastille and the rise of egalitarianism in France: "Men of every rank are joining in the chorus. Stupidity and guilt have had a long reign, and it begins, indeed, to be time for justice and common sense to have their turn…. May other nations, at the time of their reforms, be wise enough to cast off, at first, the contemptible incumbrance"—meaning, in this last reference, kingship.

Traveling in Europe in 1807, his name now changed to reflect his patrimony, Smithson was detained in Denmark. An outspoken critic of Napoleon Bonaparte, the military leader who had become emperor of France, he ended up in prison, possibly as a suspected spy. Smithson wrote to Sir Joseph Banks, president of the Royal Society, that "The dampness and unwholesomeness of that place, which is situated in the middle of the

The splendidly attired 1st Duke of Northumberland, Sir Hugh Smithson, married into the powerful Percy family in 1740. In 1764 his extramarital affair with Elizabeth Hungerford Keate Macie produced a son, James Smithson, above, whose bitter determination that the Smithson name "shall live in the memory of man" longer than those of the Northumberlands and the Percys led to his bequest to found the Smithsonian Institution.

fens, & the vigorous manner in which the English were treated, & which occasioned the death of several, threw me into a state of dangerous illness & brought on a spitting of blood."

Smithson finally was released after five years, but the experience stayed with him. He seems to have continued to oppose social inequity, but also resented the limitations imposed upon him by the circumstances of his birth. He once wrote, in a document subsequently destroyed by fire: "The best blood of England flows in my veins. On my father's side I am a Northumberland, on my mother's I am related to kings, but this avails me not. My name shall live in the memory of man when the titles of the Northumberlands and the Percys are extinct and forgotten...."—words suggesting that he had a plan.

SMITHSON LIVED MOST OF HIS ADULT LIFE ON THE Continent, in the company of such scientific enthusiasts as André-Marie Ampère and Jöns Jakob Berzelius. But his interests were not exclusively scientific. French astronomer and physicist Dominique François Arago sought to direct Smithson's attentions more to science and less to the gaming tables that had captured the Englishman's attention. Even if Smithson's gambling was excessive, it apparently made no serious inroads into his inheritance.

By 1826, Smithson was back in London, on Bentinck Street, in the Marylebone district. There he stipulated in his will that, should his nephew and only heir, Henry James Hungerford, die childless, the bulk of Smithson's fortune—worth about $500,000, an enormous sum at the time—should go "to the United States of America, to found at Washington, under the name to [sic] the Smithsonian Institution, an Establishment for the increase & diffusion of knowledge among men."

The Royal Society reportedly had declined to publish Smithson's later papers, although the reasons for

this—a perceived lack of originality or insight, perhaps—
aren't known. The society may well have been left out
of his will for what Smithson considered a slight. His
death three years later, in Genoa, set off speculation
that continues today: Why did Smithson choose a country he had never visited as his ultimate beneficiary?
What exactly did he mean by "the increase & diffusion
of knowledge"?

An avid mineralogist, James
Smithson traveled widely
throughout Europe in the 1790s,
spending perhaps the most time
in Italy. Lava samples from
Mount Vesuvius, whose cata-
clysmic eruption in A.D. 79 was
re-envisioned by the artist Jean-
Baptiste Génillion (1750–1829),
would have been of considerable
interest to Smithson.

    Early on in the Revolutionary War, Smithson's
half-brother, Earl Hugh Percy, the second Duke of
Northumberland, had fought for the British at the battle
of Concord and other engagements, but even so the Percys
had advocated peace and commerce with the new
United States of America. James Smithson himself had
been moved by the spirit of the Enlightenment and the
ideals of philosophers like John Locke, David Hume, and
Voltaire, and of Americans like the revolutionary writer
Thomas Paine and Benjamin Franklin, statesman, inventor, and scientist.

    Smithson's contemporary, Joseph Priestly, also
a chemist, had been forced to leave England because
of his political beliefs, and had found asylum in
America. Priestly had predicted that greater scientific
discoveries would be made on the American side of the
Atlantic than on the British, and Smithson must have
known of this, as well as of American poet and patriot
Joel Barlow, who had spoken of the capital city of
Washington as an "Athens of the future rising on the
banks of the Potomac."

    Oddly, Smithson's library contained only a pub-
lished paper and two books about America, one of which
was written by the secretary of the Royal Society, Isaac
Weld. In *Travels Through North America*, Weld speculated
about Washington, D.C., "If the affairs of the United
States go on as rapidly as they have done, it will become
the grand emporium of the West, and rival in magnitude
and splendor the cities of the whole world."

Smithson's inspiration was probably more general, and idealistic. The intellectual fires still burning at the outset of the 18th century in Europe were stoked with individualism, opposition to accepted authority, and cultural examination—traits the young America seemed to embody—as well as with the empirical method in scientific inquiry. The Enlightenment had produced optimism and a fervor for knowledge that approached the religious, absolutes that James Smithson no doubt valued "beyond a mere and fruitless admiration."

Smithson died on June 26, 1829. Six years later, his nephew died, leaving no heirs. A long, unpredictable, unprecedented, and quite fascinating process was set in motion, one that would transcend national boundaries and politics.

IN JULY 1835, THE AMERICAN CHARGÉ D'AFFAIRES in London received a copy of a will making his country the beneficiary of a sensational bequest—£100,000 for the creation of a theoretical "institution" in the United States. The puzzled chargé sent the will to John Forsyth, U.S. Secretary of State, along with a letter suggesting that the benefactor may have been insane.

President Andrew Jackson, reporting the existence of the bequest to Congress on December 17, 1835, was less than enthusiastic. Jackson, the avowed common man, claimed he had no authority to accept it. Fortunately, in the House of Representatives, in the aging John Quincy Adams, former President and now a Representative from Massachusetts, the bequest found an energetic advocate, unashamed of the pursuit of knowledge. Adams took up the cause of the Smithson bequest, a cause he would champion for a decade.

The arguments for and against the creation of a Smithsonian Institution revealed contradictory aspects of the American character. As chairman of the Select Committee on the Smithson Bequest, Adams wrote: "To

furnish the means of acquiring knowledge is therefore the greatest benefit that can be conferred upon mankind.... If, then, the Smithsonian Institution ...should contribute essentially to the increase and diffusion of knowledge..., to what higher or nobler object could this generous and splendid donation have been devoted?"

Adams, perfect defender of the inchoate Institution, was himself a scientist, and only two years younger than Smithson would have been, had he lived. Adams had spent years in Europe, and had been touched by the Enlightenment. But his eloquence and depth of feeling were lost on some of his fellow statesmen, whose antipathy toward the gift and its implications prefigured a struggle that would outlast them all.

Some Congressmen viewed the bequest as an attempt by a foreigner to acquire immortality, overlooking the obvious benefits to America. William C. Preston, a Representative from South Carolina, thought the gift "too cheap a way." If Congress accepted it, he said—illogically—"every whippersnapper vagabond...might think it proper to have his name distinguished in the same way."

Preston's fellow South Carolinian in the United States Senate, John C. Calhoun, said it was "beneath the dignity of the United States to receive presents of this kind from anyone," an indication that the young nation harbored some insecurity, as well as an indifference to intellectual pursuits—hardly New World versions of the Greek philosopher-statesman.

But others did speak in favor of the bequest, including Senator James Buchanan, of Pennsylvania, later to become America's 15th President. Both houses of Congress eventually agreed to accept Smithson's extraordinary gift, and passed a bill that President Jackson signed on July 1, 1836. Included in the legislation was the provision of $10,000 to cover the expenses of shepherding the bequest through the English courts. Richard

Rush, son of the famous physician and himself a former Secretary of State under James Monroe, was enlisted to travel to London on Congress's behalf.

Again the still abstract "Smithsonian" was fortunate in its advocate. U.S. Minister to Great Britain from 1817 to 1825, Rush had proven an adept operator in the Court of St. James. Now he was able to advance consideration of James Smithson's bequest ahead of some eight hundred other petitioners to the Court of Chancery, and, in July 1838, he supervised the loading of eleven boxes of gold sovereigns onboard the U.S.S. *Mediator*, and sailed with the treasure chest to New York. From there the gold was shipped to Philadelphia, melted down, and re-coined as native specie worth precisely $508,318.46.

THE SMITHSONIAN'S PROBLEMS OF DEFINITION and finance were just beginning. Martin Van Buren, Jackson's successor in the White House, announced at the end of the year that the money was in hand, and reminded Congress of its obligation "to fulfill the object of the bequest." But the United States was suffering from an economic depression, and the Congress—like those to follow it—sought solutions wherever it glimpsed them.

Science was still a murky concept. Institutions to further knowledge were in short supply. The city of Philadelphia, not Washington, was the intellectual center of the nation, with its American Philosophical Society, its Franklin Institute, and its Peale Museum. This last was founded by the indefatigable artist and collector Charles Willson Peale and was the country's first natural-history museum. Boston could claim the American Academy of Arts and Sciences, and other large cities boasted of scientific associations. But despite the rising tide of scientific interest, many members of

(Text continued on page 31)

A medieval physician consults a pharmacist in this woodcut from French surgeon Hieronymus Brunschwig's *Liber de arte distillandi...*(*Book on the Art of Distilling*), an early-16th-century "how-to" book of medical remedies and methods of chemical distillation. Three centuries later, young James Smithson worked to advance "so new a science" as chemistry.

IN SERVICE TO THE SMITHSONIAN
by SONIA REECE

Just after nine on the evening of December 14, 1993, Linda Underwood, a volunteer behavior watcher with the Friends of the National Zoo (FONZ), noticed that Shanthi, the National Zoo's pregnant Asian elephant, was beginning to act strangely. "She was straining and squatting," Mrs. Underwood said, "and her keepers noticed this, too." As it turned out, Shanthi was about to give birth to the first elephant to be born at the National Zoo in that institution's 104-year history. "The entire delivery took less than 40 minutes," Underwood related. "It was extremely exciting, but you couldn't hear anything above the horrendous noise that Nancy, the big African elephant, was making."

Because of the dedication of thousands of volunteers like Mrs. Underwood, the Smithsonian is able to undertake numerous projects that would not otherwise be possible. In 1994 alone, some 5,256 volunteers contributed an estimated 574,816 hours of service to the Institution, figures that are particularly compelling in light of the fact that, for that same year, the Smithsonian employed roughly 7,000 federal and trust-fund workers and spent approximately $465 million on salaries and expenses each year.

The Institution has fostered a tradition of volunteerism since its founding in 1846. Unlike the British at that time, who were spending £50,000—about $235,000—a year on acquisitions to build up the British Museum's collections, Smithsonian officials early on felt it was "not...expedient for the...Institution ever to do much for its cabinet by direct purchase." The "employment or assistance of collectors," it was felt, would produce an equally effective result.

To this end, Smithsonian Secretary Spencer F. Baird, the consummate collector, encouraged people to send specimens of all sorts to the Institution. Baird made sure that whenever an exploring expedition set out east, west, north, or south, someone—be it surveyor, soldier, budding naturalist, or celebrated reporter—would be collecting material for the Castle. To keep these troves coming, the Smithsonian's first Secretary, Joseph Henry, and his successor, Baird, reported that "With scarcely an exception, every expedition of any magnitude...received more or less aid from the Smithsonian Institution."

By definition, a volunteer is a person who performs or offers to perform a service of his or her own free will. Such a description certainly describes Smithsonian crab specialist Mary Jane Rathbun, who resigned in 1914 so that her salary could go to her young protégé, Waldo L. Schmitt.

A crew of behind-the-scenes Smithsonian volunteers works in anthropologist Gus Van Beek's archaeology lab at the National Museum of Natural History, skillfully reconstructing pots from thousands of shards collected at Tel Jemmeh, Israel. Above, a volunteer puts the finishing touches on a pot.

She then continued her work at the Natural History Museum for some 30 years as an honorary research associate, publishing 84 of her 166 manuscripts during this period.

Over the years, many other Smithsonian staff members have continued to work at the Institution on a volunteer basis after their official date of retirement. These include Secretaries, whose enduring commitment

is exemplified by Secretary Emeritus Charles Greeley Abbot: Leaving his post in 1944 at the age of 72, Abbot continued to work at the Smithsonian until his death in 1973 at the age of 101.

From counting bird skins to translating manuscripts, answering the Institution's public-information phone lines, and performing a myriad other jobs involving conservation, archival, administrative, clerical, educa-tional, and other skills, volunteers are engaged daily in almost every aspect of Smithsonian activity, both in the public and behind-the-scenes. For what-ever reasons Smithsonian volunteers give so generously of their time, effort, and expertise, their work, as recently acknowledged by Secretary I. Michael Heyman, has "made us a stronger and more viable institution."

Sonia Reece is an Associate Editor at Smithsonian Books.

National Museum of Natural History's wet-lab specimens are preserved in much the same way as those in Dutch merchant Levin Vincent's private collection, illustrated above in *Collection of the Wonders of Nature*, 1719. Both this book and British mathematician Roberte Recorde's *The Castle of Knowledge*—an explanation of ancient astronomy—belong to Smithsonian Institution Libraries.

Congress were concerned more with material benefits.

As head of the nine-member committee overseeing the formation of the institution, John Quincy Adams sought to block self-serving suggestions. He wanted an enlightened electorate and he wanted Washington to be the country's intellectual center, and he treated opponents to those ideals with hyperbolic disdain: "Not so easy it will be to secure, as from a rattlesnake's fang, the fund and its income, forever, from being wasted and dilapidated in bounties to feed the hunger or fatten the leaden idleness of mountebank projectors, and shallow and worthless pretenders to science."

These "pretenders" included, in Adams's opinion, a retired college president who envisioned a postgraduate university specializing in mathematics, science, and agriculture (his "very breath is pestilential") and a Senator who wanted an institution "to provide…a course of education and discipline." Adams warned Congress against creating colleges or schools for specific studies. He had for years advocated a national observatory, and although he wasn't able to convince his colleagues of the wisdom of that course after the Naval Observatory was built in 1844, he did prevent them from squandering, as he put it, "a stranger's munificence to rear our children."

Others honestly attempted to conform to Smithson's wishes. Richard Rush advocated a grand lecture bureau that would promote scientific knowledge and also serve as a catchall for natural-science specimens, cultural objects, and information picked up around the world from representatives of the United States. The president of Columbia College proposed lectures and professorships covering all aspects of learning and life in America. When a Senator suggested creating an agricultural college that also taught house-building and navigation, Senator Rufus Choate, of Massachusetts, derided his "narrow utilitarianism." Choate proposed instead a national library as "durable as liberty, durable as the Union."

THE GREATEST THREAT TO AN AUTONOMOUS SMITH-sonian came from the Secretary of War, Joel Poinsett, an amateur naturalist after whom the poinsettia was named. He had already brought together in Washington some men who were interested in science, creating the National Institution for the Promotion of Science and the Useful Arts, and he also helped organize Lieutenant Charles Wilkes's expedition to the South Seas (1838–42), the first U.S. government-sponsored maritime explo-ration. Poinsett wanted funds for his institution for the creation of a museum of natural history, and had received authority to act as curator for the specimens Wilkes brought back.

Crowds descend on the White House in Robert Cruikshank's 1841 illustration, *President's Levee or all Creation going to the White House, Washington*, above. During a brief but destructive British invasion some 27 years earlier, right, most of the nation's capital was consumed by flames. Charles R. Parsons' 1880 lithograph, *The City of Washington*, depicts a burgeoning city, home to the Smithsonian Castle (center).

Poinsett's organization was renamed the National Institute, and he was succeeded as its president by Levi Woodbury, the former Secretary of the Treasury. Woodbury had already threatened the viability of the Smithson bequest by investing the half-million dollars in state bonds, most of which were from Arkansas and almost all of which were in default. This prompted an outraged John Quincy Adams to demand that the gov-ernment make up the losses from Woodbury's unwise investment and that it ensure the Smithsonian, whatev-er form it took, a rightful return on its original invest-ment, plus interest. Meanwhile, the politically astute National Institute continued to seek access to any funds that might become available from the Smithsonian financial debacle.

Senator Benjamin Tappan, the Jacksonian Democrat from Ohio who vigorously opposed the National Institute, suggested in 1844 yet another shape the Smithsonian Institution might take, one that would combine a museum, a laboratory, and a library, and would emphasize practical information for the benefit of

THE TAKING OF THE CITY OF WASHINGTON IN AMERICA

THE CITY OF WASHINGTON THE CAPITAL OF THE UNITED STATES OF AMERICA WAS TAKEN BY THE BRITISH FORCES UNDER MAJOR GEN? ROSS On Aug? 24 1814 When we burnt and destroyed their Dock Yard with a Frigate and a Sloop of War Rope-walk Arsenal Senate House Presidents Palace War Office Treasury and the Great Bridge With the Flotilla the public property destroyed amounted to thirty Millions of Dollars. Published Oct 14 1814 by G Thompson N?43 Long Lane West Smithfield

Washington, under the name to the Smithsonian institution, an establishment for the increase & diffusion of Knowledge among men.

I think proper here to state that all the money which will be standing in the French five per cents, at my death in the names of the father of my above mentioned nephew, Henry James Hungerford, & all that is in my names, is the property of my said nephew, being what he inherited from his father, or what I have laid up for him from the saving upon his income.

James Smithson.

common people. During that debate, William Allen, of Ohio, derided the National Institute's "pompous title," and let some air out of its claims of deserving public money. Poinsett's organization, Allen said, had discovered "a Capitol here and a public Treasury...."

Senator Rufus Choate, the Whig from Massachusetts, took issue with Tappan's bill on grounds that it would create something akin to a national university, which he saw as a federal arrogation of local responsibility. However, both Choate and his ally in the House, George Perkins Marsh, of Vermont, wanted a great library.

By now the idea of a national museum was lodged in the public consciousness. So were the notions of scandal associated with the financial aspects of the bequest, as a result of the defaulted state bonds and the ineptitude and bickering among politicians about the Smithsonian's ultimate makeup.

Robert Dale Owen, a Congressman from Indiana and the son of the famous English utopian, denounced libraries as "clouds of windy verbiage," and proposed, in another bill, a natural-history museum, agricultural plots, a school for training teachers, and a laboratory. To this, Representative Marsh, library proponent, responded contemptuously, "Sir, a laboratory is a charnel house." As for the provision for a teachers' school, Adams told his colleagues that, rather than sanction this, he would see "the whole money thrown into the Potomac." The acerbic Adams kept the government's feet to the fires of responsibility for restoring the money lost on the defaulted bonds, which Owen also favored.

THE CONTINUING DEBATE OVER THE "SMITHSONIAN problem" now included Representative Andrew Johnson, of Tennessee, destined to be the country's 17th President, who opposed the bill on the grounds that his constituents should not have to pay for faulty investments. Jefferson Davis, from neighboring Mississippi, favored making

An excerpt from James Smithson's will appears here with the obverse and reverse of one of the 1838 gold sovereigns from his bequest. At top, a military escort receives Smithson's remains from the U.S.S. *Dolphin*, in Washington, D.C., on January 25, 1904. Moved from their original resting place in Italy, his remains were re-interred in a crypt, above, in the Smithsonian Castle.

the federal government meet its moral obligation.

Adams prevailed, through political astuteness and inspired denunciation of what he considered the enemies of enlightenment. The 29th Congress finally passed a bill without most of the specific provisions for a Smithsonian Institution, except those for a national museum for government collections, a laboratory, an art gallery, and a library. On August 10, 1846, President James K. Polk signed the bill, restoring the original half-million dollars and the interest that should have accrued during the eight years of Congressional wrangling, $242,129.

The bill also set out the rules for governing an institution dedicated to "the increase & diffusion of knowledge." It established a Board of Regents made up of the Chief Justice of the United States, the Vice President, the mayor of Washington, D.C. (later abolished), all ex officio; as well as three Senators, three Representatives, and six private citizens, two of whom had to be Washingtonians. It further authorized a site for the Smithsonian Institution to be selected, and a building put up "of plain and durable materials and structure, without unnecessary ornament."

The new Institution, a trust to the public, would be presided over by a Secretary, like the various government cabinets, and supervised by the board. Of the interest on the Smithson fund, amounting to $30,000 a year, Choate and Marsh succeeded in providing that a sum "not exceeding an average of $25,000 a year" would go to the creation of the library. Otherwise, the Smithsonian's managers were to spend the income from the fund "as they deem best suited for the promotion of the purposes of James Smithson"—a victory for Adams and other advocates of an autonomous and somewhat high-minded institution that had been 10 years in the making.

The crucial stipulation—"as they deem best suited"—allowed the Smithsonian to grow without rigid Congressional oversight. John Quincy Adams, who would live for less than two more years after this legislative victory, said of the Smithsonian in one of his last speeches, "Of all the foundations of establishments for pious or charitable uses which ever signalized the spirit of the age, or the comprehensive beneficence of the founder, none can be named more deserving the approbation of mankind than this."

THE ARGUMENT OVER THE SMITHSONIAN'S ULTIMATE makeup, far from resolved, was set aside for a more pressing question: What sort of "plain and durable" structure would be built to house it, and who would design the building? Already, powerful voices among the Regents were being raised in support of various plans and architects. Two days before President Polk walked on the Mall that hot September morning in 1846, the others had gathered at the Post Office Building for the first Board of Regents meeting. There, Vice-President George M. Dallas was elected interim president, but the three most influential Regents would come to be Dallas's nephew, Alexander Dallas Bache; Robert Dale Owen, proponent of the teachers' school; and Rufus Choate, the library advocate.

Bache, the youngest Regent, was the great-grandson of Benjamin Franklin and the superintendent of the United States Coast Survey. He had influential relatives and friends in Washington, among them Senator Jefferson Davis, of Mississippi, a proven friend of the Smithsonian. Bache also was acquainted with an architect in New York, James Renwick, Sr., whose son, James, Jr., sent in one of the thirteen plans eventually submitted for the Smithsonian building.

While a student at Columbia, Renwick, Jr., had exhibited, according to classmate George Templeton Strong, the "vanity and pretension" of an artist, but had proven businesslike and had acquired recognition as the designer of several Gothic and Romanesque churches in Manhattan. He would design St. Patrick's Cathedral and,

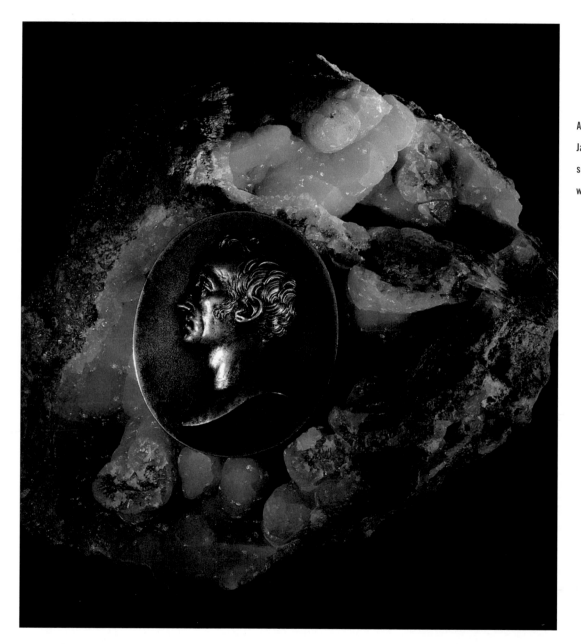

A bronze medallion portrait of James Smithson rests on smithsonite, a mineral he discovered that was later named in his honor.

in Washington, D.C., the original Corcoran Gallery of Art, but, for the moment, at age 28, his fame rested upon New York's Grace Church, known as "Renwick's toothpick" for its elegant, wooden steeple.

On November 30, 1846, Renwick's design for a Smithsonian building was chosen by the Regents over those of the competition. On paper lay the basics for a solid if somewhat whimsical structure, its towers and extensive crenelation constituting what might be considered excessive ornament. Renwick's plan was described as "Norman," but was really an amalgam—like the Smithsonian itself—of history and intellectual fashion.

Once completed, a process that would take a decade, the building captured the attention of people of all ages, a highly wrought vision in an otherwise deserted field, a latter-day castle built of varied, contentious dreams.

Between 1832 and 1839, artist George Catlin recorded many aspects of Plains Indian life, such as the regalia of the Mandan Medicine Man Mah-to-he-ha ("Old Bear"), far left. Above, in a rare self-portrait, the artist works among a group of Mandans as he paints their Second Chief Mah-to-toh-pa ("Four Bears").

FORERUNNERS

In the summer of 1846, in an action that received little attention elsewhere, Congress's Joint Committee on the Library recommended to the Senate that the bill establishing the Smithsonian Institution be amended to allow the purchase of specific works of art. These were intended for the Smithsonian's gallery, and the subject, fittingly, was the American Indian.

The prolific artist, George Catlin, displayed an appreciation of the mythic qualities of a people already in tragic decline. Then living in Paris, a controversial figure, Catlin had vividly portrayed on his numerous canvases people descended from the North American continent's first inhabitants.

Born in Wilkes-Barre, Pennsylvania, in 1796, Catlin had grown up on the edge of the frontier, and studied law, but his passions were painting and Indians. This happy conjunction produced, in 1826, a stunning portrait of the Seneca warrior Red Jacket. Nonetheless, Catlin decided not to become a portraitist, and moved to St. Louis, jumping-off place for "the West" at a time of determined expansion.

In 1832, he traveled by steamboat 2,000 miles up the Missouri River to Fort Union, at the mouth of the Yellowstone River. On the way, at Fort Pierre, Catlin painted the portraits of the Sioux (Dakota), the most warlike of the Plains tribesmen who had come to trade with the American Fur Company. Farther along, in Assiniboine country, he also painted the Crow, the Blackfoot, and the Ojibwa.

Catlin captured colorful, spirited Indian rituals that would soon vanish. He returned downriver by canoe, painting Hidatsas and Minitaris along the way, as well as Mandans, a tribe that would be eradicated by smallpox. Working under difficult circumstances with limited supplies and time, he traveled to Comanche country in 1834, and to the Red Pipestone Quarry in what is now Minnesota in 1836. He was one of the first white people to see this quarry; the stone from which the pipes were carved, catlinite, bears his name.

The painter also traveled to Florida and Georgia. He produced more than 500 Indian portraits and sketches, and amassed both authentic artifacts and notebooks filled with details of Indian life. An exhibition known as "Catlin's Indian Gallery" opened in New York in 1837 to popular acclaim before Wild West shows gained popularity, but its success wasn't repeated in other American cities. The exhibition moved to London in 1839; Catlin published his first book on the subject of American Indians in 1841. Despite these accomplishments, Congress declined to purchase his collection, and Catlin spent his last years in undeserved obscurity.

Artist, explorer, observer of indigenous cultures, Catlin embodied the various concerns that would help characterize the Smithsonian. He was also a reformer, ahead of his time, known as "Indian-Loving Catlin" to critics, who viewed his subjects only as impediments to Manifest Destiny.

Catlin wrote, two years before his death, "I love a people who are honest without laws.... I love a people who worship God without a Bible.... I love a people who have never raised a hand against me.... I love the people who have never fought a battle with white men, except on their own ground...."

Also in 1846, the United States government found itself owning, stored away in the Old Patent Office a few blocks from the Mall, thousands of specimens and hundreds of charts, maps, and paintings brought back from an extraordinary around-the-world expedition. The voyagers had discovered the continent of Antarctica, and established claims on the West Coast of America. The leader, Lieutenant Charles Wilkes, embodied another type that would contribute significantly to the Smithsonian's development: the government agent, charged with recording new facts and collecting new specimens

George Catlin's 1834 painting *Ball Play of the Choctaw* was one of the hundreds of his original Indian Gallery canvases, which were exhibited on the walls of the old National Museum (now the Arts and Industries Building), above, at the turn of the century. A few years before his death in 1872, Catlin, at the invitation of Joseph Henry, lived and painted in a room in one of the Castle's towers.

in uncharted terrain, all the while pursuing the American dream of territorial expansion.

His great-uncle, John Wilkes, the English opponent of monarchy, had inspired the name of Wilkes-Barre, the town in Pennsylvania where George Catlin had grown up. Charles Wilkes, a scientist and career naval officer, set out in the summer of 1838 with a flotilla of six ships, the first maritime exploration sponsored by the government and part of a growing tradition that began with President Thomas Jefferson's dispatching of Lewis and Clark westward in 1804 and included the Western explorations of Captain and later General Zebulon Pike.

Although the Wilkes expedition was organized in the interests of the American whaling industry, pure

science also provided inspiration. With a complement of scientists and naturalists, Wilkes visited, among other exotic places, Fiji, Tahiti, Samoa, and Australia, and sailed enough of the coast of Antarctica to convince himself of the continent's existence.

But it was his reconnaissance of the Northwest Coast of North America and overland excursions to determine which westward-flowing rivers were navigable that meant most to the United States, and helped establish the 49th parallel as the country's northern boundary. The loss of a ship—the Peacock—trying to cross the bar at the mouth of the Columbia River, for instance, indicated that better harbors should be sought in Puget Sound.

These explorations and the data amassed were invaluable, as were the charts brought back in 1842, but Wilkes and his men received little recognition. The significance of their journey escaped public notice, and English geographers rejected their evidence of a new continent at the bottom of the world. Furthermore, Wilkes was court-martialed for forcibly removing Con-federate agents from an English ship during the Civil War, and, although he later rose to the rank of commodore, like Catlin he ended his years in relative obscurity.

The Wilkes expedition's collections—including 10,000 species of plants, 500 of birds, and more than 500 of fishes—first came under the auspices of the National Institute. There they were neglected and mismanaged by ignorant or careless curators, but they were destined for better treatment at the new Smithsonian Institution.

A HOLE IN THE FLOOR

In 1846, the Smithsonian Board of Regents chose Joseph Henry, opposite, as the Institution's first Secretary. Seal, below, is set into the floor in front of the Regents' Room in the Castle. Created by Augustus Saint Gaudens in 1893–94, this large mosaic features the Smithsonian's mission statement and two torches, classical emblems of truth and knowledge.

"You can <u>be</u> a new institution...."
—ALEXANDER DALLAS BACHE

The Smithsonian, its house provided for but not yet built, remained more theoretical than real. It needed an exemplar, someone of recognized accomplishments who embodied both administrative ability and the ideals of science. The Secretary of the Institution would have to build on the hazy vision of James Smithson; he would have to withstand pressures from those in Congress and from his peers, who had their own ideas about what the Smithsonian should be. The first Secretary would need a vision of his own.

The Regents' choice seems, in retrospect, extraordinarily wise. Joseph Henry, a 48-year-old professor of "natural philosophy" (physics) at the College of New Jersey, which became Princeton University in 1896, was a broad-featured, self-made and self-assured man, who was known for his experiments with electromagnetism, a subject no American scientist since Benjamin Franklin had so avidly pursued. In demonstrating his electromagnetic relays in 1831, Henry had transmitted over distance enough power to ring a bell. This was the basis of the electromagnetic telegraph that later brought fame and money to Samuel F.B. Morse, but Henry had refused to patent his discovery—on principle.

For him, science represented the apex of civilization. Henry later wrote to a friend, in reference to the electromagnetic relay, "I did not then find it compatible with the dignity of science to confine benefits which might be derived from it to the exclusive use of any one individual." He added, tellingly, "The only reward I ever expected was the consciousness

of advancing science, the pleasure of discovering new truths, and the scientific reputation to which these labors would entitle me."

In later life, Henry would admit, "I might have been a little less fastidious." He would never be as famous as Morse, or British physicist and chemist Michael Faraday, whose discoveries had also been paralleled by Henry working in America.

Born poor in 1797 in Albany, New York, he was an unlikely candidate for scientific renown. The son of a Presbyterian laborer, Henry was placed with relatives at the age of seven, badly schooled, and assigned to work in a country store at age 10. After his father's death, Henry, just 14, returned to his mother's house, and was apprenticed to a watchmaker and silversmith. This man found him "dull," which is not surprising, given Henry's intelligence and interests and the hardships he had already known and eventually overcame.

He read novels after gaining access to the church library through a hole in the floor. The book that most impressed him in life, however, was not fiction but George Gregory's *Popular Lectures on Experimental Philosophy, Astronomy, and Chemistry*. Years later, giving a copy of the book to his only son, Henry wrote on the flyleaf, "This…opened to me a new world of thought and enjoyment; fixed my attention upon the study of nature, and caused me to resolve at the time of reading it that I would immediately devote myself to the acquisition of knowledge."

For Henry, this meant mathematics, chemistry, and natural philosophy. But his interest in science did not prevent him from participating in amateur theatricals, which he apparently took quite seriously.

Henry enrolled in the Albany Academy in 1819, at the age of 22, older than the other students. He supported himself for a time as a kind of circuit-riding grammarian and schoolteacher, earning $8 a week by

tutoring the children of well-to-do families. He taught the elder Henry James, religious writer and the father of William James, the philosopher, and Henry James, the novelist.

Henry's early career also included surveying. One summer, he headed a party assigned to establish the route of the proposed Great Road in New York State. Ironically, he was denied an appointment with the Corps of Topographical Engineers of the United States Army, a unit that would someday well serve the purposes of his Smithsonian.

Henry became professor of mathematics and natural philosophy at the Albany Academy in 1826, and librarian of the Albany Institute, a learned society, in 1829. He married his cousin, Harriet L. Alexander, the following year. His experiments with hot-air balloons gained him some recognition, and he began his experiments with electromagnetism and meteorology, interests he would pursue with enthusiasm at the Smithsonian.

Henry published articles in the *American Journal of Science and the Arts*, which was edited by Benjamin Silliman, a leading light in natural science. Along the way, Henry became acquainted with other prominent men of science, among them Alexander Dallas Bache and Robert Hare, the noted chemist at the University of Pennsylvania. In 1832, Henry joined the faculty of the College of New Jersey, where he continued his research.

In 1837, he traveled to Europe, where he met some of the most highly regarded scientists of France and England. In London, he dined with American envoy Richard Rush, and it seems reasonable to assume they discussed Rush's pursuit of the Smithson bequest on behalf of the United States.

By 1846, the pivotal year for Henry and for the Smithsonian, he was an admired professor who could be proud of his accomplishments. The de facto orphan, child laborer, novel reader, amateur actor, impoverished

A student of galvanism, young Joseph Henry, above, constructed his most powerful electromagnet, left, in 1831 for fellow scientist Benjamin Silliman of Yale College. The magnet now resides in the Smithsonian's National Museum of American History.

Secretary Joseph Henry, at right at desk in rear, and other leading 19th-century American scientists gathered in the Castle's West Wing in 1871 for a meeting of the National Academy of Sciences. Their discussions centered on theories of the natural world and their scientific applications, represented, opposite, clockwise from top, by the construction of the U.S. Capitol, Benjamin Franklin's analysis of waterspouts, and a diagram of comet observation.

schoolmaster, and inventor had climbed to a level of eminence no one could have predicted.

Asked by his friend, Bache, how he would interpret the intent of James Smithson's will, a matter of great importance to American science, Henry wrote: "The object of the institution is the increase and diffusion of knowledge. The increase of knowledge is much more difficult and in reference to the bearing of this institution on the character of our country and the welfare of mankind much more important than the diffusion of knowledge." Henry's priorities were clear.

The role of scientist was as much a matter of character to him as of learning. Because of the stature and reputation afforded men of science, pretenders abounded, and they and their schemes had to be guarded against. When the position of the first Secretary of the Smithsonian was formally offered to him, Henry agreed to take on this administrative, politically charged post with characteristic solemnity and premonitions of a

struggle: "The office is one which I have by no means coveted and which I accepted at the earnest solicitation of some friends of science in our country, to prevent its falling into worse hands, and with the hope of saving the noble bequest of Smithson from being squandered on chimerical or unworthy projects."

In view of Henry's subsequent acts, these "worse hands" can be identified as those of advocates of an art gallery, a national library, a national museum, an agricultural institute, or anything else that diluted the increase of knowledge. It didn't matter that some of these Chimeras had been mandated by law as aspects of an evolving Smithsonian.

This was the outset of a golden age of scientific advancement in America. Intellectual currents were sweeping across the Atlantic, with exciting advances being made in physics, astronomy, geology, and other disciplines; in science lay the future, its practical aspects

(Text continued on page 50)

Vietnamese calligraphers used one-hair brushes and watercolors to produce these exquisitely detailed illustrations of Southeast Asian stomatopods, a kind of marine crustacean. French carcinologist (crab specialist) Raoul Serène commissioned these drawings in the 1940s. All *Gonodactylus* species, such as the one depicted opposite right, employ the brightly colored spot on the inside of each claw in ritualized displays.

A STOMATOPOD ALLIANCE

by BRYAN KENNEDY

What small marine invertebrate has better color vision than humans and a claw with the penetrating power of a .22-caliber bullet? A stomatopod. What, you may well ask, is a stomatopod? Stomatopods are members of a marine crustacean order that currently includes some 400 species in more than 100 genera. Sometimes called mantis shrimp, they vary in length from two-fifths of an inch to a foot, and live in tropical coastal waters around the world, where they may be found as deep as 4,300 feet.

All stomatopods were of special interest to the late French crab specialist, Raoul Serène, who worked at the Oceanographic Institute, in Nhatrang, Vietnam. Serène published more than 130 works on crustaceans, the first of which, in 1939, established the systematics of stomatopods. By 1954, only 180 stomatopod species were known, 150 of them from the Indo-West Pacific. Serène drew attention to size, habitat, and sexual dimorphism as important species characteristics for stomatopods. He also recognized that the 225 papers on the systematics of these animals provided little information on their biology. So Serène pioneered the study of live specimens.

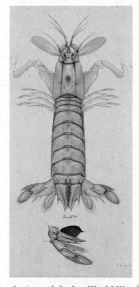

Unfortunately, Serène was unable to publish a monograph on stomatopods before he died in 1980. Raymond Manning, however, a curator at the National Museum of Natural History, picked up where Serène left off, and his monograph, *Stomatopod Crustacea of Vietnam*, includes exquisite watercolors that Serène commissioned from Vietnamese artists. Since stomatopod colors fade rapidly with death, these paintings of live specimens are invaluable for classification, all the more so in light of the fact that the Oceanographic Institute's collections in Nhatrang were largely destroyed during World War II and the Vietnam conflict. There is no current research on the taxonomy of Southeast Asian stomatopods.

Stomatopod eyes are unique: most species have a divided cornea, with a middle band of specialized cells used in color vision and, in two genera, as polarization filters. Not all stomatopods have color vision, but each species has eyes that can function independently, scanning for distance, shape, even angular velocity of moving prey. And every stomatopod's eye structure allows for binocular vision.

Combative by nature, stomatopods exhibit complex behaviors during confrontations. In some species, fighting individuals are known to employ several hundred distinct actions within a 10-minute period. One, *Gonodactylus sensu lato*, features a brightly colored spot on the inside of each claw, which it uses in ritualized displays. Generally, stomatopods are well equipped to back up their threats: the enlarged, second maxilliped

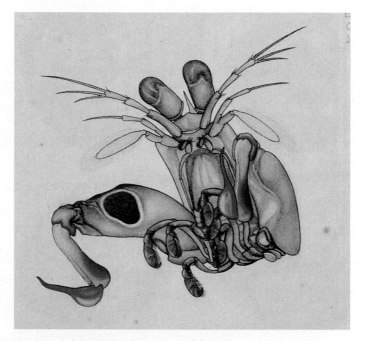

claw, which in large species can be as long as three inches, is adapted for spearing or smashing prey—similar to tactics employed by the praying mantis—or for defending their burrows and fending off predators. The striking speed of this weapon exceeds 390 inches per second underwater.

We now know that stomatopods live in burrows, such as the cavities found in coral rubble, or in holes that they dig in level bottom habitats. Some hunt from their holes, others actively search for prey, and certain species hunt only at night. Some are numerous enough to be natural predators of commercial shrimp populations.

In 1966, when he retired, Serène donated all the research for his monograph, along with the plates, to Manning. No doubt he would be proud of the finished product.

Bryan Kennedy is an Associate Editor at Smithsonian Books.

increasingly apparent. The reorganization of the U.S. Coast Survey by Bache two years before, in 1844, had preceded ambitious and productive oceanic studies. That same year, Samuel Morse had demonstrated the practical use of the telegraph, and Elias Howe and Richard March Hoe did the same for the sewing machine and the rotary printing press, respectively.

Also in 1846, a Boston dentist used anesthesia successfully. The decade also saw the founding of the Lawrence Scientific School (at Harvard), the Cincinnati Observatory, the Yale Analytical Laboratory, the centennial celebration of the American Philosophical Society, and the expansion of Silliman's scientific journal. John James Audubon, already noted for his *Birds of America*, began publishing *The Viviparous Quadrupeds of North America*. Names of those contributing to scientific development in America included Maury, Agassiz, Gray, Dana, Morton, and Owen. In 1845, John C. Frémont concluded his third expedition in the trans-Mississippi West, the great new theater of exploration and scientific inquiry that would have a profound impact upon the Smithsonian.

The city of Washington that received the Secretary was no Athens on the Potomac, as James Smithson may have once envisioned it. According to Henry Adams, grandson of the Smithsonian's legislative champion, writing in his autobiography, the United States's capital at the time was notable for its "want of barriers, of pavements, of forms; the looseness, the laziness; the indolent Southern drawl; the pigs in the streets…the freedom, openness, swagger, of nature and man…."

Hardly the place for a man interested in natural philosophy and "galvanism" (the study of electricity produced by chemical action). It is difficult to imagine the uncompromising Henry standing happily on the threshold of the Capitol, facing a new career as he figuratively faced the weedy expanse of mall, soon to be home to him and his wife and their son and three daughters. There his Institution would rise, and the rest of his life play out, but he had no certain knowledge of the Smithsonian's makeup or even of what shape its physical structure would take.

Paramount among the Chimeras to Henry was any edifice that might be built to house collections. This would deplete Smithsonian funds in the purchase of what he referred to contemptuously as "bricks and mortar." Such a museum might have limited use in furthering inquiry, but to use it for casual study or entertainment seemed to him the antithesis of the Smithsonian's responsibility. And constructing such a building with funds from the bequest was not consistent with what he saw as the intent of James Smithson.

Henry opposed the museum from the outset. He met officially with the Board, and a majority of the Regents seemed to agree with him. "I have succeeded beyond my most sanguine expectation in molding the opinions of the Board of Regents," Henry wrote happily to his wife, Harriet, in December of 1846.

In 1851, five years after the founding of the Smithsonian, England hosted the first World's Fair. In London's Crystal Palace, above, the fair exhibited American machinery of the Industrial Revolution. The palace was built during the reign of Queen Victoria, whose image appears on this coin from the Smithsonian's collections. Back home in America, small factories, right, were a common sight by the 1860s.

But Congress was another matter. Henry feared that the legislators' desire for a suitable building "will absorb so much of the annual interest...that there will be but little left for the proper purposes of the Institution," which to him were intensely intellectual. No egalitarian when it came to science, Henry believed that "like the poet, the discoverer is born, not made." Only the chosen few should bother pursuing the "high and holy office of penetrating the mysteries of nature."

In Mathew Brady's 1863 photograph of Independence Avenue, the Smithsonian Castle stands alone on the Mall, the U.S. Capitol and a few private residences its only neighbors. At right, Smithsonian Secretary Joseph Henry enjoys a relaxed moment on the Mall around 1865 with his wife, Harriet, and their three daughters, Mary, Helen Louisa, and Caroline.

Such a man was himself a mystery to most politicians, who considered Henry one of the "zealots for discovery" but were impressed by his seriousness. They would discover that this stern, principled New Yorker had some political talents as well.

Henry devised a "Programme of Organization." Printed in the first *Annual Report* given to the Regents, it reflected his belief in the primacy of original research and the dissemination of findings to as broad a scientific audience as possible. Henry later wrote, "The most prominent idea in my mind is that of stimulating the talent of our country to original research...to pour fresh material on the apex of the pyramid of science, and thus to enlarge its base...."

Three broadly based initiatives contributed to this end. First, Henry decided that meteorological observations would be made throughout the country, and correlated at the Smithsonian. The idea was to establish a base for a burgeoning science of meteorology with extensive, long-range data related to climate. By providing practical information as well as discreet scientific variables and by using ordinary Americans as well as professionals as observers, the Smithsonian could both broaden its base of support and offer services that would lead eventually to the National Weather Service.

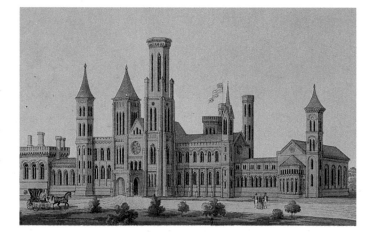

Second, Henry launched an ambitious, logistically challenging international exchange of new scientific information. The findings of American research were to be published and distributed to other institutions of learning abroad in exchange for publications featuring foreign research, which would then be disseminated in this country.

Third, in 1848, Henry initiated publication of the series *Smithsonian Contributions to Knowledge* with the appearance of a quarto-size volume, *Ancient Monuments of the Mississippi Valley*, about mound-building Indians, by Ephraim George Squier and Edwin H. Davis. This thick, illustrated work served as a milestone not only in the development of American anthropology but also in the Smithsonian's association with that branch of science.

In his book *Hints on Public Architecture*, Smithsonian Regent Robert Dale Owen advocated a medieval architectural design for the Castle because of this style's association with collegiate institutions and its expression of the American character—which he defined as vigor, independence, and practical economy. At right, this ornate mirror and a chair designed by Castle architect James Renwick, Jr., survived the fire of 1865.

The production of this book early in his administration proved that Henry would be a determined leader. Insisting upon high standards, he personally edited the work before it was published, at times heavily, excising all ethnological and racial speculation. He wanted *Ancient Monuments* to represent the best of descriptive science in the tradition of Francis Bacon, the English philosopher. Bacon was a proponent of the inductive method, whereby scientific truths were arrived at through close observation and the elimination of non-essential elements.

The Secretary lacked the assistance he needed, and, in 1850, chose as his right hand a young naturalist whose passion was collecting. His name was Spencer Fullerton Baird, and he was "to take charge of the cabinet and to act as naturalist of the Institution," Henry declared.

The word "cabinet" referred to the general, polyglot assortment of natural specimens arriving on the federal government's figurative doorstep, many of them without merit in Henry's eyes. (In Europe, such collections were referred to as "cabinets of curiosities.")

Although Henry opposed the operation of a museum by the Smithsonian, he understood the importance of collecting and classifying natural phenomena from the continent's far reaches, which were just opening to exploration, and thought it appropriate to use Smithsonian funds to obtain type specimens for such study. Any duplicates should be passed on, however, to other institutions.

This practice prefigured the Smithsonian's later contributions to taxonomy, the study of classification. The paradox of Henry's career was that the Smithsonian was already set on the path toward becoming the greatest museum complex in the world, one in which bricks, mortar, and "curiosities" would play a significant role. Inherent in that contradiction was the choice of Baird as the Institution's second most influential person.

The Henry family's residence on the second floor of the Castle's East Wing featured eight rooms, including a dining room, above, a music room, two bedrooms, and a private study. After Henry's death in 1878, the rooms were converted into offices.

Mary Henry's art studio was given over to John H. Richard, top, an illustrator whose colorful fish casts helped the Smithsonian win the grand prize at the 1880 Berlin International Fishery Exhibition.

One wonders what Henry thought when Baird arrived in Washington with two boxcar loads of natural specimens he had already collected. The energetic Baird had been the first individual to receive a Smithsonian grant, made earlier by Henry. Baird had put together a collection of freshwater fishes, but he was interested in—and highly knowledgeable about—all of North America's flora and fauna.

Since Baird had had some experience in the publishing of original research, an endeavor essential to Henry's international-exchange program, he was assigned the responsibility of both publishing and distributing new research inspired by the Smithsonian. He and the Secretary seem to have agreed on most philosophical and scientific points. Undoubtedly, Henry saw his new assistant as a potent ally in the unresolved struggle over the composition of the Smithsonian, one that threatened Henry's vision of the Institution. This early struggle involved not the creation of a museum, but of a national library.

The Library of Congress, established in 1800 and originally housed in the Capitol, contained the manuscripts of George Washington, Alexander Hamilton, Thomas Jefferson, and others. A law would eventually be passed that required a copy of every book copyrighted in the United States to be deposited there, but at this time the library was not yet an exceptional one. Advocates of a separate Smithsonian library constituted a powerful faction on the Board of Regents, led by the voluble former Senator Rufus Choate, who had stated, "we cannot do a safer, surer, more unexceptionable thing with the income…than to expend it in accumulating a grand and noble public library."

All the Smithsonian required, Choate had said, was "a plain, spacious, fireproof building; a librarian and assistants; an agent to buy your books; and a fire to sit by"—words bound to inflame Joseph Henry. The Senator had inserted into the Smithsonian's original mandate a clause allocating "not exceeding $25,000 annually" of the interest on the Smithson fund "for the gradual formation of a library." Since the total annual interest on the fund amounted to only $30,000, this clearly threatened the Smithsonian's viability.

The Regents instructed Henry to hire a distinguished librarian, Charles Coffin Jewett, who loved literature but was no bookish recluse. A few years older than Baird but much younger than Henry, he had graduated from Brown University, where he later compiled and published the library catalog, which brought him recognition. He and his brother had toured the European libraries.

Henry managed to have the amount of money for the library reduced to 50 percent of the interest on the bequest, but this figure, too, was unacceptable to him. It meant that Jewett was in at least theoretical control of half the Smithsonian's budget, and Jewett considered himself responsible to the Regents, not the Secretary.

Jewett and Henry agreed on the need for a bibliographical file to assist scholars in America. Jewett, ahead of his time in library science, was the first to propose a central national catalog of library stock by book title, a system eventually adopted in principle by the Library of Congress. But he and Henry did not agree on the desirability of a national library at the Smithsonian, or on who ultimately was boss.

Meanwhile, Spencer Baird had assumed a job that would have destroyed someone less robust. Among his publishing duties were the Institution's annual reports, book-length enterprises that included scholarly papers. The International Exchange Service required extensive physical labor, much of it performed by Baird.

On June 21, 1852, for instance, he sent out, with some assistance, no fewer than 271 packages of books, reports, and journals. In the course of a year, he wrote

(Text continued on page 62)

T. Lucreti Cari. poetæ philosophici antiquissimi
de rerum natura   liber primus incipit foeliciter.

Eneadū genitrix hominū diuūq; uoluptas
Alma uenus: cæli subter labentia signa
Quae mare nauigerum quae
terras frugiferentis
Concelebras: per te quoniam genus omne animantum
Concipitur. uisitq; exortum lumina solis.
Te dea te fugiunt uenti: te nubila cæli
Aduentumq; tuum: tibi suauis dædala tellus
Submittit flores: tibi rident equora ponti.
Placatumq; nitet diffuso numine cælum.
Nam simulas speties patefacta est uerna diei
Et reserata uiget genitalis aura fauoni
Acriæ primum uolucres te diua tuumq;
Significant nutum: perculse corda tua ui
Inde fere pecudes persultans pabula læta
Et rapidos tranant aranis: ita capta lepore.
Te sequitur cupide quocunq; inducere pergis.
Deniq; per maria ac montis flouiosq; rapacis
Frondiferasq; domos auium: camposq; uirentis
Omnibus incutiens blandum per pectora amorem
Efficis: ut cupide generatim sæcla propagent.
Quae quoniam rerum naturam sola gubernas:
Nec sine te quicq̃ dias in luminis oras
Exoritur: neq; fit lætum: neq; amabile quicq̃.
Te sotiam studio scribendis uersibus esse.
Quos ego de rerum natura pangere conor
Meminiadæ nostro. quem tu dea tempore in omni
Omnibus ornatum noluisti excellere rebus.
Quo magis æternum da dictis diua leporem
Effice: ut interea fera monera militiai
Per maria ac terras omnis sopita quiescant.
Nam tu sola potes tranquilla pace iuuare
Mortalis. quoniam bellifera munera mauors
Armipotens regit. ingremium qui sæpe tuum se
Reficit. æterno deuictus uulnere amoris.
Atq; ira suspiciens cereti ceruice reposta
Pascit amore auidos inhians in te dea uisus.
Atq; tuo pendet resupini spiritus ore.

a ij

ONE FOR THE BOOKS

by NANCY MATTHEWS

If the Smithsonian's first librarian, Charles Coffin Jewett, were alive today, he would surely applaud—and no doubt be amazed by— the Institution's current library system. Appointed by the Smithsonian's Board of Regents in 1847, Jewett was a brilliant and innovative man whose ambition it was to build a national library for the Institution.

The Smithsonian's first Secretary, Joseph Henry, recognized the need for a library, but not one that would conflict with or drain funds from his priorities, especially that of scientific research. In 1855, following a dispute with Jewett over the Institution's goals, Secretary Henry fired him, and, without the guidance of a "librarian in charge of the Library," the Smithsonian's acquisition, housing, and care of books and journals became fragmented. For a time, Henry himself oversaw the library collections, relying on the help of such staff members as Miss Jane A. Turner, whose beautiful and meticulous "Turner records" of accessions are still on file.

After the disastrous Castle fire of June 1865, Henry transferred the Smithsonian library—some 40,000 volumes—to the Library of Congress for safekeeping, and instituted a daily messenger service to retrieve books. But by the early 1880s, with the establishment of the U.S. National Museum, scientists and curators needed faster, easier access to books, and this service became wholly inadequate. Spencer Fullerton Baird, who had succeeded Henry as Secretary, thus created the National Museum Library in 1881, donating his extensive private library to augment the small reference collection that had remained at the Institution.

Early on, the Smithsonian received a wealth of printed material through the International Exchange Service, which Secretary Henry had

De rerum natura liber (Book on the Nature of Things), 1486, by Titus Lucretius Carus, and *The Naturalist's and Traveller's Companion*, 1774, by John Coakley Lettsom, are in the Smithsonian Institution Libraries' special collections. In the Jewett Room, center—named for Charles Coffin Jewett, left—a librarian consults a 19th-century folio on Brazilian birds.

The Smithsonian libraries' special collections range from natural history to the history of science and technology: above, a copy of German scientist Willy Ley's *Die Möglichkeit der Weltraum-Fahrt (The Feasibility of Interplanetary Travel)*, 1928; and, far right, a 1930 Sears, Roebuck & Co. trade catalog.

established in 1849 for the sharing of literary, scientific, and cultural publications between American and foreign scientific societies and libraries. Beginning in 1892 and continuing over a period of 22 years, William H. Dall, a prominent zoologist and explorer, donated 3,600 manuscripts and pamphlets to the library. Since that time, the library's holdings have been greatly enriched by a number of noteworthy donations, including the Larry Zim World's Fair collection and the Mel Heinz collection of machine-tool trade catalogs. Today, a special gift-and-exchange program brings in a multitude of books and about 3,000 journals annually—many of which are unavailable commercially—from some 1,800 organizations.

In 1967, Russell Shank, of Columbia University, was named director of the newly established Smithsonian Institution Libraries (SIL). Soon thereafter, Secretary S. Dillon Ripley called for the establishment of branch libraries as access points to better serve the entire Institution, and, in the early '70s, Shank established the Jewett Room, the Smithsonian's first rare-book library, in the Arts and Industries Building. This was followed in 1976 by the opening of the Dibner Library of the History of Science and Technology in what was then the National Museum of History and Technology—today's National Museum of American History. Donated by the Burndy Library, this stellar collection of 8,000 books and 1,600 manuscript groups had been assembled by Bern Dibner, founder of the Burndy Engineering Corporation, in Connecticut.

Shank also established a Book Conservation Laboratory; the SIL now houses two additional rare-book facilities: the Admiral DeWitt Clinton Ramsey Room, at the National Air and Space Museum; and the Bradley Room, at the Cooper-Hewitt National Design Museum, in New York.

Today, Smithsonian Institution Libraries is a major research facility, with 18 branches serving national and international museum and research communities and the public. Its collections of 1.2 million volumes, 15,000 journal titles, 40,000 rare books, and 1,800 manuscript groups, all of whose records are accessible on the Internet, continue to grow, often through the lasting tradition of generous donations from individuals and organizations.

Nancy Matthews is Publications Officer and Special Assistant to the Director of Smithsonian Institution Libraries.

thousands of letters, dealt with specimens arriving from expeditions in the American West and elsewhere (whiskey was bought by the barrel as a preservative because it was cheap), and sent off duplicate specimens. The naturalist's prior existence as a largely self-taught ornithologist and instructor must have seemed idyllic compared to what he had taken on.

Baird thought Henry overly strict and unyielding, sometimes authoritarian. The Secretary lectured Baird, checked even the most trivial of his expenditures, and had no compunctions about breaking into Baird's desk if he needed to obtain documents while the Assistant Secretary was elsewhere. Henry was the master and Baird still the pupil, and it rankled.

And Henry viewed with suspicion Baird's friendly relationship with Jewett. The librarian had telegraphed Baird the news of his appointment first; it was natural that the two rising intellectuals would find common ground in this still undefined Institution, but Henry suspected connivance. Both young men had passions the Secretary didn't entirely approve of, at least not as a Smithsonian mandate, Jewett's being books and Baird's specimens.

According to Jewett, Henry once told him, in what must have been a moment of frustration and perhaps of despair, "I have traitors in my camp."

Henry had concerns at the time extending beyond the library and Baird's possible disloyalty. Another proposal for the use of Smithsonian funds had been put forward by Stephen A. Douglas, the Senator from Illinois with Presidential aspirations. Douglas, one of the inhabitants of "Buncombe"—a word used to connote empty talk and Henry's contemptuous characterization of Congress—was wooing the rural vote, and proposed creating an agricultural bureau at the Smithsonian. In 1852, he staged a debate on the subject, and packed the audience with farmers, but Henry was not intimidated. He

A taxidermist at the Smithsonian mounts bird specimens from the U.S. Exploring Expedition of 1838–42. Paleontologist Fielding B. Meek, below, studied and described fossil specimens from 1858 until his death in 1876.

flatly told them that such a proposal was contrary to the wishes of James Smithson.

The bricks-and-mortar question remained. This entailed problems with the Smithsonian's architect, James Renwick, Jr.; with the contractor; and with the builders. At the outset of 1853, the "Castle," as it came to be known unofficially, consisted of two wings and ranges, each containing a large, empty space. Henry controlled the east wing and what would be the main building, but not the west wing, which was to house the library.

By now books were a source of open conflict. Jewett's manner became "pugnacious," according to his biographer, leading the Smithsonian toward its first crisis.

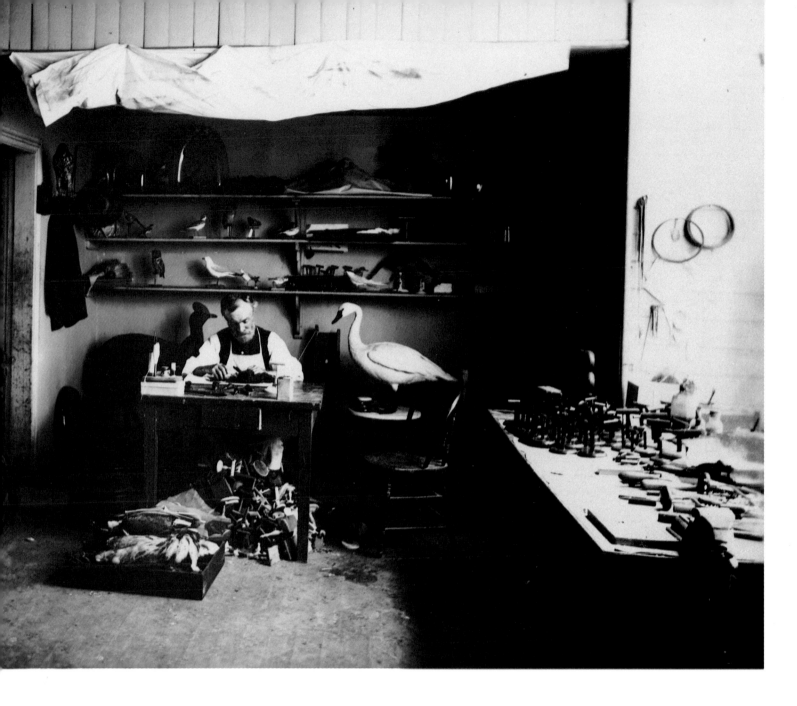

Jewett sought to undermine Henry, who accused him of insubordination. The stresses of office were showing on the Secretary. He still considered Baird not altogether trustworthy, and had a blunt talk with him, described in a letter to Bache. "[Baird]…was as pliant and affectionate as a young dog, but I fear he will sin again, and nothing but a strong arm and a few hard knocks will keep him in the right course.…"

This particular disagreement derived from information leaked to the press regarding the struggle at the Smithsonian over books. Henry believed Baird to be the source of the leak, and his words demonstrate his sometimes imperious attitude and the narrow line to which

Baird had to hew. No doubt concerned about his own career, sensing in the possible defeat of the library at least a chance of creating a museum, Baird distanced himself from the librarian.

Henry's preoccupations did not prevent him from dealing adroitly with some people, among them a majority on the Board of Regents. He discussed the Jewett problem with them, and then, in December of 1854, after gaining the Regents' approval, fired the librarian. But literature did not bow readily to science. Choate resigned from the Board in indignation; Congress got involved. A standing committee was established to look into the management of the Smithsonian, and for a brief period the Smithsonian's linen was aired, with Henry and Jewett exchanging recriminations.

This time Buncombe served the interests of the Secretary. He—and Baird—were exonerated of any misconduct, and the Smithsonian's library designated to go to the Library of Congress. It would be known as the Smithsonian Collection, but forever after would be the responsibility of someone else, pleasing Henry and, in the process, enhancing the Library of Congress.

Henry announced Jewett's dismissal in the *Annual Report* with typical reserve and without elaboration, writing that "a difficulty which occurred between the librarian and myself has led to his separation from the Institution." So much for Charles Coffin Jewett.

Henry was now in clear control of the Castle. Symbolically, what he referred to as the "dirt and rubbish" of building materials had been removed from the new Smithsonian building. In 1855, the great lecture room on the second floor was completed, and the east wing fitted out as the Secretary's residence. The Henrys—the Castle's first family—moved in.

The Secretary's relationship with Baird had lost its warmth. But, as if in response to Baird's supporters—among them the museum faction in Congress and among scientists—Henry had written in the same *Annual Report* in which he announced Jewett's dismissal, "Though the statement may excite surprise, yet I may assert, on the authority of Professor Baird…that no collection of animals in the United States, or indeed in the world, can even now pretend to rival the richness of the museum of the Smithsonian Institution in specimens which tend to illustrate the natural history of the continent of North America."

Henry still opposed the concept of a national museum on grounds that it was an inappropriate use of Smithson's money. The "increase & diffusion of knowledge" was to extend to all people and all nations, he

One of America's foremost naturalists, Louis Agassiz published numerous reports on the reptiles and amphibians collected during the Western expeditions and surveys of the 1840s to late 1870s. *A Conical Hill, 500 Feet High* was sketched by Heinrich Baldwin Möllhausen, an artist who accompanied Lieutenant Amiel Weeks Whipple's 1853 survey of the 35th parallel route for a transcontinental railroad.

thought, and the Smithsonian could not support such a venture while funding its own unprescribed research. However, Henry let it be known that he did not object to taking on the responsibilities of a museum, provided they came with outside support—in other words, with money from Buncombe.

The Secretary had so far successfully resisted Congressional pressure to transfer the natural history and anthropological collections from the Wilkes and other expeditions from the U.S. Patent Office to the Smithsonian. But two years after the Jewett affair, Congress voted to do just that, and provided federal money for the purpose. Later, Henry wrote to a friend, "Now comes the danger. The appropriations of Congress for the Museum are fitful...."

Those words would resonate for a century and a half. They indicate that Henry saw the museum as both inevitable and as a lasting source of concern.

Henry and Baird acted in accord from that point on. Neither took a formal position on Darwinism, for instance, the revolutionary theory put forward in 1858 by Charles Darwin in *On the Origin of Species by Means of Natural Selection*, which split the scientific community. Louis Agassiz, the famous geologist, was a determined creationist, but Henry maintained his distance, writing

to Asa Gray on the subject of Darwinism, "I...have come to the conclusion that it is the best working hypothesis which you naturalists have ever had"—a thoroughly objective conclusion.

Baird apparently understood the political problems that a public avowal of evolution would entail, and followed his superior's lead. He had another arena in which he intended to assert his independence. That same year, 1858, the United States National Museum was created with some fanfare, to be funded separately by Congress through the Department of the Interior, the only arrangement acceptable to Henry. It was to be curated and managed by none other than Assistant Secretary Baird.

This had always been his dream. Five years before, Baird had written to his supporter, the noted geographer George Perkins Marsh, "I expect the accumulation of a mass of matter thus collected...to have the effect of forcing our government into establishing a National Museum, of which (let me whisper it) I hope to be director."

The time for whispering had passed. Spencer Baird, devoted naturalist, conscientious omnium-gatherer, possessed his "cabinet." Joseph Henry, man of principle, avatar of American science, had maintained his vision of a Smithsonian that was devoted to the increase of knowledge and, for the moment, autonomous.

Lieutenant Charles Wilkes, commander of the U.S. Exploring Expedition of 1838–42, painted this portrait of the expedition's flagship, *Vincennes*, at anchor in Disappointment Bay, Antarctica, in 1840. The need to accommodate objects collected on Wilkes's voyage led to the establishment in 1858 of the National Museum in the Smithsonian Building, right, now known as the Castle. Today flags from around the world adorn the Castle's portico, while a statue of Joseph Henry, the Institution's first Secretary, looks out over the Mall.

Smithsonian naturalist Spencer Baird's image, such as the one above, found its way into 19th-century advertising. *Sterna aleutica bairdii*—drawn by Smithsonian bird curator Robert Ridgway—was one of a number of animals named for Baird, whose Wooten desk, left, is exhibited in the Arts and Industries Building (originially the United States National Museum) he founded and administered as its first director.

PROFILE
SUBLIME PACK RAT

Spencer Fullerton Baird, only 27 when appointed Assistant Secretary of the Smithsonian Institution, was the antithesis of the man who hired him. Born to a large family in Reading, Pennsylvania, Baird moved to Carlisle after the premature death of his father when Baird was 10. His mother was a Biddle, and consequently her son never felt the pinch of poverty familiar to the young Joseph Henry.

Baird enjoyed easy access to those with social and political influence; the Victorian precepts of the era, the attentions of a reigning matriarch—his grandmother—and the male distractions afforded by small-town America, including hunting and fishing, encouraged his inquisitiveness. He gathered the specimens that went into an extensive natural-history collection—his passion.

Enrolled in Dickinson College, in Carlisle, at age 13, the precocious Baird performed without distinction. He already knew what he wanted to be, and, at age 16, began a journal in which he detailed daily excursions—sometimes covering as much as 40 miles a day—and the skinning and preservation of his natural quarries. His meticulous observations included even the weight of his knapsack, but no personal reflections.

In an era in which there were few museums and no laws protecting wildlife, those interested in natural history often depended upon their own collections for study. Baird contacted noted collectors, and exchanged specimens with them. When he was 17, he wrote to John James Audubon, "I am but a boy and very inexperienced...." He went on to describe two species of flycatcher he could not identify, both of which proved to be new to science. This impressed Audubon, and he began a collaboration with the enthusiastic young naturalist.

In 1840, Baird enrolled in medical school, because, as his brother pointed out, "There is no living in ornithology." The dissections interested him, but not enough to stay with medicine. He dropped out to pursue his real interests, and for four years continued his walks in the environs of Carlisle, collecting and teaching himself foreign languages so he could read natural history in French, German, Italian, and Danish.

He traveled to Philadelphia and Boston to meet other naturalists, among them the already famous, Swiss-born Louis Agassiz. In Washington, Baird worked for geologist James Dwight Dana, helping identify crustacea from the Wilkes expedition.

Nearer to home, at Dickinson College, Baird was appointed professor of natural history and other science. At first unpaid, he was later given a salary sufficient to enable him to marry Mary Helen Churchill, who had an annuity of her own, in 1846, the year the Smithsonian was formally established. Baird was only 23. His enthusiasm and broad-ranging intelligence made him immensely popular with students, and also impressed adults. He soon received a letter from Dana, who had become a Regent of the Smithsonian, advising him to apply for the post of Assistant Secretary. Baird's application was seconded by Audubon, Agassiz, and George Perkins Marsh, another Regent.

Baird's natural-history collection, transported to Washington in boxcars, may not have pleased Joseph Henry, but the Secretary recognized Baird's dedication, ability, and connections. Baird's wife was the daughter of the Inspector General of the U.S. Army, a vital contributor to scientific research in the American West.

With Henry's approval, Baird wrote a letter circulated among Army personnel requesting that specimens be sent to him as an agent of the Smithsonian. Through his father-in-law, he was able to send naturalists on Army exploring expeditions and to train a number of officers who had been assigned to the Smithsonian. By 1850, the Smithsonian possessed some 6,000 specimens from 26 Army expeditions and from naturalists working abroad.

Shortly after becoming head of the National Museum, Baird described himself, in a rare bit of whimsy, as "a rather lanky, angular specimen of humanity, with red beard, rough hair, crooked legs and the biggest feet in Washington, wearing a long white coat...."

These bird skins are but a few of the many Spencer Baird brought with him to the Smithsonian. Below, the second Secretary's stereo magnifier, the Institution's only example of this unusual device.

TO THE TERRITORIES

Fossil specimens, excavation tools, and research publications evoke 130 years of discovery in the National Museum of Natural History's paleobiology division. John Bell Hatcher found the *Triceratops* skull sketched below in the 1890s.

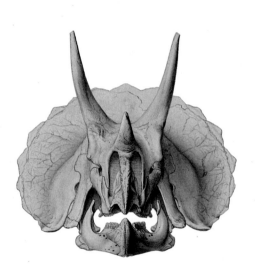

"All goes onward and outward...."
–WALT WHITMAN,
SONG OF MYSELF

As Congress sought to resolve the issue of a National Museum in 1857, a unique adventure was beginning on the far side of the Rocky Mountains, one with indirect but significant links to the Smithsonian. At the mouth of the Colorado River, at the top of the Sea of Cortez, an ambitious U.S. Army officer, Lieutenant Joseph Christmas Ives, and his men assembled a 54-foot paddle wheeler and steamed upstream, through Yuma, Chemeheuvi, and Mohave Indian country.

They fended off hostile Mormons and ran aground, and then a few men set out overland. Eventually they came into view of the awesome gorge of the Grand Canyon; so powerfully desolate was the spectacle that the men felt an irrational fear of falling. Some assumed they were not only the first white explorers to see that unforgiving country, but would also be the last.

A keen observer among them was John Strong Newberry, the geologist associated with the Smithsonian's inner circle of naturalists, who were already proving crucial to the scientific evaluation of the continent. Newberry, more detached than other members of his party, examined the canyon floor and the surrounding landscape, and wrote, "The broad valleys, bounded by high and perpendicular walls, belong to a vast system of erosion, and *are wholly due to the action of water....*"

Newberry's insights into this uplifted province had profound significance for science everywhere. Yet his observations were but a small part of a general assessment of the American territories that was then

being undertaken by men attached to expeditions of all sorts. These scientists and non-professionals recorded, collected, and classified unceasingly in what William H. Goetzmann has described in *Exploration and Empire: The Explorer and the Scientist in the Winning of the American West* as "the great empty laboratory of the West."

Lieutenant John Frémont could be seen as the first explorer to receive Smithsonian help. He had operated under the Army's Corps of Topographical Engineers, which was reorganized in 1838 into a separate arm of the military dedicated to exploration and development. Plant specimens collected on Frémont's second and third expeditions—to the Great Salt Lake and the Pacific Northwest and to California, respectively—became the subject of the sixth volume in the *Smithsonian Contributions to Knowledge*, written by John Torrey, the Princeton botanist, and published in 1854.

After Frémont's expeditions came the railway surveys, which probed Western ranges for egress to the Coast and the fulfillment of a dream that only a few years before had seemed preposterous—transcontinental travel. The Smithsonian was already on board. Taken together, these expeditions—military and adventurous—formed the "grand reconnaissance" of the Western regions of the continent that was carried out by government and augmented by private institutions, state universities, and occasionally by private initiative, with overlapping jurisdictions and mandates. They usually counted among their members at least one representative of the Smithsonian.

JOHN TORREY WAS JUST ONE OF SEVERAL PROMInent naturalists to offer early assistance to Spencer Baird. Another was Asa Gray, also a botanist. (Baird's only interest in the object of their study was as fodder for his vertebrates.) Anatomist Joseph Leidy received assistance from Baird, who considered some of the men in the field

A contemporary painting depicts President Abraham Lincoln with the founding members of the National Academy of Sciences. Second from left is Alexander Dallas Bache, Coast Survey head, academy president, and Smithsonian Regent. Smithsonian Secretary Joseph Henry is third from left, followed by Louis Agassiz, also a Regent. Lincoln often visited Henry in the Castle to discuss science or watch the Secretary's experiments.

to be members of what he, now the authoritative curator of the National Museum, thought of as his scientific sect.

Among the far-flung soldiers, surveyors, and scientists were a relative few who enjoyed an extraordinarily warm relationship with the high priest in the Castle and those around him. John Strong Newberry was one of these. Staying in a Mohave village while on the Grand Canyon expedition, Newberry wrote to fellow geologist Ferdinand Hayden, then in Washington, "I should be very happy to be one of your pleasant circle at the Smithsonian this winter." Newberry complained good-naturedly of sand in his fare; he missed, he added, "eating comforting food,

sleeping on good beds, washing clean and dressing neatly every day, and having a good time generally."

This tension between wilderness and civilization, between hard, empirical reality in the field and the ideal of science pursued beneath the gaslights of the Smithsonian, paid rich dividends. The early piggybacking of research onto Western exploration can be seen as science's taking advantage of activities of the state, with Spencer Baird as the chief instigator and provisioner.

With the tacit approval of Joseph Henry, Baird's scientific preparations included the occasional diplomatic trip to the White House. His efforts in this regard in-

creased, and, by the end of the 1850s, Baird had recruited and trained hundreds of staff members and associates to carry out his procedures. At one time, he had as many as 1,000 people collecting for the Smithsonian, with the help of various branches of government.

The Institution's bounty quickly grew from 6,000 natural-history specimens to 150,000 items, all cataloged. For his "missionaries," as he termed them, Baird often assembled the provisions himself. These included scientific instruments of various sorts, guns, powder and shot, dissecting tools, preservative whiskey doctored to make it unpalatable, arsenic, beads, mirrors, and egg blowers.

Opposite, a detail from Thomas Moran's *Cliffs of the Upper Colorado River, Wyoming Territory*. Painted in 1882, it is now at the National Museum of American Art. In return for specimens, U.S. Army Topographical Engineer John C. Frémont, left, received aid from the Smithsonian for the later of his five Western expeditions, which stretched from 1842 to 1853. A commemorative stamp celebrates Frémont's 1842 scaling of what he mistakenly called "the highest peak of the Rocky Mountains."

Military officers who collected for the Smithsonian made up a long and distinguished list. Significant expeditions so affiliated with the Institution included that of Captain Howard Stansbury, who explored and surveyed the valley of the Great Salt Lake in 1849–50; Captain Lorenzo Sitgreaves' expedition down the Zuni and Colorado rivers in 1851; Captains Randolph B. Marcy's and George B. McClellan's Red River exploration in 1852; the United States and Mexican Boundary Survey under Major William H. Emory; and the four major railway-surveying explorations. In fact, for three years, 1851 through 1854—the height of the library controversy and the clamorous erection of the Castle—Baird dealt with specimens and information collected on no fewer than 26 expeditions.

The 13 *Pacific Railway Reports*, lavishly published between 1855 and 1860, marked "the advent of specialization and teamwork in the study of natural sciences," as Herman J. Viola wrote in *Exploring the West*. Baird himself wrote the zoological sections for three volumes, as well as the one for Sitgreaves' Zuni River trip. Despite a plethora of geological, botanical, biological, ethnographic, and cartographic material about the West, the *Reports* presented, of necessity, a somewhat scattered view of what was still a great empty laboratory.

The huge store of specimens, reports, and artifacts lodged at the Smithsonian waited to be examined. Sturdy exhibit cases in the Great Hall of the Castle constituted the National Museum, minuscule compared to the bulk of accumulated material, and meanwhile more objects arrived—bird skins, pickled snakes, bows and arrows, skeletons, fossils, dried plants, artworks.

Meanwhile, the Smithsonian's secular missionaries endured more than the sand in the food John Strong Newberry had written of. John Feilner, a Bavarian mapmaker with the U.S. Army in the Pacific Northwest, was

(Text continued on page 80)

THE STAR-SPANGLED BANNER

by HAROLD D. LANGLEY

Guarding the entrance to Baltimore harbor via the Patapsco River during the War of 1812, Fort McHenry faced almost certain attack by British forces. Major George Armistead, the stronghold's commander, was ready to defend the fort, but he wanted a flag that would identify his position, and one whose size would be visible to the enemy from a distance. Determined to supply such a flag, a committee of high-ranking officers called on Mary Young Pickersgill, a Baltimore widow who had had experience making ship flags, and explained that they wanted a United States flag that measured 30 feet by 42 feet. She agreed to the job.

With the help of her 13-year-old daughter, Caroline, Mrs. Pickersgill spent several weeks measuring, cutting, and sewing the 15 stars and stripes. When the time came to sew the elements of the flag together, they realized that their house was not large enough. Mrs. Pickersgill thus asked the owner of nearby Brown's brewery for permission to assemble the flag on the building's floor during evening hours. He agreed, and the women worked by candlelight to finish it. Once completed, the flag was delivered to the committee, and Mrs. Pickersgill was paid $405.90. In August 1813, it was presented to Major Armistead, but, as things turned out, more than a year would pass before hostile forces threatened Baltimore.

After capturing Washington, D.C., and burning some of its public buildings, the British headed for Baltimore. On the morning of September 13, 1814, British bomb ships began hurling high-trajectory shells toward Fort McHenry from positions beyond the reach of the fort's guns. The bombardment continued throughout the rainy night.

Anxiously awaiting news of the battle's outcome was a Washington, D.C., lawyer named Francis Scott Key. Key had visited the enemy's fleet to secure the release of a Maryland doctor, who had been abducted by the British after they left Washington. The lawyer had been successful in his mission, but he could not escort the doctor home until the attack ended. So he waited on a flag-of-truce sloop anchored eight miles downstream from Fort McHenry.

During the night, there had been only occasional sounds of the fort's guns returning fire. At dawn, the British bombardment tapered off. Had the fort been captured? Placing a telescope to his eye, Key trained it on the fort's flagpole. There he saw the large garrison flag catch the morning breeze. It had been raised as a gesture of defiance, replacing the wet storm flag that had flown through the night.

The original Star-Spangled Banner, right, seen here in the National Museum of American History, survived the September 1814 bombardment of Baltimore harbor's Fort McHenry, below right, by the British Royal Navy. The flag was photographed in 1874 in the Boston Naval Yard, below. Inspired by this flag, Francis Scott Key wrote our national anthem, bottom, to the tune of an English drinking song.

Thrilled by the sight of the flag and the knowledge that the fort had not fallen, Key took a letter from his pocket, and began to write some verses on the back of it. Later, after the British fleet had withdrawn, Key checked into a Baltimore hotel, and completed his poem on the defense of Fort McHenry. He then sent it to a printer for duplication on handbills, and within a few days the poem was put to the music of an old English song. Both the new song and the flag became known as "The Star-Spangled Banner."

For his leadership in defending the fort, Armistead was promoted to brevet Lieutenant Colonel. When he retired from the Army in 1815, he was, according to custom, given the garrison flag. A few weeks after the battle, he had granted the wishes of a soldier's widow for a piece of the flag to bury with her husband. In succeeding years, he cut off additional pieces to gratify the similar wishes of others; the flag itself was seen only on rare occasions.

When Commodore George H. Preble, U.S. Navy, was preparing a history of the American flag, he borrowed the Star-Spangled Banner from a descendant of Colonel Armistead, and, in 1873, photographed it for the first time. In preparation for that event, a linen backing was attached to it; soon thereafter, it was put in storage until the Smithsonian borrowed it and placed it on exhibit in 1907.

The flag had become a popular attraction; in 1912, the owner, Eben Appleton, of New York, believing that the flag should be kept in the National Museum, donated it to the Smithsonian on the condition that it would remain there forever. Once in its possession, the Smithsonian hired an expert flag restorer to remove the old backing and sew on a new one to prevent damage during display.

The Star-Spangled Banner remained in the Arts and Industries Building (the old National Museum) as the new National Museum was constructed across the Mall. In 1964, when the Museum of American History opened, the flag was moved to a prominent place inside the museum's Mall entrance, an awe-inspiring testament to our nation's independence.

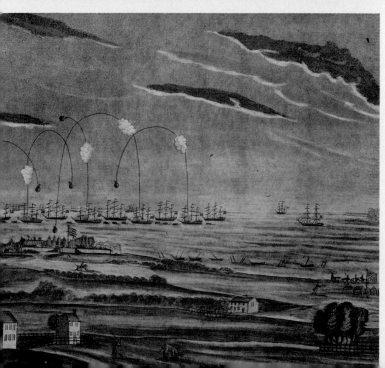

Harold D. Langley is Curator of Naval History in the Armed Forces History Collections at the National Museum of American History.

Artist John Mix Stanley portrayed the vibrant, early-19th-century Plains Indian culture in this painting, opposite, from the National Museum of American Art. Lieutenant Joseph Ives' 1858 expedition, above, up the Colorado River employed the 54-foot paddle wheeler *Explorer*, and included Smithsonian associate John Strong Newberry. Another of Spencer Baird's recruits, Ferdinand Hayden, was sketched bottling insect specimens in the field.

involved in a battle with Modoc tribesmen near Klamath Lake, in California, killing a chief. Feilner himself was later killed by Sioux along the upper Missouri while collecting for the Institution.

Lieutenant Gouverneur Kemble Warren, a member of the Topographical Engineers, conducted three surveys of the Great Plains, all the while collecting. Present at the Blue Water Creek massacre of the Sioux by U.S. cavalrymen in what would become Nebraska in 1855, a saddened Warren picked up 100 of the Smithsonian's finest Indian artifacts.

A year later, Warren led an expedition to Yellowstone country that included Baird's protégé, Ferdinand Hayden, a dreamer and a ladies' man who was destined

to become a renowned geologist. During the first month, Hayden sent 291 specimens back to the Institution. He and Warren eventually fell out over who should receive the most credit for the items collected, and, on an 1857 trip to the Black Hills, the question of loyalty arose: Should it be paid to the War Department or to the Smithsonian?

Hayden came down unabashedly on the side of science. Despite differences and intense acrimony in the field—Hayden later blustered to Baird about Warren, "I intend now either to whip him or shoot him"—the two rivals sent back 2,647 specimens, including 423 of Hayden's beloved rocks.

Hayden then joined the last of the Topographical Engineers' expeditions, to the upper Yellowstone, in 1859, another contentious, demanding, cartographically incomplete but scientifically fruitful trip. It led Hayden to conclude, with some understatement, "Such expeditions *as these* are great things to bring out the weakness of human nature."

Receiving Hayden's geological treasures back home was Fielding Bradford Meek, a balding, somewhat deaf, fine invertebrate paleontologist who was often disturbed by the mostly young, avid naturalists known collectively as "the Megatherium Club." The club was named for the extinct sloth once found in Pleistocene America. The name was frivolous, but the association was highly valued, reflecting the interests of this tightly knit group of Smithsonian naturalists.

In the 1850s, Army Lieutenant Robert Williamson's party searched the "Colorado desert," above left, for possible rail routes. Artist Thomas Moran produced his magnificent 7-foot-by-12-foot *Grand Canyon of the Yellowstone*, left, after accompanying the 1871 Hayden Survey. In 1850 Topographical Engineer Lieutenant John Gunnison collected the woven basket, horn ladle, and flask, above, from the Ute people for the Smithsonian.

In addition to Hayden, Torrey, and Newberry, Castle life included James G. Cooper, who had grown up in the presence of friends of his father—Audubon, botanist and paleontologist Thomas Nuttall, and Henry R. Schoolcraft, ethnologist; Edward D. Cope, a Philadelphia Quaker who in his lifetime would name and describe fully a third of North America's fossil vertebrates; and the prominent naturalists William Stimpson, William Healey Dall, and the Midwestern explorer of the Northwest territories, the enthusiastic but moody Robert Kennicott, who was only 22 when he first arrived at the Smithsonian.

Other young scientists came and went at the Castle, catered to by Baird while they were between the often dangerous, always difficult fieldwork and the brilliant, fraternal classifying factory the Smithsonian had become. Accommodations were found for them in Renwick's excesses, the Castle towers. "By the kindness of professor Henry," Baird's daughter, Lucy, later wrote, "many of the unused rooms, too high up for business purposes…were assigned to such young students as lodgings. They supplied their own furniture and linen…."

They dined in the basement, their exchanges of bright "conduction"—conversation—lubricated with oysters and ale when there were private funds available, although one Megatherium rule was "Never let your evening's amusement be the subject of your morning's reflections." Such a pleasant, unprecedented social collaboration, an American scientific Camelot, seemed equal to any challenge. But even the Megatheria, like the grand reconnaissance of the American West, felt the chill of civil war.

Slavery overrode all other questions in the public's mind. Before slavery ended in the District of Columbia in 1850, slave pens could be seen not far from the Castle's doors. Now talk of secession complicated all discourse in America, and at the Smithsonian, too.

Personally, Henry felt that the Union was untenable, and that the South should be allowed to secede. He counted among his friends Southerners and Southern sympathizers, including Jefferson Davis, the Senator from Mississippi who was to become president of the Confederacy; Davis was the chief proponent of the transcontinental railway, and a long-standing friend of the Smithsonian. But Henry also could claim, if not close friendship with, at least the warm personal regard of Abraham Lincoln, the Republican from Illinois who opposed the extension of slavery to the territories and who was elected President in 1860.

Henry took no public position on slavery, as he had taken none on Darwinism, a characteristic avoidance of politics. The Smithsonian had never convinced some in Congress of the Institution's importance, or even made clear to them the nature of its mission. As late as 1861, there were still Senators who considered the Smithsonian "a sort of lying-in hospital for literary valetudinarians," in the words of liberal newspaper editor Horace Greely, and Henry was careful not to provide ammunition for any more weighty accusations.

Later, Lincoln and some of his cabinet members attended an anti-slavery lecture at the Smithsonian that was given by Greeley, a war radical. Henry had a dim view of even this show of partisanship within the Institution, and endured the ridicule of abolitionists by insisting upon total objectivity. After war broke out and throughout its duration, no flag flew from Smithsonian towers—a tacit statement of scientific neutrality and a considerable display of willpower.

A week after the fall of Fort Sumter, in April 1861, Baird, who had been busy putting away duplicate birds from the Wilkes expedition, wrote, "City in wild state of confusion in consequence of the refusal of Maryland to permit the passage of [Union] troops." He prepared for a possible Confederate assault on the city by

packing away rare eggs and birds. His wife, Mary, had an "hysterical attack," but recovered. By early May, Baird was back to "labelling exotic reptiles," while crowds of soldiers visited the Smithsonian. The curator was not to be distracted.

Some members of the government thought federal troops should be billeted at the Smithsonian; Henry deflected this idea, suggesting instead that, if the need became pressing, the Institution could be used as an infirmary while carrying out its scientific mission. The Patent Office Building saw temporary duty as a hospital—the poet Walt Whitman served there as a nurse—and, in the meantime, Joseph Henry beseeched his friend George G. Meade, of the Topographical Engineers, who led the Great Lakes Survey, not to leave science to become cannon fodder.

The various goals of Henry and Baird must have seemed unattainable. At the end of 1861, Baird noted, "Terribly gloomy here. I don't know what is to become of Smithsonian matters." Publicly, Henry put the Institution at the service of the government, seeking, as historian and former editor of the Joseph Henry papers Nathan Reingold has written, "a way of accomplishing a disagreeable but necessary task."

In the *Annual Report* of 1862, Henry wrote, "Although the immediate object of war is the destruction of life and property, yet [it] is not a condition of evil unmingled with good. Independent of the political results which may flow from it, scientific truths are frequently developed…. New investigations as to the strength of materials, the laws of projectiles, the resistance of fluids, the applications of electricity, light, heat, and chemical action…are all required."

Among the opportunities provided by war were the collection of facts about the Army's "moral and economical condition," statistics of all sorts, and "illustrations

(Text continued on page 88)

A stereograph of Joseph Henry's daughter Mary's art studio, above, was taken in the East Range of the Castle in 1878. Meanwhile, a terracotta reproduction of *America*—a life-size copy of a marble corner piece in London's Hyde Park—occupied the Castle's West Wing.

THE MEGATHERIUM CLUB by RON VASILE

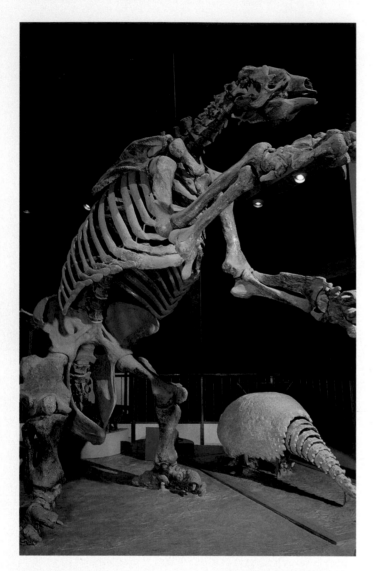

Giant ground sloths like the one favored by a group of 19th-century Smithsonian scientists are on display in the National Museum of Natural History. Right, Smithsonian Megatherium Club scientists (from left) William Stimpson, Robert Kennicott, Henry Ulke, and William Bryant mug for the camera.

"[T]hey are all Doctors and Professors and all that, and they talk about their books and all that just as if they *was* [sic] *somebody* and after all they are just a parcel of boys." The "boys" referred to here by Bruno Kennicott, younger brother of scientist Robert Kennicott, were members of the Megatherium Club, a group of naturalists based in Washington between 1857 and 1866. The Smithsonian's rapidly growing natural-history collections attracted young students from all over America, many of whom had received no formal education but instead had come to a deep understanding and love of nature through direct observation. By 1857, several of these fun-loving naturalists had formed the Megatherium Club, which was named after an extinct sloth.

The leader of this wild and raucous company was 25-year-old William Stimpson, at the time America's finest scientific dredger and an expert on marine invertebrates. After three years of duty as a naturalist on the U.S. North Pacific Exploring Expedition (1853–56), Stimpson rented a house near the Smithsonian and took in scientific boarders. The dwelling quickly became known as the Stimpsonian, and notable early members of his Megatherium Club included Robert Kennicott, Ferdinand Hayden, James G. Cooper, John S. Newberry, and Fielding B. Meek. According to Kennicott, Stimpson was "one of those chaps…who make you like them whether you will or no." Stimpson's boundless enthusiasm and love of social life served as the glue that held the club together.

Club members spent their days at the Smithsonian in the rigorous and exacting work of describing and classifying species, and afterwards they threw off all restraint. Like other gatherings of naturalists, the Megatherium Club functioned as a place where like minds could blow off steam, consume large quantities of food and spirits, and revel in the company of scientific brotherhood. On Sundays, they recuperated from the previous nights' excesses by taking long walks in the woods, "the true <u>Church</u>" according to Stimpson. The fun was often short-lived, however, as most of the naturalists left Washington periodically to spend time in the field. The club was thus transitory, meeting sporadically over a nine-year period.

The Megatheria benefitted from the counsel of Spencer F. Baird, then the Smithsonian's Assistant Secretary, who served as an informal overseer of the young men. While he admonished them to cut down on their drinking, he generously allowed them the freedom to pursue their own research. Smithsonian Secretary Joseph Henry kept his distance from the group, although he encouraged individual naturalists.

Perhaps the most interesting period in Megatheria history occurred from January to June 1863, when most of the club lived in the Smithsonian Castle. The club's resurgence during the middle of the Civil War was sparked by a reunion between close friends Stimpson and Kennicott, who, because of their wide-ranging travels, had not seen each other for three years. The two friends quickly rigged up a trap door between their rooms, and, on rainy days, led footraces through the Castle's Great Hall.

Others living in the Castle at this time included Theodore Gill, who tackled all manner of zoological subjects, and took an endless amount of kidding for his vanity; Edward D. Cope, who was not yet feuding with

Othniel Marsh over dinosaur discoveries; and invertebrate paleontologist Fielding Meek, a balding, nearly deaf "bachelor par excellence" who worked over his fossils with a vengeance.

The Megatheria did in fact tone down their antics during the war, but for a few hours each week they tried to forget the conflict by immersing themselves in group discussions on various aspects of the natural world. Older visitors to the Castle during this time included eminent naturalists Louis Agassiz, John Torrey, and John Cassin, who, perhaps despite themselves, enjoyed the boyish enthusiasm of the Megatheria. As Kennicott accurately observed, the best naturalists "never grow old."

Ultimately, tragedy stalked several of these hard-living men of science. In 1865, Kennicott departed on an exploration of what is now Alaska. After many delays and frustrations, he died in May 1866, at the age of 30, presumably of heart failure, although some claim suicide. Stimpson, who agreed to oversee the Chicago Academy of Sciences in Kennicott's absence, was appointed the academy's director permanently in 1867. He soon built its collections into one of the most significant repositories of natural-history specimens in the United States. The great Chicago fire of October 1871, however, incinerated the "fireproof" museum building. Along with the priceless specimens, Stimpson lost many important unpublished

manuscripts; seven months later, at a mere 40 years old, he died of tuberculosis. Four years later, the same disease also took the life of Meek, who had lived a solitary life in the Castle.

By 1866, the Megatherium Club had become as extinct as its namesake. Today, history has all but forgotten the triumphs and struggles

The Castle's mid-19th-century naturalists took their informal club name, Megatherium, from an extinct ground sloth, a plaster cast of which was displayed in the Upper Main Hall as late as 1872.

of many of the men who made up the club, but these naturalists were among the most dedicated America has ever seen. Stimpson summed up their philosophy beautifully and eloquently thus: "What more noble pursuit for immortal souls? Riches? War and Butchery? Political chicanery? Superstition? Pleasure? What we seek is the TRUTH!"

Ron Vasile is a Curator and an Archivist at the Chicago Academy of Sciences.

of surgical anatomy which is perhaps unrivalled," if bar-
baric. Clearly, Henry's scientific objectivity had in no way
been compromised.

He deplored the disruption of his meteorological
observations and other programs; the Smithsonian continued to support expeditions where possible, but the
endowment was affected by inflation and the decline in
the value of state bonds in which it had again been
invested. Work was further hampered by the rising costs
of printing and international exchange.

But the Smithsonian still served as the medium
for scientific and literary communication between the
United States and Europe, Canada, the Caribbean, and
Latin America. In the first year of the war, it added to
the store of meteorological data important observations
from the English expedition sent to the Arctic in search
of the Franklin party, observations relating to temperature, wind, atmospheric pressure, and "miscellaneous
phenomena, such as auroras, weather, specific gravity of
sea-water, ozone, &c."

To date, the Institution had distributed more
than 80,000 specimens and 10,000 publications to learned
societies around the world. Its burgeoning "Miscellaneous
Collections" provide an indication of the vast variety of
Smithsonian concerns. (A set of tables acquired for con-
verting various foreign measurements included "the
standard adopted in the great trigonometrical survey of
Austria.") The Smithsonian was far from moribund.

Early on in the war, Henry supported the efforts
of experimental balloonist Thaddeus S. C. Lowe, and
introduced him to President Lincoln as a military inno-
vator. Lowe's balloon hovered above fields in proximity
to the Castle's towers, with a wire strung from his wicker
basket; he sent the President the first aerial telegram:
"Sir. The city, with its girdle of encampments, presents a
superb scene." Subsequently, observations of Confederate
troop movements were made with other balloons, part of

The British Royal Navy ship of the
line H.M.S. *Agamemnon* lays tele-
graphic cable in the Atlantic in
1857. Below right, these two telegraph "sounders" from the 1850s
were used to receive messages as
a series of clicks. Opposite, a canceled Pony Express letter recalls
the 18 months that this Western
postal system operated prior to the
completion of the transcontinental
telegraph in 1861.

the Union's Aeronautic Corps, the first aerial force in American history and a popular target for Rebel marksmen.

In 1862, the Smithsonian manufactured 1,000 bottles of Laborraque's disinfectant for use in Washington's hospitals. Experiments went on in the Castle. Special devices cast light to distant navigational stations, inspiring conflicting interpretations of what went on at night at the mysterious Smithsonian. Henry was supposedly aiding the War Department in perfecting signaling. "Many a time," according to Paul H. Oehser in *Sons of Science*, "Professor Henry's companion in these studies was President Lincoln, glad to leave the scene of turmoil...."

One night the President and the Secretary were visited by a citizen who believed Confederate spies to be at work in the Castle. "What do you have to say to that, Professor Henry?" Lincoln reportedly asked his host, in mock severity. Henry explained to the man that every night a meteorological instrument had to be read with the aid of a lantern, and that nothing was taking place that might aid the Confederacy.

In 1863, Smithsonian Regent and Congressman George E. Badger, of North Carolina, was voted off the board by Congress for "giving aid and comfort to the enemies of the Government," and was replaced by Louis Agassiz. That same year, Henry, Smithsonian Regent Alexander Dallas Bache, and Rear Admiral Charles Henry Davis were placed on Lincoln's special commission to investigate "and to report upon any subject of science or art," thus establishing the National Academy of Sciences.

Like the Permanent Commission to advise the Navy on "questions of science and art," founded earlier and made up of the same three men, the academy accomplished little. As Nathan Reingold put it, "Physics and chemistry in the mid-nineteenth century were not obviously pregnant with warlike possibilities."

(Text continued on page 96)

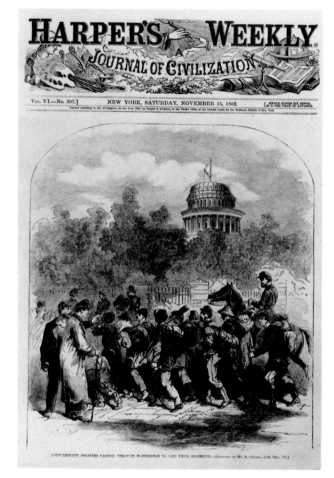

Thomas Buchanan Read's 1871 painting of General Philip Sheridan during the 1864 Civil War battle of Cedar Creek, near Winchester, Virginia, resides in the National Portrait Gallery. Sheridan's horse, Rienzi, is preserved and on display in the National Museum of American History. A *Harper's* cover portrays the Capitol dome as a work in progress.

Light Artillery Corporal

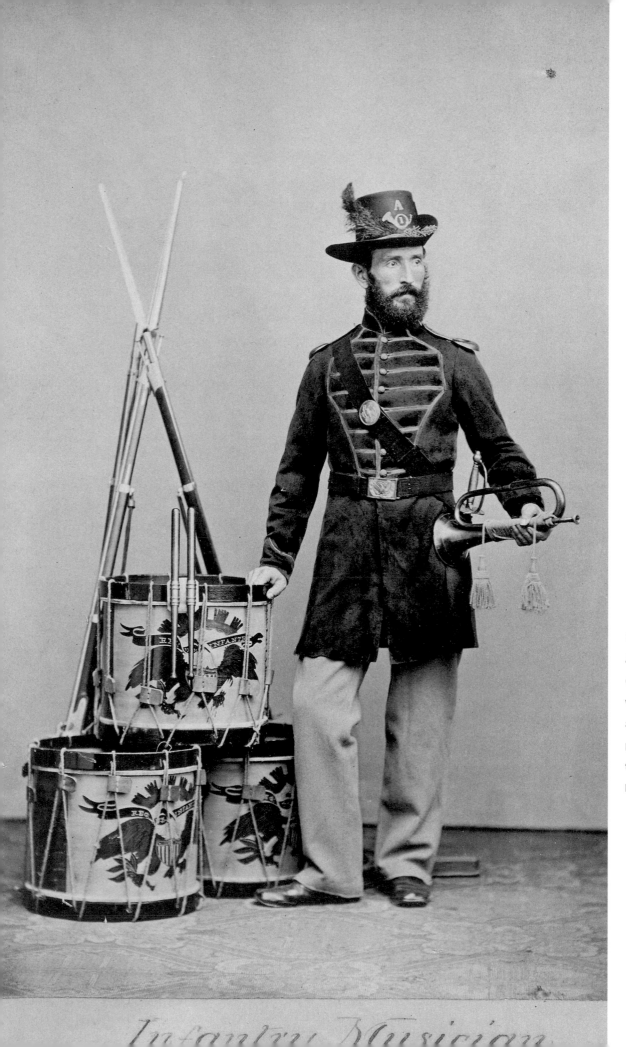

Infantry Musician

Photographs portray men in Union Army uniforms from the early part of the Civil War. Such uniforms would have been seen frequently around Washington in 1861. The photographs are part of a series in the collections of the National Museum of American History.

Long-time Smithsonian employee Solomon Brown, seated below at left forefront, appears with the staff of the International Exchange Service.

Opposite, a delivery to the exchange was photographed outside the Castle about 1910.

SOLOMON G. BROWN by TERRICA M. GIBSON

"I have engaged in almost every branch of work that is usual and unusual about the SI," noted Solomon G. Brown, the Smithsonian's first full-time, African-American employee. A trusted confidant of the Institution's second Secretary, Spencer F. Baird, Brown arrived at the Smithsonian in February 1852, even before the completion of the Castle, and stayed on through the administrations of its first three Secretaries, Joseph Henry, Baird, and Samuel P. Langley. During the course of his 54-year Smithsonian career, he worked for the U.S. National Museum, the International Exchange Service, the Bureau of American Ethnology, and the National Zoo.

Brown began as a general laborer, building exhibit cases, cleaning, and moving furniture. He also drew maps and sketches to accompany scientific lectures at the Smithsonian, as well as for talks he delivered to local church organizations and civic groups. He soon came to supervise a small group of fellow Smithsonian workers that included both blacks and whites, and was so well thought of by the staff that, in several instances, he was designated the executor of their wills. Although lacking any formal education, Brown proved himself, and gained responsibility. In August 1866, for example, he was sent to the residence of Colonel William Winston Seaton, the late mayor of the District of Columbia, to "examine the private library of that family and to enter ways to have it transported to the SI."

Much is known about Solomon Brown from the many detailed letters that he wrote to Secretary Baird during the summers, when the Baird family was away. In fact, he often served as Baird's "eyes and ears" while the Secretary was out of town, and his letters convey a clear sense of the early workings of the Smithsonian and of the young nation's capital.

Brown also performed clerical duties for Baird, entertaining visitors, opening and forwarding mail, making the family's travel arrangements, and doling out wages to workers in the Baird household. Indeed, Brown's letters show that he and Baird enjoyed a relationship that was far more than that of supervisor and subordinate. For instance, in an 1855 letter to the absent Secretary, Brown wrote, "it appears at home that some one were dead, and at the Smithsonian like I have lost some dear playmate."

The expansion of the Smithsonian through new hires and the construction of a new building, coupled with Baird's death in 1887, had a pivotal effect upon the latter half of Brown's career. He was listed as Clerk in Charge of Transportation in the Institution's early *Annual Reports*, but, by 1890, he was listed merely as a packer in the Exchanges.

Brown had great stature in the local African-American community. An accomplished and well-known poet, he was superintendent of the Pioneer Sabbath School and of the North Washington Mission Sunday School. He served on the D.C. House of Delegates, was a trustee and honored member of the 15th Street Presbyterian Church, and a trustee of Wilberforce University. The *Washington Bee*, one of the local African-American newspapers in which some of Brown's poetry appeared, reported that he delivered poems and presided over lectures to scientific and literary societies throughout the city.

In 1906, five months after retiring from the Smithsonian, Solomon Brown died. Smithsonian Assistant Secretary Richard Rathbun penned this emotional missive to the Institution's staff: "While the taking away of Mr. Brown is regretted, because of his long and faithful service, yet he was suffering pain, and death came only as a release."

Few African Americans of the time were able to claim such strong ties with influential Smithsonian staff; indeed, most were hampered by the escalating disenfranchisement of black people throughout the nation. However, Solomon Brown succeeded in opening doors of opportunity for generations of African-American employees.

Terrica M. Gibson is a Historical Researcher in the Smithsonian Institution Archives.

TREE TRUNK

Henry performed at least one unusual service for Lincoln. The President asked him to interview one of the spiritualists popular at the time in whom Lincoln's wife, Mary Todd Lincoln, had faith. The man produced sounds that seemed to come from various parts of the room, and Henry could not explain the phenomenon. He later learned of the existence of a mechanical device that could be attached to the arm and activated by flexing the biceps, setting off electrical impulses. The public exposure of this device reportedly earned Henry the enmity of the nation's mediums.

Meanwhile, the Smithsonian's bright young men continued to labor in various parts of the Castle. A typical day began with their emergence from odd places, uttering the imaginary call of the megatherium ("How! How!"). They breakfasted together, spent an hour afterward fraternizing in Baird's office, and then went off to deal with the bounty of the Smithsonian, much of it specimens from the American West.

"It is five o'clock, when the Megatherium takes its prey," Robert Kennicott wrote in the winter of 1863, "that the most interesting characters of the animal are seen. Then it roars with delight and makes up for the hard work of the day by much fun and conduction...."

Anyone could sup with the Megatheria, but they respected only scientific accomplishment, and could be wickedly critical. Hop-and-jump races about the Great Hall were not uncommon. A photograph of four Megatheria reveals William Stimpson formally posed, and Kennicott with his arm draped over another man's shoulder in an obvious burlesque. Such lightheartedness may have been in reaction to the paroxysms of war, opportunism, and fierce political combat beyond the insulating sandstone walls.

Kennicott wrote poignantly, also in the winter of 1863, "...D—n civilization. Not that I see much of it either for I live constantly here at the Smithsonian

The remains of a tree cut down by musket fire attest to the ferocity of the fighting at Virginia's Spotsylvania Courthouse in May 1864. The Confederate banner at right no doubt served as a rallying point for troops in the field.

among a set of naturalists nearly all of whom have spent their lives in the wilderness."

Joseph Henry kept his distance from Megatherium exuberance. The sudden death of his son late in 1862 left him graver than usual; life in the Castle seemed at times almost intolerable. During the summer, the Henrys' living quarters, exposed to the afternoon sun, turned into a furnace, made worse by fleas that Henry blamed on Baird's interminable collections. The visiting scientists burned too much gas, in Henry's view, illuminating their studies and, presumably, their revels. Henry wrote a note to Baird suggesting that the "making [of] the Smithsonian building into a caravansary has been carried a little too far."

Things quieted down for a time, and then, as

Stimpson wrote to Hayden in February 1863, "The Megatheria is revived. Kennicott, God bless him, has come back. Barrel of ale in the cellar. Digestion howls in the Den at Dinner. Jolly Conduction."

The Institution performed extemporaneous services for various branches of government. Henry, as head of the Government Lighthouse Board, experimented with substitutes for whale oil that could be used in lighthouses. And the collections continued to grow: "the great Ainsa or Tucson meteorite" from the Southwest, shells, reptiles, fishes from Cuba, and birds, birds, birds, which made up a significant portion of the 50,000 duplicate specimens distributed that year.

The Smithsonian reprinted lectures by such

scientists as W.D. Whitney, of Yale, and Charles M. Wetherill ("the modern theory of chemical types"); members of the French Académie des Sciences and the Royal Society of London also expanded the sources of the Institution's knowledge.

Ethnological research included work on "American aborigines" by foreign scientists. The 500-page book of meteorological observations published by the Government Printing Office contained diverse information pertaining to plants, birds, and other animals. The Smithsonian distributed meteorological bulletins from abroad, as well as star charts and tables, and expeditions continued to probe the United States and Mexico, Central and South America, Hudson's Bay Territory, Labrador, and the West Indies.

Henry pointed out that for the four years of the war, much time had also been devoted "to investigations required by the public exigencies"—in other words, the hostilities. These investigations included experiments to verify aspects of various governmental reports and the inspection of materials sold by government contractors and inventors, many of them frauds. "These facts," Henry wrote, "will be deemed a sufficient answer to those who have seemed disposed to reproach the Institution with the want of a more popular demonstration...."

The Civil War was an unprecedented disaster for the country, and a great trial for the Smithsonian. Despite Henry's efforts to remove its science from the overriding political issues of the day, the Institution was subject to divisions of loyalty and purpose that mirrored the country's. The various, far-flung scientific endeavors, like the Megatheria's sporadic conviviality, belied what seems to have been a general sense of malaise.

More of the Smithsonian's wartime activities would be known but for the fire that broke out on a cold day in January 1865, on the second story of the main building. A stove set up temporarily by men working on

THE FUNERAL OF PRESIDENT LINCOLN, NEW YORK, APRIL 25.TH 1865.
PASSING UNION SQUARE.
The magnificent Funeral Car was drawn by 16 grey horses richly caparisoned with ostrich plumes and cloth of black trimmed with silver bullion.

Alexander Gardner's photograph of President Abraham Lincoln—complete with crack that appears in the original glass negative—was taken just days before the President was assassinated in 1865, and is today preserved at the National Portrait Gallery. A contemporary print depicts Lincoln's funeral procession through New York City.

the art gallery had been improperly vented, and around three in the afternoon Henry heard a "loud crackling noise." To his dismay, he discovered the western section of the roof burning.

During the scramble that followed, his chief clerk, the assiduous William J. Rhees, saved a box of bonds deposited in the Secretary's office. Baird gathered up museum catalogs, correspondence, and—naturally—those collections he could evacuate with assistance. Fielding Meek brought up buckets from the basement, only to discover that the water in them was frozen.

Before they could be extinguished, the flames consumed most of the collected papers and effects of James Smithson. Also lost were perhaps as many as 80,000 copies of letters Henry had written and received, his notes on scientific experiments, two complete libraries obtained by the Smithsonian, manuscripts to be published, and $10,000 worth of equipment. Charles Bird King's entire collection of portraits of prominent Indians who had visited Washington also burned. Worst of all, approximately 190 of John Mix Stanley's portraits of members of 43 Western tribes, his life's work, perished in what Secretary Henry termed the "sad catastrophe."

Meanwhile, the career of Robert Kennicott, the most irrepressible and appealing of the Megatheria, an exemplar, would take on tragic overtones. Kennicott may

Christian Schussele's 1862 painting, *Men of Progress*, envisions a gathering of leading American inventors. Smithsonian Secretary Joseph Henry, standing at center, is the sole research scientist of the group. Other notables include dentist William Morton, far left, who pioneered the use of ether; John Ericsson, standing to the right of the column, designer of the U.S. Navy ironclad *Monitor*; Elias Howe, far right, inventor of the sewing machine; and Samuel Morse, seated in right foreground, who perfected the telegraph.

have been impulsive, but he was also dedicated, and he had a grand vision of scientific achievement that played a part in an important moment in American history.

A natural-history curator at Northwestern University before coming to the Smithsonian, in 1857 Kennicott had conducted a four-month collecting expedition in what became western Canada. His boyish enthusiasm masked a determination that, two years later, took him as the Institution's representative deep into both British America and Russian America—Alaska. "As a devotee to science," he wrote, "I think it decidedly my <u>duty</u>...."

He gained the respect and cooperation of the

men of the Hudson's Bay Company, to the immense benefit of Baird, the Smithsonian, and the United States. From the missionaries, trappers, Indians, and Eskimos Kennicott met, precious artifacts and previously unknown species flowed south to the Smithsonian. These connections were sustained by Spencer Baird, and proved of incalculable benefit to the Smithsonian over the years.

Back from Washington would come the usual collecting tools and items requested by Kennicott, to be used for barter and gifts. In one letter, Kennicott asked Baird for no fewer than 5,000 sewing needles, three pounds of thread, five dozen pipe beads, and "gold and silver tinsel hatcords." The whiskey to be used for preservation that Baird sent, presumably undoctored, was often consumed before it reached its destination.

Kennicott traveled as a native, enduring hardship and isolation. Civilization seemed most tolerable to him when he was away from it. Near the Arctic Circle on Christmas morning in 1861, in minus 40 degree weather, he smoked his last cigar—to the health of the Megatheria, according to his journal—and set out on a 12-hour "constitutional" by dogsled.

Back at the Smithsonian in the winter of 1862–63, dealing with his materials, Kennicott yearned for the harsh extremities of the natural world. In 1865 he was chosen as one of the principals in the Western Union Telegraph Expedition, a massive effort to locate a cable route to Asia that would take him and his men across unexplored territory from the Yukon River—which flows from far northwest Canada through central Alaska—to the Bering Strait.

From the beginning, Kennicott's efforts were hampered by the expedition's ranking military officers, ambitious men who lacked both experience in the North and a respect for science, referring derisively to the naturalist's concerns as "bugs." Kennicott had chosen not to

(Text continued on page 104)

NATURAL HISTORY REVEALED

by MARILYN SCHOTTE

J.H. Richard engraved a puffer fish, left, collected during the U.S. Exploring Expedition of 1838–42. National Museum of Natural History illustrator George Venable continues the tradition of natural-science illustration with his 1977 snow monkeys, right. Venable has employed a computer for his more recent illustrations.

Art has always accompanied the science of natural history, often serving as the most effective means of communicating newfound information. From ancient Greek herbals to medieval medical texts and accounts of the great exploratory voyages of the 15th through the 20th centuries, scientific illustrations have elucidated written text and educated us about the natural world.

The Smithsonian Institution's mandate to collect the cultural, economic, and natural resources of a newly settled continent spawned innumerable exploratory expeditions, many with illustrators in tow. Vast numbers of specimens, artifacts, and curiosities from these forays, which included the U.S. Exploring Expedition to the Pacific (1838–42), eventually became the foundation of the U.S. National Museum collections. And the energy and vision of Spencer F. Baird, the first curator in charge of the National Museum, led to the establishment of a monumental program of publications on natural-history subjects.

In Baird's view, the reputation of a publication depended equally on text and illustration, and, at a time when the study of natural history and zoology was evolving into a true profession, he wanted each work to be "unexcelled." He also was convinced that only high-quality lithographic illustrations would help persuade the U.S. Congress to fund more expeditions.

In 1878, when Baird became Secretary, he also became editor-in-chief of federal science publications, directing the production of volumes with excellent illustrations on the U.S. Exploring Expedition specimens and on the botanical, zoological, geological, and anthropological resources of the U.S. An expert on printing technologies, Baird always sought the most current drawing tools, and allowed specimens—even living plants and animals—to be sent away for illustration. Artwork of the time was reproduced with copper, steel, and wood engravings, and by lithography done largely by skilled immigrants from Europe.

Working in Paris, artist John H. Richard drew thousands of animal sketches for the mammal and reptile reports written by Baird and others,

become professional illustrators. Even Charles Doolittle Walcott, fourth Secretary of the Institution, prepared and published some of his own illustrations of the famous Burgess Shale fossils, which he discovered in the Canadian Rockies in 1910. His wife, Mary Vaux Walcott, a largely self-trained botanical watercolorist, produced paintings for a four-volume set, *North American Wildflowers*, which was published by the Smithsonian in 1925.

By the 1890s, photographic printing was commonplace, and allowed for quick reproduction of either ink illustrations, with lines, stipples, and cross-hatching, or continuous tone, involving graphite, carbon dust, and charcoal. But this new kind of printing never really replaced illustration. Photographs, while useful, cannot reconstruct, simplify, or delineate important details, which depend on an illustrator's interpretation. Illustrations are more informative, especially with microscopic subjects.

Around the turn of the century, several illustrators were in the employ of the National Museum. Frederick A. Walpole, for example, produced fine botanical line drawings with a sable two- or three-hair brush. Notably, botanical art was open to women even when higher education was not, and more than one woman began her science career by illustrating specimens and then taking on research. One such woman was Mary Agnes Chase, who worked by day as an illustrator for the U.S. Department of Agriculture and by night in the National Museum herbarium. After 30 years, she became a senior Smithsonian botanist in charge of the collection of grasses.

By the 1960s, the National Museum of Natural History employed several full-time illustrators, and many others who lived nearby worked for the museum as contract artists. Meeting regularly to share illustration techniques, in 1968 these skilled artists incorporated as the Guild of Natural Science Illustrators, now an international group with more than 1,100 members. A professional society that grew out of the grand tradition of natural-science illustration, the guild promotes the teaching of techniques and standards of excellence in publication for which the Smithsonian, in great part because of its first naturalist and second Secretary, has so long been known.

including *Report on the United States and Mexican Boundary Survey*. Steel engravings were made in the U.S. by master engravers, and later from daguerreotypes, which would eventually lead to photographic printing. Lithographic landscape illustrations, such as those painted by William Henry Holmes, who accompanied John Wesley Powell to the Southwestern U.S. and, much later, became the first director of the National Gallery of Art, depicted localities in which species new to science had been discovered.

For many years, hand-colored lithographs provided the only means of publishing colors and patterns of subjects, such as those in *A History of North American Birds: Land Birds*, by Baird, Thomas Brewer, and Robert Ridgway. In 1886, National Museum ornithologist and illustrator Ridgway published "Nomenclature of Colors," a chart of colors for standardizing taxonomic description that helped scientists describe colors based on his hand-colored plates.

A student of John J. Audubon, Baird encouraged young men to

Marilyn Schotte is a Museum Specialist-Illustrator in the Department of Invertebrate Zoology at the Smithsonian's National Museum of Natural History, and a past President of the Guild of Natural Science Illustrators.

fight in the Civil War, and this, plus his knowledge of Northern terrain, made him the object of the officers' resentment and jealousy.

Many of the supplies Kennicott requested were denied him. Eventually this brightest hope of Arctic exploration found himself stranded on the lower Yukon with only two companions, essentially abandoned. One morning in May 1866, Kennicott was found dead near the encampment, apparently of a heart attack.

He had been only 30. His equally young assistant, William Dall, termed his death a kind of murder. "Not by the merciful knife but by the slow torture of the mind," Dall wrote to his future wife. "By ungrateful subordinates…by anxiety to fulfill his commands, while those that gave them were lining their pockets in San Francisco."

Dall took over command of the expedition's scientific corps, and became extremely important to science. Western Union canceled the expedition after a successful laying of the transatlantic cable, but Dall stayed on in the North to fulfill his mission. His perseverance in the field added to the store of charts, notes, and thousands of specimens of incalculable value to science and, as it turned out, to politics.

Armed with this knowledge, Baird was able to testify convincingly about the resources of the great Northwest, and to tip Congressional scales toward "Seward's Folly"—the purchase of Alaska—one of the most important acquisitions in American history and one that was indirectly affected by the enterprise of young Robert Kennicott.

After the Civil War, the opening of the American West began in earnest, with a new vision building upon those previously held. The West had been seen periodically as a land of deliverance, of desolation ("the Great American Desert"), of serenity, and, finally, of bounty, this last inspired in part by the Homestead Act and practical scientific advances. "The last ten years," Henry Adams wrote of years following the war, "had given to the great mechanical energies—coal, iron, steam—a distinct superiority in power over the old industrial elements—agriculture, handwork, and learning…."

Tied to America's more muscular expansionism were dreams of fortunes to be made in real estate, in minerals, in farming, and in countless schemes, but the naturalists dreamed of another bonanza: new species and revelations awaiting discovery in the physical resources beyond "the shining mountains."

The Army set out to obtain accurate information about the West; it was particularly concerned with belligerent Indians and potential new American settlements. Surveys were envisioned, to be conducted by latter-day scientific argonauts with strings attached to the Smithsonian. However, the Institution was not limited to the American West. In 1866 alone, expeditions with Smithsonian assistance could also be found in British and Russian America, Cuba, Haiti, Puerto Rico, Mexico, Guatemala, Honduras, Panama, and the Sandwich Islands (today known as the Hawaiian Islands). Even W.H. Hudson, the future author of *Green Mansions*, wanted to provide specimens—birds—from "Buenos Ayres," but he also wanted more money than the Smithsonian was willing to provide.

Two famous Western surveys became de facto extensions of the Castle. In 1867, Baird told his friend Ferdinand Hayden that the state of Nebraska needed a leader for a survey of the state's resources. A doctor of medicine as well as a geologist, Hayden undertook the job with typical enthusiasm, and over the years sent Baird all his natural-history specimens. His trans-Missouri exploits so captivated Congress that in 1869 it underwrote an expansion of the effort, and named it, under the aegis of the Department of the Interior, the United States Geological Survey of the Territories.

Hayden's dedication to collecting earned him the nickname, among the Sioux, of "Man-who-picks-up-

BURNING OF THE SMITHSONIAN INSTITUTE AT WASHINGTON, JANUARY 24, 1865.—SKETCHED BY PHILIP WHARTON.—[SEE PAGE 94.]

Melted coins evoke the intensity of the fire that engulfed the Castle in January 1865. *Harper's* portrayal of the misnamed "Smithsonian Institute" depicts the entire building in flames. In fact, only the central section burned.

stones-running." Among scientists, the speed and exuberance of his scientific travels brought into question the reliability of his reports, although no one discounted the awesome amount of terrain covered by the former Megatherium.

Hayden's accomplishments included a thorough reconnaissance of western Wyoming and Colorado. Some of his best "acquisitions" were people, among them his resident paleontologist, Edward Drinker Cope, of the Philadelphia Academy of Natural Sciences. Cope convinced Hayden in 1873 to issue bulletins that gave quick credit to scientists for their discoveries. A year later, Cope discovered the Eocene fossil beds of northern New Mexico that contained distinctive remains of early mammals. (Cope would later become embroiled in a famous paleontological controversy with the equally renowned Othniel C. Marsh, a long-time friend of Baird's.)

Hayden's young photographer, William Henry Jackson, with whom he spent nine expeditionary seasons, essentially invented the role of intrepid photographer in the American West. Working with a heavy box camera and tripod, a portable darkroom, chemicals, easily shattered glass plates, and a mule, Jackson took thousands of photographs, including the first and most memorable of the headwaters of the Yellowstone River. (Hayden wanted that unique country set aside as a national park, a suggestion originally made by George Catlin as early as 1832.)

Another artist, Thomas Moran, was allowed by Hayden to accompany the expedition out of Ogden, Utah, that entered the little-known and even less understood Yellowstone country. In 1872, Moran produced the great, heroic American landscape painting, *The Grand Canyon of the Yellowstone*, which today hangs in the Smithsonian's National Museum of American Art.

Photographer and painter influenced each other's work, lending detail and scope. The photographs had the most scientific value, however. Hayden wrote in his fifth annual report that they were "of the highest value…nearly 400 negatives of the remarkable scenery of the routes as well as the canyon, falls, lakes, geysers and hot springs…. They have proved…of very great value in the preparation of the maps and this report." Jackson would go on to produce the first photographs of Colorado's Mountain of the Holy Cross, as well as of that state's ancient cliff-dwellings in the Mancos Valley of Mesa Verde.

In 1867, the Army hired the leader of the California Geological Survey, Clarence King, a renaissance man of daunting intellectual and social abilities, to conduct a scientific appraisal of the 40th parallel from California to the Great Plains. This roughly coincided with the transcontinental rail route that was expected to attract both trains and settlers. King contributed to the Smithsonian; he also exposed a massive gem hoax that put both science and himself in a good public light.

In 1871, Lieutenant George Montague Wheeler, of the Army's Engineer Corps, began a massive survey beyond the 100th meridian, an ambitious attempt to systematically partition and map the American West. King's survey served as a model. Wheeler, who lost three men to the Apaches in the Southwest, donated more than 62,000 specimens to the Institution.

The Western surveys contributed substantially to the knowledge of geology, ornithology, paleontology, botany, entomology, and zoology in the inter-mountain West—and to the Smithsonian's collections. They involved the Institution in the ongoing drama of the unraveling of the continent's past, a colossal study of ancient formations and cultures, and, as scientists began to see, of the present, too.

The best known "surveyor" of them all, the name most resonant of the West during this period, was John Wesley Powell, who would go on to play a significant role at the Smithsonian Institution.

THE FLAG THAT HAS WAVED ONE HUNDRED YEARS.

A Scene on the morning of the Fourth day of July 1876.

Raising the flag on America's 100th birthday—1876—as the Smithsonian's collections continued to grow.

PROFILE
BEYOND THE PLATEAU

John Wesley Powell is described by one biographer, the late novelist Wallace Stegner, as "the personification of an ideal of public service that seems peculiarly a product of the American experience."

In 1867, while in Washington, Powell had sought help from the War Department and the Smithsonian for an expedition into the Rocky Mountains. Henry and Baird offered him advice and instruments, including a barometer that was crucial in determining elevation. Powell completed that trip, and then decided to attempt a reconnaissance of the Colorado River country; Henry was more enthusiastic this time, but still didn't under-write the trip.

Powell planned an unprecedented descent of the Colorado River. The idea that a physically impaired man—Powell had lost his right arm as a Union artillery captain at the battle of Shiloh—and nine companions could survive 1,500 miles of uncharted cataracts in four wooden boats no doubt seemed unlikely. So Powell cobbled together contributions from the Illinois Natural History Society and Illinois Industrial University, instruments from the Chicago Academy of Sciences and the Smithsonian, and government rations.

In the spring of 1869, the expedition set out from Green River, Wyoming Territory. It soon caught the public's fancy; for a time during the 99-day ordeal, the party was feared lost. Powell and his men endured hunger and deprivation, and three who left the expedition prematurely were murdered by Shivwit Indians. Powell's emergence from the Grand Canyon, in that forbidding landscape described by John Strong Newberry a dozen years before, made him a national hero, and riveted public attention. Powell's first river-running party had survived, as Stegner wrote, by "observation, caution, intelligence, skill, planning—in a word, Science."

Powell returned to Washington in glory, and met with, among many others, Joseph Henry, who was

John Wesley Powell confers with a Paiute Indian in this photograph from the 1870s. Largely on his own initiative, the one-armed Civil War veteran explored the Green and Colorado rivers, and in 1879 founded the Bureau of American Ethnology to study Native American cultures.

Thomas Moran painted this water-color, top, from Powell's Plateau on the Colorado River in 1879. Above, an engraving from one of Powell's reports depicts his boat in a rapid. Opposite, Powell (left) takes a break during one of his early explorations.

pleased with the expedition's geological specimens. Powell wished to map and collect extensively in the plateau country, and Henry recommended appropriations from Congress.

In 1871, the one-armed river-runner received $10,000 for what was officially named the "Geographical and Topographical Survey of the Colorado River of the West." Over the next decade, Powell would formalize his theories about the slow uplift of land masses and the effects on them of water, the element that shaped the West and remained a crucial factor in its divination and development. He would also seek to preserve the essence of Indian cultures on the brink of extinction, and to maintain a cautionary view of Western settlement.

That same year—1871—Powell undertook another descent of the Colorado, with a chair lashed to the deck of the *Emma Dean*, named for his wife, and a copy of Walter Scott's *The Lady of the Lake* for reading aloud. He had the most serious intentions, among them mapping the entire Colorado Plateau.

Powell left the expedition to cross from the Colorado to Salt Lake City, observing the country first-hand, and traveled to Washington to consolidate his power base while his men continued the expedition. He answered only to the Smithsonian now, which had enfolded him in the scientific community that dominated research in the West and protected him from government bureaucracy.

Meanwhile, Powell's surrogates on the river, and later in the Plateau Province, served him and science well. They included his brother-in-law, Almon H. Thompson, who became an expert topographer; a young artist, Frederick Dellenbaugh, who produced the first sketches of the interior of the Grand Canyon; and teamster-turned-photographer John K. Hillers. Powell returned to complete the second descent, which stopped short of Black Canyon.

In the summer of 1872, Thompson and his party discovered the last unknown river in the continental United States, the Escalante, named for the first white man to pass through the area almost a century before, and the last unknown mountain range, which Powell later named for his friend Joseph Henry. Powell was in Washington again in 1873, arranging more backing, when the first map of the Grand Canyon arrived from his party, now in Utah, delivered in a homemade tin tube and sent east by railway.

Powell's expeditions neglected botany, zoology, and minable minerals in the interests of geology, mapping, and environmental research, all of which informed his very important publications, *Exploration of the Colorado River of the West and Its Tributaries* (1875) and *Report on the*

Geology of the Eastern Portion of the Uinta Mountains (1876). He became convinced that techniques of farming and general livelihood developed in the humid Eastern United States were ill suited to the arid West, and that Indian lore, including myths, language, and other cultural manifestations, should be preserved and studied to best understand Native Americans.

Somewhat religious, Powell believed that humans had evolved separately from other animals. He embraced the popular thesis put forward by Lewis Henry Morgan, the American evolutionist who attempted to systemize the sciences into a coherent whole, that human evolution involved three distinct stages—savagery, barbarism, and civilization.

Archaeology had come of age in Europe in the 1860s. Joseph Henry had foreseen its applications in North America, and recognized its considerable popularity, although he doubted the probability of tracing human origins on this continent. Baird, a true Baconian, believed that "general truths in science would surface of themselves from the comparative study of many specimens," according to his biographers, E.F. Rivinus and E.M. Youssef. This would soon lead to a conflict between Baird's emphasis on archaeological collections—and his consequent transfer to the National Museum of funds that Powell felt were rightfully his—and Powell's insistence upon cultural analysis through primary study of language, myths, and so on.

Only about a quarter of the archaeological specimens at the Castle prior to the Civil War came from North America, and the emphasis among those was on cultures east of the Mississippi. The gradual shift to peoples in the West was hampered by ongoing warfare with the Indians and by the politically expedient notion that they were rootless and unworthy of scholarly attention. Powell was one of the people who worked to change this attitude, and with it the course of the Smithsonian.

CENTENNIAL 1876

"Is not science a growth?"
—HERBERT SPENCER
The Genesis of Science

This slide-valve mill engine in the Arts and Industries Building was built in 1864 by the railroad division of the U.S. War Department. Patent-model makers, above, fashioned miniatures of these and other engines for the U.S. Patent Office.

The International Exhibition of Arts, Manufactures and Products of the Soil and Mine opened in Philadelphia in the spring of 1876. It celebrated the 100th anniversary of American independence, the country's emergence from Reconstruction, and the successes of science, industry, and cultural exchange. The visual extravaganza included such disparate elements as a giant Corliss steam engine, a Turkish scarf dancer, and hundreds of replicas of fishes.

From the exhibitions, Americans gained an unprecedented view of, among other things, their country's intellectual and material progress. The Smithsonian gained recognition and esteem through its organizing efforts and the contributions it made. The National Museum would eventually acquire enough additional objects from the Centennial to make serious physical expansion inevitable.

The Smithsonian's part in the Centennial was, predictably, the responsibility of Spencer Fullerton Baird. He had responded to a request from President Ulysses S. Grant in 1874 to join other government representatives, and had been made a member of the Centennial Board. In January 1876, he affixed to Henry's annual report an appendix describing the preparations. "[T]he most suitable exhibition on the part of the Smithsonian Institution should embrace, in the first place, the history, condition, functions, workings, and general results of the Institution itself; in the second, a display of the mineral and animal resources, as well as of the ethnology, of the United States...."

PHILADELPHIA EXHIBITION 1876

Memorial Hall, left, at Fairmount Park, Philadelphia, site of America's 1876 Centennial Exposition, housed works of art from around the world. A centennial souvenir banner, above, displays images of an eagle, George Washington, Memorial Hall, and objects exhibited at the exposition, including the *John Bull* (right), an 1831 locomotive now at the Smithsonian.

Baird was careful to distinguish between the Smithsonian's publications, international exchanges, meteorological observations, and expeditions, on the one hand, and, on the other, the possessions of the National Museum, which would clearly predominate in Philadelphia. His thorough, dutiful reporting—"The birds will include all the forms that are appreciated as being eatable and as supplying feathers, plumes &c.... The kinds specially beneficial or injurious to the farmer will also be exhibited"—must have concealed his inner glee.

The Centennial became a triumph not of ideas but of things, most of which were unlikely to appeal to the pure scientist. All the states and most nations were represented in more than 30,000 displays, at least a quarter of them belonging to the United States, whose facility at the Centennial covered two acres. The Smithsonian shared the U.S. Government Building, put up at a cost of $110,000, with the departments of War, Interior, Navy, Treasury, Agriculture, and the Post Office, but the Institution's plot was the largest, and included space devoted to the Fish Commission, of which Baird was head.

His young assistant, George Brown Goode, only 25, from Wesleyan University, put together the exhibits of fish and animals. Goode's compilation of North American mammals in a 351-page encyclopedia and his exhibits of stuffed specimens standing side by side, offset by the weapons used in their capture, riveted public attention. Among the animals encountered by visitors from all over the country who came to Philadelphia during the six months were a 15-foot walrus, a polar bear and other bears, an elk, and a musk ox.

In the end, Baird's beloved birds were too numerous to be included. But the fishes included man-eating sharks, a stingray, a swordfish, various pickled specimens, and more than 400 plaster casts painstakingly painted by a Smithsonian artist. Vessels, tackle, and other implements used in domestic fisheries also were

In the Centennial Exposition's Government Hall, far right, the Smithsonian displayed numerous Indian artifacts, including totem poles from the Northwest Coast that had never before been seen in the East and a tepee that is still on exhibit at the National Museum of Natural History. Assembled by curator George Brown Goode, the Smithsonian's animal display, right, featured moose, elk, caribou, and other North American mammals.

displayed. These objects were reduced to categories with sub-headings, an attempted scientific rendering of the real, empirical, work-a-day world.

Two hundred varieties of fresh fish were presented in two enormous refrigerators with transparent sides; some of the fish were even sold to restaurants on the grounds by the enterprising supplier. Displays of minerals included stunning crystals, ores, building stone, coal, and other examples of the geologically arcane and useful.

They had come to Baird from amateur collectors and professionals; some mineral specimens were cut into blocks, and others exhibited on pedestals. Meteorites, marble, and petrified wood added to the display of the elements gold and silver, of such interest to Americans.

These had real competition among the engineering marvels of the age: electric lights and elevators powered by the 1,400-horsepower Corliss; locomotives; and all manner of engineering feats heralding the rise of

technology that would dominate American society in the future. But the Smithsonian's displays of natural phenomena, including new agricultural products, "was considered by all visitors," *Leslie's* magazine reported, "as decidedly the best part of the International Exhibition, in view of the extent and exhaustiveness of the collection and the method and order of its display," something that redounded to Baird's credit—and to Goode's.

Among the exhibits most heatedly discussed was that of the American Indian. A joint project of the Smithsonian and the Department of Interior, the ethnology exhibit was calculated to impress a public already much interested in the subject, one that entailed the last vestiges of the frontier and the problem of continuing guerrilla warfare in the West. Baird had sent out directives to obtain "objects illustrating the habits, customs, peculiarities and general condition of the various tribes, and also...

(Text continued on page 122)

JOHN BULL

by WILLIAM L. WITHUHN

It may look pretty modest, but the *John Bull* locomotive is the world's oldest still operable self-propelled vehicle. Much more than that, it is in the ancestral line of piston-driven wheeled vehicles that have been transforming our planet since the 19th century. Furthermore, since the *John Bull* was steam-powered, it was part of the steam revolution that thrust humankind into the industrial age.

Late in August 1831, after a six-week voyage from Liverpool, England, the *Allegheny* docked at a Philadelphia wharf. Lashed aboard were the parts for "one locomotive steam engine" that had been purchased by New Jersey entrepreneur and engineer Robert Stevens. Stevens was building a railroad, one of the first in the United States; he had hired Isaac Dripps as a skilled mechanic.

A sloop carried the parts upriver to Bordentown, New Jersey. There, on September 4, young Isaac and his assistants received the crates. None of the men had ever seen a locomotive before, and there were no instructions for its assembly. But Dripps had had some experience with steamboats.

Eleven days later, Dripps and his crew had put the engine together on a short length of track. A fire was lit, and steam raised. To everyone's relief, the machine moved, although it would need considerable fine-tuning before it worked properly. In November, Stevens held a party to display the engine to politicians whose support he needed to complete his railroad. Napoleon Bonaparte's nephew, Napoleon-Lucien-Charles Murat, attended the festivities, and his wife became the first woman in America to ride aboard a steam-pulled train.

After the party, Stevens put his engine in a shed for two years while he worked on his railroad, laying rails between Camden and South Amboy, New Jersey (hence the name Camden and Amboy Railroad). Travelers then took ferries at either end to reach the cities of New York or Philadelphia. The Camden and Amboy became one of the most successful early railroads in the U.S.

Meanwhile, the *John Bull* that greets visitors to the Smithsonian's National Museum of American History today looks quite different than it did when first completed. Back in 1831, Stevens had traveled to the Newcastle, England, factory of Robert Stephenson & Co. to negotiate the engine's specifications. The two Roberts, builder and client, settled on a design for the locomotive based on Stephenson's *Samson* model, which had four

In a shower of sparks, the *John Bull* rides again, left. Acquired in 1884 as the Smithsonian's first large engineering artifact, this 1831 English-made locomotive served on one of the United States' first railroads, the Camden and Amboy. A letter from one of *John Bull*'s first passengers appears above. In 1981, the tiny patriarch returned to life on the old Georgetown Branch, top, in Washington, D.C., on the 150th anniversary of its first run in America.

equal-sized wheels that were powered by two steam cylinders. Numerous other details reflected British practice of the day.

In the spring of 1833, the *John Bull*, named some time later for England's counterpart to Uncle Sam, along with several other engines that Stevens had built, helped finish construction of the Camden and Amboy Railroad. Soon thereafter, the engine got its famous cowcatcher, whose real function was not to deflect livestock: A major alteration to the engine's basic design, the cowcatcher included a new pair of wheels to better keep the locomotive on the track.

Because investment capital at the time was scarce and the distance between major cities often was long, American track was built on the

cheap. In this frontier environment, unless the design of the locomotives could be modified and improved to navigate uneven track, railroads might not pay.

Stevens and Dripps thus combined their ideas with those of American engineer John Jervis. The extra wheels—joined by beams to the large front wheels—were rigged into the engine's suspension. The new front axle acted to steer the locomotive over rough spots without derailing. The cowcatcher, added in front of the new wheels, was more or less an afterthought.

For 35 years, the faithful patriarch locomotive served the country in one capacity or another, retiring in 1866 at the end of the Civil War. It appeared thereafter at several fairs, most notably the 1876 United States Centennial Exposition, in Philadelphia. In 1884, the Smithsonian acquired both the locomotive and the Institution's first curator of engineering,

J. Elfreth Watkins, from the Pennsylvania Railroad, which had taken over the Camden and Amboy.

John Bull left its home at the Smithsonian a couple of times to run before an admiring public—in 1893, at Chicago, and in 1927, at Baltimore. In the 1970s, curator John White posed a question: Could *John Bull* run one last time on the 150th anniversary of its first steaming in America?

On September 15, 1981, after considerable analysis, a careful examination by a boiler-inspection firm, and a 1980 trial run on a branch-line track in Virginia, *John Bull* displayed its magic before a rapt audience. Belching fire and smoke under the care of White and colleague John Stine,

Back for a day of action after 115 years in retirement, *John Bull*, right stops for a rest along Washington's C & O Canal, itself a victim of expanding railroads. At left, Smithsonian staffers in period costume watch as the 10-ton engine emits smoke and steam.

the locomotive ran on the old Georgetown Branch rails beside the C & O Canal in Washington.

To the museum staff, *John Bull* had always appeared a Rube Goldberg-like contraption, an ungainly concatenation of many years' modifications. Surprisingly, however, the little engine proved agile, easy to fire and to operate, even peppy, its pilot wheels providing an uncannily steady ride. All the engines contemporary to *John Bull* had gone to the boneyard years earlier. The reason for this locomotive's longevity became clear: The *John Bull* had escaped that fate because it was so *useful*.

William L. Withuhn is Curator of Transportation at the National Musuem of American History.

such relics of their predecessors as may be procurable." Among those who received them were John Wesley Powell and James G. Swann, who brought back a formidable collection from Alaska.

Baird sought optimum effect at the Centennial through the use of live Indians, a possibility that did not excite the Department of the Interior; he pressed the issue with stipulations to ensure that only "the cleanest and finest looking" Indians would be displayed, those who could speak English and who brought with them a child, a dog, and a pony. Indians truly representative of the tribes were considered unpresentable, and although the plan to use live Indians was endorsed by President Grant, Congress refused to appropriate funds for moving and housing even "the cleanest and finest looking" such people.

Life-size manikins were substituted for the missing real Indians. The ethnology exhibit lacked the meticulous, taxonomic approach Baird and Goode had brought to mammals and fishes, but it still triumphed in the sheer accumulation of objects. Stone-age specimens from the West Indies were included, but North American tribes predominated. From those of the Southwest—Ute, Paiute, Shoshone, Navajo, Hopi, and Apache—came implements of daily life, including baskets, weapons, and buckskin garments. From the Northwest Coast tribes—Tlingit, Haida, and Bella Bella—came majestic painted canoes and totem poles that rose solemnly above the other artifacts.

A number of grim ironies might have been read into this array. Indians were fast disappearing at the hands of the culture that was including them in its Centennial exhibition. During the height of the celebration, far across the continent, Lieutenant Colonel George Custer led a frontal assault on a Sioux encampment on the Little Bighorn River. The Sioux, under the leadership of Sitting Bull, Gall, and Crazy Horse, annihilated Custer and his 225 cavalrymen—the greatest single Indian victory in the West. It cast a pall over the Centennial celebration, eliciting calls for revenge, despite the fact that Little Bighorn marked the end of meaningful Indian resistance.

BAIRD SPENT MOST OF THE SUMMER IN PHILADELphia serving on judging panels and committees and working behind the scenes to obtain the exhibits he wanted for the Smithsonian. His personal agent visited representatives of individual states and countries with a letter from Baird to "explain more fully the plan of the Smithsonian Institution in connection with the National Museum, and show in what way the contribution desired may be of benefit to yourself as well as to the cause the Smithsonian has at heart."

The Smithsonian eventually acquired the exhibits of 34 countries and numerous states, "a quantity," Baird noted, "far beyond the storage capacity of the Smithsonian building." Once again collections beloved by Baird began to head south for Washington by rail; this time the number of freight cars required to transport them was not two but some number between 40 and 78, depending upon who was counting.

In Baird's triumph lay the seeds of the modern Smithsonian and what can be seen as the eclipse of Henry's ideal of contained, autonomous research. This came about in part through the sheer force of material accumulation. Congress authorized transferral of ownership of the Armory building between Sixth and Seventh streets—now the site of the National Air and Space Museum—to the Institution, and there the bulk of the collections sat.

Henry, close to the end of a remarkable career, once again called upon Congress to take responsibility for the National Museum, beseeching the Regents, and presumably posterity, to remember the intent of James Smithson—the increase and diffusion of knowledge. In the 1876 annual report, he praised the Smithsonian

By the end of the American Revolution, George Washington was the country's most famous figure. The Smithsonian's bicentennial exhibition featured a number of his personal effects, which lend a human touch to this often idealized man. Family legend maintains that Washington wore the uniform seen here when he resigned his commission as Commander-in-Chief in December 1783. Washington's sword, whose hilt appears at right, also resides at the Smithsonian.

exhibits—one can only guess at the self-discipline
required to list all those stuffed animals and the "dried,
smoked, salted, pickled, and canned" food exhibited
with them, the sort of thing Henry often characterized
as "trash"—and those acquired at Philadelphia. But, he
reminded the Regents, "To preserve and exhibit this
increase, or to render it available for education and scientific purposes, an additional building is imperatively
demanded."

Henry went on, "the experience of the last year
has strengthened my opinion as to the propriety of a
separation of the Institution from the National Museum....
[T]he Museum is destined to become an extensive establishment involving a large annual expenditure for its
support and a variety of complex operations having no
necessary connection with...the 'increase & diffusion of
knowledge....' Smithson gave *his own* [Henry's italics]
name to the establishment which he founded...and in
strict regard to this item of his will the endowment of
his bequest should be administered *separate from all other
funds*, and the *results achieved by it should be accredited to his
name alone*."

The museum was for education through exhibits,
Henry pointed out, whereas the Smithsonian "does not
offer the results of its operations to the physical eye, but
presents them to the mind in the form of new discoveries, derived from new investigations and an extended
exchange of new ideas with all parts of the world." Every
civilized nation had a museum, he added, "while there is
but *one Smithsonian Institution....*"

The Centennial had been a financial success—in
other words, it broke even—and Congress agreed to put
the money from its loan to the Centennial, now repaid,
into a new building to house the National Museum. This
was estimated to cost $250,000; Baird, by accession,
would be its director, and Goode, the avid organizer and
exhibitor, the museum's second in command.

(Text continued on page 129)

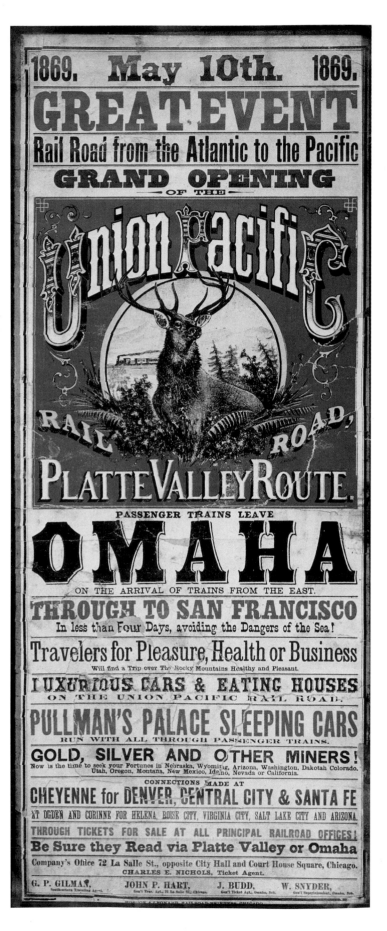

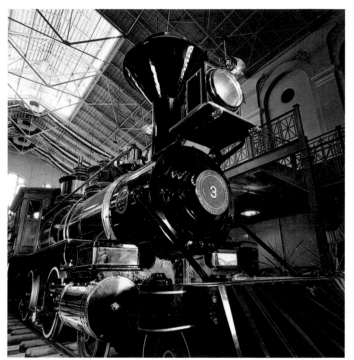

With the last rail laid at Promontory, Utah, in 1869, locomotives of the Central Pacific and Union Pacific touch cowcatchers, opposite top. After the linkup, the Union Pacific flooded the country with copies of the poster at left. The 1876 *Jupiter*, originally Santa Cruz Railroad's engine No. 3, appears in the Arts and Industries Building during the bicentennial exhibition, above, and, opposite, is attended by two Smithsonian staffers, Alex Doster and Ed Robinson, dressed as railroad roustabouts.

MODELS OF AMERICAN INGENUITY
by SONIA REECE

Between 1858 and 1883, the U.S. Patent Office in Washington, D.C., awarded patents for these nine clothespins. On November 13, 1877, William N. Whiteley, of Springfield, Ohio, received a patent (No. 197192) for his reaper, a model of which, left, is one of some 10,000 in the Smithsonian's collection.

The American Patent Act of 1790 initially required inventors to submit a model of their device, along with a written description and a drawing of their invention, to the Patent Board before a patent could be granted. Around 1802, the board officially became the United States Patent Office, and in 1810 it was located in Washington's Blodgett's Hotel. The patent models were placed on public display there until 1836, when the hotel and all the models were destroyed by fire. Four years later, the doors to a magnificent new Patent Office Building opened, and its halls quickly filled with models, establishing not only a monument to American genius and ingenuity but a major tourist attraction as well.

For the 1890 centennial celebration of the Patent Act, the Patent Office loaned part of its collection to the Smithsonian to be displayed at the U.S. National Museum. At this point, the Patent Office Building was drowning in models, and, by 1908, rising maintenance costs and dwindling exhibition space prompted Congress to begin dispersing the collection. The Institution selected 1,061 models that were associated with famous inventors, and

those remaining were either auctioned off or placed in storage. Several years later, a Congressional commission developed a plan to donate models that were considered to be historically important to the Smithsonian and other institutions.

According to Douglas E. Evelyn, former Deputy Director of the Smithsonian's National Museum of American History, "The Smithsonian Institution played a key role in making certain that a significant proportion of them [the models] would remain in the public domain, as immediate and tangible evidence of American ingenuity in the 19th century." Of the hundreds of thousands of patent models that once existed, approximately 10,000 can be found today at the American History Museum . The Institution also came into possession of the former Patent Office Building itself, which, in 1968, became home to the Smithsonian's National Portrait Gallery and its National Collection of Fine Arts (renamed the National Museum of American Art in 1980).

Sonia Reece is an Associate Editor at Smithsonian Books.

No. 76,547
Clothes Pin
Patented April 7th
1868.
No. 141740
Vincent D. Urso
and
Benj. Charles
Clothes Pin
Patented August 12th
1873.
No. 47,223
H. W. Sargeant, Jr.
Clothes Pin.
Patented April 11th
1865.
1867.
D. M. Smith.
Clothes Pins
Patented Apl. 9th
1867.
No. 45,119
J. Greenwoo
Clothes Pin.
Patented Nov 15th
1864.
Patented Dec 18th
1866.
No. 119,938
Henry
Patented Oct 17th
1871.
1858.
Dexter Pierce.
Clothes Pin.
Patented May 25th
1858.
No. 272,762.
1883.
R. B. Perkins.
Clothes Pin.
Patented Feb. 20.
1883.

Hand-operated models of the Gatling gun—invented by Richard Gatling in 1861—were displayed both in the War Department's exhibit at the country's Centennial Exposition and 100 years later in the Smithsonian's bicentennial exhibition, which also included such medical paraphernalia of the centennial period as this pharmaceutical display. The surgical set of John Maynard Woodworth, the first U.S. Surgeon General—serving from 1870 to '79—is part of the National Museum of American History's medical-sciences collection.

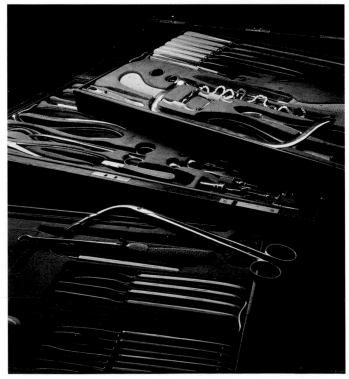

GEORGE BROWN GOODE, KNOWN AS BROWN GOODE to colleagues, was, like Baird, a naturalist of extraordinary early promise who grew into one of the best museum men of the age. Born the year after Baird was made Assistant Secretary, Goode studied under Louis Agassiz at Harvard, and, because of his strong ichthyological bent, was taken on as a volunteer by Baird at the U.S. Fish Commission. Then he joined the Smithsonian. Goode became what a later Secretary described as "the one administrator…who had seemed to grasp the essential need of combining the recording and documenting function of museum collections with original research and with public education," a happy synthesis of Henry and Baird.

Goode's fragile physique, inauspicious considering the Smithsonian's tradition of settling Herculean undertakings on the shoulders of its assistants, was indeed unsuited to the rigors of Castle life. His health suffered specifically under the load of the Centennial, but he soon became curator of the Smithsonian and one of the seminal figures in its development, both as scientist and historian.

Goode would later write, "The people's museum should be much more than a house full of specimens in glass cases. It should be a house full of ideas, arranged with the strictest attention to system." And, "A finished museum is a dead museum…." To his mind, a museum had three basic functions: as a place of record, with objects identified as "permanent landmarks of the progress of the world"; as a place of research, complete with reference collections; and as a place of education for the interested citizenry. Here he differed from Henry and Baird.

A prime tool in the diffusion of knowledge, in Goode's opinion, was the label, seemingly insignificant in the late 19th century but in fact a world of its own, with paramount future importance. "An efficient museum," Goode wrote, "…may be described as *a collection of*

Sioux chief Red Horse's 1881 depiction of a scene from the Battle of Little Bighorn resides at the Smithsonian. A newspaper article, opposite, theorized that some 10,000 Indians took part in the June 25, 1876, battle, in which Sioux and Cheyenne warriors killed Colonel George Armstrong Custer and his 225 troopers. After the battle, a requiem was composed in honor of the slain colonel.

instructive labels, each illustrated by a well-selected specimen [his italics]."

Goode also wrote, "The collections should form a museum of anthropology, the word *anthropology* being applied in its most comprehensive sense. It should… illustrate human culture and industry in all their phases; the earth, its physical structure and its products, is to be exhibited with special reference to its adaptation for use" by people.

JOSEPH HENRY POINTED OUT IN HIS LAST ANNUAL report, 1877, that anthropology "is at present the most popular branch of science." A vast amount of material was now available, much of it stored at the Smithsonian, which had put thousands of dollars into the collection of artifacts. The seemingly imminent disappearance of North America's original inhabitants, forecast by many, contributed, paradoxically, to their popularity with the public as a subject; so did the desire by some scientists to make sense of the aboriginal experience, as well as the desire, among those

like John Wesley Powell, to preserve myth and language.

Archaeology may have concentrated on the Eastern half of the continent, but ethnology focused on the Western, and on often hostile tribes. All materials relating to Indians ended up in the Smithsonian's "division of ethnology," which had three paid assistants, all protégés of Baird: Charles Rau, Edward Foreman, and Frank Hamilton Cushing.

Despite Henry's antipathy toward museum management, he valued the broad-based collection of implements under the Smithsonian's roof, those from Europe as well as North America. A new room was devoted to the anthropological exhibits, and in it, Henry wrote proudly to botanist Asa Gray, "I shall make a grand display."

In the same report, Henry wrote: "Nothing has occurred…to change my opinion" that the essential Smithsonian required nothing more than modest accommodations so scientists could do their research and receive and distribute publications and collections. The

(Text continued on page 134)

HE LITTLE HORN MASSACRE

ATEST ACCOUNTS OF THE CHARGE.

FORCE OF FOUR THOUSAND INDIANS IN POSITION ATTACKED BY LESS THAN FOUR HUNDRED TROOPS—O NIONS OF LEADING ARMY OFFICERS OF THE DEED AND ITS CONSEQUENCES—FEELING IN THE COMMUNITY OVER THE DISASTER.

Special Dispatch to the New-York Times.

The dispatches giving an account of the aughter of Gen. Custer's command, pub-shed in THE TIMES of yesterday, are con-rmed and supplemented by official reports om Gen. A. H. Terry, commanding the expe-ition. On June 25 Gen. Custer's command me upn the main camp of Sitting ull, nd at once attacked it, charging thickest part of it with five companies, ajor Reno, with seven companies attack-g on the other side. The soldiers were pulsed and a wholesale slaughter ensued. n. Custer, his brother, his nephew, and a brother-in-law were killed, and not e of his detachment escaped. The dians surrounded Major Reno's com-and and held them in the hills ring a whole day, but Gibbon's command me up and the Indians left. The number killed is stated at 300 and the wounded 31. Two hundred and seven men are id to have been buried in one place. The t of killed includes seventeen commis-oned officers.

It is the opinion of Army officers in Chi-go, Washington, and Philadelphia, that nding Gens. Sherman and Sheridan, that n. Custer was rashly imprudent to at-ck such a large number of Indians, Sit-g Bull's force being 4,000 strong. Gen. erman thinks that the accounts of the aster are exaggerated. The wounded diers are being conveyed to Fort Lincoln. dditional details are anxiously awaited roughout the country.

NFIRMATION OF THE DISASTER

PATCHES FROM GEN. TERRY RECEIVED AT SHERIDAN'S HEAD-QUARTERS — THEORIES OF THE BATTLE—PROBABLY TEN THOUSAND SIOUX IN POSITION— THE ATTACK CONDEMNED AS RASH BY OFFICERS OF EXPERIENCE—DISPOSI-TION OF THE WOUNDED.

CHICAGO, July 6.—At the head-quarters Lieut. Gen. Sheridan this morning, all was tle and confusion over the reported massa-e of Custer's command. Telegrams were coming constantly received, but most of em were of a confidential nature and hheld from publication. It is also known at the unfortunate command broke camp on North Rosebud on June 22 for the purpose proceeding in a direction which would bring the point named about the 25th, at which e. The following dispatch, the last re-ved at head-quarters in this city previous to news of the massacre, confirms the ac-unts given to the extent of showing that Cus-intended to go to that place.

CAMP ON THE NORTH ROSEBUD, June 21, 1876.
ut. Gen. P. H. Sheridan, Commanding Military
　　　Division of the Missouri, Chicago :

o Indians have been met with as yet, but traces arge and recent camp have been discovered nty or thirty miles up the Rosebud. Gibbon's mn will move this morning, on the north side of Yellowstone, for the mouth of the Big Horn, where will be ferried across by the supply steamer, and nce it will proceed to the mouth of the Little ... in, and so on. Custer will go up the Rosebud orrow with his whole regiment, and thence to te-waters of the Little Horn, thence down the tle Horn.

　　　　　A. H. TERRY,
　　　　　Brigadier General Commanding.

dispatch received at the quarters of Gen. eridan this morning at 11 o'clock confirms the first reports received. The dispatch states the forces were falling back, and that the nded had been sent to Fort Lincoln. No ails were given, but the officers at head-rters regard it as a full confirmation of the agement reported. In reply to an inquiry whether the attack was made by Custer of his own accord, or under ers from the department, an answer was en that Custer made the charge of his own A still later dispatch from Lieut. zie, of the Seventh Cavalry, was received, ing that he be transferred from the depart-at where he is now on duty to the scene of ion. This is also regarded as another con-ation of the bloody massacre reported. Gen-ster's family are at Fort Lincoln, to which at the wounded are being conveyed.

o far as an expression in regard to the wis-of Gen. Custer's attack could be obtained

thinks the first dispatch giving the details of the battle was mislaid, or else some enterpris-ig newspaper correspondent bought up the messenger and sent the account East, thus keeping the War Department in ignorance of the occurrence. From what he knows of the occur-rence he believes that Gen. Custer attempted a battle without reconnoitering the position, and that he was too bold. He does not think the slaughter so great as at first reported. The first dispatch received by Gen. Sheridan was as follows :

CAMP ON YELLOWSTONE, NEAR MOUTH OF }
　　　　　BIG HORN, July 2. }

On the evening of the 28th we commenced moving down with the wounded, but were able to get along but four miles, as the hard litters did not answer the purpose. The mule litters did excellently well, but they were insufficient in number ; therefore, the 29th was spent in making a full supply of them. On the evening of the 29th we started again, and at 2 A. M. the wounded were placed on the steamer at the mouth of the Little Big Horn. The afternoon of the 30th they were brought down to the depot on the Yellowstone. I send them to-morrow by steam to Fort Lincoln, and with them one of my aids, Capt. E. W. Smith, who will be able to answer any questions which you may desire to ask. Col. Sheridan's dispatch informing me of ... Rosebud ... hear ... a hun ... alymn ...

Tha ...
I th ... in pos ... While ... my pl ... that ... move ... Reno ... shoul ... Horn ... keep ... so as ... in th ... He wi ... Tollas ... of wh ... him ... count ... take ... the ... sweep ... requin ... co-op ... that ... asked ... He sai ... miles ... battou ... with ... sugge ... me to ... we ha ... gettin ... the ba ... ing th ... strong ...

nn ...
the a ... cannot ... cessful ... theme ... from ... cavalry ... five m ... forty-fi ... ther, r ... miles, ... not ... struck ... examin ... tell yo ... action ...

The ... Sherm ... orrow ... and w ...

GEAP ...

boys approached the river, but the attempt was made, and though one man was killed and seven wounded the water was gained and the command relieved. When the fighting ceased for the night Reno further prepared for attacks.

There had been forty-eight hours' fighting, with no word from Custer. Twenty-four hours more of fighting and the suspense ended, when the Indians abandoned their village in great haste and confusion. Reno knew then that succor was near at hand. Gen. Terry, with Gibbon commanding his own infantry, had ar-rived, and as the comrades met men wept on each other's necks. Inquiries were then made for Custer, but none could tell where he was. Soon an officer came rushing into camp and re-lated that he had found Custer, dead, stripped naked, but not mutilated, and near him his two brothers, Col. Tom and Boston Custer. His brother-in-law, Col. Calhoun, and his nephew Col. Yates, Col. Keogh, Capt. Smith, Lieut. Critten-den, Lieut. Sturgis, Col. Cooke, Lieut. Porter, Lieut. Harrington, Dr. Lord, Mack Kellogg, the Bismarck *Tribune* correspondent, and 190 men and scouts. Custer went into battle with Companies C. L. I. F. and E. of the Seventh ...

vegetables, the latter are at their worst cruel, cowardly robbers. The former are as much like the brave and war-like red men represent-ed by the *Last of the Mohicans* as ever existed outside the covers of fiction and ro-mance. This difference between the foes in the North and South-west seems not to have been well counted upon, nor provided for, and formed, as it might, prudently, no restraint upon the reckless fatal charge of the 300. If the tale told by the courier Taylor is true, the charge has scarce a parallel in the history of civilized or savage warfare. The massacre of Major Dade and his command in the Florida war is alone comparable with it in American history. The reason for an expedi-tion against the Indians this Summer is not well understood, nor has any satisfactory ex-planation been published. The wild Sioux had never been willing to live upon the reservation marked out for them, and the understand-ing has been that they were to be whipped into submission, and compelled to live like Red Cloud and Spotted Tail, with their bands, about the Government agen-cies. The question of the policy and right of the war will now be renewed and discussed.

mand which had started while he was detained as a witness before a Congressional Investi-gating Committee.

Gen. Custer's old comrades in this city will hold a meeting on Saturday evening for the purpose of taking some action ex-pressive of their esteem for him as a citizen and soldier, and adopting suitable resolutions regarding his death.

MISCELLANEOUS DISPATCHES.

A LIST OF OFFICERS KILLED—FEELING OVER THE DISASTER—A REGIMENT OF FRON-TIERSMEN OFFERED FROM UTAH.

ST. LOUIS, July 6.—A telegram from Gen. Ruggles at St. Paul to Capt. Green Hale, commanding the cavalry at the arsenal here, gives the following as the names of the officers killed in the fight between the Sioux and Gen. Custer's command :

Gen. Custer,	Lieut. Smith,
Col. Custer,	Lieut. Porter,
Col. Yates,	Lieut. Harrington,
Col. Keogh,	Lieut. Calhoun,
Col. Cook.	Lieut. Reilly,
Lieut. McIntosh,	Lieut. Sturgis.
Lieut. Hodgson,	
Lieut. Harrington is missing.	

Gen. S. D. Sturgis, in command of this post, received a telegram this afternoon from Assist-ant Adjt. Gen. Ruggles, at St. Paul, Minn., notifying him that his son was killed in the fight between the Sioux and Gen. Custer's command.

SALT LAKE, July 6.—The citizens here are very much excited over the Custer massacre, and several offers have been made to the Secre-tary of War to raise a regiment of frontiers-men in ten days for Indian service.

SAN FRANCISCO, July 6.—A dispatch from Virginia City reports great excitement at Cus-ter's death. A meeting has been called to or-ganise a company.

TOLEDO, July 6.—A special to the *Blade* from Monroe, Mich., the home of Gen. Custer, says the startling news of the massacre of the Gen-eral and his party by Indians created the most intense feeling of sorrow among all classes. Gen. Custer passed several years of his youth at school in Monroe, and his parents have re-sided there many years. The town is draped in mourning, and a meeting of the Common Council and citizens was held this evening to take measures for an appropriate tribute to the gallant dead.

SKETCH OF GEN. CUSTER.

Major Gen. George A. Custer, who was killed with his whole command while attacking an encampment of Sioux Indians, under command of Sitting Bull, was one of the bravest and most widely known officers in the United States Army. He has for the past fifteen years been known to the country and to his comrades as a man who feared no danger, as a soldier in the truest sense of the word. He was daring to a fault, gener-ous beyond most men. His memory will long be kept green in many friendly hearts. Born at New-Rumley, Harrison County, Ohio, on the 5th of December, 1839, he obtained a good common education, and after graduating en-gaged for a time in teaching school. In June, 1857, through the influence of Hon. John A. Bingham, then member of Congress from Ohio, he obtained an appointment to the United States Military Academy at West Point, and en-tered that institution on the 1st of July of the year named. He graduated on the 24th of June, 1861, with what was considered the fair standing of No. 34 in one of the brightest classes that ever left the academy. Immediately upon leaving West Point he was appointed Second Lieu-tenant in Company G of the Second United States Cavalry, a regiment which had formerly been commanded by Robert E. Lee. He reported to Lieut. Gen. Scott on the 20th of July, the day preceding the battle of Bull Run, and the Com-mander in Chief gave him the choice of accepting a position on his staff or of joining his regiment, then under command of Gen. McDowell, in the field. Longing for an opportunity to see active service, and determined to win distinction Lieut. Custer chose the latter course, and after riding all night through a coun-try filled with people who were, to say the least, not friendly, he reached McDowell's head-quarters at daybreak on the morning of the 21st. Prepara-tions for the battle had already begun, and after delivering his dispatches from Gen. Scott, and hastily partaking of a mouthful of coffee and a piece of hard bread he joined his company. It is not necessary now to recount the disas-ters of the fight that followed. Suffice it to say that Lieut. Custer's company was among the last to leave the field. It did so in good order, bringing off Gen. Heintzelman, who had been wounded in the engagement. The young officer continued to serve with his company, and was engaged in the drilling of volunteer recruits in and about the defences of Washington, when upon the appointment of Phil Kearny to the position of Brigadier General that lamented officer gave him a position on his staff. Custer continued in this position until an order was issued from the War Department prohibiting Generals of Volunteers from appointing officers of the regular Army to staff duty. He then returned to his com-pany, not, however, until he had been warmly ...

DISPATCHES ... TO RENEW OPERATIONS EFFECTIVELY DISCUSSED— THE PERSONNEL OF THE CHARGING PARTY STILL UNDIVIDED.

Special Dispatch to the New-York Times.

WASHINGTON, July 6.—The news of the fatal charge of Gen. Custer and his command against the Sioux Indians has caused great excitement in Washington, particularly among Army people and about the Capitol. The first impulse was to doubt the report, or set it down as some heartless hoax or at-

forwarded from there to Philadelphia, where Gens. Sherman and Sheridan now are.

VIEWS AT THE WAR DEPARTMENT.

THE CONFIRMATORY DISPATCHES FROM SHERIDAN'S HEAD-QUARTERS IN CHICAGO —FEELING AMONG CUSTER'S FRIENDS.

WASHINGTON, July 6.—Not until late this afternoon did the War Department re-ceive confirmatory reports of the news pub-lished this morning of the terrible disaster in the Indian country. The absence of ...

FOR TWO DAYS—EVERY MAN OF CUS-TER'S DETACHMENT KILLED EXCEPT ONE SCOUT—AFFECTING SCENES WHEN RELIEF ARRIVED.

Special Dispatch to the New-York Times.

CHICAGO, July 6.—A special to the *Times* to-night from Bismarck, recounts most graphic-ally the late encounter with the Indians on the Little Big Horn. Gen. Custer left the Rosebud on June 22, with twelve companies of the Sev-enth Cavalry, striking a trail where Reno left ...

REQUIEM TO THE MEMORY OF

Gen. Geo. A. Custer.

Composed by CHARLES GLOVER

NEW YORK

Published by Wm. A. POND & CO.　547 Broadway

BRANCH STORE　　No. 39 UNION SQUARE

SAN FRANCISCO M. GRAY.　BOSTON CARL PRÜFER.　BALTIMORE OTTO SUTRO.　PITTSBURG H. KLEBER & BRO.　MILWAUKEE H. N. HEMPSTED.　SAVANNAH LUDDEN & BATES.　SAN JOSE A. WALDTEUFEL.　CINCINNATI F. W. HELMICK.　NEW HAVEN C. M. LOOMIS.

Entered according to Act of Congress in the year 1876 by W.A.Pond & Co. in the office of the Librarian of Congress at ...

THE MAJOR & KNAPP ENG. MFG & LITH CO. 56 & 58 PARK PL.

SOME ENGINES!

by ROBERT LOCKHART

On opening day of America's 1876 Centennial Exposition, in Philadelphia, the huge Corliss engine loomed over all the other machines that had been gathered for the occasion. Nearly 70 feet tall and weighing more than 650 tons, it was the largest steam engine ever built. Not for show only, the Corliss produced enough horsepower—1,400 units of it, generated by the engine's 56-ton, 30-foot-in-diameter gearwheel—to power the Exposition's entire Machinery Hall. The Corliss clearly symbolized America's unlimited potential as it came of age in the post-Civil War era.

There were thousands of other, less imposing but equally fascinating objects on hand at Philadelphia's Fairmount Park that day, and Smithsonian Assistant Secretary Spencer Fullerton Baird knew it. As a naturalist, he immediately recognized the Exposition's importance as an unparalleled source for natural-history specimens from around the world that could enrich the Institution's fledgling collections. With this in mind and the Exposition underway, Baird and his assistants, William P. Blake and Thomas Donaldson, quietly persuaded representatives of both foreign countries and American states to donate material. Soon after the Centennial celebration closed, some 60 boxcars full of new acquisitions for the Smithsonian arrived in Washington. In fact, so much new material was garnered that the first National Museum was built on the Mall just to house and present it.

One hundred years later, in May 1976, in this same building—now called Arts and Industries—the Smithsonian gathered some 30,000 objects of the centennial period, and, in its largest special exhibition ever, celebrated the nation's 200th birthday by recreating the atmosphere of the Philadelphia Exposition. About 500 Smithsonian staffers, dressed in period costumes that were supplied by a professional designer, lent the exhibition an added air of authenticity.

Many of the artifacts on display in the "1876" exhibit, however, had been loaned to the Smithsonian from outside sources, for when the Institution's collections had been searched in preparation for the exhibition, few objects from the Exposition were found.

As for the inimitable Corliss, industrialist George Pullman bought it in 1880, four years after the Exposition; had it shipped to Chicago in 35 boxcars; and used it to power his sleeping-car works. After 30 years of grand service in the name of progress, it was sold as junk for $8 a ton.

Robert Lockhart is Assistant Editor at Smithsonian Books.

Dwarfing visitors, the 70-foot-tall Corliss steam engine powered the Centennial Exposition's entire Machinery Hall. Built by George Corliss, it was the largest steam engine in the world. Of engines like the Corliss, William Dean Howells wrote, "In these things of iron and steel the national genius speaks."

Castle itself was too large, to Henry's mind, with excess space and activities like those of the proposed new National Museum to stand next door. That should be supported by the government of the United States, not by the Institution. But the Castle couldn't contain all the specimens and amassed objects, and he worried about the financial drain they caused.

A man of contradictions, Henry understood the power and importance of the imagination, yet disliked the whimsical building in which he had lived for so many years. He recognized the need for objects, yet he despaired of meeting the responsibility for the burgeoning collections. And what he considered one of his duties— to preserve type specimens and unique phenomena—was leading directly to the demise of the small research institution he favored.

The force of Henry's personality contributed greatly to the Smithsonian's reputation at a time when its operating revenues were minuscule compared to the funds available to other scientific organizations with government support. The Coast Survey, for instance, received 10 times the income of the Smithsonian. Nathan Reingold wrote in *Science in Nineteenth-Century America* that the Smithsonian "had acquired the status of a venerable symbol...strange in an institution so relatively young." On the other hand, "limited resources...prevented it from acquiring a major role in the growth of science in America. The organization is a good example of institutional proclivities for drifting into the path of least resistance." But a museum had been stipulated in the bill establishing the Smithsonian.

It is difficult to imagine how Henry or anyone else, even without Baird and Baird's strong propensity to gather, could have resisted participating in and collecting from the pursuit of Manifest Destiny and the general, highly diffuse scientific enthusiasms of the period. The Smithsonian may have had no signal scientific break-

through to which it could point then, no latter-day equivalent of Henry's telegraph. But the collections and the work done on them, like the exchanges of scientific information, satisfied one interpretation of the will of James Smithson.

Even if Henry's vision of a more limited Institution did not prevail, he "laid the basis for the intellectual advances of future generations of American scientists," historian Wilcomb E. Washburn has written, "who...clearly comprehended the fundamental necessity for support of basic research untrammeled by practical considerations."

In December 1877, Henry had his first attack of what was diagnosed as Bright's disease, a complication of the kidneys. He was 80, and had, according to his doctor, only six months to live. He became the de facto Secretary only, with Baird tending to business and looking anxiously toward the transition. Baird had succeeded in shaping the Smithsonian, and he feared a political appointee to replace Henry might undo all the Secretary and Baird had accomplished. More, Baird badly wanted the position of Secretary himself.

As in the past, he proved capable of political expediency when his career was at risk. He had thoroughly learned the lesson of subservience in the Jewett affair a quarter of a century earlier. In the spring of 1878, Baird wrote confidential letters to his two strongest supporters on the Board of Regents, James D. Dana, dean of geology in the United States, and Asa Gray, botanist and resolute Darwinian. Gray had championed Baird in a fight with Agassiz over Baird's admission to the National Academy of Sciences, one of many squabbles that erupted among America's leading scientists of the day.

Baird confided to him, "I have a right to look forward to the succession, even though I may be unfit to occupy in all respects Prof. Henry's chair. I doubt whether there is anyone who has a poorer opinion of myself than I have in many respects; but I think I can continue in the

Crowds flock to the recently opened U.S. National Museum—today called the Arts and Industries Building—at the turn of the century. Above, artist Paul Takacs' rendering of the National Museum depicts totem poles that had been exhibited in the Centennial Exposition's Indian display.

4995

future as well as in the past, the general routine of the Smithsonian." He asked Gray to help prevent "rivals to supplant me in the Institution"—and affirm the status quo ante.

Baird was 55, about the age Henry had been when he became Secretary. He had grown into a bearded, portly patriarch, but the words might well have come from the eager young naturalist whom Dana had urged on the Smithsonian, way back in 1850.

HENRY DIED ON MAY 13, 1878, IN THE BUILDING about which he had ambiguous feelings at best. His funeral was attended by President Rutherford Hayes and his cabinet, the Supreme Court, and both houses of Congress. The Government Printing Office published 15,000 copies of a 528-page *Memorial of Joseph Henry*, the title embossed in gold, and Congress appropriated money for the statue of Henry that stands in front of the Castle today.

Henry's accomplishments were legion, and included meritorious service as a member of the U.S. Lighthouse and other boards. He was known for discoveries in electromagnetism and telegraphy, but his experiments with lard as a replacement for whale oil in lighthouse beacons and with Fresnel lenses had broad, practical impact. He had successfully stewarded the Smithsonian through its contentious, formative years; more importantly, his strength of character and the natural respect accorded Henry made him the symbol of the Smithsonian and the key element in the achievement of the Institution's status.

The day after Henry's funeral, May 17, 1878, the Regents unanimously elected Spencer Baird second Secretary of the Smithsonian Institution. His ascendancy came on the eve of the Institution's, and the country's, transformation—the Smithsonian into a multi-faceted reflection of the nation's culture, the United States into an industrial power, with, sadly, a vanishing frontier.

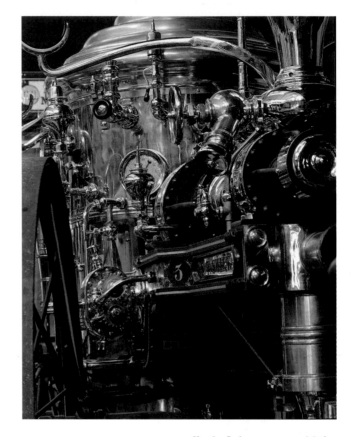

Massive Rodman guns, a model of the 312-foot U.S.S. *Antietam*, and other military and naval objects in the Arts and Industries Building recall the War Department's display at the Centennial Exposition. The steam-driven fire engine above appeared with other machines of the period.

THE SCIENTIST AS ARTIST

Out of the reconnaissance of the American West had arisen a man who combined two salient aspects of the future Smithsonian: science and art. William Henry Holmes, just 32 at the time of the transferal of power from Henry to Baird, had proven to be the most accomplished artist cum topographer in America.

  Born in the year the Smithsonian was founded, he came to Washington to study art in 1871, and met Mary, Joseph Henry's daughter. Invited to visit the Institution, Holmes was recognized as a talented illustrator, and soon was employed to draw fossils for Fielding Meek and William Dall. In the words of a friend, Holmes saw himself as "an original predestined member of the [Smithsonian] family."

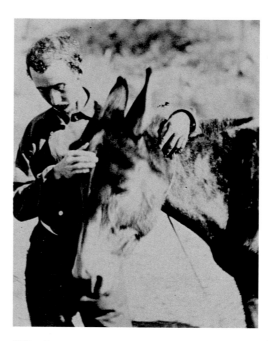

William Henry Holmes completed *Panorama From Point Sublime*, far right, and his illustration of the valley of the Virgin River, right, during Clarence Dutton's 1879 survey of the Grand Canyon. Smithsonian Butte, named for a fancied resemblance to the Institution's Castle, rises in the background. Above, Holmes and his mule rest during Ferdinand Hayden's 1874 survey of Colorado. Photographer William H. Jackson also accompanied Hayden's surveys of the 1870s, at some point capturing Holmes, left, beside his tent writing letters.

In 1872, Holmes obtained a position on the Hayden survey, during which he revealed an ability to deal convincingly with vast, intimidating landscapes, his detailed drawings of natural panoramas doubling as meticulous topographical work. He took an active role in the two-year study of the San Juan region of what would become Arizona and New Mexico in the company of William Henry Jackson, and found in the lost cliff dwellings in the Mancos Valley, part of the Mesa Verde complex, a romantic vision augmented by his ongoing study of archaeology and ethnology.

  Holmes's highly detailed, subtle illustrations of

the geology of the Colorado River country combined intimate scientific knowledge with an imaginative use of light and shadow, creating the best illustrations ever done of the demanding Grand Canyon terrain.

Curtis M. Hinsley, Jr., wrote in *Savages and Scientists* that Holmes knew natural "emotion required restraint.... He fought that battle for years, resolving the issue only by harnessing his imagination to the service of a strongly inductive science." This sympathy between knowing and imagining also affected the Smithsonian, where Holmes would play an increasingly vital role.

A year after Henry's death, Holmes traveled to Europe to study art, but he was soon back in America as a ranking member of John Wesley Powell's Geological Survey. His interest in the origins of primitive art, so closely tied to scientific discovery and evolutionary theory, prefigured the later expansion of anthropology and the amassing of art at the Institution.

As William H. Goetzmann wrote in *Exploration and Empire*, Holmes was "a central figure in the development of so many scientific surveys, bureaus and art galleries that his career is a palimpsest of the cultural and institutional history of late-nineteenth-century America."

Holmes, like his Smithsonian "family," was about to re-invent himself.

II UNIVERSE: 1879–1949

The men visiting the construction site of the National Museum had about them an unmistakable air of propriety. The Smithsonian, in little more than three decades, had become a recognized force in American life, reflected now in silk top hats, in the handkerchief in the jacket pocket of Secretary Baird, and in the cape worn by Lieutenant General William Tecumseh Sherman. The man who had broken the will of

The architecture firm of Cluss and Schulze based their plans for the Smithsonian's new National Museum (today the Arts and Industries Building) on the 1877 drawings of U.S. Army General and consulting engineer Montgomery Meigs. Here, Meigs's vision for the National Museum's rotunda.

The Castle rises in the background of artist Robert Sivard's painting of a 19th-century trolley in Washington, D.C. Riding on the trolley are contemporaries (from left to right) Smithsonian Secretary Spencer Baird, Gallaudet College cofounder Edward Miner Gallaudet, Secretary of the Interior Carl Shurz, and Secretary of War Robert Todd Lincoln.

the Confederacy in Georgia during the last campaign of the Civil War had gone on to become a Smithsonian Regent and chairman of the Institution's Building Committee.

General Sherman's fellow Regent, General M.C. Meigs, had supplied Sherman's forces down south, and had commanded a division of civilians within the War Department when Jubal Early, a Confederate general, threatened Washington. A brilliant engineer, Meigs had also directed the construction of the Washington Aqueduct, which brought water to Washington from the Potomac River at Great Falls, and the building of the Cabin John Bridge, for a time the longest masonry arch in the world. As a member of the U.S. Army's Topographical Engineers, he had distinguished himself by surveying much of the Mississippi River.

That day on the Mall, Meigs, as consulting engineer, showed considerably more interest in the particulars of the rising museum than its architect, Adolf Cluss, who leaned raffishly against an unfinished doorway. Cluss had stated in his 1879 report that the building would require even more material than had originally been proposed: five million bricks, 3,000 barrels of cement, 4,000 cubic yards of sand, 470 tons of wrought iron, 31,000 square feet of glass, and 60,000 pieces of slate.

Meigs kept track of this phenomenal load; Baird, true to character, was also intimately involved in the overseeing. Spending the $250,000 approved by Congress was so closely monitored, in fact, that a few thousand dollars would be left over when the building was completed in 1881 and the doors opened to an inquisitive public.

By then the collections, including the avalanche of accessions from foreign and domestic exhibitors at the 1876 Philadelphia Centennial Exposition that had been assiduously sought by Spencer Fullerton Baird and his assistants, would be so great that even the new National Museum could not contain them.

THE AMERICANS

"…the people of the world have left their history most fully recorded in the works of their hands."

—OTIS T. MASON

The fight in Congress to formally establish the United States Geological Survey (USGS) spilled over into early 1879. It was an attempt to extend the range of scientific knowledge in the American West, and the surveys of Ferdinand Hayden, Lieutenant George Wheeler, Clarence King, and John Wesley Powell were consolidated to avoid duplication. The USGS was opposed by members of Congress who did not want any limitations placed on Western development, including limitations that might also serve to promote knowledge, and debate about its establishment brought together powerful egos from both sides.

Among those in favor of the USGS were Othniel C. Marsh, the famous Yale paleontologist, and King himself, who was named first director of the USGS. Of the reformers, however, the most notable was Powell. His political contributions made the Survey's survival possible.

As important as the creation of the USGS, at least for the Smithsonian, was the addition, instigated by Powell and included in the same legislative bill, of a little-noticed item. "For completing and preparing for publication the contributions to North American ethnology," it read, "under the Smithsonian Institution, twenty thousand dollars: Provided, that all of the archives, records and material relating to the Indians of North America, collected by the geographical and geological survey of the Rocky Mountains, shall be turned over to the Institution, that the work may be completed and prepared for publication under its direction…."

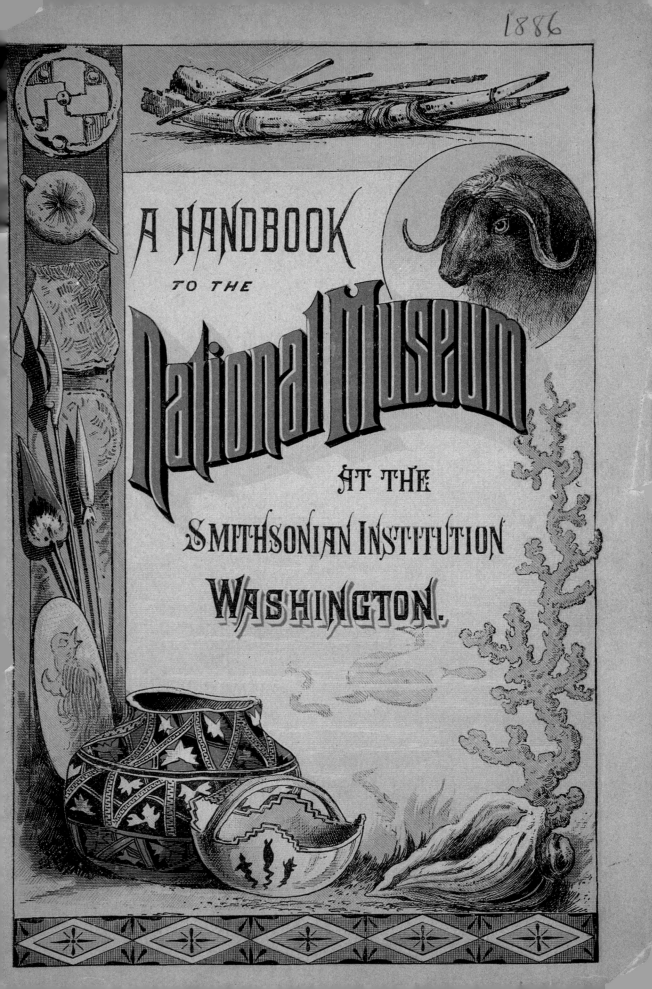

This was the seed of the Bureau of Ethnology—later renamed the Bureau of American Ethnology (BAE)—and a personal triumph for Powell. As its director, he launched himself on a second career. And by making the bureau an adjunct of the Smithsonian, rather than of the Department of the Interior, he had it removed from national politics.

Two years later, in 1881, Powell succeeded King as director of the USGS. He then combined the administrative offices of the survey with those of the BAE, hired new people, and set about mapping the entire United States while initiating broad-ranging research in archaeology, ethnology, linguistics, and physical anthropology.

The BAE was the first government agency formed solely for the study of humans. Intended as a permanent anthropological survey, it had grown out of Powell's experiences in the field. He had become convinced that American Indians were faced with eradication through unplanned development of the West and attempts to "civilize" them, and he wanted to record all aspects of their cultures.

Intellectuals of the period sought unity in chaos, a rational explanation of the cosmos and of humanity's place in it. Anthropology was already a serious endeavor at the Smithsonian, considered an admixture of science and religion. Joseph Henry's main anthropological interest had been origins. He pushed for classification of human habitation of the North American continent, and earlier had turned the head of Powell from geology to anthropology. The first Secretary had always stressed the value of research.

The current Secretary, Spencer Baird, was also committed to anthropology and other natural sciences, but as a Baconian he believed that truth would emerge from the diligent study of many specimens. This brought him and Powell into philosophical conflict, and pushed the Smithsonian toward intellectual frontiers it

Director of the Bureau of American Ethnology and one of the most formidable figures of American science during the late-19th century, John Wesley Powell works in his Smithsonian office in 1894. Artist and archaeologist William Henry Holmes incorporated a cloud-and-rain symbol, a depiction of cliff dwellings, and pictograph motifs from the Southwest into his 1879 bureau insignia.

would ultimately reach after the real Western frontier had been declared closed.

A year before the completion of the new National Museum in 1881, the Smithsonian's enduring, punctilious chief clerk, William J. Rhees, produced a second guide to the Institution that attempted to classify objects roughly according to geography and Indian tribe. It revealed—again—the exponential growth and dismaying diversity of collections that still contained such oddities as a "tomahawk presented to Davy Crockett by the young men of Philadelphia" and fragments of an iron bolt "to which Columbus was chained in Santa Domingo."

The character of the collections was matched at times by the Institution's anthropologists, a diverse lot. Some were quite eccentric, and some would clash with Powell. Among them was Charles Rau, a German, who had corresponded with Henry in search of a job and finally had been hired by Baird to help with the Centennial's ethnological exhibit.

Baird made Rau curator of the museum's Department of Antiquities, a fitting appointment since Rau was no field collector but a thoroughgoing museum man who believed that paleolithic hunters had crossed from Siberia on the Bering land bridge to America. This theory brought him into conflict with Powell, who thought humans had not dwelled on the continent before neolithic times.

More versatile than Rau was Otis T. Mason, who had taught anthropology and other subjects at Columbian Academy in Washington. In 1869, then a devoted scholar of Eastern Mediterranean cultures, Mason had been called to the Smithsonian to explain some Semitic inscriptions to Henry and Baird. Afterward, Baird suggested that Mason give up Near Eastern studies for those of the Americas, where opportunities for firsthand, significant research abounded. Baird's arguments were compelling, and Mason, in his own words, was "born again that day."

Mason believed that invention was the basis of human culture, that a person was an "artificializing" animal, and that therefore the key to human identity lay in what was concocted. Invention was construed as any action directed toward some new objective, including societal ones. But things were most important to him, as they were to Baird, who considered Mason the Smithsonian's resident anthropological expert.

Like Rau, Mason was a museum man rather than a field worker. He started the list of Indian tribes that provided the seed for Powell's "synonymy," a card catalog of tribal names that would grow into the Bureau of Ethnology's *Handbook of American Indians North of Mexico.* Like Powell, Mason believed in the thesis of Lewis Henry Morgan that all humankind progressed through three successive stages from savagery to barbarism to civilization.

Both men tended to shoehorn findings into these categories, to which Powell added a final stage of "enlightenment"—meaning rational, scientific society. But Powell believed that language, religion, and folklore, not collections, were the primary objectives of the committed anthropologist.

Powell's reigning inner circle at the BAE included four men. One, James Stevenson, formerly with the USGS, was chosen to lead the BAE's first expedition to the Southwest in 1879, the year the bureau was formed. This was to prevent the ransacking of ethnological sites there, as well as to study pueblo cultures and collect objects.

Another member of the inner circle and also a friend, James Pilling accompanied Powell on field trips, compiled notes, and assisted with the synonymy. Making up in diligence what he lacked in imagination, he assembled a valuable set of bibliographies of publications dealing with Indian languages, the focus of so much BAE activity.

Colonel Garrick Mallery, a retired Army officer, contributed a study of Indian pictographs and sign language. He worked mostly in Washington, conducting his

research through correspondence, a method of which Joseph Henry would have approved. It was Mallery who skewered the popular notion that Indians believed in a "Great Spirit"—a notion that appealed to Victorians because it suggested that the Indians were prime candidates for conversion to Christianity. Mallery pointed out that Indians tended to give answers they thought would please their white interlocutors, and that, in fact, many Indians didn't even understand the concept of a single divinity.

The sickly Henry Henshaw became Powell's linguistic coordinator. Formerly a member of the Wheeler survey, Henshaw was a naturalist and an ornithologist. He believed, as Powell did, that "biologic training was a prerequisite to a successful career in anthropology." To Henshaw fell the task of devising a sound scientific nomenclature for anthropology, a task to which he was singularly devoted.

Others, though not intimates of Powell, depended heavily on him for work in the field. The Reverend James Dorsey, an Episcopal minister and missionary whose linguistic talents led him to become an authority on the languages of the Omaha, Ponca, Kansas, and Quapaw tribes, did not believe, as Powell did, that Indian cultures became more homogeneous as they progressed toward "civilization." But he added support to Mallery's debunking of the Great Spirit myth—a notable contribution, coming from a Christian missionary.

An early link between Powell's BAE and the Smithsonian was Frank Hamilton Cushing, one of the Institution's most colorful and controversial anthropologists. Originally hired by Baird to help Rau assemble the Centennial exhibits in Philadelphia, Cushing had been annoyed by the irascible German's strict requirements for placement and description.

Although Cushing lived in the towers of Baird's Smithsonian, he wasn't entirely suited to its prevailing

This 28-inch-tall Underwater Monster tepee model was collected by ethnologist James Mooney from the Kiowa around the turn of the century. During the 1897 Tennessee Centennial Exposition, Mooney hired Kiowa artists to construct models, right, for a miniature camp circle to explain tepee heraldry. Far right, a watercolor records the exquisite details of two Native American pots in the Smithsonian's collections.

ethic; he believed, as Curtis M. Hinsley, Jr., later wrote in *Savages and Scientists*, that the anthropologist "must understand motive through ethnographic data, and method through personal experiment." Cushing was assigned as the Smithsonian's representative to Stevenson's BAE expedition of the Southwest, thus initiating one of the Smithsonian's most colorful and resonant professional contretemps.

Baird directed Cushing to concentrate on a single pueblo—the Zuni—and report directly to him. At first Cushing was disgusted with the physical privations and the food, but later he wrote to Baird, "I am far from sorry you have decided to keep me down here...." He stayed behind after the others moved on, sometimes assuming the guise of a Zuni, and set the stage for the bitter feud that followed.

THE NATIONAL MUSEUM WAS COMPLETED BUT still unoccupied in the spring of 1881, when it was used for President James A. Garfield's inaugural reception. Located on Independence Avenue, just east of the Castle, the building suggested a French museum, with a center hall and radial wings designed for flow and space, but it was more a testament to industry than science. There was much to display under the vast iron roof topped with flying banners, steel girders, and colonnaded second-story walkways; some exterior brick had been glazed with different colors, achieving a striking pattern.

The cost, much heralded, was a mere $250,000—quite economical for a federal construct. So economical, in fact, that plaster began to fall in patches from the ceiling shortly after the museum opened. The *Annual Report* of 1881 pointed out that this situation "greatly endangered life and property in the Museum." It would have to be dealt with over the summer, after the new building had filled up with steam engines and other fine examples of America's burgeoning industrial power.

Smithsonian anthropologist Frank Hamilton Cushing demonstrates a Native American pottery-repair technique. He was photographed by John K. Hillers at Zuni Pueblo, New Mexico, in 1881–82, above, where his unorthodox style of research caused controversy. In 1884 he was recalled to Washington after siding with the Zuni in a land dispute.

It was already apparent that the Smithsonian required yet another new building to accommodate all in its possession.

MEANWHILE, STORIES FROM THE SOUTHWEST about a "white Indian" began to appear in print. This "Indian" was Frank Hamilton Cushing, the Smithsonian's brilliant young ethnologist, who was also, in the words of Curtis M. Hinsley, Jr., "chronically ill, eccentric, and uncontrollable...."

Some scientists raised questions about Cushing's methods, which involved dressing like his subjects and trying to assume a Zuni persona; others wondered if Cushing was emotionally stable. But Baird at the Smithsonian, like Powell at the administratively independent BAE, was interested in Cushing's work, and they both stood behind their unorthodox anthropologist.

Cushing sought not just to record evidence of primitive thought, but to enter it. "As gradually their language dawns upon my inquiring mind," he wrote to Baird about his experiences in the field, "not the significance of these ceremonials alone but many other dark things are lighted up by its meanings." These "dark things" were of less interest to Baird than specimens, but he and Powell both valued Cushing's spiritual approach.

Cushing became a member of the Zunis, and was elected Bow Priest, but some thought he exaggerated the level of his true acceptance. The unorthodox ethnologist did broaden traditional areas of inquiry, and he made the significant discovery that much of the Zuni's formal life was governed by what he called "formulas" passed down by word of mouth. But he became involved in Zuni affairs that some thought he should have been merely studying, rather than seeking to influence.

James Stevenson and his wife, Matilda, who disliked Cushing, heavily criticized him. In 1881, returning

(Text continued on page 156)

A close-up from a photograph taken at the National Museum building site in 1880 depicts Secretary Spencer Baird. At a cost of $3.00 per square foot, the museum was the cheapest permanent U.S. government building ever built. Years later, workers installed a new floor.

A spectacular array of ancient giants fills Dinosaur Hall, right, in the National Museum of Natural History (NMNH). *Diplodicus*, center, looms over *Triceratops*, foreground, while a reconstruction of *Stegosaurus*, at far right, appears beneath both *Albertosaurus* (curved in its death pose) and *Edmontosaurus*. Suspended overhead is *Quetzalcoatlus northropi*. NMNH staffer Marguerite Noga, opposite, adds the finishing touches to a skull cast of *Tyrannosaurus rex*.

DINOSAUR WARS

by MICHAEL BRETT-SURMAN

In the late 1860s, a private feud erupted that would affect children all over the world. Eventually, the feud became a war, a war whose unlikely bones of contention were those of dinosaurs. Some of the most famous spoils of this conflict are now on display in the Dinosaur Hall at the Smithsonian's National Museum of Natural History.

The two protagonists—paleontologists Edward D. Cope and Othneil C. Marsh—started out as friends. Cope once took Marsh on a tour of his favorite collecting sites in New Jersey. When Cope returned the next summer, he discovered that Marsh had secretly bought the mineral rights to these areas, and that he could no longer collect there. Their friendship declined abruptly. Cope then concentrated on the fossils collected during the Ferdinand Hayden surveys in what is now Colorado, Wyoming, Montana, and the Dakotas, surveys that produced better material than Marsh was obtaining on the East Coast.

Marsh quickly expanded his operations out West, and their territorial squabbles escalated. In 1872, Joseph Leidy, the father of American vertebrate paleontology, took both men on a joint expedition to Wyoming in an attempt to resolve their differences. It was to no avail, however; by the end of the summer, an all-out war between the two had begun. Both Cope and Marsh were more than a little egotistical: Each was determined to be the first to scientifically name and describe new fossil species, including dinosaurs, and each considered his own work superior to anyone else's.

Most of their competition centered on the rocks of the Morrison Formation. This original "Jurassic Park" produced some of the most spectacular dinosaur fossils ever discovered, which, unlike the partial remains found in the East, included complete skulls and skeletons.

By 1891, the arguments boiled over into the national press. Cope accused Marsh, who was the official vertebrate paleontologist for the U.S. government, of misusing government money. He argued that Marsh took advantage of both his position and federal tax dollars to enhance his own fossil collection. In fact, Marsh also used his own money for collecting, but, because of Cope's claim, he was ordered to turn over all material that had been collected with government funds to the Smithsonian.

The Marsh collection became the foundation of the National Museum of Natural History's dinosaur collections. Many specimens found by Marsh's field crews from the 1870s through the late 1890s are here: The predatory *Allosaurus* is one of the most complete skeletons ever mounted in a museum; *Ceratosaurus*, another meat-eater, is known for its complete skull, unique in the world. Our knowledge of this animal is based on the Smithsonian fossil. The museum's *Stegosaurus* is displayed as it was found, in its flattened death position. For more than 100 years, this remained the most complete known specimen of this creature. Other Marsh specimens in the paleobiology collection include *Triceratops* and *Edmontosaurus*, favorite dinners of *Tyrannosaurus rex*.

The public's fascination with dinosaurs has continued long after Cope's death in 1897 and Marsh's in 1899. From 1903 until 1940, Charles W. Gilmore upheld their legacy. He discovered the first large accumulations of

baby dinosaurs in North America, and the massive *Diplodocus*, *Camarasaurus*, and *Brachyceratops* in the Dinosaur Hall were collected by Gilmore's crews. The Dinosaur Hall exemplifies the Smithsonian's percentage of type specimens on display, a percentage that is unrivaled in the museum world. (A type specimen is the original one used to name a new species.)

Even today the public can see many of the fossils Marsh described during his race for fame with Cope in naming new dinosaurs. *Ceratosaurus nasicornis*, *Edmontosaurus annectens*, *Stegosaurus stenops*, and *Camptosaurus nanus* are among them. Other type specimens on exhibit include Gilmore's *Brachyceratops montanensis*, *Thescelosaurus neglectus*, and *Camptosaurus browni*.

From 1959 until his retirement in 1993, Nicholas Hotton III served as the Smithsonian's "dinosaur curator." In 1979, I joined him in the Department of Paleobiology as a museum specialist, and together we have led expeditions to Big Horn County, Wyoming. To this day, dinosaur fossils outnumber that region's human inhabitants.

Michael Brett-Surman is a Museum Specialist in the Department of Paleobiology at the National Museum of Natural History.

to the pueblo country on a lavish collecting expedition, the Stevensons didn't like what they found: Cushing in Indian regalia, acting like a native. They were jealous both of Cushing's access to the culture and of his claims of findings based on long residence in the pueblo. The Stevensons were known to be somewhat insensitive when dealing with their subjects, and they tended to leave after a brief stay, often taking collectibles back to their Washington home.

With Powell's approval, Cushing moved over to the BAE. Then, as a Bow Priest in the tribal council, he took the side of the Indians in a land dispute involving a Senator's son-in-law, a political misstep. He was recalled to Washington in 1884, and accused of being a fraud by politicians and the envious Stevensons, who had powerful connections.

But Cushing was still held in high regard by most of his colleagues, who recognized the value of his introspective ethnology. In an extraordinary "interview" he conducted with himself in 1883, Cushing judged himself "sincere in his motives, honest in his assertions, and in spite of his undeniable but voluntary and acknowledged 'degradation' to have retained fully his moral character and self-respect...."

THE ROMANTIC IMPULSE IN SOME OF POWELL'S—and the Smithsonian's—anthropologists was augmented by powerful intellect, perseverance, and idiosyncracy. Among such independent spirits owing allegiance first to knowledge and only then to humanity's institutions was Jeremiah Curtin, who was hired to collect Indian myths for the BAE. A linguist with considerable detachment, Curtin believed that tribes' underlying religious beliefs were essentially the same, differing only in details. To Curtin, the myths were representative of the best of the primitive imagination, important in themselves and in need of preserving.

The exterior and interior of the National Museum building as proposed by the architectural firm of Cluss and Schulze. The skylights and balconies were added between 1897 and 1902, and the original wooden floors were replaced with cement between 1891 and 1900. The roof leaked constantly, and sagged under the weight of heavy snowfalls.

Curtin collected myths from members of various tribes, often in lonely, difficult circumstances, with singular devotion. Of his work among the Modocs, Klamaths, and Wintus on the West Coast, Curtin wrote in his memoirs, "Whenever one Indian failed me, I sent for another and, while waiting, I kept my nerves steady by reading Persian."

In 1883, Powell brought into the Geological Survey a self-taught, determined young Iowan named W.J. McGee, who wrote a dense volume on glacial geology but was ultimately bound for anthropology. Powell recognized a kindred spirit, and once told him, "McGee, I know what I want; you know what I want. Figure out a way to do it...."

When Powell resigned from the Geological Survey in 1894 and withdrew from the ongoing political struggle, he moved into the BAE and took McGee with him. There, McGee was his assistant, and the man most likely to succeed him.

In 1885, an Irish-Catholic journalist named James Mooney joined the BAE without salary after having applied annually for years, and began to make his mark on anthropology. Mooney possessed a political consciousness and an interest in the ongoing traditions of oppressed peoples, and he sought to record Indian cultures through careful reconstruction of the past.

Mooney's first monograph, on the Cherokees, was based upon living memories of those involved in Cherokee history, and seemed to prove that, among the Cherokees, past tribal experiences were still vital to their lives and beliefs. A later monograph included stories of the abuse inflicted upon Indians by whites at the battle of Wounded Knee, a subject that was a political liability in Washington.

Like Powell, Mooney believed that American Indian cultures were doomed. But he clashed with Powell—and with the next Secretary of the Smithsonian—over some of the old theoretical practices of natural science. The social environment of the tribes was changing rapidly, and required an ethnological approach closer to

(Text continued on page 161)

Grover Cleveland became the first—and only—U.S. President to be married in the White House when he wed Frances Folsom—who became, at 21, the youngest First Lady ever—in the Blue Room, right, in June 1886.

As seen in this advertisement, President Grover Cleveland's marriage to Frances Folsom captivated the nation. As the Clevelands left the White House in 1889, Mrs. Cleveland told the servants, "I want to find everything just as it is now when we come back again…four years from today." Four years later, during her husband's second inauguration, she wore the gown, opposite, that now resides in the Smithsonian's First Ladies' collection.

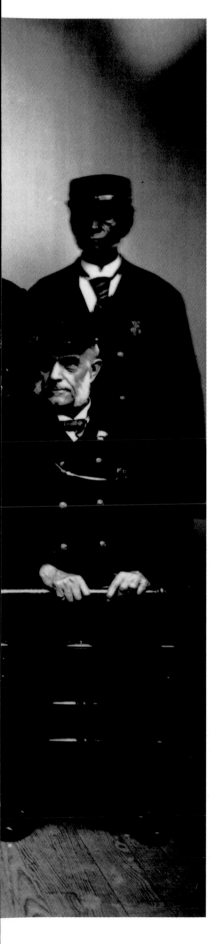

A portrait of guards from the National Museum, probably taken before the turn of the century. James Thomas Gant, standing at right, may have been the Smithsonian's first full-time African-American guard.

Cushing's than to Powell's, Moody thought. He considered the continued classification of tribes by linguistic stock outmoded, and said so—a source of annoyance to the old guard.

POWELL AND BAIRD MANEUVERED CONTINUALLY around the questions of authority and money. Baird respected Powell, and had recommended him to President Garfield as a replacement for Clarence King at the USGS. He described Powell as knowing "more about the live Indian than any live man," but that did not mean Baird deferred to him.

When Powell wanted to send geologist Clarence Dutton to Hawaii to study volcanoes, and another scientist to Spain to study quicksilver, he couldn't justify using USGS funds; Baird financed the missions. But Baird had insisted from the beginning that he wanted acquisitions—things—from the BAE for the National Museum as well as studies of language and culture, and he continued to press Powell on this.

A quarter of the BAE's budget of $20,000— known as the "Secretary's reserve"—went toward purchases for the museum. Powell was not happy with this arrangement. Baird may have been Secretary of the Smithsonian, but Powell was a national hero, locus for Washington's intellectual elite and, in 1878, along with Baird, Dutton, Henry Adams, Clarence King, Colonel Mallery, William Henry Holmes, Otis Mason, and others, a founder of the Cosmos Club. Powell was highly regarded within the National Academy, the Philosophical Society, the Association for the Advancement of Science, and Congress. He was an early protégé of the Smithsonian, perhaps, but he was now probably the most influential scientist in the country.

Baird must have felt if not envy, at least the burden of Powell's arguments for BAE autonomy. Their relations remained cordial, however, and Powell remained a strong supporter of the Institution. He proposed that Congress create a National Department of Science that would include the USGS, the Coast and Geodetic Survey, the Signal Service, the Fish Commission, the Hydrographic Bureau, the National Observatory, and the National Museum, all under the authority of the Smithsonian's Regents rather than as adjuncts of government agencies that were therefore subject to politics. Powell described Baird as a committed scientist who "knew how to marshall significant facts into systems, and to weld them into principles," and, in 1879, he stepped down as president of the Cosmos Club to allow Baird to be elected.

Still, conflicts arose over the Secretary's reserve fund. Powell considered the dispensation of BAE his prerogative; Baird was determined to be Secretary of all Smithsonian bureaus. The Secretary's reserve remained at $5,000, while the BAE appropriation increased to $40,000, and Powell's research ambitions rose, too. He resented being deprived of even the $5,000, but Baird wouldn't relinquish it.

Baird told Powell that Congress wanted more material from North American Indian sites to prevent other countries from plundering them. He hired James G. Swan to collect artifacts on the Northwest Coast, and paid Swan's generous salary of $3,600 out of BAE funds. Baird predicted that the returns from the expenditure would "compare favorably with the result of outlays of a similar amount by the Bureau," in a clear statement of authority. Baird added that Swan would report to Baird "without the formalities of reference to the director of the Bureau of Ethnology."

The BAE was also expected to pay some of the salaries within the United States National Museum's Department of Anthropology, and generally to submit to Smithsonian overview. Powell protested. "I beg permission to state that I think it unwise that the fund should

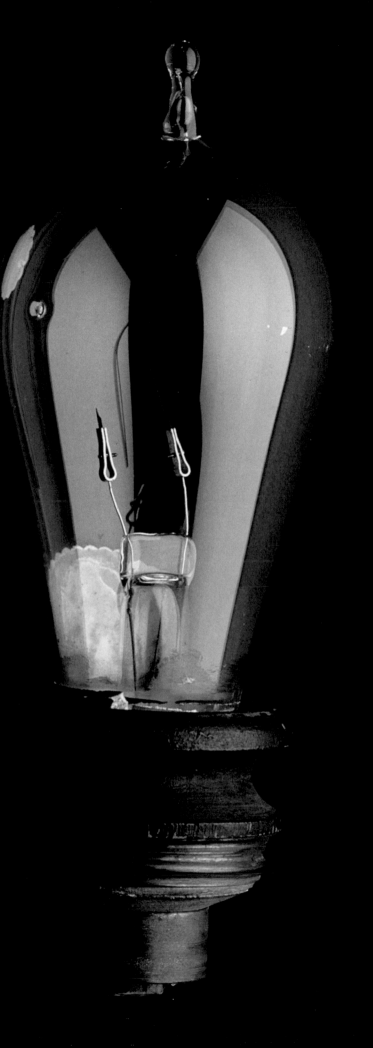

In 1880 Thomas Edison patented his first bamboo-filament light bulb, left, which featured one of the first screw bases. The Cosmochronotrope, opposite top—a clock that displays the time of sunrise and sunset for

any location at any date, as well as the position of the sun in the zodiac—was first patented in 1879 by James F. Sarratt. These steam-engine models, pictured here in the Arts and Industries Building, once resided at the Patent Office Building, above, which now houses the National Museum of American Art and the National Portrait Gallery.

be diverted from the purpose for which the appropriation was made," he wrote, "namely for research…. I also wish to express a regret that the Secretary of the Smithsonian should take a part of the fund from under my control…."

Baird pointed out that Powell had asked that the BAE be placed under the aegis of the Smithsonian, and that Congress was far more interested in museum acquisitions than in the study of language and tribal nomenclature. But he had reasons for wanting to keep Powell within the Smithsonian camp, one of them being his plans for a new natural-history museum. "I do not want anyone to think that Major Powell is in antagonism to [sic] the National Museum," Baird wrote to a BAE administrator. "It will require the concurrent efforts of both to get the new building…."

RELATIONS IN THE SMALL, FERVENT SCIENTIFIC community on the Mall were highly personal. Slights—both real and imagined—were taken seriously. Chief clerk William Rhees resented Baird's tight control of

A plaster model of "Freedom," the statue that caps the dome of the U.S. Capitol, adorns the fountain in the Arts and Industries Building's rotunda in the 1890s.

Smithsonian staffers regarding their duties and their general views of the Institution. Most were short, agreeable documents, but Rhees presented Baird with two extraordinarily lengthy screeds.

The first listed 66 specific duties of the chief clerk, with a nine-page addendum highlighting Rhees's other jobs and a request for a raise. The second, "Memorandum of Some of the Work That Ought to Be Done," contained 66 suggestions for improvement, plus a 13-page addendum that generally condemned Baird's tight-fisted control. Typically, Baird dismissed the suggestions, many of which no doubt were needed. To the end, Baird remained extraordinarily defensive in the face of criticism, determined that the Smithsonian would reflect his, and only his, vision of the multifaceted museum.

FOR YEARS BAIRD HAD SUFFERED POOR HEALTH, burdened, like others attached to the Smithsonian, with work he loved. On November 18, 1885, he wrote a note to himself: "Heart. Irregular in beating sometimes intermitting every ten or fifteen beats then starting again with a throb…. Sometimes a little pain about the heart…."

A year later, in an internal memo, Baird wrote: "It has been understood among men of science in this country that the Secretaryship of the Smithsonian, which represents perhaps the chief scientific prize of the country, should be…held alternately by a physicist and a naturalist." The physicist he had in mind to replace him was Samuel Pierpont Langley, director of the Allegheny Observatory near Pittsburgh. One reason Langley was chosen was the relatively low pay the Secretaryship carried. "Other gentlemen have been thought of, but unfortunately they all occupy high positions in Universities and establishments where they receive a salary far beyond that which the Institution can afford…."

Baird's physical ailments grew worse, exacerbated by the squabbles involving Rhees, Leech, and others.

Smithsonian affairs, and the fact that the Secretary was distracted by his duties at the Fish Commission and other agencies. Too, Baird treated Rhees as a social inferior, another source of ill will. And Rhees and the Smithsonian's correspondence clerk, Daniel J. Leech, argued continually, and brought these disputes to Baird.

Rhees also fought with the administrators of the various agencies. The rapid growth of the Institution, with its overlapping jurisdictions, added to internal tensions, and, in 1884, Baird requested statements from all

The Baird family—Mary, Spencer, and daughter Lucy—pose in 1887 at their summer home in Woods Hole, Massachusetts, where Baird was to die on August 18. A few months earlier, Baird had appointed curator George Browne Goode, below, director of the National Museum. Opposite (top to bottom), photo engravings illustrate activities Baird oversaw as director of the Bureau of Fisheries: the collection of saltwater samples; the releasing of artificially hatched fry; and research at the National Carp Ponds, then located on the Mall.

Baird had made George Brown Goode director of the National Museum, but he felt obliged to find a successor for himself outside the Institution. In late 1886 he brought Langley to the Smithsonian as Assistant Secretary in charge of Library and Exchanges, but with a much loftier, unspecified final designation.

THE FOLLOWING SUMMER, BAIRD TRAVELED TO Woods Hole, the fishing village on the coast of Massachusetts that had become a highly regarded center for biological and oceanographic research. Over the years, Baird had participated in much of that research for the Fish Commission.

For a time, Baird's heart condition seemed to improve, but then it grew worse. In a wheelchair, he was rolled past work stations and vessels he had helped design; he spoke with other scientists in what was a tacit, touching farewell. Then he was confined to his room in the official residence of the fish commissioner.

Baird died there of heart failure on August 18, 1887. His body was taken by special train back to Washington, where flags flew at half mast.

Among Baird's contributions to the Smithsonian were his personal collections, which had led, indirectly, to the colossal amassing of specimens—by now two and a half million of them—from almost every niche of natural science. To the discipline in general, he had contributed a systematic approach, characterized by his biographers as "the introduction into American scientific description of a degree of precision which had not been there before."

While Baird had controlled the Smithsonian more assiduously than Joseph Henry, he had served as example and mentor to many scientists and scientific observers, as well as a general inspiration: The accrual of knowledge, to Spencer Baird, was inseparable from the objects in which that knowledge resided.

CRAZY TO GET AWAY

A prime example of the idiosyncratic collector's supplying the Smithsonian with rare and exotic objects was set in 1887 by William Louis Abbott. A Philadelphian who had studied medicine here and in England, Abbott gave up his profession to travel to Madagascar, the Seychelle Islands, East Africa, and Turkistan. His wanderings eventually included the Malay Peninsula and Archipelago, and continued until 1923.

Abbott's close relationship with ethnologist Otis Mason recalled the early days of the Smithsonian, and the tradition of independent operators working for the Institution. In this case, the adventurer provided a vicarious life for the scientist who stayed behind in the Castle.

Wealthy and misanthropic, Abbott undertook the expeditions on his own. He lived for months aboard his ship, the *Terrapin*, amassing natural-history specimens first and then, later, ethnological ones. From Singapore he shipped collections by the ton back to the Smithsonian, where they were eagerly received by the older Mason, the quintessential museum man.

Abbott grew addicted to wild places. He wrote to Walter Hough, Mason's colleague, "I never feel as if life were worth living in Europe, until the scorching wind from the desert strikes the ship in the Red Sea, east bound." Abbott considered the polluted air in America and England oppressive, and the houses stifling; Singapore's tourists made him "crazy to get away and smell the water and the coral beaches again."

A collector pure and simple, always moving, Abbott was interested in what he found, but far more interested in a new landfall beyond the grasp of "civilization." He made no pretense of scientific observation, and, in the descriptions of objects he sent back to Washington, forbade Mason from discussing his travels.

Abbott's collections from Malaysia suggested to his friend Mason that an evolutionary stage of industrial development might exist between the savage stage of American Indians and civilized society. Mason toyed with this notion, based on a thorough examination of Abbott's objects, and speculated about Malaysia as the possible point of origin of American Indians. These musings, inspired by the peripatetic Abbott, led to no conclusions.

While collecting for the Smithsonian, William Louis Abbott, left, traveled throughout the Indonesian archipelago. In 1902 he encountered inhabitants of Tekako (now Taikako) village, right, on North Pagai Island off Sumatra's west coast. In 1906 he explored mainland Sumatra, where his ship, the *Terrapin*, lies anchored in the Little Siak River. During his travels, Abbott visited island groups from the Mergui archipelago off Burma (Myanmar) to the north coast of Dutch New Guinea (Irian Jaya).

Mason gradually lost interest in American ethnology, which had become crowded with scholars, and responded to the appeal of Abbott's new, distant encounters. "A lot of young men, God bless them," Mason wrote to Abbott in 1904, "are rummaging the Western Hemisphere for ethnic fame. If I can quietly steal aboard the *Terrapin* in spirit...I would follow you anywhere."

That same year, Mason published his *Aboriginal American Basketry*, full of details gathered over many years, but his heart was in the South Seas. His heavily illustrated and detailed work, *The Vocabulary of Malaysian Basketwork*, dependent upon his long association with Abbott, appeared in 1908—on the day of his funeral.

ICARUS ON THE MALL

"Nature had solved
it [flight], and
why not man?"
—SAMUEL PIERPONT LANGLEY

Broken into its component colors by a 17th-century prism, white light falls on Sir Isaac Newton's monumental 1704 volume, *Opticks*. In the late-19th century, Smithsonian Secretary Samuel P. Langley, right, invented the bolometer to measure solar radiation.

Innovative, shy, brilliant, aloof—all these words have been used to describe the scientist who took on the mantle of Joseph Henry and Spencer Baird in the fall of 1887. Langley, the son of a prosperous wholesale merchant in Boston, had been professor of physics and astronomy at Western University of Pennsylvania, in Pittsburgh, for 20 years.

Langley's astronomical work as director of the Allegheny Observatory, particularly with regard to solar energy, had made him famous. His bolometer, then the most accurate instrument for measuring radiation, encouraged new investigations of solar composition and power.

Tall and reserved, an impressive lecturer and an accomplished prose stylist, Langley at age 53 was a perennial if most eligible bachelor who enjoyed hard, often tedious work. Highly motivated, he embodied the contradictory aspects of the Gilded Age: a strict outward propriety and a taste for material and intellectual adventure. His professional strength lay in testing current theories, and in experimentation.

Though known for precision, Langley sometimes rationalized his own research to obtain what he thought were the proper ends, and he also consistently overvalued the solar constant, the density of solar radiation at the outer layers of the Earth's atmosphere—an error that would be corrected by his successor. Langley insisted upon privacy, and distrusted reporters, allowing the grass to grow around the Castle to discourage their visits.

He would get more adverse coverage than either of the Secretaries

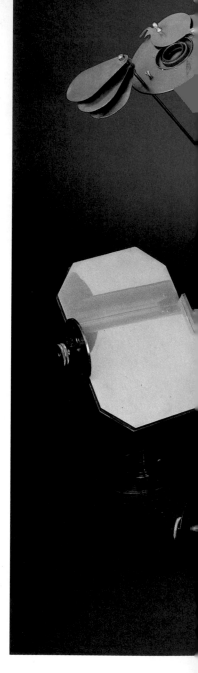

who preceded him. Already disposed toward difficult, some would say impossible, problems, Langley's passions—the sun and aeronautics—led him to demand of others the same toil and devotion he evinced, and many at the Smithsonian came to fear his irritability and impatience.

Langley had little regard for precedent, and quickly abandoned the Smithsonian's tradition of correspondence, using telegraph wires on the theory that telegrams brought results more quickly than letters. His view of the world and his role in it was paternalistic and aristocratic. As Secretary, he felt he should receive credit for Institution work regardless of his involvement. Though by nature cautious, he harbored another characteristic of the Gilded Age: As one biographer has pointed out, "a certain part of Langley was attracted to the spectacular."

LANGLEY MOVED INTO THE COSMOS CLUB AFTER arriving in Washington. There he dined with Supreme Court justices and United States Senators. At the Smithsonian, he quickly established himself as the august director of projects and studies. The Institution now had a curatorial and clerical staff of about 100. Because of Langley's administrative duties, his purely scientific investigations began to flag.

This he protested, but he found time to pursue such pet projects as "lighter than air" machines and to maintain control of the Allegheny Observatory. There, in the summer of 1887, he helped design a "whirling table," two 30-foot armatures on a revolving vertical shaft capable of speeds of 70 miles an hour. With it, he hoped to reproduce mechanically the aerodynamics of flight.

Langley wanted to see if sufficient lift for flight could be generated by a flat plane. Eventually, electric motors with propellers were attached to the whirling table, as were model airplanes, which he called "aerostats," and stuffed frigate birds and California condors borrowed from the Smithsonian—thus conducting what at the

Instruments at right—including a water-cooling component for a bolometer (far right)—gathered data for the Smithsonian's pioneering astrophysical research. Above, Charles Greeley Abbot, acting director of the Smithsonian Astrophysical Observatory, uses a bolometric apparatus to record solar radiation from an eclipse in 1900.

time were imaginative, daring experiments. Langley was determined to prove that the impediment of gravity could be overcome through science.

In Washington, he pursued his other passion: the sun. In his 1888 report to the Regents, he announced that he would seek funds from Congress for an astrophysical observatory. When Congress proved unwilling, Langley raised money himself to augment Smithsonian funds, including $5,000 from Alexander Graham Bell, for any research the Secretary deemed necessary.

The Institution's earlier patron, John Quincy Adams, would have approved of the project, at least in principle, though the wooden structure that went up in

the 20-acre "Smithsonian Park" south of the Castle—where the Enid A. Haupt Garden now blooms—was unsuited to pure science, surrounded as it was by commerce and, in summer, more oven than laboratory. (It looked like a stable, and housed the astrophysical observatory until 1955, at which point the observatory was moved to Cambridge, Massachusetts.

Langley eventually installed refrigerated coils—an early version of air conditioning—and there employed his bolometer to measure the capital's abundant solar energy. He was not so much interested in the sun itself as in its effects: "My intention [is] to give greater place to one of the chief objects of the Institution, the direct

addition of knowledge by original research"—an echo of Joseph Henry.

ANOTHER FLEDGLING BUREAU OF THE SMITHSONIAN was emerging: the National Zoo. Talked about for years, its creation was the inspiration behind the Washington Zoological Society, to which Spencer Baird had belonged. Baird had discussed the possibility of having P.T. Barnum finance the zoo and then use it as a repository for his animals.

The real, eponymous force behind the zoo was William T. Hornaday, a taxidermist for the National Museum. On behalf of the Smithsonian, Hornaday had traveled to Montana to obtain bison skins and skeletons for mounting, and had returned fearful of the species' extinction. He urged the Smithsonian to found the zoo specifically to prevent this, even though it was a politically unpopular cause. (General Phil Sheridan suggested that medals be given to buffalo killers, who, he believed, had done more than the Army to bring American Indians into subjugation.)

At Hornaday's urging, George Brown Goode, Assistant Secretary and director of the National Museum, created the Division of Living Animals. The justification for this new bureau was the supposed need for live animals as models for Hornaday's large cadre of taxidermists. Prior to this, donated animals were turned over to the U.S. Insane Asylum. It was Goode who sent Hornaday west again to search for live animals, which were brought back in empty boxcars used by the U.S. Fish Commission: a "cinnamon" bear, a white-tailed deer, a Columbian black-tailed deer, some prairie dogs, a red fox, badgers, and a golden eagle.

Friends and collectors sent more animals, and, by 1888, the Smithsonian possessed 58 animals, which lived in pens set up between the Castle and the National Museum. The first bison arrived later, followed in 1889 by several more, one of which became the model for the buffalo on an American $10 bill.

Langley approved of the proposed zoo, although many in Congress did not. When the Secretary requested an appropriation of $200,000, a Congressman from Tennessee suggested that the Vice President of the United States, a member of the Board of Regents, "has not the time to go out and look after the monkeys, and the members of the Senate and House…have no time to give to bear farming."

A Representative from Texas stated more succinctly, "I do not believe it is ever proper to tax men and women to support monkeys and bears…." Despite this

Secretary Samuel P. Langley's steam-powered, unmanned *Aerodrome Five*, left, first flew successfully on May 6, 1896. Paintings of the aircraft in flight (top) and in preparation for launch (above) were reproduced for *McClure's* magazine from photographs taken by Langley's close friend Alexander Graham Bell. Langley's success with this aerodrome inspired him to build a manned version of the machine.

opposition, funds were voted, and the famous landscape architect Frederick Law Olmsted was retained to draw up plans for a zoological park near Rock Creek.

Langley involved himself closely in the project. He clashed with Hornaday, who had enjoyed an easy relationship with Baird but found his successor dictatorial. Finally Hornaday resigned, and was replaced by the anatomist Frank Baker, who acceded to Langley's demands. One of these was that a large portion of the zoo grounds be reserved for Langley's astrophysical observatory, something that Congress did not allow.

On April 30, 1891, a procession led by two donated elephants, Dunk and Gold Dust, made its way to the new zoo, and the National Zoo was formally inaugurated. The hiring of William H. Blackburne, head animal keeper of the Barnum & Bailey circus, brought in to tend the animals a professional who would remain for 53 years.

Langley, typically, found his own use for the zoo: He spent hours in specially erected towers observing the flight of birds, particularly vultures. Photographers used electronically synchronized cameras with telephoto lenses to photograph the vultures, producing simultaneous images. The cameras were designed by his young assistant at the Astrophysical Observatory, a graduate of the Massachusetts Institute of Technology named Charles Greeley Abbot.

MEANWHILE, THE CENTURY OF DISCOVERY THAT began with the daring trek of Lewis and Clark ended with another expedition, this one led by a captain of industry who embodied the optimism and extravagance of the age. The lavish Alaska trip of railroad tycoon Edward Henry Harriman in 1899 launched the notion of large-scale forays by American philanthropists into the groves of quasi-science. In this case, it was to collect specimens, make observations, and afford Harriman the chance to shoot a Kodiak bear.

William H. Blackburne, the National Zoo's first head animal keeper, feeds a baby camel on the zoological park's grounds at the turn of the century. At right, Secretary Langley (facing camera) and others survey the proposed site for the park in Northwest Washington. In 1890 noted landscape architect Frederick Law Olmsted produced this preliminary study for the zoo's layout.

Possibly there was a hidden agenda: reconnaissance for Harriman's dream of a New York-to-Paris railway. Two years earlier, the railroad tycoon had merged the Union Pacific Railroad with the Southern Pacific, and had taken on a struggle for control of the Northern Pacific; he was rumored to be interested in a tunnel under the Bering Strait.

More realistic goals gained the cooperation of the Smithsonian. Interdisciplinary socializing was to be done by 25 of the nation's top natural scientists, professors from schools as distant from one other as Harvard and the University of California at Berkeley, photographers, and artists, all under the sway of triumphant capitalism.

Harriman also brought along a number of friends and relatives, numerous personal servants, two stenographers, a doctor and a nurse, a chaplain, 11 hunters, and assorted packers and camp assistants. The entourage traveled first class from New York to Seattle, where it boarded the ship *George W. Elder* and steamed slowly up the Alaskan coast.

Among the notables leaning on the ship's rails were William Healey Dall, now the grand old man of Alaskan exploration; geologist G.K. Gilbert; the British-born naturalist John Muir; Henry Gannett, chief geographer with the USGS; C. Hart Merriam, physician and chief of the Biological Survey; John Burroughs, ornithologist and writer; Robert Ridgway, curator of birds at the Smithsonian's National Museum; artist Frank Dellenbaugh; George Bird Grinnell, editor of *Forest and Stream*; several veterans of the surveys of the American West; and a young Seattle portraitist, Edward Curtis, who would become famous for his photographs of American Indians.

In two months, the party covered 9,000 miles, and made about 50 stops. There were lectures ranging in subject matter from glaciers to Somaliland. A certain easefulness reigned, uncharacteristic of the society of scientists and academicians, exemplified by an expedition cheer: "Who are we? Who are we?/We are, We are H.A.E."—the initials "H.A.E." standing, of course, for the Harriman Alaska Expedition.

Muir, who had been promised access on the Harriman Alaska expedition to parts of the country he had not visited, wrote on the way home, "We had...much twaddle about a grand scientific monument of this trip, etc...." But a huge collection, including 5,000 pinned insects and 600 species described as "new to science," was brought back, and the shrimp that were collected inspired a review of all 50,000 specimens at the National Museum, from lower California to the Arctic.

After the expedition, a dozen well-bound, illustrated volumes were published in a cooperative arrangement between Harriman and the Smithsonian. They included narratives of the journey and studies of starfish and mollusks. Overall, in Dall's judgement, it was a venture "of which America may justly be proud."

HISTORIANS DIFFER ON THE SUBJECT OF LANGLEY'S happiness while in Washington. He has been seen as both a social lion and a lonely figure of authority without family, longing for friends. An essentially closed person, he was interested in children—the Children's Room was installed during his tenure, later subsumed in the Smithsonian's wartime activity—and yet without children of his own. His Assistant Secretary, Cyrus Adler, wrote of long winter carriage rides with Langley: "We could both be silent for hours, and thus established a friendship which was free from dialectics."

Among those who considered Langley a worthy, even inspiring, companion was Henry Adams, the intellectual light of late-19th-century Washington who turned to Langley with questions about scientific phenomena. "Langley listened with outward patience," Adams wrote. "He, too, nourished a scientific passion for doubt...."

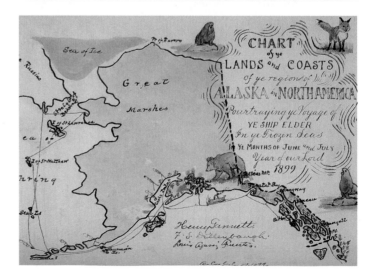

1. TUFTED PUFFIN, LUNDA CIRRHATA
2. HORNED PUFFIN, FRATERCULA CORNICULATA

Louis A. Fuertes

A. HOEN & CO. BALTIMORE.

Aboard the steamer *George W. Elder*, above, in 1899, railroad magnate Edward H. Harriman and his 125-member entourage explored the Alaskan coast. At far left (top), expedition members pose in front of an Indian village at Cape Fox, Alaska. Participants collected thousands of artifacts and photographed such scenes as that of a woman (center) outside her winter dwelling. Henry Gannett, chief geographer of the U.S. Geological Survey, and artists F.S. Dellenbaugh and Louis Agassiz Fuertes collaborated on this illuminated chart of the voyage. Fuertes also produced numerous other illustrations, such as that of the tufted (top) and horned puffins.

Langley also professed "to know nothing between flashes of intense perception"—an uneasy condition for the administrator of the Smithsonian Institution.

WHAT LANGLEY STYLED "AERODROMICS," BASED on the Greek word *aerodrome*, meaning a place where machines traverse the air, remained his focus. He had transformed the Smithsonian's workshops into amateur aeronautical-assembly plants, and regularly inspected them in striped trousers and morning coat. He had found support among the growing cadre of Washington aeronautical enthusiasts, among them Carl Barus, of the Bureau of Standards, and Charles Doolittle Walcott, director of the U.S. Geological Survey. Langley's demands for perfection and his domineering attitude, however, took a toll on the nerves of some of his underlings.

They had turned out various rubber-band-driven model airplanes and steam-powered machines that lifted themselves at speed. But the twin problems of weight and power plagued the initial versions of Langley's "aerodromes." The engines of Aerodromes 1 and 2 proved inadequate to their task, while Aerodrome 3—equipped with a new type of fuel burner—was also too underpowered to fly.

A much larger version came next, weighing just over 10 pounds, its four front and rear wings covering 14 square feet. It had an improved steam-powered engine, and was launched from a specially adapted houseboat—called the "scow" by the Secretary—on the Potomac River. After nine unsuccessful attempts during the winter of 1896, however, a new design was sought.

In May 1896, the year the Smithsonian celebrated its 50th anniversary, an unmanned *Aerodrome Five* flew for more than half a mile before setting down in the water. It then was dried off and flown again. Alexander Graham Bell photographed *Aerodrome Five*, and later

(Text continued on page 184)

Artist Thomas Wilmer Dewing's *America Receiving the Nine Muses* decorates the inside lid of Steinway & Sons' 100,000th grand piano. Presented to the White House in 1903, it became part of scheduled music performances and such courtly receptions as the one at right during President Theodore Roosevelt's administration. In 1939 the White House donated the piano to the Smithsonian.

KNOWLEDGE BEGINS IN WONDER

by CYNTHIA FIELD

In 1901, convinced that museums could provide a special learning environment for children, Secretary Samuel Pierpont Langley created the Children's Room at the Smithsonian Castle. In staff directives, he ordered that exhibit shelves should be lowered for small viewers and that poetic inscriptions should replace the Latin labels typically found in museums of the day. Placing himself in the role of the child, he wrote, "We are not very interested in the Latin names, and do not want to have our entertainment spoiled by its being made a lesson."

Langley intended that the room inspire young visitors to learn about the wonder of the natural world. He believed that "to interest the little minds in such things is to lay the foundation for more serious study in after life." His guiding principle for the room thus became "knowledge begins in wonder," a phrase loosely translated from Aristotle and later painted on the transom above the room's entrance.

Grace Lincoln Temple, a professional interior decorator, carried out the designs for the Children's Room, choosing colors that not only reflected the natural focus of its contents but that also were sure to "delight the child" and appeal to his or her "sense of wonder." She selected luminous shades of green that were set off by gilded moldings for the walls. A frieze of stylized birds and sinuous ribbons wrapped around the room at eye level. The ceiling was decorated with a painted trellis, intertwined with grapevines and leaves, on which perched small, colorful birds.

The room contained several displays of live animals: colorful fish in a mammoth aquarium and songbirds in gilded cages. The birds were a particular favorite of Langley, reminding him how, as a child, he had been inspired by their flight to pursue his future professional interest in aviation. He wrote: "Lying down in a New England pasture and looking at the mysterious soaring of a hen hawk far above the sky has led me to give many years of mature life to the study of the subject of traveling in air."

From this early start, the Smithsonian has developed several

The Children's Room, above, created in 1901 by the Smithsonian Secretary Samuel P. Langley in the Castle's South Tower Room, was the first of its kind at the Institution. Today, all manner of activities engage young visitors: Children in the National Museum of American History's Hands on Science Center learn about radioactivity; Smithsonian gardener Sung Do Kim displays orchids to children at the National Museum of Natural History; and a musician plays jazz for a young person at Arts and Industries' Discovery Theater.

innovative rooms designed to stimulate the curiosity of children of all ages. The original Discovery Room in the National Museum of Natural History opened in 1974. It was the first of its kind in the nation, a place where visitors could handle real objects from the museum's collections, including natural-history specimens similar to those Langley had put in the Children's Room. New items also were added: a microscope for viewing small specimens, an elephant tusk, and, recently, a 10-foot-tall polar bear standing on its hind legs. Unique objects called "stumpers" are everywhere, with labels asking "Is it a fossil?" or "Where does the tail begin?" while enticing visitors to "Look Inside!" and "Smell them!"

The National Museum of American History now has two "hands-on" rooms: "Hands On History," which opened in 1985 and was expanded in 1990, and "Hands On Science," which opened in 1994. Each has dramatically expanded children's appreciation of cultural history and physical science through interactive experiences that stimulate their senses—touch, sound, even smell—rather than trying to reach them through traditional, behind-the-glass exhibits.

The first thing visitors notice upon entering Hands On History is children and their parents pedaling two stationary penny-farthing bicycles. Although these and other objects in the room are not authentic historical pieces, they are accurate reproductions of artifacts in the museum's collections that enable visitors to literally touch America's past. An 1897 Singer sewing machine, a Native American buffalo-hide painting, and a rope-making machine await the curious hands and minds of visitors eager to experience history.

From Langley's novel idea, which set the precedent for children's programs at the Institution, the Smithsonian has become a leader in promoting knowledge through wonder among visitors of all ages.

Cynthia Field is Director of the Smithsonian's Office of Architectural History and Historic Preservation.

wrote that "no one who was present on this interesting occasion could have failed to recognize that the practicability of mechanical flight had been demonstrated."

This was revolutionary—the first successful engine-driven, heavier-than-air flight in history. In November, Langley's next craft, *Aerodrome Six*, flew farther—4,200 feet. Langley claimed that he had proved his thesis, and that a larger aerodrome would be capable of carrying a person on a sustained flight.

He continued his search for funds, including among potential donors the government. Money was needed on a scale beyond the available resources of the Smithsonian. Walcott suggested the military option, and placed Langley's proposal before President William McKinley. The country faced a conflict with Spain, and airborne fighting machines suggested military advantage. (Assistant Secretary of the Navy Theodore Roosevelt also became interested in the project.)

Langley met with the Board of Ordnance and Fortification in November 1898 to present his work and answer questions. He insisted on sole responsibility for the project and its funds, and also on absolute secrecy. He was thus shocked and dismayed when, two days later, the Washington *Post* reported on the meeting and the purpose of the project: "an investigation of the possibilities of flying machines for reconnoitering purposes and as engines of destruction in time of war." He subsequently sent a letter to the board reiterating the conditions of their agreement, and was awarded $50,000 to develop an airplane.

The following year, Langley received a request for information about aeronautics from a bicycle maker in Ohio named Wilbur Wright. Apparently Langley wasn't the only person working on the prospect of manned flight.

AMONG LANGLEY'S FRIENDS WAS JOHN WESLEY Powell. Langley and the major had exchanged papers on scientific philosophy; according to Assistant Secretary Adler, they quarreled "violently on the subject as to whether there was or was not a soul, or whether there was or was not a future life." They even vacationed together; in 1900, Powell traveled to Cuba with William Henry Holmes, and Langley asked them to join him in Jamaica, where he was studying the flight of turkey vultures.

Langley's earlier attempt at taking control of BAE personnel and money had been deflected by Powell, who had written, "To have these duties assumed by the Secretary of the Smithsonian, would place the Secretary in the position of performing the duties of a Bureau officer...." Powell prevailed, and their friendship survived through the last years of Powell's life.

The Secretary's reserve remained a source of friction, however. W.J. McGee, Powell's alter ego in the BAE, now objected to it. No field anthropologist—McGee's second expedition in search of "wild" Seri Indians in Mexico had approached farce—he was, however, an astute inside operator who consistently promoted Powell's views—and his own.

McGee enjoyed the support of Franz Boas, the influential professor of anthropology at Columbia University and honorary philologist at the bureau who believed in the importance of linguistics and mythology. Boaz—and McGee—thought the "museum school" of Holmes, Mason, and others focused too much on the collections and not enough on original research.

The various tensions between the Smithsonian and the bureau did not approach the antipathy Langley developed toward McGee, even as the Secretary continued to tolerate the bureau's independence. McGee's referring to himself as "ethnologist in charge" during Powell's tenure didn't help matters.

Another source of friction between Langley and the BAE was James Mooney, whose emphasis on cultural deprivation, later to become a mainstream view in 20th-century anthropology, struck Langley as deviant. Mooney's suggestion that Christianity had been founded on dreams and visions seemed to Langley a kind of blasphemy. Although Powell was not fond of Mooney's ideas either, he valued his abilities as an ethnologist.

Then Mooney wrote an account of the massacre of Sioux men, women, and children by the U.S. Army during the battle of Wounded Knee that was sympathetic to the Indians' side. Published in 1896, it angered both Langley and Powell. Such candor brought on more criticism of the Smithsonian in Congress, which already was thick with opponents of the limited and orderly Western development Powell had championed. The victim of this renewed criticism was the BAE.

JOHN WESLEY POWELL DIED IN 1902, AND WITH HIM went the notion of an independent Bureau of American Ethnology. Langley already considered McGee too outspoken on current social issues and lacking in scientific objectivity, as well as personally irritating. He thus decided to clean out and subordinate the bureau, which had lost favor with the politicians. Charles Royce's *History of Land Cessions of the Indian Tribes* was the only publication Langley had as evidence of the BAE's ability to produce useful information, its primary reason for existence. McGee's writings on the Seri, like Mooney's description of the massacre and his *Myths of the Cherokees*, had aroused pointed Congressional criticism.

Soon after Powell's death, Langley appointed a reluctant William Henry Holmes "chief"—not director—of the BAE after informing him that from then on the bureau would have the same relationship with the Smithsonian as its other divisions, and that "...its work must be popularized and shown to be practical."

A storm of controversy followed, with attacks on Langley's entire administration by McGee, whose position Langley had abolished. Appeals on McGee's behalf came

Uncle Sam springs to action during the Spanish-American War. During this 1898 conflict, the U.S. Army developed a strong interest in the possible use of airborne fighting machines and lent support to Secretary Langley's experiments.

from noted scientists, among them Boas, but to no avail. Langley claimed that by disciplining the BAE—by insisting that various studies finally be completed and that the bureau's informational function be reinstated—he was saving it from the Congressional budget knife. "On [Powell's] death," Langley wrote, "a new day begins for the Bureau—partly a reversion to the policy of his own vigorous years." He focused the BAE on the completion of *The Handbook of American Indians*.

This had been a fight between institutional administrators and anthropologists, and the former had triumphed. No self-respecting choice remained for McGee than to leave the Smithsonian, which he did in July 1903. He had become a symbol of the decline of highly individualistic, sometimes idiosyncratic pursuits in anthropology and other natural sciences. Personal achievement and the pursuit of one's life work had been subordinated to the bureaucracy.

McGee's life seemed to fall apart during the next four years, but then he rallied. In 1907, he went to work for the Department of Agriculture; that summer, he and Gifford Pinchot, head of the U.S. Forest Service, conferred on a plan for conserving parts of the country, which has since been characterized as the basis of the modern conservation movement.

FOR FIVE HECTIC, OFTEN FRUSTRATING YEARS AFTER *Aerodrome Six*, Langley experimented with different designs and various components: a light, rotary-radial engine, an improved catapult for launching, biplane and monoplane—all coordinated by Charles Matthews Manly, his chief aeronautical assistant and, later, recipient of the Langley medal. It was Manly who had to deal with talented, unpredictable inventors—chief among them Stephen Balzer—and who finally succeeded in perfecting an engine of sufficient power to support manned flight.

Its revolutionary Manly-Balzer radial engine in view, Secretary Langley's Aerodrome rests by the Castle, opposite. One of pioneer glider Otto Lilienthal's originals, above, hangs in the National Air and Space Museum. Even after Lilienthal's accidental death in 1896 in a similar machine, the passion for flight continued to soar.

In 1901 they ran out of money, and were forced to dip into general research funds established earlier by Alexander Graham Bell and English-born Thomas George Hodgkins. By October 7, 1903, the new Aerodrome was ready for test piloting. Manly, at the controls, revved up the engine, and started the craft along its track mounted on the roof of the modified houseboat. "Just as the end of the track was reached," he later wrote, "and at the moment when the machine should have become entirely free from the launching car, I experienced a slight jerk...." He quickly found himself in the water.

Langley's disappointment was compounded by public exposure. A reporter described the Aerodrome as entering the Potomac "like a handful of mortar." On top of the flight's failure, further damage was done to the craft as it was towed back to the houseboat.

The Secretary blamed the catapult for the plunge, but the craft itself was at fault, according to numerous authorities, among them Tom Crouch, a historian of aeronautics. After consulting with aeronautical experts who later reconstructed the Aerodrome, Crouch wrote in *A Dream of Wings*, "The weakness of the smaller models suggests that the scaled-up version was incapable of even marginal flight."

Unwilling to admit structural weakness, Langley forged ahead. On December 8, Manly again took the controls, wearing a cork-lined vest to keep him from drowning in the chilly Potomac. Again he felt a jerk at the end of the catapult, but this time the Aerodrome flipped over backwards before plunging into the river. Manly narrowly escaped from beneath the icy water, and the project was a shambles—technically and politically.

Some members of Congress, always quick to ridicule the intellectual and erudite, took full advantage of Langley's embarrassment—as well as the Smithsonian's and the War Department's. One Representative described Langley as "a professor...wandering in his dreams of flight...." Another mused, "[I]f it cost us $73,000 to construct a mud duck, how much is it going to cost to construct a real flying machine?"

Langley had been trying for 18 years to build a flying machine. His critics in and out of government agreed that many more years and thousands of dollars lay between Langley's dream and reality, if indeed such reality was possible. Langley disagreed. In his essay "The Laws of Nature," he wrote, "We must not consider that anything is absolutely settled or true...." He still believed in the possibility of his dream, and he was soon proven correct.

On December 17, 1903, a mere nine days after Langley's humiliation and as the recriminations continued, Orville Wright took the controls of a gasoline-powered biplane near Kitty Hawk, North Carolina, and traveled 120 feet through the air in 12 seconds—officially becoming the first human being to fly.

Probably the most significant shortcoming of Langley's machine was the fact that it couldn't be steered. The Aerodrome, with its four wings in tandem pairs, was inherently stable, and thus couldn't be diverted easily from a straight line. The Wright brothers, on the other hand, realized that control was one of the essential secrets of flight. That realization made them the recognized pioneers in the field.

LANGLEY ENTERED A PERIOD OF DECLINE, BUT HIS work at the Smithsonian was not done. Opportunity had arisen that same year in the unlikely guise of art. With the death of Mrs. Harriet Lane Johnston, President James Buchanan's niece, had come news of her bequest of a collection of paintings and other objects to a national gallery, should one ever be established. A friendly suit was brought in court determining that the Smithsonian, as originally set up by Congress, was qualified as the recipient; a national gallery was an inevitability.

(Text continued on page 192)

In December 1903 the ill-fated Langley Aerodrome, above right, sits on its houseboat launcher on the Potomac River. Pilot and engine designer Charles Manly, above (left), photographed here with Secretary Langley, is about to be repeatedly dunked and nearly drowned in the frigid water. Pitching downward, right, the Aerodrome refused to fly; on its second launch attempt, the back wings broke off. Following the Wright brothers' successful flights, Manly's 53-horsepower engine languished at the Smithsonian.

PAUL GARBER
by E.T. WOOLDRIDGE

In 1907 he received instruction from Alexander Graham Bell on the finer points of kite flying. During World War II, he passed along a few tips to Eleanor Roosevelt during her visit to a target-kite factory. On April 30, 1928, Charles Lindbergh delivered the *Spirit of St. Louis* to him in Washington, D.C., with the brief statement, "Well, Paul, here it is." And his pleas to Senator Jennings Randolph, of West Virginia, resulted in the creation of the National Air Museum in 1946.

"He" was Paul Edward Garber, whom journalists over the years labeled the "grand patriarch of American flight," "a living treasure," and the "soul of aviation history." He was at the top of his profession during the most exciting, romantic period in aviation history, the golden age of flight between the two world wars, when air racing, record breaking, and aerial exploration made daily news headlines.

When Garber signed on as a "preparator" at the Smithsonian's National Museum in 1920, he was honing the skills he would need in pursuing his aviation career. His love of flight was inspired by such experiences as a 1909 visit to Fort Myer, Virginia, at the age of 10, to witness a demonstration of the U.S. Army's first airplane, with Orville Wright at the controls. His fascination for all things aerial grew, stoked by membership in local model clubs, visits to airfields, and the building and flying of kites and model airplanes.

A few days short of his 16th birthday, he soloed in a homemade glider, whose design was based on that of an 1896 Octave Chanute model. This feat qualified him for membership in a distinguished fraternity, the Early Birds of Aviation, which was composed of pilots who soloed before December 17, 1916.

During World War I, Garber joined the D.C. National Guard, transferred to the Army, and emerged determined to pursue some kind of career in aviation. Following a brief tour with the Postal Air Mail Service as a ground crewman at College Park, Maryland, he joined the staff of the Smithsonian's National Museum, beginning an association that lasted 72 years and was interrupted only by World War II.

Paul first worked in the Division of Mechanical Technology, where he prepared and repaired exhibits. He also managed to find time to construct aircraft models for display and to acquire an occasional aeronautical artifact for the collections. In 1932 he was placed in charge of the newly created Section of Aeronautics, and more accessions followed. As he

grew in his job, Garber's circle of friends and associates in the aviation world expanded, eventually including such renowned personalities as Grover Loening, Al Williams, Charles Lindbergh, and Jimmy Doolittle.

Garber had both the unique style and the foresight to amass an incredible array of one-of-a-kind aviation artifacts. He played a key role in the acquisition of the 1903 Wright *Flyer*, as well the U.S. Navy's Curtiss NC-4, the first aircraft to cross the Atlantic.

Garber's many years of experience prepared him well for his role during World War II, when Lieutenant Paul Garber, then in the U.S. Naval Reserve, found himself assigned to the Navy's Bureau of Aeronautics, employed in the Special Devices Division model shop. There he worked on scores of projects for training personnel with simulators and models. His kite-flying instincts led him to construct a target kite; by the end of the war, more than 300,000 of these kites had been manufactured for training

A 1940s photograph shows Lieutenant Paul Garber, U.S. Naval Reserve, with one of his target kites, which bears the likeness of a Japanese Zero fighter. In the 1990s, when the Ryan NYP *Spirit of St. Louis* was cleaned and conserved, Garber had his picture taken with the aircraft he had acquired from Charles Lindbergh in 1928.

shipboard antiaircraft gunners. The target kite allowed them to practice shooting at moving targets.

Garber arrived back at the Smithsonian in 1946, just in time to become the first curator of the new National Air Museum. His first task as such was to find room for scores of World War II military aircraft from around the world that had been earmarked for the national aeronautical collection. With Garber's patience and ingenuity and the cooperation of many sources, the Institution's Silver Hill facility opened in nearby Suitland, Maryland. In 1980 it was named the Paul E. Garber Preservation, Restoration, and Storage Facility, a place where part of the Garber legacy—hundreds of flight-related objects—can be viewed by an enthusiastic public.

Although Paul Garber officially retired from civil service in 1969, he remained at the National Air and Space Museum, working as the Ramsey Fellow five full days a week on " …the increase and diffusion of knowledge pertaining to United States Naval Flight history." Until his death, on September 23, 1992, at the age of 93, Garber continued to work on his "aerobiography," as he called it, and welcomed frequent visitors of all ages who came to hear his stories.

There are no more Jimmy Doolittles, Charles Lindberghs, Wiley Posts, or Amelia Earharts, and there will probably not be another Paul Garber. Airplanes with romantic names like the *Spirit of St. Louis* and *Winnie Mae* are rare, and there are no more oceans still to cross, no more continents to discover, and few records left to set. Paul Garber's passing may have marked the end of a "golden age of curators."

E.T. Wooldridge is a Historian at the National Air and Space Museum.

Then, in the spring of 1904, just a few months after his disastrous experiment with flight, Langley had a second such opportunity. He received a visit from a retired Detroit industrialist named Charles L. Freer, who was prepared to give the Smithsonian more than two thousand art objects, among them unique collections of American painters, most notably James McNeill Whistler, and an unparalleled assemblage of Asian art and pottery going back to the 10th century.

The highly conventional Smithsonian Secretary, no doubt still despondent, was faced with a fastidious aesthete and wealthy former industrialist who knew what he wanted in all categories, whether it be Chinese porcelain, stone for his Detroit mansion, caviar, his dandified clothes, or the flower artfully placed in the vase by a precisely instructed servant. Years before, Langley had recalled the paintings, engravings, and etchings that Joseph Henry entrusted to the Corcoran Gallery of Art, but he was not knowledgeable about Freer's valuable, highly focused collection, nor appreciative of it.

Yet neither Freer's collection nor the fact that it came with half a million dollars for a proper gallery could be taken lightly. Langley put the collector off temporarily, and, at a board meeting in January 1905, raised the proposal with the Regents, who were equally indecisive. They asked Freer to put his offer in writing, which he did, adding, "No addition or deduction shall be made to the collections after my death, and nothing else shall ever be exhibited with them...." He also specified that no work of art could ever be removed from the building.

Freer suggested the Regents travel to his home in Detroit to view the treasures he had so passionately collected. This was considered an ordeal by the Regents, all of whom were elderly, as well as by Freer, who wrote to a fellow collector, "What they do not know about art would fill many volumes...."

(Text continued on page 196)

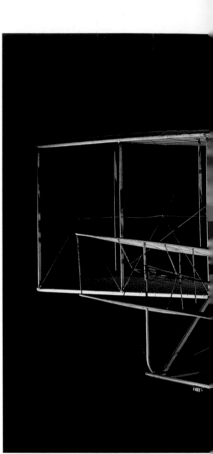

A manikin of Orville Wright at the controls, the Wright brothers' 1903 *Flyer* hangs in the Milestones of Flight gallery at the National Air and Space Museum. "I am an enthusiast, but not a crank," wrote Wilbur Wright to the Smithsonian in May 1899, right (center), requesting information on heavier-than-air flight. American dominance of the skies in the early 1900s, celebrated at far right, was short-lived: As the Wrights fought to protect their patents, Europeans improved on their invention.

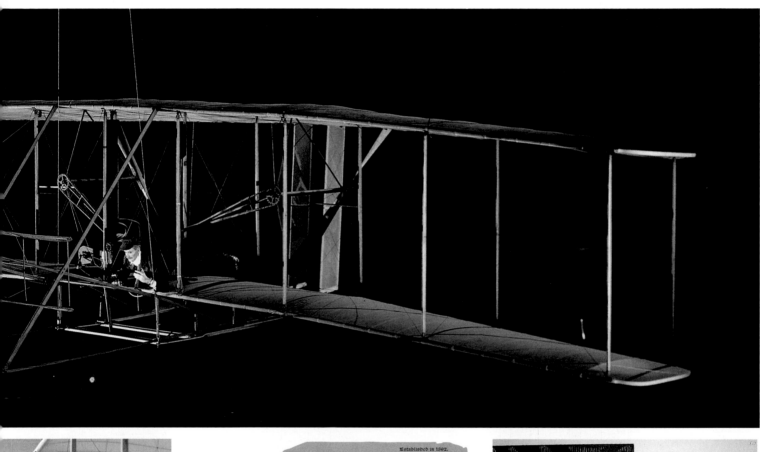

RESTORING THE *FLYER*

by PETER L. JAKAB

Like the Star-Spangled Banner and the Hope diamond, the Wright *Flyer* is one of the priceless relics that Smithsonian visitors expect to see when they come to Washington. In the early 1980s, however, after nearly 50 years of almost constant museum exposure, the *Flyer*'s tattered, worn appearance had become a serious concern to curators at the National Air and Space Museum (NASM).

The famous aircraft had last been restored under Orville Wright's direction in late 1926 and early 1927. New fabric had been applied, and many broken and missing parts repaired or replaced. But after 58 years, the 1927 fabric was severely discolored, badly stained, and covered with numerous small patches. Alarming rust blemishes suggested corrosion on the underlying metal fittings. In addition, the wooden structure and the engine were long overdue for a thorough inspection and cleaning.

On the evening of January 29, 1985, with television cameras rolling, the historic airplane was lowered from its place of honor in NASM's Milestones of Flight gallery. In order not to disappoint visitors who had traveled to Washington to see the *Flyer*, NASM officials decided to restore the aircraft publicly in one of the museum's other exhibition galleries.

And so, behind plexiglass walls, a team of experienced Smithsonian professionals began the four-month task of disassembling, inspecting, preserving, and documenting the flying machine that first carried humans aloft in 1903. Photographers and draftsmen helped technicians record details that led to the first set of truly accurate and complete drawings of the Wright *Flyer*.

As the restoration progressed, a number of interesting details emerged, adding a human dimension to the revered museum piece. When craftsmen stacked the disassembled wing spars in the proper order, for example, the words "Wilbur Wright, Elizabeth City, North Carolina" and "Wright Cycle Co., Dayton, Ohio," written in crayon, appeared across the bundled parts.

Other hidden markings on the structure offered clues to the *Flyer*'s design. The name "Brown's," stenciled on the inside of a wingtip bow, prompted NASM researchers to check the Wright financial records in the Library of Congress. It turned out that S.N. Brown and Co., a Dayton carriage manufacturer, had made the bows. The conclusion was that the bows were probably off-the-shelf items used to support leather carriage tops.

The airplane's wooden structure was in surprisingly good shape,

requiring only a thorough cleaning. After chemical treatment to prevent corrosion of the metal fittings, the airplane was ready for reassembly. NASM restorers were able to use the only remaining intact panel of wing covering dating from the original 1903 flights—recently donated to the museum by the Wright family—as a pattern for the new wing covering.

The engine restoration was the final, and in some ways the most interesting, aspect of the project. The original engine's crankcase had been broken when the aircraft overturned in a gust of wind on December 17, 1903, after its final flight. The crankshaft and flywheel disappeared after being displayed at a 1906 New York aeronautics show. When Orville Wright first reassembled the *Flyer* for public exhibition in 1916, he substituted engine components that had been used to power subsequent 1904 and 1905 aircraft.

By 1985 there was some confusion regarding which of the *Flyer*'s engine components were original. A study of the engine conducted by NASM propulsion curator Rick Leyes and metallurgist Martha Goodway of the Smithsonian's Conservation Analytical Laboratory demonstrated that most of the internal components were in fact from 1903. The crankshaft, flywheel, and crankcase were from 1904–1905.

The history of the original, broken crankcase had always been a mystery. On several occasions, Orville had indicated that the original crankcase no longer existed. Yet the Wright Brothers National Memorial, in Kitty Hawk, North Carolina, has on display a Wright engine crankcase broken in a manner consistent with the Wrights' description of the December 1903 accident.

In an attempt to sort out the mystery, NASM borrowed the Wright Memorial artifact to perform a side-by-side comparison during the *Flyer* restoration. The internal components of the NASM engine, along with remnants of sealant material, matched the Kitty Hawk crankcase perfectly. The Wright Memorial crankcase was almost certainly part of the original engine.

In an even more significant finding, Martha Goodway's analysis of the microstructure of the aluminum alloy from which the 1903 crankcase was cast showed it to be the earliest known example of the precipitation-hardened alloy process. Prior to her discovery, the first documented use of this technique—which would become essential to the future aerospace industry—was in the structure of German airships after 1909.

The 1985 Wright *Flyer* restoration project was a marvelous example of how the diverse divisions and professionals that constitute the

In 1985, after being lowered from its place of honor in the Milestones of Flight gallery, bottom, the Wright *Flyer* was publicly restored at the National Air and Space Museum. Below, restorers re-attach the new wing covering, which was patterned after that of the original 1903 craft. At right (top and center), the *Flyer*'s chain drive, fuel line, and control mechanism appear before and after restoration; lastly, a rust-stained outboard attachment wire.

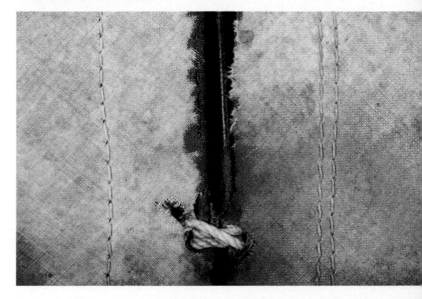

Smithsonian Institution collaborate not only to preserve our great national treasures, but also to enhance our historical and technical understanding of the collections we hold in the public trust.

Peter L. Jakab is a Curator in the Department of Aeronautics, National Air and Space Museum.

In Detroit, Langley, Alexander Graham Bell, Dr. James Burrill Angell, and Senator John B. Henderson sat through four days of viewings conducted by Freer. "The things are all very well of their kind," the Senator confided to a companion, "but damn their kind!" The decision to accept the collections was put off yet again.

The Regents were concerned about lack of space and the ultimate shape of a national gallery, and uncertain how to maintain Freer's collection before his Florentine Renaissance gallery could be built. Then, in December, President Theodore Roosevelt instructed the Regents, "Gentlemen, accept this collection whether you care for it or not."

This they did, on January 24, and Freer telegraphed Roosevelt, "Without your good influence it could not have been accomplished."

The Johnston bequest and Freer's generosity performed a function larger than just providing treasures; they enhanced the popularity of the Institution's already existing art department, and forced the Smithsonian to deal with America's growing interest in the highest expressions of imagination.

The man given immediate responsibility over the collections and thus a new component of power was the veteran of geology, ethnology, and art—William Henry Holmes.

AT THE TIME OF THE REGENTS' ACCEPTANCE OF Freer's bequest, Langley was dying in South Carolina, where he had gone after suffering a stroke the previous November. He had been a bold, controversial, and, to the end, enigmatic Secretary. The failure of his flying machine had overshadowed real accomplishment, including publication of the *International Catalogue of Scientific Literature*, which continued for decades.

Langley's research efforts had furthered the goals of the first Secretary—Langley's name would eventually

Among Secretary Langley's friends was explorer and anthropologist John Wesley Powell, who died in 1902 and was buried, above, in Arlington National Cemetery. Soon thereafter, Langley himself died, leaving a legacy of scientific achievement that inspired the collection of such items as this Wright J-5 radial aircraft motor from the 1920s.

be used to define a unit of solar radiation, the *langley*—and one of his last official acts would have been equally pleasing to Spencer Baird. In 1904 Langley turned the first spadeful of earth on the north side of the Mall, launching the construction of a new museum building.

This structure, when completed, would dwarf the existing Smithsonian buildings, and solve—at least for a time—the Institution's perennial problem of increasing the collections while promoting the search for knowledge.

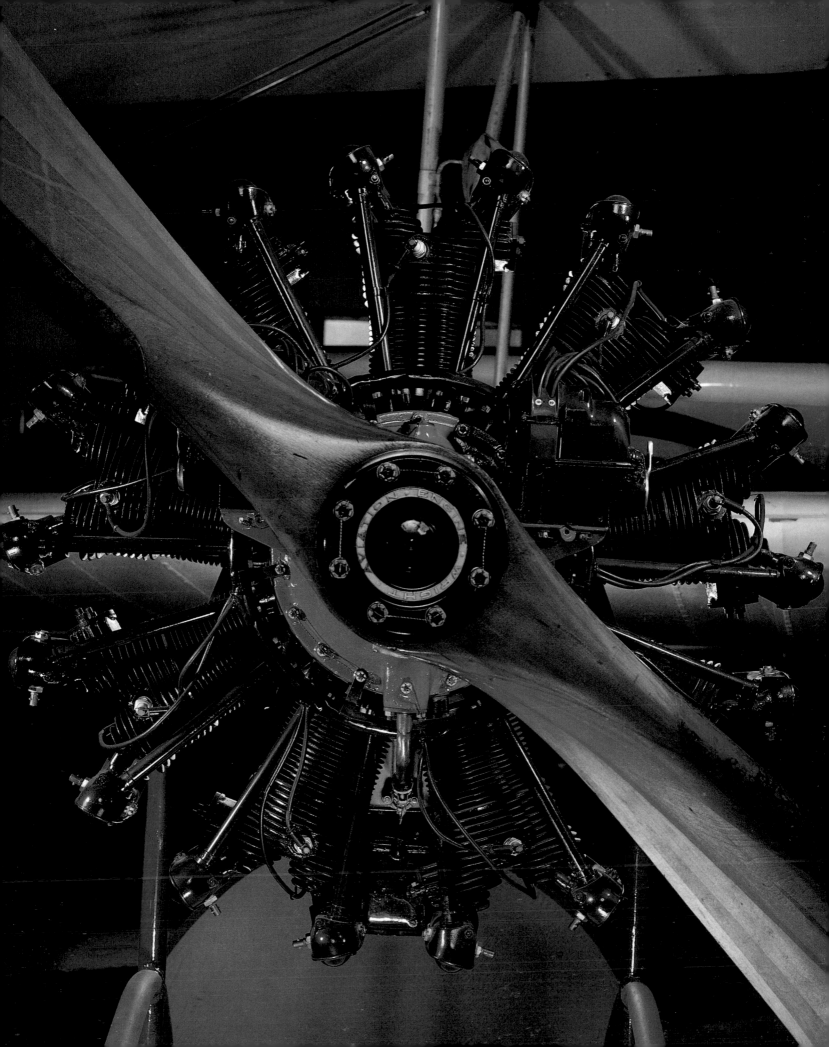

Bureau of American Ethnology affiliate anthropologist Alice Cunningham Fletcher appears in a photograph taken late in her career. Her illustrations of Pawnee rattles, below, and "The Kurahus in Ceremonial Dress," opposite, were included with transcribed music in her 1904 report, *The Hako: A Pawnee Ceremony*.

PROFILE
HARMONIOUS

The Victorians' interest in the American Indian and in the "progress" of humanity generally was related in part to the great disparities in class society at the end of the 19th century. The Industrial Revolution, rather than freeing all people, seemed to relegate some to inferior roles, a subject of interest to preachers and scientists alike.

One ethnologist who shared James Mooney's concern with history and the effects of mistreatment of American Indians was Alice Cunningham Fletcher, an early "applied" anthropologist—one who attempted to solve practical problems through science. Fletcher worked for a decade in the Indian reform movement to help the subjugated tribes, and at the same time sought to document their often distressed cultures, particularly through her interest in Indian music.

Fletcher considered her version of anthropology a means of improving the conditions of those she studied, and, in 1905, she wrote: "There is much in [the Indians'] past that should be conserved, for no people can be helped if they are absolutely uprooted. It is just here that the ethnological student can become a practical helper to the philanthropist."

Her personal relationship with the Omaha tribe contributed to her advocacy of the policy known as "severalty," whereby Indians' economic opportunities would be improved through individual land allotments. In 1882, the Omaha were granted land—and eventually citizenship—through her efforts. It was a process of assimilation that she felt Indians wanted.

Fletcher's strong belief in basic human rights did not affect judgment of her science. While chief of the Bureau of American Ethnology, William Henry Holmes chose Fletcher for inclusion in the *National Cyclopedia of American Biography*. The only other woman he so honored was Matilda Stevenson, the enemy of Frank Hamilton Cushing who had shown considerably less concern for her subjects than Fletcher.

A voracious reader and prolific correspondent, Fletcher was intimately involved in the crosscurrents between the Smithsonian and the BAE. She defended W.J. McGee for his promotion of anthropology as a respectable science; she objected to the practice by some in the BAE of withholding materials from scholars outside the agency. As the anthropologist Charles Lummis observed of Fletcher's confrontations within the bureau, "Some of her opponents were never quite sure what quiet, deep river had just drifted along and left them stranded far from their selfish hopes."

Fletcher was a pioneer in the direct transcription of music during ceremonies. When gramophones later came into use, the recorded music contained the exact melodies and harmonies that Fletcher had noted earlier. Her two most significant works of ethnography, *The Omaha Tribe* and *The Hako*, both contain music and reflections of her belief in crucial environmental as well as cultural influences.

In her essay "Leaves from My Omaha Notebook," Fletcher expressed her hope "that by the lifting of the veil here and there upon days passed in Indian homes, something of the human life of the lodge may be seen, and the touch of nature there revealed may 'make the whole earth kin.' "

A VOICE FROM THE CAMBRIAN

"Do things!...after due deliberation."
—CHARLES DOOLITTLE WALCOTT
TO PRESIDENT WOODROW WILSON, 1914

Geologist Charles Doolittle Walcott, who became the Smithsonian's fourth Secretary, lifted the veil on the Cambrian, bringing to light— and to science—such organisms as *Anomalocaris*, right, which swam in ancient seas.

On the high Colorado Plateau of southern Utah and northern Arizona, a largely self-taught geologist and paleontologist named Charles D. Walcott had worked with Clarence Dutton, a member of the United States Geological Survey (USGS) and a geologist whose descriptions of the Western landscape were as spectacular as the paintings by William Henry Holmes. Walcott later succeeded Powell as director of the USGS, made some major discoveries in the Cambrian rocks of New York State and other North American sites, and, in 1897, was chosen by Secretary Langley as acting Assistant Secretary in charge of the National Museum.

As Assistant Secretary, Walcott nonetheless retained his USGS position. Although officially a separate government entity within the Department of the Interior, the USGS kept its ties to the Smithsonian— an unusual, productive, and enduring tradition. The much smaller Biological Survey, established in 1885 under mammologist and ornithologist C. Hart Merriam to gather information on North American fauna, was merged with the Bureau of Fisheries to become the U.S. Fish and Wildlife Service. It also would maintain a permanent liaison with the Smithsonian.

Walcott had immediately set about organizing the chaos of the natural-history collections and their curatorial staff. (At the time he took over, only 26 of the 63 employees were paid a salary.) He established three departments—Anthropology, Biology, and Geology—and a clear chain of command whose effects are still felt today.

Upon Langley's death in 1906, Walcott had not been the Regents' first choice to succeed him. That honor was offered to Henry Fairfield Osborn, of the American Museum of Natural History, in New York. He declined, and only then did the Regents turn to Walcott—over the objections of President Theodore Roosevelt. Walcott had helped defeat a bill seeking to exploit the national-forest preserves, and the President wanted to keep him at the highly political USGS as an ally. The Regents exerted considerable pressure on Roosevelt to convince him that this commanding workhorse was indeed needed more at the Smithsonian than in the President's own conservation efforts.

Walcott's breadth of interest would now have to accommodate everything from 500-million-year-old fossils to nascent rocketry. One of his immediate and most pressing tasks was to oversee the National Museum's transition from the old to the new.

ON THE DAY WALCOTT WAS SWORN IN AS FOURTH Secretary of the Smithsonian, January 31, 1907, the new National Museum building loomed on the north side of the Mall, its neoclassical outlines seemingly the answer to all the Smithsonian's space problems. Delays in the delivery of granite stalled for a time the museum's inevitable completion, but by the fall of 1908 enough was in place to allow it to host the Sixth International Tuberculosis Congress.

What a spectacle the new museum presented in comparison to the doughty old Castle and the old National Museum building south of the grassy expanse. In the new museum, three massive wings and a stately rotunda—at that point still without its Roman dome—took up almost 11 acres. A full five acres of exhibit space was supposed to satisfy the needs of all curators, present and future. The top floor, when added, along with the north wing, would accommodate all conceivable research. This

During the 1880s, as a paleontologist for the U.S. Geological Survey, Charles Walcott discovered this Cambrian trilobite fossil, *Olenellus vermontanus*, on one of several expeditions to the mountains of western Vermont. In 1909, as Smithsonian Secretary, Walcott discovered the Burgess Shale in western Canada, a site that was to become almost synonymous with life in the Cambrian seas some 525 million years ago. At far left, Walcott takes a respite from work at the Burgess Shale's Phyllopod Bed quarry.

was an edifice to impress, despite the fact that the huge statue of a winged Victory envisioned by the architect, J.D. Hornblower, had been nixed by Langley.

At a cost of $3.5 million, the new museum was to represent the best design and building in the nation, as had the Capitol and the Washington Monument in their time. Suddenly, in the eyes of many, it was the Smithsonian Institution.

The National Museum's move out of what came to be called the Arts and Industries Building began in the summer of 1909. It was supervised by the redoubtable Assistant Secretary, Richard C. Rathbun, who had to contend with everything in the new building, from threat of fire to acres of leaking roof. The collection of mollusks crossed the Mall first, and found a home on the third floor, although the division's curator, William Healey Dall, had pronounced the proposed floor plan "a hopeless muddle." By the end of the year, renowned scientists in many fields had unpacked their books and specimens, and were at work in offices throughout the heroic structure.

On March 17, 1910, the museum's great doors were opened, and members of the public entered the north hall, where, according to paleontologist Ellis Yochelson in his book, *The National Museum of Natural History*, "the sawing of mahogany and pine wafted a pleasant smell."

By 1912, the three Smithsonian buildings held 2,724 exhibition cases, almost 5,000 steel specimen drawers, and about 33,000 of wood. To the ethnology exhibits were added zoology and paleontology specimens, the specialty of the current Secretary. Stately wooden cases marched the length of high-ceilinged rooms where both the committed and the merely curious could browse—even on Sundays.

Among the viewing possibilities were a temporary display of selected Freer art objects, six buffalo originally mounted by William T. Hornaday in 1888, plants, stuffed birds, and archaeological specimens from sites ranging from the top of the world to the Antarctic. Knowing these things were significant, visitors enjoyed

gazing upon assembled objects of scientific and cultural interest; they were satisfied by the mere proximity of the arcane and exotic, with written explanations offered by recognized experts.

As the Smithsonian's fourth Secretary, Walcott enlivened the *Annual Report*, and tried to make the public more aware of what the Institution was up to. He represented Baird's legacy in the natural sciences, but, like President Roosevelt, he was also an outdoorsman and a demonstrably "vigorous" administrator. During the summer that thousands of specimens crossed the sunbaked Mall to the new museum, Walcott was recovering fossils in British Columbia. Leading a pack train along a trail near Burgess Pass in the Canadian Rockies, he picked up a piece of shale, split it open, and found inside the carbonized bodies of trilobites and other small animals in what became the foundation for studies of the Cambrian Period in Western North America.

It was this small yet significant discovery that led Walcott to a larger quarry farther up the mountain.

The following summer, that of 1910, and for many years thereafter, Walcott, dressed in knee-high boots and often with dynamite in hand, immersed himself in his work there, and produced examples of more than 70 genera and 130 fossilized species. He collected approximately 65,000 specimens, a trove that represents one of the treasures of the Smithsonian. Yochelson has written that "were it not for the hard, physical labor of quarrying performed by a man in his sixties, the unique Burgess shale fauna would never have been made available for study by biologists and paleontologists."

The Secretary's approach to his science was teleological: He believed in an orderly progression from the pre-Cambrian to the more modern, "higher" forms of life. Those scientists belonging to the "spontaneous-generation" school challenged this approach, but no one doubted the potential value of Walcott's discovery.

Ironically, Walcott himself undervalued the importance of follow-up research on the Burgess shale, incorrectly classifying many specimens and failing to address

On May 11, 1909, laborers set the last stone of the new National Museum, right, which in 1969 became the National Museum of Natural History. Specimens from the museum's multifaceted collections include an ancient insect preserved in amber and a shell, *Chicoreus palmarosae*. In 1973 the great pachyderm in the building's rotunda provided an apt centerpiece for an inaugural celebration staged by partisans of President Richard M. Nixon.

their broader biological ramifications. He simply did not have the time, given his administrative duties. It was said that he "defined the Cambrian," but the significance of the Burgess shale material was realized only later, after others had studied it more thoroughly.

THE RELATIONSHIP BETWEEN THE SMITHSONIAN and the 26th President, Theodore "Teddy" Roosevelt, proved mutually beneficial. As Vice President under William McKinley, Roosevelt had served as a Smithsonian Regent, and, in his first message to Congress as President, he publicly endorsed the Institution's objectives—the increase and diffusion of knowledge—and attested to the worth of all its related projects.

"There should be no halt in the work of the Institution...," Roosevelt said, "for the preservation of the vanishing races of great North American animals in the National Zoological Park. The urgent needs of the National Museum are recommended to the favorable consideration of the Congress."

Roosevelt's practical assistance to the Smithsonian began before the Freer gift. In 1904, he ordered an American ship, the U.S.S. *Dolphin*, to transport the remains of James Smithson from New York—where they had been shipped from Genoa, Italy—to the Washington Navy Yard. Representatives of the U.S. and Italian governments had agreed that the Institution's founder should be interred at the Smithsonian. And, in 1905, he instructed his Attorney General "to back the Smithsonian up" in its interpretation of Harriet Lane Johnston's will, which stipulated that her art be given to the National Gallery.

Then, in 1908, Roosevelt wrote to Walcott of his plans to travel to East Africa after his Presidency. "Now it seems to me that this opens the best chance for the National Museum to get a fine collection not only of the big game beasts, but of the smaller animals and birds of

(Text continued on page 210)

EMBLEMS OF STYLE AND STATUS

by DENISE D. MERINGOLO

In 1912, with great foresight, Mrs. Cassie Myers James and Mrs. Rose Gouvenor Hoes started a costume collection at the Smithsonian. Shortly after they began their work, the Institution's *Annual Report* described the collection as "illustrative of the fashions of the women of the United States ...." A radical step for its day, it promoted women and "women's sphere of home life" as legitimate and important categories in the study of history. And it was to incorporate what has become one of the Smithsonian's most popular group of objects—that of the First Ladies.

Thirty-one years after the collection was begun, the Smithsonian hired a professional curator, Margaret Brown Klapthor, to care for and interpret it. By the mid-1950s, Klapthor had separated the First Ladies' gowns from the rest of the costumes, grouped them together by period, and put them on exhibit in a separate First Ladies Hall in the Arts and Industries Building. In Klapthor's words, "The idea for the First Ladies Hall came about because of the Smithsonian's large collection of presidential and White House furniture and household accessories. The hall was already being planned when we had the opportunity to add architectural details available after the [1948 White House] renovation."

The new Museum of History and Technology (now the National Museum of American History), which opened in 1964, also featured a First Ladies Hall, again curated by Klapthor. The collection gained visibility, and the donation of inaugural gowns by new First Ladies became a Smithsonian tradition.

In 1983, after 40 years as curator, Klapthor retired. Her influence had ultimately transformed the First Ladies collection into one of the Institution's biggest attractions. In 1990, Edith P. Mayo, a curator in the Division of Political History, assumed responsibility for the collection, her background in women's political history and her museum experience adding a new dimension to the collection's interpretation.

For Mayo, as for Mrs. James and Mrs. Hoes, the collection offered an opportunity to examine the contributions of women in American life. She saw the individual dresses as emblems of style and social status that were important in communicating the power and potential of the First Ladies' position. Her exhibit, "First Ladies: Political Role and Public Image," which opened in 1992, placed the first ladies in the context of both Presidential and women's history.

Today, visitors often ask what will happen to the collection when

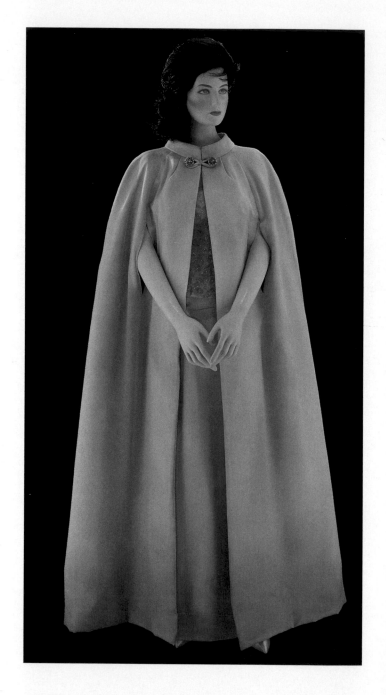

a woman is elected President. Any changes would, of course, be the decision of the curator in charge at that time. But if the collection continues to document the role of the President's spouse, then the clothing of the "First Gentleman" will change the interpretation of the collection once again.

Denise D. Meringolo is a former assistant in the Division of Political History at the National Museum of American History.

First Lady Mamie Eisenhower and President Dwight D. Eisenhower, above, opened the First Ladies Hall in Arts and Industries on May 24, 1955. On March 6, 1995, First Lady Hillary Rodham Clinton presented her inaugural gown to Smithsonian Secretary I. Michael Heyman. Far left, Jacqueline Kennedy's inaugural gown.

Africa; and looking at it dispassionately I believe that the chance ought not to be neglected." And so did Walcott and the Regents.

In addition to Baird's two boxcars of natural specimens, the museum also had received the 1,200 mammal and bird specimens that had been sent from Borneo and Polynesia by William Louis Abbott. There were innumerable other contributions as well, but the new, spacious museum was about to see a hefty increase.

Roosevelt pointed out that his expenses and those of his son Kermit would be covered in part by his publisher. But he also wanted on the expedition "one or two professional field naturalists" to prepare the specimens for return to Washington. These expenses, as well as considerable logistic and material costs, would be covered by the Institution.

Three naturalists from the National Museum were chosen to make the trip with Roosevelt: Edgar A. Mearns, ornithologist, and the mammologists J. Alden Loring, a specialist in small mammals, and Edmund Heller, a specialist in large ones. Meanwhile, Roosevelt read an average of five books on African wildlife weekly, some provided by a friend at the American Museum of Natural History, in New York.

An amateur taxidermist and ornithologist, Roosevelt wrote to a friend during these preparations, "I am much more pleased at making the trip a scientific one with a real object than merely a holiday after big game."

On April 21, 1909, the Roosevelt entourage set out from Mombasa, armed and ready for preserving specimens with no less than four tons of salt and portable skinning tables. Roosevelt's interest in science was genuine. Heller wrote that Roosevelt "had at his command the entire published literature concerning the game mammals and birds of the world, a feat of memory that few naturalists possess. I constantly felt while with him

A campaign postcard asks which "Bill"—William Howard Taft or William Jennings Bryan—will win the 1908 Presidential election, while another exhorts voters to cast their ballots for the former. Both cards and this 1956 wind-up toy reside in the Smithsonian's political-history collection.

Willie T or Willie B

It's bound to be a BILL

COPYRIGHTED 1908 ALBERT J. MOORES

that I was in the presence of the foremost field naturalist of our time…."

Eight months later, the expedition ended its journey in Khartoum. Soon the National Museum received its bonanza: 5,013 mammals, 4,453 birds, 2,322 reptiles and amphibians, and similarly large numbers of fishes, invertebrates, shells, and plants. "No longer was there any need to apologize to the London or Berlin museums," P.R. Cutright wrote in *Theodore Roosevelt, The Naturalist*, referring to the largest collection ever brought out of Africa by a single party. "The series of skins of such animals as the white rhino, giant eland, reticulated giraffe, northern sable antelope, and Vaughn's kob were unrivalled in any other museum."

And yet the Roosevelt donation was just a fraction of the 100,000 zoological and botanical specimens the National Museum received in 1910 alone.

LIKE HIS PREDECESSORS, SECRETARY WALCOTT had duties that extended beyond his chosen field, paleontology, and the Smithsonian. He was one of the founders of the Carnegie Institution of Washington, D.C., and served the National Academy of Sciences both as president and as a discreet lobbyist for changes in the academy's constitution, which had to be approved by Congress.

He managed all his enterprises well, and established crucial connections among those who kept Washington functioning. He oversaw the reopening of Langley's aerodynamic laboratory, and helped set up a corporation to administer grants for governmental and private research; eventually he headed the National Advisory Committee for Aeronautics. All the while he endured extraordinary personal loss: his wife, Helena, was killed in a train wreck in 1911; his oldest son Charles died of consumption two years later; and, in 1917, another son, Benjamin, was killed in the war.

Walcott worked his way through these losses. As

he later wrote to President Woodrow Wilson, "Steady, systematic work is one's salvation." In 1914, he married artist Mary Vaux, who accompanied him to British Columbia in the summers and whose voluminous illustrations of wildflowers were published by the Smithsonian. The marriage was a boon for the tall, athletic Secretary, who strode through the Smithsonian's buildings with an authoritative and patrician bearing. Unlike Langley, Walcott left no impression of condescension or impatience, but no one questioned who ran the Institution during his tenure.

There was an unspoken rule that the Secretary was not to be disturbed between ten in the morning and two in the afternoon, during which time he worked in a small room on the third floor of the Castle pursuing his passion through layers of Burgess shale. Walcott produced weighty manuscripts that would prove his most enduring contribution to science. One, *Cambrian Brachiopoda*, published in 1912 by the USGS, contained 872 pages and 104 plates, and remains a primary reference in the field.

Walcott's efforts on behalf of the Institution were often behind the scenes, unknown to the majority of the staff. He raised at least $40,000 from outside sources to cover the costs of Roosevelt's African expedition, financed his own efforts in the Burgess shale, and, with his new wife, established a research fund.

He was also instrumental in persuading Freer to move his collection to Washington before his death, traveling to Detroit with William Henry Holmes and displaying an appreciation of Freer's objects that Walcott's predecessors had failed to show. He further persuaded Freer to contribute $1 million to the building of his own museum.

"We had only to point out to Mr. Freer," Walcott told a friend, in a typical disclaimer, "…[that] it would be of immense value to us during the period of construction and installation. We would be able to draw upon his

(Text continued on page 218)

On April 16, 1912, Harriet Quimby, above, became the first woman to fly across the English Channel. The sheet-music cover, far right, offers a song honoring the 1912 Boston Aero Meet, during which Quimby fell to her death after wind gusts upturned her airplane. Right, a World War I-era sheet-music cover depicts airplanes as engines of war.

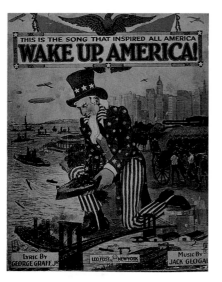

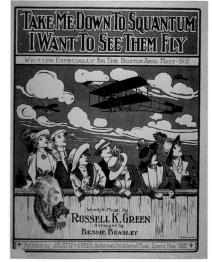

One of eight artists the U.S. Army commissioned to chronicle the World War I American Expeditionary Forces, Harry Everett Townsend painted this portrait of a U.S. infantryman, right. In the end, the artists produced some 500 paintings, all of which reside in the National Museum of American History (NMAH). Volunteer civilian artists created these posters, which today are part of NMAH's Archives Center collections: above, Haskell Coffin's 1918 poster for the War Savings Stamps program and, far right, a 1917 poster for the American Red Star Animal Relief fund. Cavalry in World War I used implements similar to these, opposite, to care for their horses.

CAPT HARRY TOWNSEND
A.E.F.

"HELP THE HORSE
TO
SAVE THE SOLDIER"

"GOOD-BYE, OLD MAN"

DRAWN BY F·MATANIA

PLEASE JOIN
THE AMERICAN RED STAR ANIMAL RELIEF
National Headquarters Albany, N.Y.

INTO THE HEART OF NEW GUINEA

by JOHN HOMIAK

Anthropology has always evoked images of travel, exploration, and adventure mixed with scientific discovery. This association reached a high point in the public imagination during the 1920s. And for good reason. This was a time when growing urban populations were increasingly subject to industrial regimentation. At the same time, technological mastery of travel and the practical applications of science fed an unbridled optimism and public appetite to learn more about a culturally diverse, but heretofore unknown, world.

Anthropologists of this generation often went to great lengths to document their expeditions through film and photography. Many believed that communicating the risks and adventure of their undertakings was as important as revealing scientific discoveries to the public. To this end, anthropologist-explorer Matthew W. Stirling, chief of the Bureau of American Ethnology, and his associates ultimately shot thousands of still photographs and more than 5,000 feet of motion-picture film documenting contact with the natives of southern Dutch New Guinea, which is today Irian Jaya, Indonesia.

For years, Stirling had been fascinated by New Guinea. He believed that it remained "a land of legend, a place of imagined geographical and biological wonders," and was "the world's last stronghold of the Stone Age." In particular, he focused on the accounts of British explorers who claimed to have encountered a small group of Pygmies (whom they called "Tapiro") in the mountains of west Dutch New Guinea. Scientists believed that sizeable populations awaited discovery in this rugged and impenetrable terrain, and Stirling was determined to explore and claim this region for ethnology.

In 1924, Stirling resigned from his post at the Smithsonian to sell real estate; the money earned from this venture helped to fund his expedition to New Guinea. With the support of the Smithsonian and the Netherlands Colonial Government, he and his group set out for the south coast of Dutch New Guinea.

A novice aviator as well as an anthropologist, Stirling hit upon the idea of using an airplane as a tool of exploration. The idea of flying into a remote location appealed to him as much for its logistical possibilities (hauling equipment and supplies) as for the swashbuckling image that was then associated with aviation. It was one year before Charles Lindbergh's 1927 transatlantic flight, and Stirling would be the first to fly over this region of New Guinea's interior.

In 1926, aboard a pontoon-fitted Breguet 14B2 named *The Ern*, above, Matthew Stirling became the first person to fly into New Guinea's interior. Carrying with him such necessities as this map of southern New Guinea (now part of Irian Jaya, the Indonesian segment of the island), Stirling also brought a motion-picture camera—seen here held by a native—which he used to make the documentary film "By Aeroplane to Pigmyland," promoted in the poster at right.

The expedition was a large-scale undertaking that involved the challenge not only of moving sizeable numbers of men and supplies from Jakarta and Surabaya (Java), but also of dealing with native peoples as part of the expedition. More than 100 Malay convicts were pressed into service as carriers, and some 70 Dyaks from Central Borneo served as canoemen. The latter proved indispensable for spotting and repelling ambushes set by hostile Papuans as the expedition moved into uncharted areas along the Rouffaer River.

Trade served as the lingua franca for much of the expedition's contact with the Papuans and Pygmies. Knives, beads, mirrors, cowries, and tobacco were among the goods expedition members exchanged for bows, bone-tipped arrows, net bags, stone axes, braided rattan armor belts, armlets, feathered headdresses, and bone, seed, or feather body ornaments. Similar exchanges were used to insure the cooperation of the natives in the taking of photographs, sound recordings, and anthropometric measurements.

The expedition ultimately reached its primary goal—the uncharted region of the Upper Rouffaer and the Nassau Mountains, which was the site of the previously isolated Nogullo Pygmies. Expedition members spent two and a half months mapping the villages of this area and collecting ethnological information and specimens. For some years after the expedition's close, Stirling made public presentations and lectured with his film—"By Aeroplane to Pygmyland"—which sought to capture the adventure and exotic appeal of his experience. Today, photographs, film, and material objects he collected remain an important part of his legacy to early Smithsonian anthropology.

John Homiak is the Director of the National Anthropological Archives at the National Museum of Natural History.

intimate knowledge of the history of the objects…and to have his advice as to the most effective method of their presentation to the public." It is difficult to imagine such deference on the part of Langley and his associates, who had been the first to deal with Freer.

The fourth Secretary staunchly defended his predecessor's aeronautical experiments. In 1914, to determine whether it had been capable of sustained flight, he agreed to a reconstruction of Langley's 1903 Aerodrome by the aeronautical pioneer Glenn Hammond Curtiss. During tests, however, Curtiss made considerable alterations. In what was one of Walcott's few lapses in judgment, when the experiments proved successful the Smithsonian published a statement describing the Aerodrome as "the first aircraft in history capable of flight with a pilot and several hundred pounds of useful load."

When the "restored" Aerodrome was put on exhibit in the National Museum in 1918, the label identified it as "The Original, Full-size Langley Flying Machine, 1903." Another label—"The first man-carrying aeroplane in the history of the world capable of sustained free flight"—was soon substituted, and later modified with the qualification: "in the opinion of many competent to judge."

These claims prolonged an ongoing patent controversy over the Wright brothers' flight designs, and seemed to align the Smithsonian with those challenging the Wrights both for the honor of being first in flight and the money deriving from that honor. They briefly cast the Smithsonian's probity in doubt, and soured relations between the Institution and Orville Wright, one of America's greatest heroes, at a time when war again aroused interest in airplanes as strategic weapons. Meanwhile, Wright sent the *Flyer* to London's Science Museum, where many feared it would remain.

ON APRIL 26, 1916, WALCOTT AND FOUR OTHER members of the National Academy of Sciences met with President Wilson, and offered to organize research in the interests of national security. The conflict in Europe had begun to draw American research and educational institutions into its orbit; war-related science of all kinds was quickly mobilized and implemented.

The weight of the Great War fell on the Smithsonian in 1917, when employees were summoned to the auditorium of the National Museum in June and strongly encouraged to buy Liberty Loan bonds for the war effort. Some employees also sponsored a Red Cross ambulance. Then Walcott's son Benjamin, a member of a French flying unit, was killed on patrol behind German lines.

Smithsonian geologists found themselves called upon to perform various experiments for the government that they thought to be related to the war. Scientists in physical anthropology and other departments were enlisted in such esoteric enterprises as providing infor-

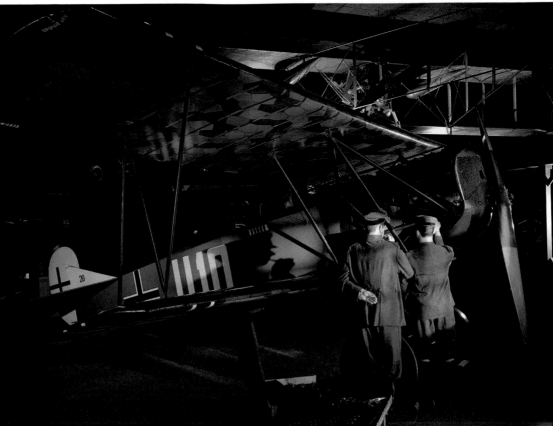

After World War I, the "tin shed," then located on the Mall near the Arts and Industries Building, displayed such military artifacts as the French-made Renault tank and the German howitzer, seen in foreground below. The German Fokker D VII, right, captured on November 9, 1918, near Verdun, is an example of the fighter aircraft many consider the best of World War I. It now resides in the National Air and Space Museum, as does this bust of Eugene Jack Bullard, opposite, who was America's first black combat pilot and flew more than 20 combat missions with a French squadron during World War I.

mation on the Balkan peoples. On the more practical side, the Astrophysical Observatory investigated wind pressure on projectiles, perfected the design of a recoilless gun, and experimented with searchlights for the Army.

In October 1917, President Wilson asked Walcott for space within the Smithsonian complex to accommodate the Bureau of War Risk Insurance, which handled the paperwork for all Americans under arms. The ground floor of the new National Museum was cleared, disrupting the division of mammals and the Biological Survey. Cases and whole collections, including corals from the Wilkes expedition and all invertebrates and domestic animals, were moved to the second floor.

A second White House request for space was also granted. Then, on July 16, 1918, in an unprecedented development, the Regents closed the museum to the public altogether, and turned it over to thousands of government clerks.

THE MUSEUM REOPENED IN THE SPRING OF 1919; the Bureau of War Risk Insurance had moved to its own quarters, leaving behind damaged plaster and exhibit halls badly in need of paint. In spite of this run-down appearance and the fact that many exhibits were still closed, attendance at the museum was heavy. The population of Washington had grown considerably during the war, and after it concluded the Smithsonian represented one of the few distractions for Washingtonians and visitors alike.

In the end, World War I provided the Institution with a huge collection of historical artifacts and memorabilia that included weapons, uniforms, insignia, decorations, captured enemy equipment, medical instruments, chemical-warfare paraphernalia, and ordnance. In the rotunda of the new museum—today the National Museum of Natural History—were displayed signaling devices and weapons. The six-inch naval gun that fired America's first shot of the war wouldn't fit into the

Teddy Roosevelt and son Kermit pose with their quarry, a cape buffalo, during their 1909 East African expedition. At right, an exhibit at the National Museum of Natural History features African cape buffalo at a papyrus swamp in Kenya. These are but a few of the thousands of animal specimens the Roosevelts collected for the Smithsonian.

building, and was thus set up in the east driveway.

The so-called War Collection was particularly popular with the public, but, as Ellis Yochelson points out in his book about the museum, "The staff had become deeply frustrated by the continued occupation of so much of their exhibit and storage space and the hindrance of their work."

THE GLORIOUS FUTURE BAIRD, LANGLEY, AND Walcott had envisioned for the Smithsonian in the resplendent Natural History building had been stymied. Appropriations from Congress for scientific work had not risen in a decade, and remained hovering at about

$300,000 even though three million new specimens had been added to the collections. Internally, the museum was growing and proliferating despite the shortage of funds; both a Division of Echinoderms and a Division of Mollusks were formed.

Art seemed to be the only prosperous enterprise. According to the *Annual Report* of 1921, an event "of great importance in the development of Washington as an art center was the organization…of the National Gallery of Art, previously a dependency of the United States National Museum, as a separate administrative unit under the Smithsonian Institution…. Art was placed on an equal footing with science…."

For William Henry Holmes, being tapped as the gallery's first director was a remarkable final appointment. He had undergone the complete transformation from young artist and man of action to scientist to aging artist and administrator. Holmes wrote, "The Smithsonian has harbored the dream of a gallery of art, but art has been in the shadow of the all-absorbing material interests of a rapidly developing nation."

Presumably the Institution, like the nation as a whole, was at last prepared for aesthetic appreciation, and Washington was poised on the edge of cultural and artistic significance, about to transcend its provincial ties to a merely expansionist federal government.

Photographed in Alphonse Bertillon's criminal-identification laboratory on March 17, 1896, while a student at the Ècole d'Anthropologie in Paris, Aleš Hrdlička was hired by William Henry Holmes in 1903 as the Institution's first physical anthropologist. Bertillon had developed a system for the Paris police that was based on anthropometry, the study of human body measurements for anthropological classification, which also influenced much of Hrdlička's research.

The opening of the stunning Freer Gallery of Art in 1921 seemed to affirm this strengthened interest in art. The event brought an extra $12,650 from Congress, and the public was treated to a carefully choreographed exhibit of unique objects, including Whistler's "Harmony in Blue and Gold: The Peacock Room" and Oriental artifacts in regal cases made of American black walnut, all housed within the sumptuous, sky-lit Italian Renaissance building. Constraints on the Smithsonian's other structures—and on the work going on within them—were made even more apparent by the gallery's luxuriousness.

Also in 1921, a Department of History was carved out of the Department of Anthropology—a crucial distinction—and headquartered across the Mall in the original museum, now known as the Arts and Industries Building. And the sheet-metal hangar that the Army Signal Corps had erected behind the Castle for experimentation during the war was re-christened the Aircraft Building. Within that homely conglomeration of metal and wood lay the unlikely nucleus of what would become the National Air and Space Museum—the most popular museum on Earth.

lection from various departments, inspired by museums of technology in other capital cities around the country and in Europe.

With the ending of World War I and the influx of military technology, Mitman got his chance. In 1920, he proposed to the Regents a Museum of Engineering and Industry modeled on the Deutches Museum, in Munich, Germany. Although the Regents did not agree to it, the proposal attracted attention elsewhere. In 1922, Mitman and a promoter named Holbrook Fitz-John Porter planned a museum complex consisting of, in the words of Smithsonian historian Arthur Molella, "a central historical museum in Washington, linked to a network of regional museums illustrating recent developments in local industries…with a system for exchanging artifacts, replicas, motion pictures, and other educational materials."

It was a curious variation on the objectives of Joseph Henry, but it failed to generate the needed funds. Mitman's dream would finally materialize some 30 years later, in different form, under the guidance of a man named Frank Taylor.

THE *ANNUAL REPORT* OF 1923 ADMITTED "DIFFICULTY in making both ends meet…. It is only by rigid economy and the omission of many things that should be done that the year ends without a deficit."

A burgeoning federal bureaucracy depersonalized much of the Smithsonian's business with Congress. The Bureau of the Budget reclassified museum positions in 1924, and raised salaries, making it at least theoretically easier to attract talent; but the bureau's influence further distanced Smithsonian agency heads from those voting for appropriations.

Even with old, warm relationships in the Senate, Walcott found his influence diminished. He had enjoyed easy access to the White House since the days of

FOR YEARS, THERE HAD BEEN AN EFFORT IN TANDEM with the Smithsonian's "pure" research to steer the institution in the direction of the history of engineering and mechanics. Carl W. Mitman, a mining engineer who had joined the Smithsonian in 1911, dreamed of a national museum of engineering and industry independent of the National Museum and its ties to anthropology. As curator of the technical collections, Mitman had separated the "engineering" artifacts from Otis Mason's Indian handicrafts. As chief of the Department of Mechanical and Mineral Technology, he gradually assembled his own col-

(Text continued on page 227)

GREAT DONORS

Since its original "donation," the $500,000 bequest from James Smithson that founded the Smithsonian, the Institution has been enriched by the generosity of many donors, including those on these pages. In 1958 jeweler Harry Winston (top right) presented the 45.5-carat Hope Diamond (right). The Mrs. James Steward Hooker Hall of Geology, Gems, and Minerals, established with a three-million-dollar gift from Mrs. Hooker, will showcase many of the 25,000 geology specimens donated in 1926 by Washington Roebling and Frederick Canfield, as well as gems and jewelry from Mrs. Hooker herself. Peter Harmatuk (below, right) has contributed some 30,000 fossil specimens, including those used by Smithsonian scientists and technicians to reconstruct accurately the jaws of a gigantic extinct shark, *Carcharodon megalodon*. Willis H. du Pont (far opposite) gave three of the rarest of U.S. coins. To his left, a portrait of Bern Dibner, whose donation of 8,000 books and 1,800 manuscripts to the Institution in 1974 established the Dibner Library of the History of Science and Technology. From the Dibner Library's collection (far right, below): an illustration from Luigi Galvani's 1791 pamphlet, *De viribus electricitatis in motu musculari.*

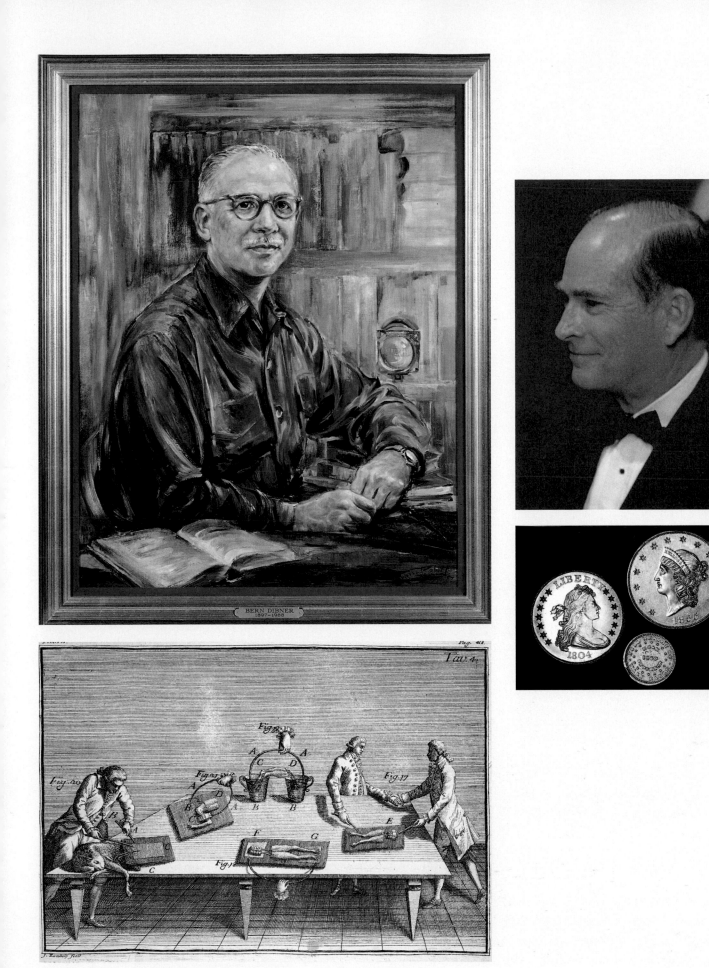

BERN DIBNER
1897-1988

Secretary Charles Walcott, photographed at his desk in 1918, gloried in the field, as did his wife, artist Mary Vaux Walcott, pictured here painting a wildflower during an expedition to the Canadian Rockies around 1921. In 1925 the Smithsonian published 400 of her wildflower illustrations, including this yellow driad.

President Grover Cleveland, but that, too, changed with the advent of a new President, Warren G. Harding. The nation was more interested in recovery, material prosperity, and "practical" science, necessitating strategic battles for public money that would endure for the rest of the century.

The Secretary sadly reported that fiscal year 1926 "marks a crisis in the affairs of the Institution. For several years it has grown more and more difficult to stretch the income from its meager endowment sufficiently to cover the steadily increasing costs of even the limited amount of research...and the administration of the eight growing government bureaus."

The cost of the Institution's publishing, for instance, had more than doubled in a decade, and the number of publications had declined. Walcott spoke so often of "rigid economy" that the phrase became almost as emblematic of the Smithsonian's mandate as "the increase & diffusion of knowledge."

The Secretary's own bound work took up about three feet of bookshelf, and, at the time of his death, represented some 70 percent of published information about the Cambrian and pre-Cambrian. His organizational and administrative talents equaled or surpassed those of any previous Secretary. But he and other members of the old guard, such as Holmes, William Healey Dall, and the geologist George Merrill, were fading, and the Smithsonian seemed to be losing some of its grip on the popular imagination.

Walcott sought to raise funds with the production of an encyclopedic work, written by National Museum staffers, called the *Smithsonian Scientific Series*, and attempted to increase the Institution's endowment by hiring consultants for the Smithsonian's first national fundraising drive. In early 1927, he suffered a stroke, and died. The fundraising drive failed in the face of the stock-market crash and the onset of the Depression.

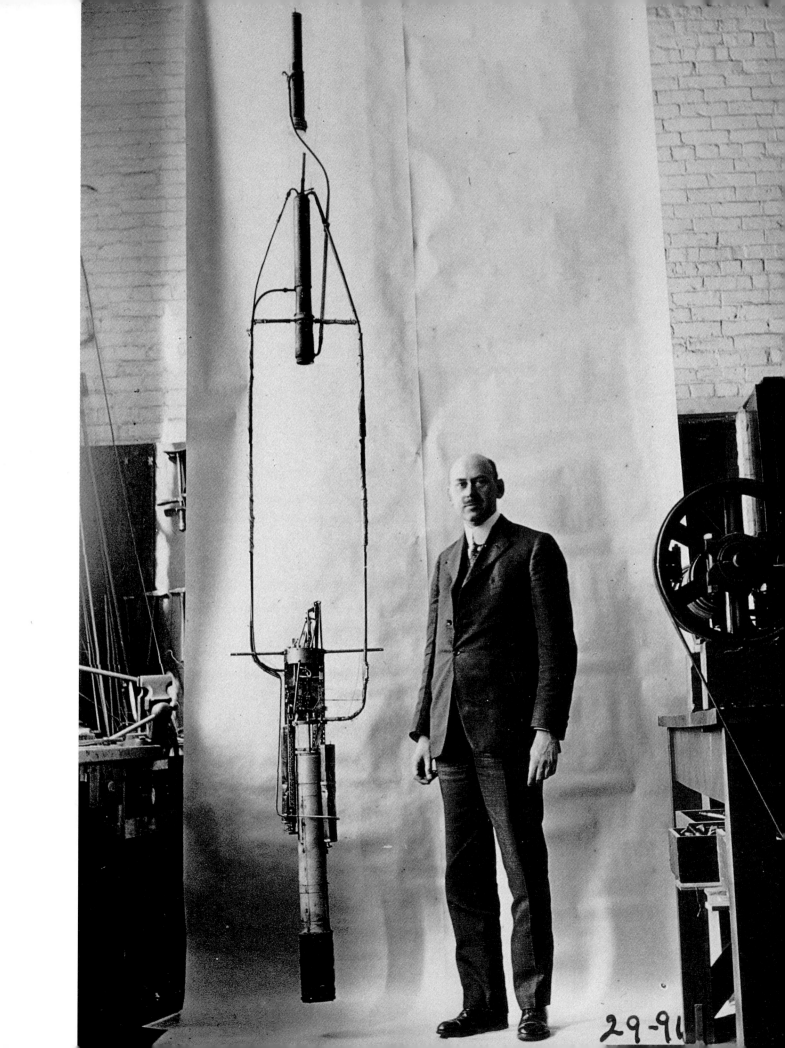

29-91

PROFILE
GOING SOMEWHERE ELSE

Rocket pioneer Robert Goddard appears at left in 1925, the year before he launched the world's first liquid-propellant rocket. Above, Goddard (foreground) and helpers carry rocket components in Roswell, New Mexico. At top, standing in front of the Roswell launch tower on September 23, 1935, are Goddard (center), Harry Guggenheim (to his right), Charles Lindbergh (to his left), and two assistants.

In 1916, a professor of physics at Clark University, in Worcester, Massachusetts, wrote a letter to "the President" of the Smithsonian Institution, requesting the Institution's support for an unusual proposal to build a rocket. "I feel," he wrote, "that it is to the Smithsonian Institution alone that I must look.... I cannot continue the work unassisted."

The author believed his invention would be capable of reaching altitudes much greater than those achieved by balloons and of transporting material—including explosives—over long distances. His name was Robert H. Goddard, and, since the age of 17, as a devoted reader of H.G. Wells, he had dreamed of devising a means of reaching outer space.

At the time Goddard's letter arrived, Secretary Charles Walcott was retrieving fossils in British Columbia, as he did every summer. This was probably fortunate for the inventor, for the letter ended up in the hands of Assistant Secretary Charles Greeley Abbot, who, as director of the Smithsonian's Astrophysical Observatory, was sympathetic toward any effort to extend science's reach into the atmosphere.

Abbot presented the letter to Walcott when he returned, characterizing it as something worthy of pursuing, and the Secretary was intrigued. He requested more detailed information, and Goddard's paper—"A Method of Reaching Extreme Altitudes"—soon arrived in a secure box. The paper outlined the mathematical and engineering work Goddard had already completed, which proved to his own satisfaction that his device could be propelled several hundred miles above the Earth's surface.

Abbot was assigned to read the paper carefully, and found it "the best presentation of a research project" he had seen. Goddard was thus awarded $5,000 to continue his research, an extraordinary show of faith by the Institution for a project with at least the potential for adverse publicity.

Goddard's paper was published in 1919. Meanwhile, a rumor spread through the press that an eccentric Smithsonian scientist, working on his aunt's farm in rural Massachusetts, was trying to get to the moon. Reporters sought him out, and requests to be included in the lunar expedition arrived from all sorts of strangers. (Even the press agent for actress Mary Pickford sent Goddard a telegram stating that America's most popular entertainer would like to send the first message to the moon.)

In truth, Goddard had yet to construct a rocket that could reach even moderate altitudes, much less extreme ones. But Walcott, convinced of Goddard's talent, interceded on his behalf with the Army Signal Corps—and later with the Ordnance Department—to obtain underwriting for his experiments. The military remained interested until the end of World War I, when the perceived need for bomb-carrying rockets, even theoretical ones, sharply diminished.

Goddard insisted on working alone, an independence that was not suited to government agencies. His experiments involved a painstaking, often disastrous sequence of trial and error, much of which was reported by the press and cost him public support. He and the

Smithsonian also felt earned a measure of the public ridicule that had followed the failure of Langley's Aerodrome.

By 1925, Goddard was so demoralized that he hesitated to accept a $500 check from the Institution. On March 16 of the following year, in the snow on his Aunt Effie's farm, he set up his ungainly invention, which was mounted on metal poles resembling a tent frame.

The 10 feet of tubing had neither the fuselage nor the fins later associated with rockets. It was a simple, skeletal dream, an exercise in pure engineering, seemingly less substantial than the overcoated inventor standing next to it and gripping a support as if to hold up the entire contraption. Attached were separate canisters containing liquid oxygen and gasoline.

When the rocket was launched, it attained an altitude of only about 40 feet, but it was still the first liquid-fuel rocket ever to fly, an achievement comparable to that of the Wright brothers.

"It looked almost magical as it rose," wrote Goddard of the liftoff, "without any appreciably greater noise or flame, as if it said: 'I've been here long enough; I think I'll be going somewhere else, if you don't mind.'"

Goddard works on one of his A-series rockets, right, in his Roswell, New Mexico, workshop in October 1935. In 1941 he produced the larger P-series rocket, left. Both rocket types, as well as Goddard's 1926 rocket, are exhibited at the Smithsonian's National Air and Space Museum.

CELESTIAL, TERRESTRIAL

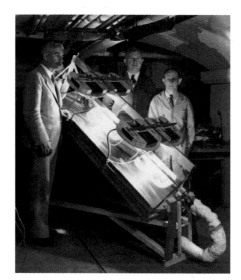

"Wouldn't you like to see my experiment?"
—CHARLES GREELEY ABBOT

Smithsonian Secretary Charles Abbot appears above (left) with the solar heater he devised in the 1920s. Twentieth-century technological breakthroughs fueled science fiction's popularity; here, a magazine from the National Air and Space Museum's collections.

In the spring of 1890, while still a student at Phillips Academy, in Andover, Massachusetts, Charles Greeley Abbot traveled to Boston with a group of classmates who were intending to take the entrance examinations at the Massachusetts Institute of Technology. Abbot was just along for the train ride, but, in the end, because he didn't want to wander around Boston alone, he also took the exams, and passed.

Five years later, wearing acid-shredded overalls in an MIT laboratory, Abbot the graduate student was introduced to an intimidating man in a silk hat named Samuel Pierpont Langley. Langley, the Secretary of the Smithsonian Institution, told the young physicist that he would indeed like to see Abbot's experiment, "but I regret that my engagements will not permit."

The following day, a surprised Abbot received an offer of $1,200 a year for a position as an assistant at the Smithsonian Astrophysical Observatory (SAO), in Washington, D.C. He had not heard of the observatory, but he accepted the job anyway and took another train, this one headed much farther south. He arrived in the capital at the height of summer, only to find Langley abroad in Europe and the temperature in the sheds where he was to work climbing to 120 degrees Fahrenheit.

Twelve years later, in 1907, Abbot was appointed director of the SAO, and, in 1928, upon the death of Charles Doolittle Walcott, he became the fifth Secretary of the Smithsonian Institution. Ironically, a significant part of Secretary Abbot's work would be to resolve controversies

NOW PUBLISHED EVERY MONTH!

25¢

STARTLING STORIES

APR.

THE GLORY THAT WAS
A NOVEL OF OLYMPIAN LAUGHTER
By L. SPRAGUE de CAMP

•

THE LAST DAYS OF SHANDAKOR
A NOVELET OF ANCIENT MARS
By LEIGH BRACKETT

engendered, directly and indirectly, by the man who had hired him 33 years earlier.

LANGLEY'S INCORRECT MEASUREMENT OF THE solar constant, for example, had hung in scientific doubt for years. At the SAO, Abbot had worked on Langley's bolometer and galvanometer, improving the accuracy of both instruments. After Langley's death, he expanded operations at the SAO and successfully corrected the solar constant.

Abbot sought clear skies for his observations, and set out to find them. On Mt. Wilson, in California, he proved that the methods of measurement he had perfected were not affected by the altitude at which the observations were made. Physically vigorous, Abbot also visited sites for observatories on mountains ranging from Harquahala, in Arizona, to Brukkaros, in Southwest Africa; Mt. St. Catherine, in the Sinai; and less satisfactory prospects in Argentina and Chile.

Abbot worked for most of his life measuring and recording the effect of solar radiation on cyclical climatic conditions, as well as its influence, through photosynthesis, on terrestrial biology. In 1929 he established the Division of Radiation and Organisms, which later became the Smithsonian Radiation Biological Laboratory and stayed in operation for nearly 60 years. Abbot's strong belief in the existence of a relationship between fluctuations in solar radiation and climate patterns and his consequent attempts to predict the weather ultimately brought criticism.

On another front, the Secretary tried to improve relations between the Smithsonian and the surviving Wright brother, Orville. From the beginning, Abbot had entertained doubts about Langley's flying machine, and he disagreed with the way the Institution had handled the reconstruction of the 1903 Aerodrome during the Walcott years. He wrote candidly that Langley's "method...

An observer makes adjustments to solar-radiation and heat-measuring instruments at an early Smithsonian Astrophysical Observatory station on Mount Montezuma in Chile. The SAO used such equipment, much of it designed by its own physicist, Charles Abbot, to collect data on the sun for some 50 years.

CHAPTER EIGHT: CELESTIAL, TERRESTRIAL

was to make rough trials at once, to improve the method as experience dictated, and at length reach the final dispositions as the result of correcting this or that detail." In other words, Abbot thought his friend and mentor had avoided thoroughly studying the details before launching tests, which led to repeated failure.

The dispute between the Smithsonian and an embittered Orville Wright had been precipitated by the Institution's dubious claim that the Aerodrome had been the original flying machine. In an ongoing patent fight between the Wrights and Glenn Curtiss, designer of the reconstructed Langley machine, Curtiss sought to escape the suits, which alleged infringement of the patents on the Wrights' flight-control system, by using the Smithsonian's claim as the mainstay of his defense. This so incensed Orville that he refused to offer the original 1903 *Flyer* to the Institution; instead, it was displayed in the Science Museum in London, in 1928.

Abbot tried to placate Orville by meeting with him, and later published a paper under the Smithsonian imprint entitled "The Relations Between the Smithsonian Institution and the Wright Brothers." In the paper, Abbot stated, "All men agree that...Orville and Wilbur Wright, alternately piloting their plane, made the first sustained human flights in a power propelled heavier-than-air machine...."

Abbot further conceded that the Institution "lacked of consideration to put the tests of the Langley plane into the hands of [Wright's] opponent, Mr. Curtiss," and that "the labels on the Langley Aerodrome shall be so modified as to tell nothing but facts." Unfortunately, he also included in the publication the original report on the Aerodrome, and Orville remained adamant.

Meanwhile, Abbot, with the encouragement of Smithsonian aviation specialist Paul E. Garber, had sent a congratulatory cable to a young man named Charles A. Lindbergh, the first flier to cross the Atlantic Ocean alone.

As a result, Lindbergh agreed to donate his single-engine transatlantic plane, the *Spirit of St. Louis*, to the Smithsonian. A beneficial relationship developed between the world's most famous pilot and the world's largest museum.

In the 1942 *Annual Report*, Abbot listed 35 differences between the original Langley Aerodrome and the restored one that was tested in 1914. At the next meeting of the National Advisory Committee for Aeronautics, Wright crossed the room to shake Abbot's hand; within the decade, the *Flyer* would be disassembled in London and sent back across the Atlantic to the Smithsonian. The long feud would be over.

DESPITE THE SMITHSONIAN'S LACK OF FUNDS AND the fading of some of its leading lights, it retained talented scientists throughout the early part of the 20th century. Most of them worked quite autonomously on projects unrelated to the interests of the current Secretary or his predecessors. One of these scientists was Aleš Hrdlička, a Czech who was brought on by William Henry Holmes in 1903 to head the division of physical anthropology.

Hrdlička generated considerable controversy among paleoanthropologists by his claim that no human had trod the North American continent prior to the last Ice Age. As the most influential physical anthropologist of his time, Hrdlička dismissed other scientists' claims that the ancestors of *Homo sapiens* may have come to the continent prior to that time. He assembled a huge collection of human skulls and bones, from which he sought to develop a comprehensive body of knowledge on the racial and cultural diversity of North America. His excursions to Alaska and the Aleutians produced a vast quantity of human remains for the Smithsonian—and eventually led to some thorny legal problems.

Hrdlička trained another anthropologist of great promise, T. Dale Stewart. In the new National Museum,

(Text continued on page 241)

Charles Abbot, above, takes caloric readings from his silver-disk pyrheliometer in 1925. At right, celebrating his 75 years at the Smithsonian, a 98-year-old Abbot displays a section of an 18-foot-long graph of his predictions—based on solar activity—for precipitation in St. Louis, Missouri, over a 104-year period. Remarkably, they have often matched the actual weather pattern the city has experienced.

THE TALES BONES TELL

by DOUGLAS H. UBELAKER

Several years ago, the remains of a missing 17-year-old adolescent from upstate New York were found charred and decomposing in a remote area. Comparison of the teeth with dental records quickly established the victim's identity, but the cause of death remained a mystery. Detective work traced the deceased's last moments to an encounter with a friend, who, under questioning, acknowledged that he was responsible for the death. He claimed that he and the deceased had been drinking, and had started to fight. In the course of events, his friend fell, struck his head on a rock, and died.

The young man claimed the death was accidental, that he had panicked and had attempted to hide the evidence by burning the body. The New York authorities submitted the remains to the Federal Bureau of Investigation—the FBI—for verification of any evidence of the alleged fatal rock blow to the head. The FBI, in turn, brought the remains to the Smithsonian, where I and my colleagues discovered 33 stab wounds to the bones of the chest and neck. The young man was convicted of first-degree manslaughter.

The National Museum of Natural History (NMNH) has a decades-old tradition of assisting the FBI and other law-enforcement agencies with the identification of human remains. Our collections in NMNH's physical-anthropology division contain one of the world's largest assemblages of human remains. Most of the skeletons originate from archaeological excavations, but others represent more recent individuals who came to us from modern forensic cases or from medical-school dissection laboratories.

Through research on our collections and on others outside the Smithsonian, we have developed techniques that allow us to learn a great deal about an individual from his or her bones. Environmental influences such as disturbance by a carnivore or exposure to the sun can be detected. And, using a process called facial reproduction, we can project the facial portrait of a person from the skull so that that person may be recognizable.

Many of the same techniques used to study ancient human remains are used to help identify remains of recently living persons. Submitted materials are examined first to determine if they are of human origin, and then to establish the age at death, sex, likely ancestry, living stature, the amount of time since death, disease history, and a variety of other features that may assist identification.

Careful study may also turn up such evidence of foul play as a cut mark, depressed fracture, or gunshot wound. Such methods enable us to learn more about the health and other biological characteristics of past popu-

lations, as well as to help identify human remains submitted as forensic cases.

My own research with recovered human remains from Ecuador is aimed at learning more about the long-term patterns of disease, and at discovering how health is correlated with both geographical environment and human behavior. Over the years, I have studied hundreds of human skeletons that have been carefully excavated from a variety of sites throughout Ecuador and that represent different time periods as well. By dating the samples, I have documented changes in disease and demographic factors in both time and space. The earliest sample dates back to about 8,000 years ago, when

Ecuadoreans were still mostly hunting and gathering their food.

Samples from more recent time periods allow me to trace the history of these ancient Americans as they developed ceramics and agriculture, became more politically complex, and eventually interacted with Europeans. Analysis reveals that they were healthiest earliest on—8,000 years ago. As they developed agriculture and began living in larger, more permanent settlements, their exposure to infectious disease increased, and other health problems intensified.

The historic period was harsh, but skeletal research indicates it had been preceded by hundreds of years of gradually increasing morbidity that was brought on by changing social conditions. In some areas, it seems that although agriculture may have given the people greater control over their food supply, it may also have resulted in a less varied and thus less nutritious diet.

I recently organized a research project to examine European populations for these same health indicators. Since European populations underwent many of the same long-term cultural changes as their American counterparts, examination of well-dated European samples might reveal the same features. Fortunately, European museums have preserved such collections, making this research possible. Bones do tell tales.

Douglas H. Ubelaker is a Curator in the Department of Anthropology at the National Museum of Natural History.

238

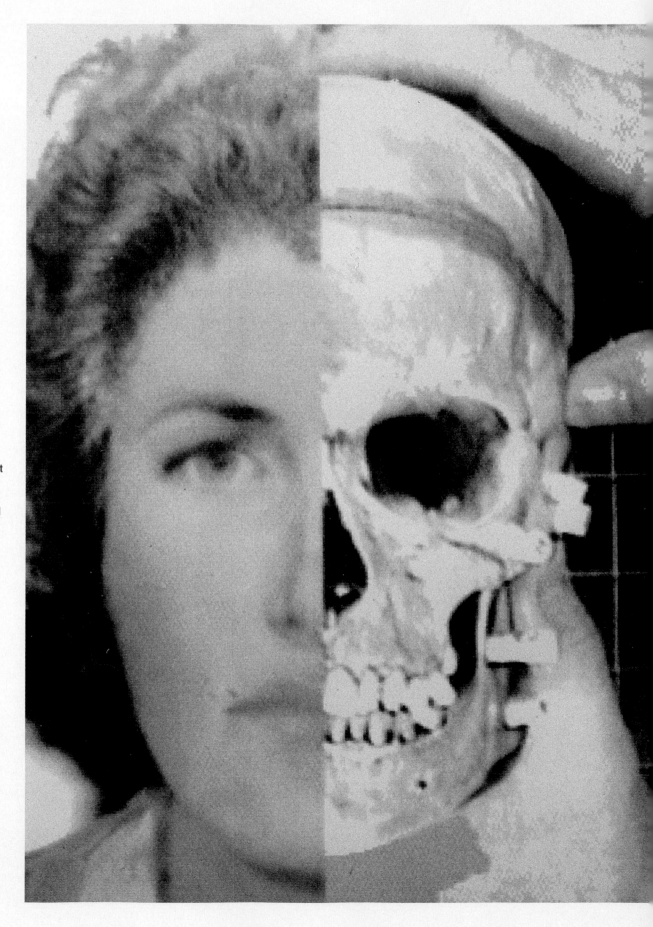

A Federal Bureau of Investigation computer reconstruction of an unknown woman is projected onto her skull, right. Used in this manner, photographs of victims and their previously unidentified skulls will match perfectly. At left, Smithsonian physical anthropologist Douglas Ubelaker takes bone measurements in his lab at the National Museum of Natural History.

Shipping magnate Frederick Leyland acquired James McNeill Whistler's 1864 painting *Rose and Silver: The Princess from the Land of Porcelain*, right, and then hired the artist to help decorate the dining room of his London townhouse. Much to Leyland's dismay, the result was Whistler's celebrated Peacock Room, center. Some years later, after the deaths of both Leyland and Whistler, American railroad baron Charles Freer, far right, bought both painting and room, which today are among the treasures of the Freer Gallery of Art.

which was to become the National Museum of Natural History, Stewart and Hrdlička developed a section of forensic specialty that became an important asset to police and to the Federal Bureau of Investigation (FBI), which often consulted with the Institution in seeking to identify the remains of potential crime victims. Stewart was one of the few people not intimidated by Hrdlička, who ran his division with an iron hand and with what he acknowledged were his own personal quirks and prejudices. He believed, for instance, that researchers should not talk during working hours, and that women should stay at home "vere dey belong."

One notable woman who not only did not stay at home but achieved distinction at the Smithsonian was Mary Jane Rathbun, who had been given a clerkship at Woods Hole by Spencer Baird and had learned zoology, marine biology, and other natural sciences largely through her own observation. The sister of Smithsonian Assistant Secretary and National Museum director Richard Rathbun, Mary Jane came to the Smithsonian in 1886 as a "copyist,"

and, by 1913, occupied an office in the west wing of the Natural History Building as assistant curator in the division of marine invertebrates.

As such, Rathbun had sole responsibility for the division's operation. She oversaw collections, handled divisional reports, and attended to all correspondence—in longhand. Her highly legible specimen labels and catalog entries, written in what has been described as a beautiful Spencerian hand, were well known and instantly recognizable.

In 1914, when it became unavoidably obvious that Mary Jane Rathbun needed help with the division's work, although no money for a new hire existed, she resigned so that her salary could be paid to an assistant. After her resignation, she worked for many years as a dedicated volunteer carcinologist—a zoologist who specializes in crustacea—and published more than 160 papers on a wide variety of scientific subjects.

The assistant hired with her salary was Waldo LaSalle Schmitt, a naturalist with the Bureau of Fisheries

Charles Lindbergh made the first solo, nonstop, transatlantic flight in history on May 20–21, 1927, in the *Spirit of St. Louis*. After the 3,610-mile, 33.5-hour, New York-to-Paris flight, Lindbergh donated his single-engine Ryan NYP to the Smithsonian. The aircraft arrived on the Mall, above left, on May 12, 1928. Lindbergh received the elaborate check, opposite, as prize money, and, literally overnight, became the world's darling, as proclaimed in this song. The medal, left, which features Lindbergh's profile on the obverse and a soaring eagle on the reverse, commemorates his feat.

While Superman leapt tall buildings, all America moved further, faster, and higher. In 1922, above, two federal workers in Washington, D.C., set out cross-country in their Ford Model T. Magazines, advertisements, and visionary art evoke America's love for machines that fly, ride, or rocket into space.

who would become curator of the Smithsonian's division of marine invertebrates. Schmitt accompanied expeditions in the Pacific, and spent summers with the Carnegie Institution's marine laboratory in Tortugas, Florida. Awarded the Smithsonian's Walter Rathbone Bacon Traveling Scholarship in 1925 "for the study of the fauna of countries other than the United States," Schmitt collected marine invertebrates along both coasts of South America. He became such a recognized authority on these animals that Captain Allan Hancock, who conducted expeditions in the Galapagos, said of him, "Well, if that fellow knows so much, we'd better take him along." Schmitt continued to study crustacea into his nineties.

Meanwhile, other departmental adjustments were made to acquire talent and accommodate certain eccentricities. For instance, the division of echinoderms had been created to provide a position for talented echinoderm specialist Austin H. Clark, who wrote voluminously while maintaining the most cluttered office in the museum building. According to Ellis Yochelson, Clark once discovered a typewriter that had been hidden for a decade under a pile of papers.

Throughout this period, the Smithsonian continued its tradition of association with far-flung collectors who provided the Institution with a steady stream of natural-history specimens and artifacts. In the summer of 1919, for example, missionary David Crockett Graham began collecting in Szechuan, China, with Smithsonian support, and made 14 additional expeditions during the next 20 years. Graham kept a detailed journal of his travels in such remote parts of China as Tatsienlu (Kangding), Chuan Hsien, and Tibet. He trained and employed native peoples to collect for him, and was eventually made an honorary "collaborator" in biology by the Smithsonian's National Museum.

In 1925 ornithologist Alexander Wetmore was appointed Assistant Secretary in charge of the National

Museum, the National Gallery of Art, and the National Zoo. A colleague described Wetmore as a "tall man of quietly distinguished presence and great natural modesty." Although jackets were not required apparel for men after World War I, employees tended to put them on before entering Wetmore's office.

UP THROUGH THE DEPRESSION, THE SMITHSONIAN remained an essentially male domain. According to Herbert Friedmann, who succeeded Robert Ridgway as curator of birds, men at the Institution felt that women "interrupted their bull sessions." Men still expected to find a fresh cuspidor beside their desks in the mornings. "We never needed a clock to tell us when it was 4:30," Friedmann later recalled. "I could hear [C.V.] Riley pounding his pipe on his cuspidor." Riley was the aging honorary curator in the Department of Biology, a founder of the division of entomology, and a sometimes obstreperous colleague.

A male curator in the division of mollusks was known for naming newfound species after women he had known, and for occasionally pursuing female employees. And there were other lapses in the pursuit of pure science. An emotionally unstable aide in the geology department threw a rock that struck a curator of minerals on the head. Depending on the source, Mary Jane Rathbun either threw a glass of water into the face of an hysterical technician faced with dismissal or stood on a chair and poured a pitcher of water over the technician's head.

When the head curator of anthropology, Walter Hough, died in 1935, none of the three curators in the division—the irascible anthropologist Hrdlička, archaeologist Neil Judd, and ethnologist Herbert Kreiger—was on speaking terms with another. Most scientists, however, were far more interested in their own research and writing than in the Institution's administrative problems or in who occupied its musical chairs.

Exhibits in the museum reflected this ordered,

staid view of science as a monument to dedication and single-minded pursuits without evidence of petty personal clashes. This aura was best represented by the 70-foot skeleton of *Diplodocus longus*, an intimidating fossil from Dinosaur National Monument on the Colorado-Utah border that was mounted to allow an ever-increasing number of awestruck visitors to pass beneath it.

BY THE STANDARDS SET BY THE SMITHSONIAN Secretaries who preceded him, Abbot was considered relatively easygoing, willing to take the time to tell an occasional anecdote or sing a sea chantey. As a dedicated scientist, he wrote *The Sun*, which correctly advanced the theory that the sun's photosphere was gaseous and not composed of liquid particles. Eleven years of solar-radiation study at various high-altitude-desert observatories

(Text continued on page 255)

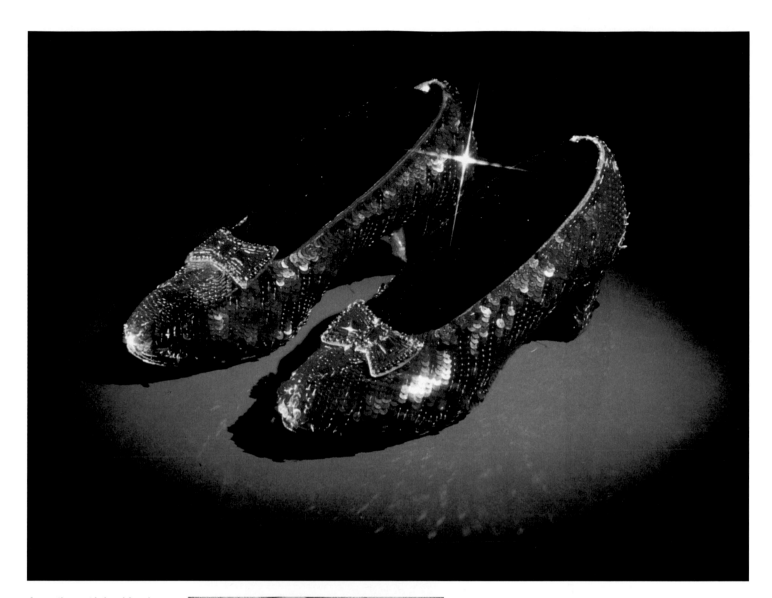

Among the most beloved American icons to be found at the National Museum of American History: the original Teddy bear, named for President Theodore Roosevelt; Dorothy's ruby slippers from the "Wizard of Oz"; music and lyrics from the movie "Bright Eyes," recalling gumdrops on Peppermint Bay; and a now world-famous mouse, who appeared for the first time in Walt Disney's 1928 "Steam Boat Willie," the earliest animated cartoon with a synchronized soundtrack.

ON—AND NOW OFF—THE ROAD
BY ROGER B. WHITE

Smithsonian curators have enjoyed an intimacy with automotive experimenters, manufacturers, and collectors for almost a century. This relationship began in 1899 when Stephen Balzer, a machinist and inventor who had been hired by Secretary Samuel P. Langley to build an engine for Langley's flying machine, donated his 1894 vehicle to the Institution. Made of bicycle parts and powered by an air-cooled, rotary engine, Balzer's prototype was one of the first automobiles in New York City. At the suggestion of J. Elfreth Watkins, at the time the Smithsonian's curator of mechanical technology, it was placed on display in the National Museum on January 12, 1899.

Since then, the Smithsonian has collected 60 additional automobiles that illustrate many facets of motoring history, including the aesthetic and mechanical changes of the 1900s to the 1920s, the growth and diversity of the consumer car market, and the history of auto racing and its famous drivers.

Today, approximately 15 automobiles from the collection are displayed in the Road Transportation Hall of the National Museum of American History. Some are on loan to other museums, and the rest are in storage. Meanwhile, the Smithsonian continues its close collaboration with donors to acquire vehicles that reflect important advances, trends, or events during more than 100 years of American automotive history.

Roger B. White is a Specialist responsible for automotive history and collections at the National Museum of American History.

Since the late-19th century, automobiles have taken America by storm (left). As seen in the rare inverted stamp at right, the earliest cars resembled carriages. The 1911 Sears Model P, below (right), was popular for its high ground-clearance and low price—under $500. Montgomery Ward later advertised its own vehicle, below right. Below (left), the 1903 Winton touring car that H. Nelson Jackson and Sewall Crocker drove across the country in a record 63 days.

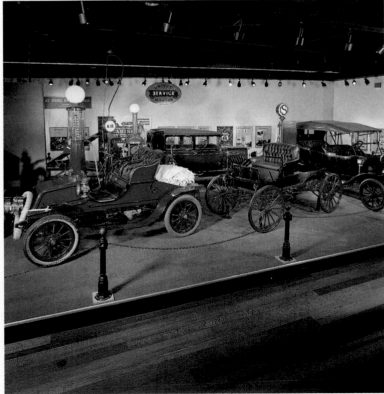

With its sleek lines, adjustable cen-
ter headlight, and front-seat pas-
senger crash cellar, the 1948
Tucker, right, one of only 51 of
these cars produced, came to the
Smithsonian from the U.S. Marshals
Service. Alexander Winton's 1903
Bullet No. 2, below, entered that

year's Gordon Bennett Race in
Ireland, but had to drop out after
breaking down. A year later, Barney
Oldfield reached a speed of nearly
84 miles per hour in this car on
Florida's Daytona Beach.

In 1990 the Smithsonian acquired "Dave's Dream," right, a 1969 Ford LTD lowrider originally owned by David Jaramillo, of Chimayó, New Mexico. Decorated with colorful folk art and lined with plush fabrics, it has a chassis capable of "hopping" more than a foot by means of battery-operated hydraulic pumps. This 1939 school bus was donated—fully restored in "double-deep orange"—in 1982 by Carpenter Body Works, of Indiana. One of the first all-steel school buses made in the United States, it was used to transport students in Martinsburg, Indiana, during the 1940s. It then became a traveling grocery store until 1962.

One of America's foremost architectural renderers, Hugh Ferriss completed the 1922 drawing, right, to illustrate possible design solutions to a 1916 New York zoning law. Today the drawing is in the collections of the Cooper-Hewitt National Design Museum. As official design consultant for the 1939 New York World's Fair, Ferriss helped create its futuristic buildings, including the triangular Trylon and the spherical Perisphere, which adorn this commemorative plate in the National Museum of American History.

went into his *Annals of the Astrophysical Observatory*. He also wrote a book about science for young people and an autobiography.

The Smithsonian continued to suffer financially under Abbot, however. In 1934, during the administration of Franklin D. Roosevelt, the Institution applied for relief under the Federal Emergency Relief Administration, and was assigned 77 temporary workers. That project ended a year later, but under another program, this one sponsored by the Works Project Administration, in 1936 the number of temporary workers grew to 88, and then to 167. The workers assisted in improving some collections, but disturbed others. As many curators discovered, their practical utility was limited. (For his part, T. Dale Stewart complained that a temporary worker could put a number on a bone when told to, but then didn't know what to do with the bone.)

In 1937 Abbot presided over the creation of the National Collection of Fine Arts. The establishment of this new bureau took place only after the National Gallery of Art had been underwritten by a gift of $15 million from industrialist Andrew W. Mellon and thus had become a mostly autonomous entity. From then on, the National Gallery, with Mellon's magnificent collection of mainly Renaissance art, would officially be a bureau of the Smithsonian, but would have its own building on the Mall, paid for by Mellon's gift, and its own endowment and board of trustees. In years to come, this arrangement would lead to the National Gallery's complete separation from the Smithsonian.

The National Collection of Fine Arts (NCFA), on the other hand, remained an integral part of the Smithsonian, the culmination of almost a century of the random assemblage of art and of conflicting opinions about the ways in which it should be administered and exhibited. The NCFA was to control the various, polyglot collections that had been brought together by five different Secretaries.

The signal acquisition during Abbot's reign was the $4.5 million purchase of John Gellatly's art collection in 1929. According to the Smithsonian's interpretation of Congress's mandate, the NCFA's mission was to encourage American art and crafts, promote art appreciation among Americans, mount traveling exhibits, provide a repository for government-sponsored art, lend works to various government agencies, and represent the government in art-related matters. Yet it would be another three decades before the NCFA would have its own gallery—the Old Patent Office Building that long ago had contained the dusty, disheveled artifacts of the Wilkes expedition.

AT ABOUT THE SAME TIME AS THE OPENING OF THE NCFA, the Smithsonian was entering into yet another collaborative expedition of scientists and wealthy amateurs. For at least a century, such expeditions to various parts of the world had served the Smithsonian well. Now, in 1937, a ship set sail from the United States—this time for southern climes—with scientists set to mingle onboard with a group that included among its unlikely participants a popular novelist and a Philadelphia socialite.

Probably no Smithsonian venture had had less claim to pure science than this one, the West Indian excursion of Huntington Hartford. Hartford's primary objective was apparently to show off the *Joseph Conrad*, the fully rigged Danish naval training vessel he had purchased from noted sailor and writer Alan Villiers. Dinner jackets proved as important as microscopes, and fine food replaced the rudimentary fare that had served the likes of Kennicott, Dall, and John Wesley Powell.

One of the scientists onboard was Waldo Schmitt, the Smithsonian's preeminent invertebrate zoologist and a veteran of Galapagos Islands expeditions. Another scientist of note whom Hartford entertained was Robert Lunz, senior entomologist at the museum in Charleston, South Carolina. Both men had intended to collect zoological

One of the first color photographs of an American President, this portrait of Democrat Franklin Delano Roosevelt was taken after he defeated incumbent Herbert Hoover in 1933 to become the 32nd President of the United States. Published that same year, this sheet-music cover today is part of the National Museum of American History's political-history collection.

In this painting from the National Air and Space Museum's collections, artist R.G. Smith captures the turning point in the Battle of Midway, June 3–6, 1942, as U.S. Navy Douglas Dauntless dive-bombers pass the mortally stricken Japanese aircraft carrier *Akagi*. Affectionately nicknamed "the barge" by pilots for its steady flying qualities, the carrier-based bomber destroyed four enemy aircraft carriers during the battle, changing the course of World War II in the Pacific. Below, a World War II poster promotes patriotism.

IT CAN HAPPEN HERE!

-UNLESS WE KEEP 'EM FIRING!

R.G.Smith

specimens, and collect they did, although, according to Schmitt's diary, they spent more time sightseeing and attending cocktail receptions and dinners hosted by governors, consuls, and senior military officers in the Caribbean than they did collecting.

The ship's other passengers included John Jacob Astor's sister-in-law; DuBose Heyward, author of *Porgy*, the novel upon which George Gershwin based *Porgy and Bess*; and A. Atwater Kent, heir to a radio fortune. All were included presumably for their social connections or

their fame. In the end, the ship visited 15 islands, and Schmitt sent back 17 barrels of specimens to the Smithsonian (Lunz assembled a similar collection) that featured mostly crustacea and invertebrates but included various fishes and two porpoises.

The Smithsonian paid only Schmitt's salary, so the expedition was judged a success financially and scientifically, and, at least for Schmitt himself, gastronomically. An additional advantage of the voyage was Schmitt's introduction to DuPont heir J. Bruce Bredin at a recep-

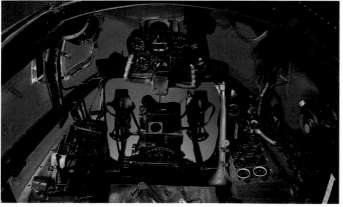

tion. Bredin conducted expeditions of his own, and in the future Schmitt would go along on some of them, both for his own edification and for the benefit of the Smithsonian's ever-growing store of specimens and artifacts.

SOON, HOWEVER, THERE WERE FAR MORE PRESSING concerns in the country—and at the Smithsonian. With the bombing of the American fleet in Pearl Harbor, Hawaii, on December 7, 1941, and the country's entry

(Text continued on page 264)

PRESERVING AVIATION'S HISTORY
by TOM HUNTINGTON

The National Air and Space Museum's Paul E. Garber Restoration, Preservation, and Storage facility, located a distance from the Mall in Suitland, Maryland, is an aviation enthusiast's heaven. A wanderer in this aeronautical realm might encounter anything from a Piper Cub to a sturdy Stearman trainer to the jet engine that would have powered the planned American supersonic transport. And, on a sunny autumn day in 1986, a meticulously restored SPAD XIII sat outside while, a hundred yards away, a German Focke-Wulf 190 poked its pinwheel nose out between half-open hangar doors.

displaced aircraft. Garber persuaded the Smithsonian to acquire Silver Hill, a parcel of unused land in suburban Maryland, and arranged to move the aviation collection there. In 1980 the Silver Hill facility was named in honor of the man who had made it possible.

For years, the collection's storage conditions were, at best, horrendous. A small staff with limited funds was unable to stem the effects of time and the elements on the aircraft. Finally, in conjunction with the planned construction of the National Air and Space Museum, funds became

A sampling of aircraft, far right, from the National Air and Space Museum's Paul Garber facility in Suitland, Maryland, includes everything from hang gliders to rocket-propelled interceptors, as well as Germany's best all-around WWII aircraft, the Focke-Wulf 190 F-8, and, at right, the newly restored Arado Ar 234 B-2 Blitz, the only extant example of the world's first operational jet bomber.

Hidden away in the Garber facility's 28 corrugated-metal buildings are nearly half of the Smithsonian's 300 aircraft, in addition to models, engines, and space artifacts, a collection that spans the history of human involvement with flight. Garber may be outside the limelight on the Mall, but it is not ignored. Each year as many as 12,000 visitors take the time for a by-appointment-only tour.

Until the outbreak of the Korean War, the Smithsonian's collection of aircraft had been housed in an unused airplane factory outside Chicago, now the site of O'Hare International Airport. When hostilities commenced, the U.S. Air Force reopened the factory, and gave the flying machines an eviction notice. At that time, Paul E. Garber was curator of the National Air Museum, and he became determined to find a home for the

available to revamp and clean up Silver Hill, and the aircraft were placed in new buildings to await eventual restoration.

Building 10 is headquarters for the restoration staff. Of the works in progress, the best known is the Enola Gay, the Boeing B-29 that dropped the atomic bomb "Little Boy" on Hiroshima, Japan, on August 6, 1945. Putting the airplane back together is itself an enormous task, but the restoration crew has to do much more than that. Each part must first be treated and chemically protected. Historical accuracy, not airworthiness, is the purpose of the restoration process. Slowly and painstakingly, the Garber craftspeople continue to salvage history from the ravages of time.

Tom Huntington is Managing Editor at Air & Space/Smithsonian *magazine.*

into World War II, the Smithsonian found itself in a unique position. Its collective, highly specialized knowledge of the Pacific made it a great asset to the Allies. And, as in the past, the Institution was able to expand its knowledge, as well as its store of specimens, by assigning scientists to various military expeditions.

Abbot convened the special Smithsonian War Committee he had created, and approximately 10 percent of the Institution's staff found itself assigned to the war. Scientific cooperation was kept under wraps both during and after the war, however. One rumor had it that a Smithsonian study of the migration routes of Pacific snapping shrimp allowed American submarines to travel the same routes and avoid detection by Japanese sonar. Julia Gardner of the USGS was credited with determining the place of origin of a recovered Japanese fire balloon by studying microfossils in its sandy ballast. And aviation specialist Paul Garber designed kite targets for the Navy's antiaircraft gunners.

Precautions also were taken to protect irreplaceable specimens at home, in the event that the war should threaten the Mall. "The work of selecting and packing this material has occupied the staff for months," stated the *Annual Report* of 1942. "Type specimens preserved in alcohol, which offer some difficulties in handling, were evacuated together with selections of insects."

Type specimens are those used for reference in identifying other organisms. The Institution transported these and other objects considered of prime importance— a collection that weighed some 60 tons—to an undisclosed location in the Blue Ridge Mountains near Luray, Virginia, where they remained hidden for three years.

The National Museum's one great auk—a large sea bird of the North Atlantic that had been extinct since 1844—was taken off exhibit and wrapped in paper, where it was attacked by moths. (The feathers later were painstakingly glued back on.) Curators moved the heavy

geological and paleontological collections from the museum's upper stories to the lower ones, and concern over works in the National Collection of Fine Arts led to the strengthening of the wall behind the mural *Diana of the Tides*.

Air-raid and blackout drills were conducted, and boxes of sand—to be used in case of fire—were placed in attics throughout the Institution. Many of these boxes would remain for decades, reminders of an uneasy time. Scientists went off to serve in the military, to assist various government agencies, and to teach. Some never returned.

The government repeatedly called upon the Smithsonian to provide information and services even as arcane as supplying mites and ticks to the military so that their effects on human health could be studied. For the first time, public attendance at the Institution declined, although it increased again at the end of the war.

THROUGHOUT HIS TENURE, ABBOT SOUGHT TO convince Orville Wright that the Smithsonian was the proper place for Wright's Kitty Hawk *Flyer*. He arranged for Charles Lindbergh to meet with Wright on behalf of the Smithsonian, and, on a steamboat voyage to the newly created Langley Field, in Hampton, Virginia, he himself beseeched Wright to donate his plane to the Institution.

On June 30, 1944, after 16 years as Secretary, Abbot became the first Smithsonian head to resign (all the previous Secretaries having died on the job), and was given an office in the Castle to continue his solar research. During his administration, Abbot had essentially continued his predecessors' expansion of the Smithsonian's role in the affairs of the nation, and had struggled to maintain the Astrophysical Observatory. He had helped the arts prosper, while increased emphasis had been placed on engineering and industry.

Overall attendance at the museums and galleries had grown dramatically during Abbot's tenure. For the

The cockpit of the Boeing B-29 Superfortress *Enola Gay*, which dropped the first atomic bomb over Hiroshima, Japan, on August 6, 1945. Bombadier Thomas Ferebee used the Norden bombsight (center), a mechanical analog computer, to help him determine the exact moment the bomb needed to be released to hit its target.

first time, the annual reports featured these statistics without reference to the quality of interest shown by the public, or to the educational merits of the exhibits. Without formal recognition, entertainment—pure anathema to Joseph Henry—had crept into the Smithsonian's equation.

ABBOT'S REPLACEMENT AS SECRETARY WAS FRANK Alexander Wetmore (whose first name was never used), the Smithsonian's modest Assistant Secretary in charge of the National Museum. Wetmore had served with the Biological Survey, participating in field investigations throughout the United States as well as in Canada, Puerto Rico, Mexico, South America, and the islands of the mid-Pacific. An ornithologist with interests similar to those of the late Spencer Baird, Wetmore was a voluminous contributor to biological journals and an author of several books, and he became an expert on the birds of Central and South America.

A contemporary of Wetmore's who wrote for *Audubon* magazine described the Secretary's "tall, wiry frame…his smooth white hair, close-cropped, his hazel eyes steady behind plain rimless glasses…. His deep, drawling voice and earnest manner command respect…. Although he likes the company of…scientists, he is

A National Museum of American History manikin models the uniform worn by the first American G.I.s in World War II. Because the U.S. Army was woefully short of equipment when the nation entered the war, it issued new recruits World War I-era gear, including this M1917 steel helmet and M1918 cartridge belt. The melton wool overcoat, first distributed around 1940, was their only new piece of equipment.

happiest when he is with birds." Indeed, Wetmore thrived in the field rather than in the office. Yet the irony remains that at various times during his career he held a multitude of posts, including director of the National Zoo, secretary-general of the Eighth American Scientific Congress, chairman of the Interdepartmental Committee on Research and Development, director of the Canal Zone Biological Area, director of the Gorgas Memorial Institute of Tropical and Preventive Medicine, and trustee of the National Geographic Society; and president of the American Ornithologists' Union, the Washington Biologists' Field Club, the Explorers' Club, the Cosmos Club, the Baird Ornithological Club, and the 10th International Ornithological Congress.

In 1946, the Institution's centennial year, the Smithsonian held a modest celebration that included a commemorative stamp issued by the Postal Service, a special exhibition in the foyer of the National Museum, and a reception there for some 1,000 guests that featured the Marine Band Orchestra on the second floor, overlooking the rotunda. Even Wetmore danced, a surprise to just about everyone. But there was no time during the centennial year to compile a written record of the Smithsonian's accomplishments over the century, and, despite the fact that they were badly needed, there was no special effort to attract public support and private funds.

The same year, Wetmore presided over the transfer to the Smithsonian of the Canal Zone Biological Area, an island in the Panama Canal that had provided scientists with prime research opportunities for years. A consortium of scientific organizations under the auspices of the National Research Council had operated there since 1923, when the Barro Colorado Island "natural park" was established. The biological area, or CZBA, was set up by Congress in 1940, with $10,000 appropriated annually for the maintenance of a laboratory and other buildings

(Text continued on page 268)

STAR STUFF FOR KIDS OF ALL AGES

by PEGGY LANGRALL

"I believe that even the most sophisticated theory can be explained to a fifth grader. If one tries and it doesn't work, I claim the storyteller hasn't been clever enough. You've got to build a bridge for the children from places that are familiar to the places where you want to take them."

The speaker, National Air and Space Museum (NASM) astrophysicist Jeff Goldstein, was explaining his philosophy of science education. It was this philosophy that got him involved in a pilot outreach program known as Learning is a Family Experience, which began in the spring of 1992 under the auspices of NASM's Laboratory for Astrophysics and its Education Division and the National Zoo's New Opportunities in Animal Health Sciences. In its one-year existence, the program reached 5,400 students, teachers, and parents from 47 Washington-area schools.

A self-described "interplanetary-weather guy," Goldstein builds instruments for NASM's Laboratory for Astrophysics, specializing in devising laser systems for use with spectrometers, which measure wind velocities in planetary atmospheres. He and his fellow astrophysicists travel to such observatories as the one atop Mauna Kea, on the Big Island of Hawaii, where they connect their equipment to the National Aeronautics and Space Administration's (NASA's) Infrared Telescope. "Considering that Venus, for example, can be some 200 million miles away and flying toward or away from us at six miles a second—fast enough to cross the entire United States in seven minutes—measuring two-to-four-miles-per-hour winds there is a pretty amazing feat!"

Advances in the study of the geology and atmospheres of other worlds in the solar system have spurred the creation of the new field of comparative planetology. No longer is Earth the sole laboratory of weather. Our planet's climate can now be compared to that of planets with faster rotation rates, greater mass, and different composition.

The Laboratory for Astrophysics plays a unique role at NASM. According to its chair, Howard A. Smith, "The department works to demystify science, empower the public, and encourage it to think about the *scientific value* of the impressive space artifacts on display. Our younger visitors, who may be considering a career in space science or a related field, especially need to understand that our universe is comprehensible. Science can be made accessible, technology is not magic, and understanding enhances our appreciation." It's increase and diffusion of knowledge pure and simple.

Meanwhile, holding a basketball in one hand, Goldstein tells audiences that if the sun were as big as the ball, the Earth would be the size of a pinhead—and 100 feet away…. He has given more than 200 such talks so far, both at NASM and around the country, to people of all ages and interests, and has taken thousands of Americans—parents, students, and teachers—on an imaginary journey to the stars.

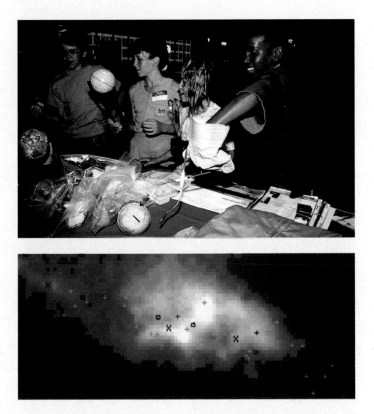

An outflow jet from a newly forming star is revealed here by an imaging system developed in part by the National Air and Space Museum.

Top, children participate in a NASM outreach program, Learning Is a Family Experience.

"The great thing about it for me is that they're here because they want to be, and I feel that maybe I can change—a little—the way they view the world. There is a reverence associated with the Smithsonian, the national museum. With some of the most important artifacts and icons of the human race within its holdings, it can launch the dreams of the next generation. It is our charge to make this happen."

Peggy Langrall is a Writer in the Smithsonian's Office of Public Affairs.

and administration by a board headed by Thomas Barbour, of Harvard's Museum of Comparative Zoology. Now Barro Colorado (today part of the Smithsonian Tropical Research Institute, or STRI) was entirely the responsibility of the Smithsonian, affording unique opportunities for research in a pristine tropical environment but facing limited means.

Also in 1946, President Harry Truman approved an act of Congress establishing the National Air Museum as a bureau of the Smithsonian. Aspiring to that grand title was the Institution's old hangar, where wartime tests, such as those on the World War I Liberty engine, had been conducted. The earliest meetings of the National Advisory Committee for Aeronautics, the distinguished predecessor of the National Aeronautics and Space administration, had been held elsewhere in the Smithsonian as far back as 1916.

The act stated that the new museum "shall memorialize the national development of aviation; collect, preserve, and display aeronautical equipment of historical interest"; and generally educate the public about aviation. Most of the Smithsonian's 3,500 aeronautical items were in storage, however, and there was no money for a new building.

TO ASSIST HIM WITH ADMINISTRATIVE DUTIES AND budgetary matters when he became Secretary, Wetmore brought John Keddy from the Bureau of the Budget to the Castle. Without a doubt, the responsibilities of the Secretary of the Smithsonian had proliferated, far outpacing the funds available to support them. So, too, had the activities undertaken in the cramped, often oven-like offices throughout the Institution, whose every department remained understaffed. "Rigid economy," the Institution's mantra in 1926, during Walcott's administration, had persisted through Abbot's, and now, in the aftermath of World War II, continued to hold sway over Smithsonian affairs.

With the dawn of the atomic age after World War II, Luis Alvarez of the Berkeley Radiation Laboratory began building the initial section, right, of a thousand-foot linear accelerator, the world's first. Above, this Albert Einstein medal, part of the numismatics collection at the National Museum of American History, was given in 1960 to Leo Szilard, a nuclear physicist who had helped establish the Manhattan Project to develop the atomic bomb.

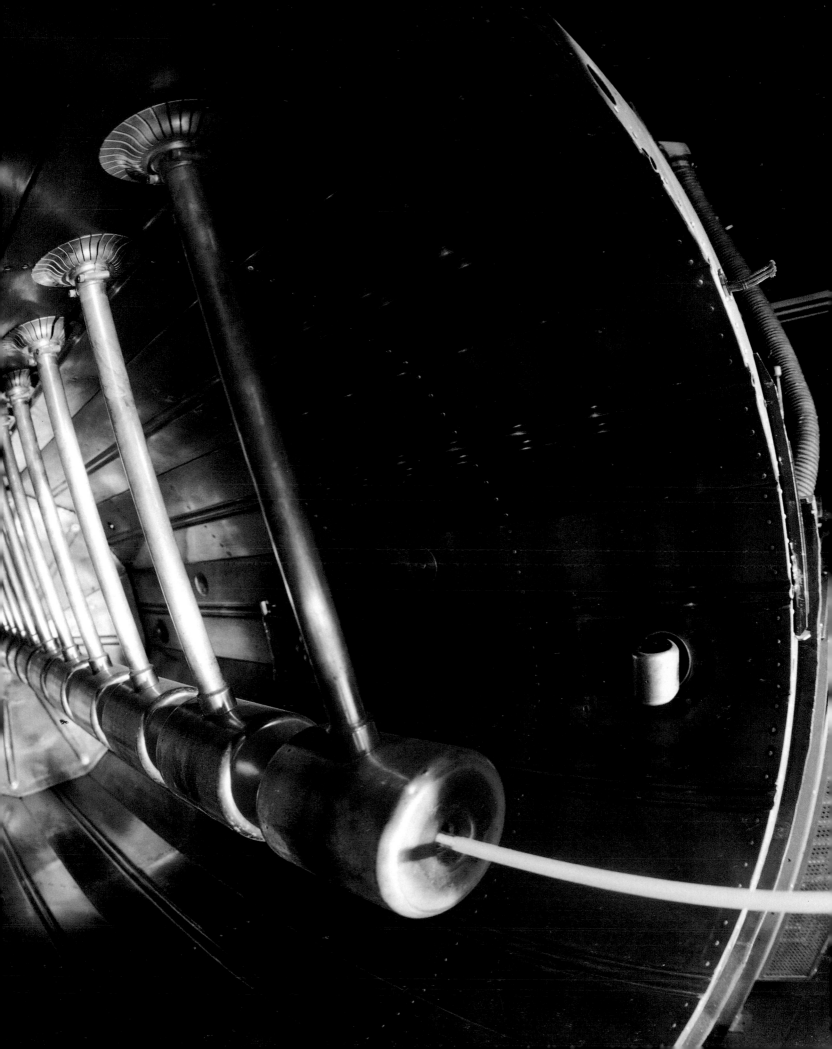

OVER THE VOLCANO

Perhaps the most spectacular expeditions involving a Smithsonian scientist were those undertaken in the 1940s by the Institution's own William Frederick Foshag to track the growth of a Mexican volcano. A member of the Smithsonian's geology department since 1919, Foshag contributed substantially to research in minerals and gems, but it was his procurement of mineral collections for scientific purposes that had the most significant and lasting impact on the Institution. Through Foshag's and fellow geology curator Earl V. Shannon's friendship with the owner of the Roebling mineral collection and their arrangement for the acquisition of the Canfield collection, in 1926 the Smithsonian received both, a trove that amounted to some 25,000 mineral specimens in addition to endowments of $200,000 for further acquisitions.

That same year, 1926, Foshag began to pursue what became a lifelong interest in Mexico's mineral deposits and, in particular, its metallic ores. Then, in 1943, he slipped almost inadvertently into volcanology when a volcano appeared in a cornfield near the Mexican town of Parícutin, in the fault-riven state of Michoacán. On-site almost from the volcano's inception, Foshag charted the inexorable rise of the volcanic cone while lava flows disrupted the countryside, and ash buried nearby towns like New World Pompeiis.

Realizing the unique opportunity El Parícutin offered to observe firsthand the step-by-step growth of a volcano, Foshag worked—often at considerable risk—with scientists from Mexico's Instituto de Geologia to compile a factual account of its development. Foshag and his colleagues visited the site often, measuring and evaluating escaping gases and attempting to collect gas samples even from a field of pieces of ejected fluid lava that formed fearful miniature cones, or "hornitos," over the already cooled and hardened lava. The atmosphere in the "hornitos" area was laden with hydrochloric acid fumes and punctuated with flying globs of molten rock. At times the heat in the vents was so intense that the glass vacuum tubes Foshag and his fellow scientists inserted to collect gas samples melted before they could extract them.

Paul O. McGrew, a scientist from the Chicago Natural History Museum, visited Foshag and his colleagues at El Parícutin in June and July of 1943, writing afterward that, during one particularly violent period of eruptions, he was "very frankly more interested in choosing a clear path of escape through the rough lava field than anything else…. [M]y companions appeared, like seasoned infantrymen, to take this barrage in their stride. Bombs would hit the ground with a dull 'plop' and bury themselves in the hard ash…. Tremendous quantities of ash and cinders were falling. The rain consisted chiefly of tiny black particles…."

Determined that the different stages of El Parícutin's growth be preserved as fully on film as on paper, Foshag at one point enlisted the U.S. Army to fly a helicopter near the volcano's rim so that scientists onboard could take color movies of its eruptions.

By the time El Parícutin finally subsided in 1952, Foshag had gathered enough material for the publication of many scientific papers, the most insightful of which detailed the volcano's gaseous and aqueous emanations; and for his and Mexican colleague Jenaro González-Reynas' seminal monograph, *Birth and Development of Parícutin Volcano*. And, in addition to a wealth of data and specimens, the Smithsonian had acquired some of the most dramatic photography ever taken of an awesome natural disaster. In 1993 a book published in association with the Smithsonian Institution celebrated the 50th anniversary of the volcano's birth.

Above, three visitors to Mexico's Parícutin volcano in August 1944 maneuver carefully around its crater. Lava flows from Parícutin's violent eruptions, right, first reached the village of San Juan Parangaricutiro, far right, in June 1944; in time, they covered the entire town.

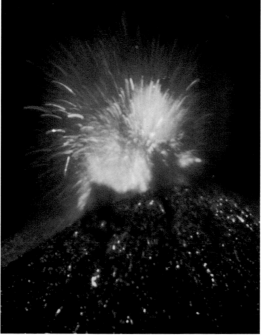

III THE LIVING MUSEUM: 1950–1996

In August 1950, a blunt, orange aircraft resembling a winged bomb dominated the National Air Show at Boston's Logan Airport. Among those on hand for the occasion were Alexander Wetmore, the Secretary of the Smithsonian Institution, and General Hoyt Vandenberg, the U.S. Air Force Chief of Staff. The craft, officially known as the Bell X-1, was nicknamed *Glamorous Glennis* for the wife of

The visor of an astronaut's helmet reflects the National Air and Space Museum's Milestones of Flight hall, home of such aeronautical treasures as the Wright *Flyer*, the *Spirit of St. Louis*, and (visible in the helmet's reflection) the Bell X-1 *Glamorous Glennis*—the first plane to break the sound barrier—and the Apollo 11 command module.

Air Force Captain Charles E. "Chuck" Yeager. On October 14, 1947, at 43,000 feet above sea level, Captain Yeager had flown the Bell X-1 700 miles per hour to become the first person to exceed the speed of sound. Now the X-1 would be coming to the Smithsonian.

Less than two years before this air show, on December 17, 1948, Wetmore had attended another ceremony for the acquisition of an even more famous aircraft: the Wright *Flyer*. After a long separation, the world's first successful airplane had been shipped back from England and placed on exhibit in the Smithsonian's Arts and Industries Building. Now Wetmore was to officially receive the utterly contemporary but equally experimental Bell X-1. The Institution would house these two very different symbols of aeronautical daring and achievement with some 100 other "heavier-than-air" craft, including the rubber-band-driven model plane designed by Alphonse Pénaud; the *Vin Fiz*, the first plane to cross the North American continent; and the globe-girdling Douglas World Cruiser; as well as various engines, instruments, scale models, and associated aeronautical objects.

The Bell X-1 was airlifted to Andrews Air Force Base, strapped to a 40-foot flatbed trailer, and driven into Washington in the middle of the night by way of the South Capitol Street Bridge. A wall had been removed from the National Air Museum, a recent addition to the Smithsonian, to provide access for the new arrival, and a crane lifted it onto a pedestal that had been supplied by the Bell Aircraft Corporation. On October 11, 1950, Carl Mitman, Assistant to the Secretary for the National Air Museum and a long-time student of technology, wrote to General Vandenberg, proudly acknowledging receipt of the "supersonic rocket airplane."

The Air Museum's curator, Paul E. Garber, a devotee of all things aeronautical, including kites, wrote to the U.S. Air Force after the museum had reopened to say that "the public is greatly interested in this

Images from the Smithsonian's annual Festival of American Folklife: quarter-horse races on the Mall in 1982 and, in 1979, colorfully attired participants from the Caribbean.

renowned...plane." In fact, *Glamorous Glennis* was a bellwether: As General Vandenberg had said of it in his airshow presentation, the aircraft "marked the end of the first great period of the air age, and the beginning of the second. In a few moments the subsonic period became history, and the supersonic period was born."

In relative terms, the Smithsonian Institution was to undergo a similar transition.

STIRRINGS

"…the Institution is by no means exclusively concerned with museum displays."
—LEONARD CARMICHAEL

An owl, the symbol of Athena, goddess of wisdom, graces this ancient Greek coin and serves today as the Smithsonian Secretary's badge of office. At right, 15-year-old Alexander Wetmore circa 1902. Wetmore went on to become a renowned ornithologist and the Institution's sixth Secretary.

At mid-century, the Smithsonian remained focused on research, predominantly in the natural sciences. The Regents, however, were growing increasingly concerned that, despite his official acceptance of the Wright brothers' *Flyer* and the Air Force's *Glamorous Glennis*, Alexander Wetmore remained resistant to activities that did not further scientific inquiry. A traditional Secretary, he was dedicated to the details of his particular discipline—that of ornithology—and determined to restore the Institution's reputation as a global leader in research.

As he had for many years, Wetmore continued to find great delight in fieldwork, and his adventures were legendary. He was frequently accompanied on collecting expeditions by the National Museum's taxidermist, Watson Perrygo, who later acknowledged that his boss suffered stress on the job in Washington, but that "After he was there [in Panama] a while, it would all clear up, and he would be fine…." These trips, noted Perrygo, were for Wetmore the equivalent of a vacation, "therapy…you go out in the hills."

The Secretary did the cooking, and insisted upon a balanced diet, whereas Assistant Secretary A. Remington Kellogg, who also loved fieldwork, would have been happy with potatoes. Despite his lack of pretension, Wetmore always wore a khaki shirt and pants with a khaki tie, and requested that others do the same. He kept his equipment spotless, even in the field, and paid close attention to details. "The table we were going to skin birds on had to be in line with the tent," Perrygo

reported, "and in line with the other chairs, and what have you, always."

Perrygo, a freer spirit, may have found these strictures a bit excessive. Once, at Petite Gonâve Island, Haiti, he laced bananas with rum to intoxicate the rhinoceros iguanas and make them easier to capture.

IN WASHINGTON, THE AURA OF THE CASH-STRAPPED Institution had not changed appreciably in two decades. Perrygo earlier had described the Smithsonian as a "typical old-time museum with a bunch of old-fashioned people running around with long whiskers and stooped shoulders, who lived in a world of their own, and didn't know when it was time to go home."

This was especially true of Wetmore, who, in addition to performing his official duties, pursued his bird studies on his own time. He spent the early morning hours working in his lab at the National Museum, and then crossed the Mall to begin official business in his office in the Castle. When his day there was done, he would often go back across the Mall and roam the museum at night to see what other scientists were accomplishing.

Wetmore's fellow ornithologist, Herbert Friedmann, who also served as the museum's head curator, feared that Wetmore would not help raise funds for the museum. However, the Secretary identified the need to reform the Institution's administrative and budgetary practices, and, with the help of John Keddy, a specialist in federal budgetary procedures, and Assistant Secretary John E. Graf, he was successful in bringing more professional management to the Institution.

Wetmore also approved plans to study ways for improving exhibits, which, because of decreased funding during World War II, had changed very slowly. Friedmann participated in the Exhibits Modernization Program, which had been created by Frank Taylor, chief of the Department of Engineering and Industry, to review exhibits

Alexander Wetmore appears in the field in Formosa, Argentina, in 1920 on a bird-collecting trip for the Biological Survey. Below left, some of the more than 600,000 bird specimens in the Smithsonian's National Museum of Natural History; at right, a computer-generated illustration by George Venable, one of that museum's scientific illustrators.

From the National Museum of
Natural History's entomology collections, two beetles from the order
Coleoptera, largest in the animal
kingdom: right, a snout beetle
(Curculionidae) commonly known as
a weevil; and, center, a leaf beetle
(Chrysomelidae). At far right, an
arachnid, or spider, drops in on Miss
Muffett in an Arthur Rackham illustration of the well-known children's
rhyme "Little Miss Muffett."

throughout the Institution. Others involved with the program included Paul Gardner, a curator with the National Collection of Fine Arts, and ethnologist John C. Ewers, who, in 1946, had been hired in part to help improve the exhibits. Meanwhile, collections continued to flow to the museum, compounding the problems arising from the lack of both space and personnel.

In 1951 Clifford Evans joined the Department of Anthropology. Intrigued by the idea of possible early human contact between Japan and South America, he and his wife, Betty Meggers, collaborated on an exhibit of maps and objects, the first new anthropological exhibit in almost 40 years. They also undertook a major revision

of the South American Indian exhibits on the museum's second floor. To the dismay of Assistant Secretary Kellogg, who was as traditional as Wetmore, the pair painted the inside of one display case red—something no one else had ever dared to do. But change was in the air, as well as the rumor of a new Secretary who might be more amenable to it. Catching the attention of visitors passing meekly through the Smithsonian's endless hallways was about to become a virtue.

In 1952 Wetmore, who believed there came a time in everyone's career when he or she should relinquish his or her position to someone with a fresher perspective,

(Text continued on page 284)

NO. 1401
by WILLIAM L. WITHUHN

"Have you seen starlight on the rails?" asked novelist Thomas Wolfe. "Have you heard the thunder of the fast express?" Growing up in Asheville, North Carolina, Wolfe often saw the starlight reflection and heard the thunder of the trains, as Americans virtually everywhere once did.

In the 1920s, the Southern Railway served Asheville, and engines of the same class as the 1401, the Smithsonian's big, green locomotive, rolled passenger trains into town every day. Built in 1926 by the American Locomotive Company, in Richmond, Virginia, the 1401 spent her working

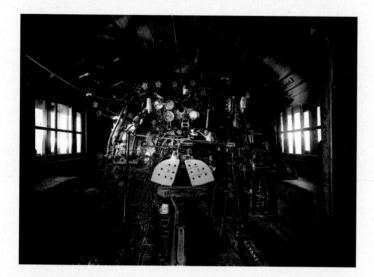

life on part of the Southern mainline between Greenville, South Carolina, and Spencer, North Carolina, and pulled such famous trains as *The Crescent*, *The Birmingham Special*, and *The Piedmont Limited*. Assigned to the Southern Railway's Charlotte (North Carolina) Division, the 1401 retains the name *Charlotte* on her cab.

Engines like the 1401 were the Boeing 747s of their age, inspiring people of all ages with their speed and huge size. More importantly, they provided the long-distance transportation that bound the disparate parts of the nation into an economic whole. At one time, more than 50,000 steam locomotives in the United States moved up to 90 percent of all intercity travelers and freight. It is the significance of steam railroads in the first half of the 20th century that makes the 1401 such an important part of the Smithsonian's collections.

In April 1945, the 1401 was one of ten locomotives of her type chosen to pull President Franklin Delano Roosevelt's funeral train in relays from Warm Springs, Georgia, to Washington, D.C. Paired with locomotive

Still the heaviest object the Smithsonian owns, the 188.5-ton 1401 steam locomotive rolls into the soon-to-be-completed Museum of History and Technology (today the National Museum of American History) in 1961. A view of the 1401's interior reveals its elaborate plumbing and the source of its power—the fire box (center).

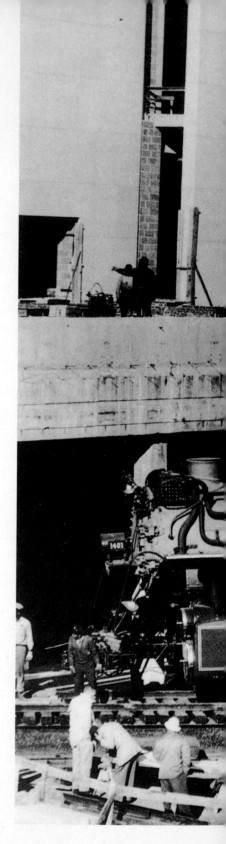

1385, the 1401 headed the somber procession from Greenville to Salisbury, North Carolina. Box Childers, fireman on the second engine, remarked: "There was a solid line [of people] on both sides of the track. I believe you could have walked on their heads all the way to Salisbury, and they all looked sad."

The Southern Railway retired the 1401 in 1952. Her days of thun-

dering along at 80 miles per hour were over; her stylish green paint—a sign of top-rank passenger engines on the Southern—was soot-stained and faded. Contemplating installations for what would become the National Museum of American History, the Smithsonian acquired the locomotive soon after.

At 188.5 tons empty, the 1401 was, and still is, the heaviest object the Smithsonian owns. Ninety-two tons of added coal and water were required to make it run. In 1961 the Southern Railway restored the engine, and moved her by crane and special trailer to her new home at American History. The museum opened to the public in 1964. No doubt Thomas Wolfe would have been pleased.

William L. Withuhn is Curator of Transportation at the National Museum of American History.

decided to step down. As Paul Oehser wrote in the quarterly journal of ornithology called *The Auk*, Wetmore had, since assuming the position of Secretary in 1945, "in his quiet way, following more or less the traditional patterns of his predecessors, fostered the Institution's laboratory and field researches in natural history, anthropology, and industrial arts...[and] laid the foundations of expanding the exhibits, buildings, and programs that came to fruition in later administrations." His was an impressive list of achievements, and Wetmore would continue his research at the Smithsonian for another quarter century.

The man who in early 1953 succeeded Wetmore as Secretary could not have differed more from his predecessor in temperament, learning, or ambition. As president of Tufts University, Leonard Carmichael was not just a university man, as Langley had been, but a psychologist rather than a pure scientist. According to precedent, Wetmore's successor should have been a physicist. Instead, the Regents chose this academic from a relatively "soft" field of inquiry, a man with no formal training in physics, history, or art, and relatively little in natural science, but who was unquestionably sophisticated and charming.

This choice suggested a plan. Carmichael was known as an effective manager and an activist, qualifications that were unusual in most of the previous Secretaries but that would be crucial to the Institution at a time when it sat in the doldrums, understaffed, burdened with conflicting mandates and aging real estate, and entrusted with the safekeeping of between 34 million and 37 million cataloged items. Carmichael was to promote change, but the question remained: how?

The new Secretary had wide-ranging interests, but, more importantly, he was socially and politically adept, and was eager to procure expanded facilities and to pursue a broader role for the Smithsonian. He gave a major

(Text continued on page 290)

Food for thought: Lunch-boxes collected by museum specialist Larry Bird in 1988–89 for an exhibit at the National Museum of American History evoke memories of popular television shows and historic events.

THE BUSINESS OF AMERICA

BY JOHN FLECKNER

It was Isadore "Sonny" Warshaw's hobby, his business, and his obsession. Warshaw, the bookseller and inveterate scavenger from Albany, New York, and, later, New York City, filled the basement of a Manhattan brownstone with boxes and piles of the documentary outpourings of American businesses. Today, the Warshaw Collection of Business Americana is the most heavily used resource in the National Museum of American History's Archives Center.

Where company officials saw old, worthless paper taking up valuable storage space, Sonny Warshaw saw a business opportunity in old advertisements, catalogs, letterhead stationery, point-of-purchase displays, and a host of other forms of business ephemera. He used items from his burgeoning collection as evidence in patent and trademark litigation. He also lent and sold these materials for corporate anniversaries and museum exhibitions.

In 1967 the Museum of History and Technology, as this Smithsonian bureau was then called, bought Warshaw's collection for $100,000. Museum staff envisioned this vast body of historical evidence as a permanent information source on the origins, nature, and uses of many of the museum's industrial and commercial artifacts. Indeed, since the collection's arrival, Smithsonian employees have used it to verify manufacturing dates, document prices and styles, and find illustrations of artifacts in actual or recommended use.

Over the years, the Warshaw collection has proven to be far more valuable than imagined three decades ago. Following new trends in historical scholarship, academic and museum researchers now pursue such topics as the emergence of a consumer-based economy, the ways in which commercial imagery reflects and shapes the larger culture, and the 19th-century origins of the information age. Moreover, today's researchers seek to augment textual information with visual images, the latter an especially strong feature of the Warshaw collection.

The story of American business enterprise continues to be a focus of new acquisitions by the Archives Center. In 1992, the children of Earl S. Tupper, the founder and inventor of Tupperware, donated their father's notes, diaries, photographs, and other records of the trials and errors in the 1930s that culminated in his famous invention.

Research materials on music; the history of the telegraph, radio, and television; and other less familiar aspects of American social and cultural history are also preserved in the Archives Center. The Duke Ellington

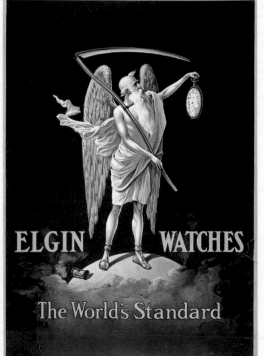

Business ephemera from the Warshaw collection in the National Museum of American History's Archives Center offers a window on American culture: far left, the cover of a Jerome B. Rice & Co. flower-seed catalog and an advertisement for Elgin watches; left, a New England Valentine Company greeting card; and, above, Westinghouse announces its Frost-Free refrigerator.

collection documents the career of one of America's great composers. This and other collections, including the Naff Arab American collection, the Hazen Collection of Band Photographs and Ephemera, the Carlos de Wendler-Funaro Gypsy Research collection, and the Iowa Button Industry collection, provide an invaluable window on American society.

John Fleckner is Chief Archivist of the Archives Center at the National Museum of American History.

The business ephemera of the Warshaw collection features a wealth of visual images: above, a J.W. Stoddard & Company trade card, with Columbia riding across the sky on farm machinery pulled by a tiger; at right, the cover of a Willow Furniture Company catalog; and, far right, a store display advertisement for Grove's Tasteless Chill Tonic.

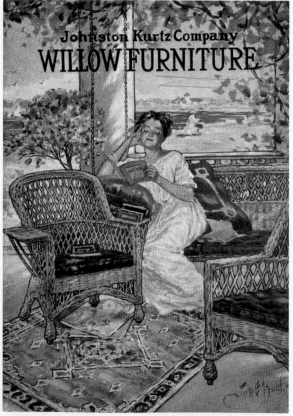

MAKES CHILDREN AND ADULTS AS FAT AS PIGS.
No Cure No Pay
Price 50 Cents.
GROVE'S
TASTELESS CHILL TONIC
ON THE MARKET OVER 20 YEARS
1½ MILLION BOTTLES SOLD LAST YEAR

boost to exhibits development, overseeing the hiring of a talented group of people whose task it would be to create engaging, informative exhibits. In fact, the Smithsonian would see the opening of at least one new exhibit hall each year of Carmichael's administration.

Carmichael's first *Annual Report*, lively and full of goals for the future, conveyed a tone of assurance and foregone accomplishment. He took up plans originally proposed by Secretary Abbot for two new buildings, one for a history museum and one for a museum of engineering and industry that was the dream of the chief curator of the Smithsonian's technological collections, Carl Mitman. Carmichael personally appealed to Congress for money to undertake these new ventures.

Up until this time, the idea of creating a Museum of History and Technology, spearheaded by Mitman's protégé, curator Frank A. Taylor, had lacked a champion. It had one now in Carmichael, who also asked Congress to transfer to the Smithsonian the Old Patent Office Building, near the Mall, as a home for the National Collection of Fine Arts. This historic edifice, which had housed the original collections from the 1838–42 United States Exploring Expedition, led by Lieutenant Charles Wilkes, and which had been scheduled for demolition in the 1950s to make way for a parking lot, was now preserved for posterity.

Carmichael also sought money for the National Zoo, the National Air Museum, and the expansion of the Museum of Natural History, which, beginning in 1957, occupied the Smithsonian's National Museum building. And his efforts were not limited to high-visibility projects in the nation's capital. The Canal Zone Biological Area (CZBA), in Panama, originally established in 1923 as the Institute for Research in Tropical America, had experienced difficult financial times from the beginning. In 1946 it was placed under Smithsonian administration; in the early 1950s, when the Department of Agriculture

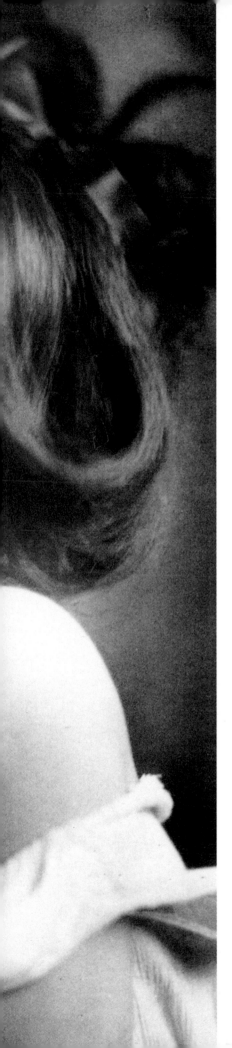

From the National Museum of American History's photographic-history collection: Rudolf Eickemeyer, Jr.'s platinum print of fashion model Evelyn Nesbit; a still-life autochrome; and an undated daguerreotype portrait of a young woman. The wet-plate camera, below, is similar to those used by 19th-century photographers on Western survey expeditions.

terminated its research activities in Panama, the Institution assumed full responsibility for the expenses and salaries of James Zetek, CZBA's entomologist and resident manager, and other scientists at the facility. Carmichael convened a conference of interested parties in an ongoing attempt to save this unique scientific effort.

By 1954 what could be characterized as "the Carmichael style" had evolved fully. The Secretary selected, as he described them, "a pink, a warm yellow, a sky blue, and a wondrous green" as the colors for the interior of the old Arts and Industries Building, unpainted since its opening 76 years earlier.

On another level, Carmichael's limited knowledge of the natural sciences was sometimes apparent. According to ornithologist Herbert Friedmann, curator of birds at the Natural History Museum, the Secretary "didn't really understand what the museum was about...he told me, 'This is a museum of dead animals.' I said, 'But there's a lot you can learn from dead animals....' "

Carmichael was never particularly sympathetic to that view, nor to the plight of the Smithsonian libraries: He had to be convinced that the Library of Congress was not the best place for housing early scientific descriptions and reports that were needed in ongoing research. He had no qualms about using the exhibits program to showcase his administration, but he was quick to compliment administrative Assistant John Keddy on his success in using the General Services Administration to negotiate contracts.

A natural and astute politician, Carmichael, according to Friedmann, "could meet congressmen and senators without feeling bashful…and could take Keddy's rather brusque demands and put them into polite language." Such skills had become essential for a Smithsonian Secretary.

THE SON OF A PHILADELPHIA PHYSICIAN AND A scholar who had done her research in logic and psychology

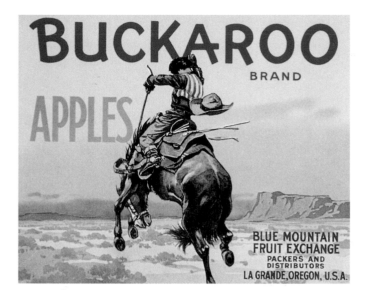

Thomas Hart Benton's 1947 mural *Achelous and Hercules*, in the National Museum of American Art, portrays the taming of the land and its bounty. From the National Museum of American History, a familiar American icon decorates an apple-crate label, above, and, opposite, an ornate show saddle crafted by Mervin Ringlero (Pima), a visiting artist at the National Museum of Natural History.

Leonard Carmichael stands in the Castle's Mall entrance in June 1960, with Joseph Henry and the National Museum of Natural History in the background.

at Wellesley College, Carmichael had grown up in the Germantown section of Philadelphia, in comfort and in the presence of books. "I made a fair collection of the butterflies and moths…and mounted them with care," he wrote in his autobiography, which revealed a domestic arrangement reminiscent of Baird's and Langley's. "From our gardener I learned something of the old-world nurture of plants…. A chauffeur of my father's taught me the proper use and care of basic woodworking and metalworking hand tools…."

While attending Tufts University, in Boston, Carmichael worked as a laboratory assistant in zoology. He obtained a Ph.D. in psychology from Harvard, and taught at Princeton and then at Brown, where he began studying prenatal behavior in mammals. Working with Dr. H.H. Jasper, he helped to develop a new model of electroencephalograph (EEG), an instrument for recording the electrical activity of the brain, and, in 1935, they published the first report of such research in North America. Eventually he wrote or cowrote several books, including *Elements of Human Psychology* and *Basic Psychology*.

In 1938, at age 39, Carmichael became Tuft's youngest president in its 86-year history. During World War II, he also served as director of the National Roster of Scientific and Specialized Personnel, in Washington, recruiting scientists and assigning them to such projects as the development of atomic energy and radar. By his own calculation, he spent more than a year of nights in railway sleeping cars, traveling between the nation's capital and Boston.

During this time, Carmichael had developed a sure sense of advocacy. He also "had a very strong competence in presenting needs…, personal persuasiveness and stature," said a colleague who was quoted in Geoffrey Hellman's *Octopus on the Mall*. "He was able to convey the great *diversity* of the Smithsonian to the Hill. And he was a master of the 'Smithsonian letter,' which is dignified,

tugs at your heart, is outrageously pompous and a bit chauvinistic, and ends with a little joke."

THE MID-1950S WERE MOMENTOUS YEARS FOR Carmichael and the Smithsonian. In 1954 the Biological Sciences Information Exchange was established. Two years later, Congress appropriated the funds necessary for the construction of the new Museum of History and Technology, as well as for the preparation of plans for the east and west wings of the Museum of Natural History. Private funds enabled preliminary architectural planning for the newly approved National Air Museum, while the Air Force agreed to pay for moving planes and other objects from storage facilities in Park Ridge, Illinois, to the Smithsonian's Silver Hill site in Suitland, Maryland.

In 1955 the Smithsonian Astrophysical Observatory moved from Washington to Cambridge, where, in 1973, it was officially associated with Harvard University to form the Harvard-Smithsonian Center for Astrophysics (CfA). On May 24 of that year, the rejuvenated Hall of the First Ladies' Gowns was officially opened to the public by President Dwight D. Eisenhower, and his wife, Mamie. Her own inaugural-ball gown would eventually be included in the exhibit, as well as the accessories she used that evening: pocketbook, gloves, shoes, even stockings and petticoats. (She once had to send a chauffeur to the Smithsonian to temporarily borrow back the pink shoes for another event.)

Meanwhile, new natural-history exhibits proliferated under the tutelage of Herbert Friedmann and others involved with the Exhibits Modernization Program. The American Indian Hall was completed in June 1955, followed the next year by Birds of the World. Three new exhibits opened in 1957: Everyday Life in Early America, North American Mammals, and North American Indians and Eskimos.

(Text continued on page 298)

ON SAFARI

by BRYAN KENNEDY

Strewn across the parched African landscape were 400 stone implements—flakes and cores—and, among them, the ribs and tusk fragments of a 990,000-year-old fossilized elephant, *Elephas recki*. In 1988 Richard Potts, director of the Smithsonian's Human Origins Program, and a team of colleagues unearthed this ancient butchery site at Olorgesailie, in southern Kenya's Great Rift Valley. Once nestled beside a Pleistocene lake, the locale is now part of a stratigraphic layer cake that has been exposed by erosion.

Back in the 1940s, world-famous paleoanthropologists Louis and Mary Leakey came to Olorgesailie to excavate, recover, and study hand axes, which were considered important hominid tools. They and other paleontologists of that period searched for artifacts and fossils on the surface, digging only in small, promising areas. Some of these areas were thought to be hominid campsites, but sediments indicative of moving water made it difficult to determine precisely how the fossils and stone tools they found had actually come together.

Today, Potts and his team are searching for more than just hand axes. Since climate, plants, and animals all affected the lives and behavior of ancient hominids, excavations now seek to uncover evidence of all three. At the Olorgesailie elephant-butchery site, pollen, root marks, and old animal burrows and bones are scattered in the soil layer on which the elephant's remains rest, awaiting analysis.

This relatively new method of focusing on the setting is called "landscape archaeology." A highly complex discipline, it requires the expertise and cooperation of a team of experts; in the case of Olorgesailie, the specialists hail from such diverse places as Yale University, the Berkeley Geochronology Center, and the National Museums of Kenya. Working alongside two dozen Kenyan excavators under the supervision of J. Muteti Nume, the Smithsonian contingent includes Potts, paleobiologist Anna K. Behrensmeyer, volcanologist Bill Melson, geologist Tom Jorstad, research technician Jennifer Clark, and photographer Chip Clark.

Their summer camp at the site overlooks eroded gullies where fossils and stone-age tools abound. Semi-nomadic Maasai people visit the outcrop during the day; lions and striped hyenas prowl it at night. One wonders what sort of neighbors hyenas and hominids were nearly one million years ago: About 490 feet west of the elephant, Potts and his colleagues discovered the remains of ancient burrows containing complete skeletons of spotted hyenas; 33 feet east of these carnivore fossils, another dense concentration of stone tools and bones appeared.

Smithsonian paleoanthropologist Richard Potts, right, examines a fossil find at Olorgesailie, Kenya, in 1994. The spotted hyena fossil shown below (its massive skull visible in the foreground) was

unearthed in an area now known as Hyena Hill. Colleague Tom Plummer, above, also a paleoanthropologist, enters information on a laptop computer run by solar panels. Photographer Chip Clark built the units that power the camp's database.

The elephant and hyena remains and the hominid tools are encased in an ancient land surface that has since been buried under diatomite-lake sediments, some of which are 12 feet thick. (The size of this freshwater lake fluctuated with the climate.) With the help of a bulldozer, the Smithsonian team uncovered this ribbon of soil, and excavated trenches along the length of the exposure, sampling an area up to two and a half miles long.

Keeping track of a project of these proportions is a challenge in itself, and calls for state-of-the-art technology. A grid generated by a computerized laser transit creates a map of the area on which all finds, along with such information as their depth within the strata, are carefully plotted. Utilizing this electronic-surveying technique, the computer produces three-dimensional maps that are accurate to within two-tenths of an inch.

Olorgesailie is unique in that this well-dated outcrop remained undisturbed over a period of time from a million to 50,000 years ago. Such an extraordinary window into Africa's past makes precise measurements crucial, particularly since large periodic shifts in climate and environment were common.

What hominids did as their habitat and climate changed may hold some important lessons for us today. Back at the Smithsonian's human-origins lab, in the National Museum of Natural History, scanning-electron microscope studies of the Olorgesailie fossils reveal whether they were scratched by hominid tools, gnawed by carnivores, or simply trampled and washed down a stream. Searching for comparative evidence, Rick Potts has even crawled into a modern, abandoned hyena burrow to retrieve old leftovers to put beside the ancient bones.

Every discovery raises new questions. Perhaps hand axes weren't used as we always imagined. Perhaps these oblong, flaked stones were really dispensers for razor-sharp flakes used for various cutting jobs.

Even earlier inhabited African locations Potts has studied present more evidence of competition between scavengers—be they hominid or hyena—for meat and marrow. And carnivores and hominids appeared not to be sharing carcasses 990,000 years ago at Olorgesailie. Whatever was happening there, one thing is for sure: The creatures who cut up that elephant didn't act like us. They were not just primitive versions of ourselves, and curator Richard Potts will continue to investigate how and why they were different.

Bryan Kennedy is an Associate Editor at Smithsonian Books.

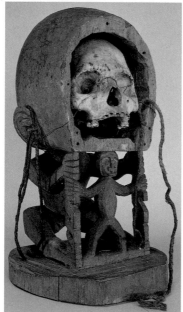

Artist John Gurche used skull fossil casts to fashion this clay, plaster, and plastic reconstruction of the head of *Homo erectus*. Opposite, Gurche's illustration links a fossilized skull of Neanderthal Man displayed (top) on a modern museum table with its discovery in Gibraltar in the mid-1800s (center) and the presence of this ancestor of *Homo sapiens* in a firelit cave about 50,000 years earlier. Crafted from wood, cloth, and beads, an Indonesian ancestral figure bears a human skull.

When it came time to dismantle the old American buffalo exhibits that had been set up by taxidermist William Hornaday in 1888, a box discovered in the plaster yielded copies of an 1887 issue of *Cosmopolitan* magazine with an article by Hornaday. On one copy, he had written a note above the article asking that the specimens not be destroyed. "Enclosed please find a brief and truthful account of the capture of the specimens…. The old bull, the young cow and yearling calf were killed by yours truly."

The *Annual Report* for 1957 stated that "The curators of the National Museum have a twofold objective in planning their halls and exhibits, to give the Museum visitor the experience of viewing objects of significant historical or scientific interest and rarity; and to show these objects in exhibits so effectively explanatory that they increase the visitor's knowledge, not only of the object, but also of the history, science, technology, or art to which the object relates." No longer would Smithsonian visitors be left simply to wander the halls, making their own deductions; an evolutionary step had been taken, one that surely would have pleased the late Assistant Secretary George Brown Goode, an early advocate of instructive labels. Carmichael wanted exhibits to contribute to the collective education and to be designed in a rational, systematic, perhaps even inspirational manner.

The new Museum of History and Technology building rising on Constitution Avenue—closest of all the Smithsonian bureaus to the Washington Monument—created an atmosphere of excitement. Slated to house collections and exhibits pertaining to science and developing technology in America, the new museum also made reorganization of the Institution inevitable. In 1957 the National Museum ceased to be administered as a single unit. (A decade later, the office of Director General of the National Museum was eliminated upon the retirement of its last holder, Frank A. Taylor.) Carmichael stipulated

(Text continued on page 302)

INFORMATION AGE
by DAVID K. ALLISON

Among the more than 700 artifacts on display in the National Museum of American History's Information Age exhibit are, at right, a prototype of the Apple personal computer; top, a collection of communication devices, including Ralph Waldo Emerson's first commercial success—a gold-stock ticker (center); and, above, Leon Scott's 1857 "phonautograph," the first machine to record sound.

In 1985 the National Museum of American History began planning an exhibition on the history of information technology. Robert McCormick Adams, then Secretary of the Smithsonian, suggested to curators that the new exhibit pioneer innovative approaches to exhibition development, focusing not on the pertinent inventors themselves, nor on how their inventions worked, but on the difference each new technological breakthrough made. Adams felt the exhibit should address the ways in which peoples' lives—and thus American history—were affected by telegraphs, telephones, television, computers, and networks, and he wanted this to be the most interactive show the Smithsonian had ever created, using information technology in creative and interesting ways.

Curators whose fields of expertise ranged from electrical, computer, business, and social history collaborated in drawing up the overall plan, selecting artifacts, and writing the script for the exhibit. They were assisted by a number of young researchers, as well as by educators, who helped identify audience interests and desires. A Baltimore firm made more than 20 life-sized human figures representing different historical periods, while a California company experienced in interactive development designed the show and a consultant from Disney Imagineering helped make the environmental pieces exciting and lifelike.

The team also received invaluable support from the information-technology companies that sponsored the exhibit. Many, such as IBM, Pioneer Electronics, Unisys, and Hewlett Packard, donated both funding and equipment—which amounted to more than 50 computers, 40 TV monitors, 3 video projectors, and a 12-screen multimedia wall. Six miles of cable connected everything into an integrated communications network. As part of its donation, the EDS corporation offered millions of lines of software to run the new exhibit, even agreeing to operate the show for the Smithsonian; their staff has been at the museum every day, to ensure that the exhibit runs effectively and continues to keep up with technology.

Information Age opened in May 1990. Since that time, more than 6.5 million people from around the world have seen it. Several area colleges routinely use it to support their history courses on information technology, and corporate training classes send students here. In addition, the exhibition has hosted dozens of special receptions for information-technology companies, trade associations, and such groups as the National Education Association.

The American History Museum's most active outreach program today is the annual *Computerworld* Smithsonian Awards. These are presented to those people whose innovations, in the opinion of *Computerworld*, a news weekly for the information industry, and the Smithsonian, are changing society. The museum has also held symposia on "Information Technology and Medicine," "Information Technology and Education," and similar topics.

Most importantly, records of new contributions to this field are created and preserved for use in updating the exhibition and as a basis for research. In June 1995, these materials became virtual: A World Wide Web site made them accessible from any location on the globe.

David K. Allison is Chairman of Information Technology and Society at the National Museum of American History.

that in the future there would be two equal entities, the Museum of Natural History, which would occupy the National Museum building, and the Museum of History and Technology, each with its own director.

At Natural History, the Secretary was so pleased with the progress of the expanded exhibits program that he held a dinner for the Regents there. The following summer saw the opening of the Hall of Gems and Minerals, organized by George Switzer and Paul E. Desautels, and, in November 1958, the Hope diamond, which had been donated by the world-famous New York jeweler Harry Winston and which carried a reputedly infamous provenance, found its unique final setting at the Smithsonian in a specially constructed, transparent safe that allowed the famous gem to be closely viewed by an overwhelmingly appreciative public.

Leonard Carmichael's energy and vision had won him allies in Congress and among the Regents and the Institution's staff, but there were those who found the Secretary to be somewhat stuffy and overly concerned with publicity. Both of these traits manifested themselves in the affair of the Fénykövi elephant, a huge bull shot near the Cuito River in Angola, where it was skinned and the entire two-ton pelt treated with a truckload of salt before being sent to Washington, along with the tusks, leg bones, and 1,800-pound skull. Most everyone agreed that the Fénykövi elephant was the perfect occupant for the magnificently empty rotunda of the Natural History Museum.

Chief taxidermist William L. Brown and others threw themselves into the complex and exhausting task of preparing and mounting what was then the largest elephant ever shot; 16 months later, they had produced what would become a symbol of the Institution's expertise and excitement for millions of visitors.

Working under plastic sheeting, with a constant flow of steam pumped in to maintain the proper humidity, the Smithsonian crew constructed a wooden armature

Demonstrating humankind's propensity to invent: at right, suspended from a silk cord, an 18th-century Persian astrolabe from the National Museum of American History, and, from the National Air and Space Museum, an eight-foot-long slide rule held by Smithsonian curator Paul Ceruzzi.

slightly smaller than the elephant, and covered it with clay. Plaster of Paris, which would be removed later, then went over the hide covering the clay model. Massive supports were installed, along with a trap door in the elephant's stomach to allow access to the interior. The animal's stance, posed as if walking with its head and trunk erect, appeared very lifelike.

The final product was unveiled in the spring of 1959. The elephant was said to have stood 13 feet, 2 inches in life; when journalists checked it with a tape measure, however, they found it short a few inches, and threatened to embarrass Carmichael over his claims about the elephant's original height. It was duly explained to them that, had the elephant been reconstructed as if it were standing still, it would indeed have measured up.

This wasn't the only pettiness associated with the grand Fénykövi elephant. In the interests of delicacy, Carmichael reportedly ordered the elephant's anus sewn up, a move that angered Assistant Secretary Kellogg, who saw it as tampering with science in the interest of public relations, and considered it a dire precedent.

THE 1950S WERE SOON GONE, AND THE SMITH-sonian was still in a state of flux. At Natural History, June of 1961 saw the opening of four new exhibits— Fossil Plants and Invertebrates, the Age of Mammals in North America, Fossil Reptiles and Amphibians, and the first of two on North American archaeology—and work began on the museum's new 260,000-square-foot east wing. Scientists also worked diligently on another ambitious new exhibit, Life in the Sea; when it opened, two years later, it would include a 92-foot model of a giant blue whale.

In the minds of many, the heart of the Smithsonian might well have been the Museum of Natural History, but that perception was about to change. The laying of

(Text continued on page 306)

INSTRUMENTS OF DISCOVERY
by JAMES CORNELL

In astronomy, perhaps more than any other science, serendipitous discovery often follows the introduction of new technology. Consider Samuel Pierpont Langley's discovery of the sun's infrared radiation. Langley, the Smithsonian's third Secretary and founder of the Smithsonian Astrophysical Observatory (SAO), was searching for the "solar constant," or average amount of energy falling on Earth, which he hoped could link the sun's radiation to a host of terrestrial phenomena. It was this obsession that led him to develop the heat-sensing bolometer with which he discovered "a new spectrum...wholly unknown to science...."

Recognizing the vital role that instruments play in astronomy, the SAO has pursued a vigorous and innovative program of telescope and detector development. It has produced some of the world's most sophisticated tools for probing the universe at wavelengths across the electromagnetic spectrum. In fact, three major instrument projects—a 6.5-meter-diameter optical telescope to be located in Arizona, a high-resolution camera for an x-ray observatory in space, and a unique array of submillimeter-wave antennae in Hawaii—are now under development. Each is designed to examine a different region of the spectrum, each represents a significant advance in its field, and all have the potential to redefine astronomical research in the next century.

In 1979 the Multiple Mirror Telescope (MMT), a joint Smithsonian and University of Arizona facility, came into use. Considered a revolutionary departure from traditional telescope design, it overcame the size and cost limitations inherent in casting and mounting giant glass mirrors by utilizing six separate and relatively small 1.6-meter mirrors arranged in six-gun fashion. Each of the mirrors collected light from a distant object, brought that light to a central focus, and combined it into one image.

Later this decade the MMT will undergo a radical transformation. Thanks to the University of Arizona's spin-casting technique for manufacturing large, lightweight mirrors, the MMT's six separate mirrors will be replaced with a monolithic mirror 6.5 meters in diameter. The converted telescope will have twice the light-gathering power of the original and will view an area of sky some 20 times larger across.

In its creation of instruments for space observatories, the SAO's most ambitious attempt to date is the high-resolution camera to be placed aboard the Advanced X-ray Astrophysics Facility (AXAF), scheduled for launch in 1998. AXAF is designed to study the violently energetic processes

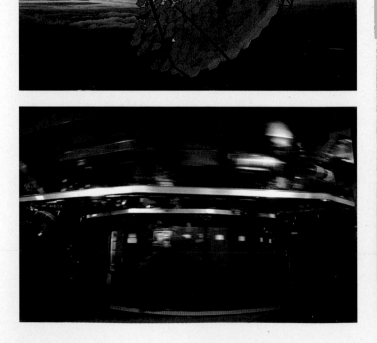

found at the centers of some galaxies, in supernovae, and in the spiraling mass surrounding black holes. In addition to designing the camera and its unusual cylindrical mirrors, Smithsonian scientists will also operate the AXAF Science Center, receiving, analyzing, and archiving data throughout the satellite's lifetime.

Not all of astronomy's frontiers are in space. Indeed, until recently, the submillimeter band of the electromagnetic spectrum—lying between radio and infrared radiation—remained largely unexplored because the technology to produce the precisely figured antennae and highly sensitive detectors did not exist. The SAO is constructing the Submillimeter Array (SMA) to observe astronomical objects and phenomena obscured or extremely difficult to study from Earth.

The array will consist initially of six 6-meter-diameter, moveable antennas capable of being positioned by a huge wheeled transporter. At their widest separation, the individual elements will act like a single, giant antenna some 500 meters wide. Using computers to combine and integrate the radio signals, the SMA will produce images with a resolution comparable to the best optical telescopes and some 10 times better than any existing single-dish submillimeter telescope.

Groundbreaking for the SMA occurred June 8, 1995, near the summit of Mauna Kea, Hawaii. When fully operational later this decade, it will probe the murky dust clouds where stars are born, peer into the explosive hearts of distant galaxies, and study the cool, faint objects—such as comets and planets—of our own solar system. Appropriately, the sensitive new detectors developed specifically for the SMA are direct descendants of the bolometer invented by Langley. The observatory's founding father would be proud of his scientific progeny—and delighted by their prospects for opening new windows on the universe.

Located on Mt. Hopkins, Arizona, the Fred Lawrence Whipple Observatory, above, named in honor of the former SAO director, left, is the site of a 10-meter-diameter optical reflector, far left, used in gamma-ray astronomy, and the Multiple Mirror Telescope, whose replacement glass mirror was cast in a giant rotating oven, below left. The Whipple Observatory produced this image of a spiral galaxy, below.

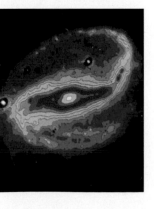

James Cornell is Publications Manager for the Harvard-Smithsonian Center for Astrophysics.

the cornerstone of the Museum of History and Technology, the first major construction in years, was a big step for the Institution in fulfilling the second of James Smithson's directives: the diffusion of knowledge, rather than simply its increase.

Among its other goals, the new museum would attempt to tell the story of America, and, in so doing, would display the country's most significant objects. As Carmichael wrote in an earlier *Annual Report*, "the strands that have been woven together in the making of our modern American civilization will be shown in a way that…will be unique and particularly appropriate to the special genius of our country."

Frank A. Taylor was named the first director of the Museum of History and Technology, which, considering that he had been advocating just such a museum for two decades, was fitting. Perhaps the best symbol of the new museum's mandate and physical ambitions was the arrival, on November 26, 1961, of the restored Southern Railway's Number 1401 locomotive, a Ps-4 Pacific type that was built in 1926 and that had weighed 280 tons while in service. Before it took up permanent, magisterial residence in the Transportation Hall, the locomotive was maneuvered into the still unfinished museum in an operation that took 11 days. (A soundtrack of a moving steam train, installed shortly after the exhibit opened in 1964, caused one startled visitor to jerk his son out of the imagined path of the locomotive.)

During Carmichael's administration, the Smithsonian's collections had grown to more than 58 million items. In 1968, the old Patent Office Building that Carmichael had secured five years earlier officially became the home of two distinct Smithsonian branches, the National Portrait Gallery and the National Collection of Fine Arts.

And things kept rolling. In 1958 Carmichael appointed Theodore Reed the new director of the bur-

geoning National Zoo. That same year, the Zoo began attracting additional public support through the Friends of the National Zoo, or FONZ, which was founded by two Washingtonians Mary Ellen Grogan and Barbara Robinson. The Smithsonian Institution Traveling Exhibition Service, created in the fall of 1952, transported Smithsonian treasures around the country. The new National Air Museum site was chosen, and the Smithsonian's central administration, not the old National Museum, had been established as the controlling entity for all the Institution's museums and galleries.

Equally impressive as all these achievements, the Smithsonian's endowment had grown from $10.5 million to $19 million, its annual appropriations from $2.5 million to more than $13 million. Carmichael's wooing of Congress and his mastery of "the Smithsonian letter" had paid off.

In 1963 the year Carmichael resigned as Secretary, some 10 million people visited the Institution, three times the number recorded for any year under Wetmore. Among his predecessors at the Smithsonian, Carmichael had most closely resembled George Brown Goode, in ambition if not in personality. Goode's prime concern had been education, and, while Carmichael did not neglect research, he had been the first Secretary to actively pursue and secure funds for the massive diffusion of the Institution's prime commodity—knowledge.

The installation of air conditioning at the Museum of Natural History the year before Carmichael retired received little attention. Fittingly, it was Frank Taylor, director of the Museum of History and Technology, who put this seminal event into perspective: "Visiting the Museum is now much more pleasant," he said; visitors "are induced to stay longer and absorb more of the instruction and inspiration that exhibits provide."

Inspiration was a pale word for what the Smithsonian was about to receive in the person of a new and, once again, utterly different type of leader.

The race for space in the 1960s fueled the public's fascination with interstellar travel, as evidenced by this movie poster and these porcelain cosmonauts from Smithsonian collections. A multiple-exposure

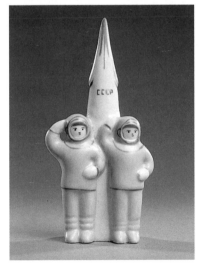

photo shows a falling gantry during the July 18, 1966, launch of Gemini 10 from Cape Kennedy, Florida.

THE END OF THE COLD WAR

by BRYAN KENNEDY

In April 1990, a fireball laced with streamers of burning rocket propellant shot up from the barren Asian plain. Gregg Herken, chairman of the Department of Space History at the Smithsonian's National Air and Space Museum, was surprised by the magnitude of the shock wave that followed. Herken had come to Kapustin Yar, the former Soviet Union's missile test base in central Asia, to take possession of an SS-20 "Saber" intermediate-range ballistic-missile trainer for the National Air and Space Museum (NASM). He now watched as the Russians destroyed two of the SS-20's live cousins with explosives.

Officially, Herken was a guest of the Soviet government, but he accompanied the U.S. On-Site Inspection Agency (OSIA) team, whose job was to observe the demolition of 24 of these weapons in compliance with the 1987 Intermediate-range Nuclear Forces (INF) Treaty. His status on the trip initially puzzled both host and guest governments: In his welcoming speech, Soviet Inspector Colonel Gennadiy Komogortsev mentioned an honored guest from the Smithsonian, and then inquired why he was there.

Two days before the explosion, "OSIA Team Deeny," named after its leader, U.S. Air Force Lieutenant Colonel Dennis Deeny, inspected the SS-20 training missile, which lacked rocket nozzles and propellant and was

outfitted with a dummy warhead. It was then crated and flown to Moscow. Much to Herken's disappointment, the SS-20 had been painted red, white, and blue, rather than left in its operational colors, as he and his NASM colleagues, who had been through so much to get this prize for the collection, would have preferred. Herken was not allowed to take pictures while at the base—but in fact his troubles were only just beginning.

On December 8, 1987, the United States and the former Soviet Union agreed to dispose of 2,692 missiles from their arsenals in Europe. The INF Treaty was the first to eliminate an entire class of nuclear weapons—those with a range of 300 to 3,400 miles. Of these, the intermediate-range SS-20 and the U.S. Army's Pershing II were the most accurate and lethal. Reading over the treaty's fine print, NASM Space History curators Frank Winter and Paul Ceruzzi discovered allowances for the preservation of up to 15 "static display" models from each side. Thus was born the idea of a joint exhibit between the two countries that would involve trading a demilitarized Pershing II trainer for an SS-20.

Senior advisor Donald Lopez broached the subject of the trade with then Secretary of Defense Frank Carlucci, while Herken and his staff approached everyone on the Soviet side from Nobel Prize laureate Andre

Far left, the official Russian photograph of an April 1990 SS-20 missile demolition in Kapustin Yar, central Asia. Another SS-20, this one bound for the National Air and Space Museum, lies stuck on a loader, center, which had broken down. The missile finally reached its destination, and was installed, right, for the opening of a June 1990 exhibit.

Sakharov and Vice-President of the Soviet Academy of Sciences Yevgeniy Velikhov to Soviet Defense Minister Dmitriy Yazov. Finally, in October 1988, the U.S. Army agreed to provide two Pershing IIs. NASM personnel, however, encountered difficulty in locating Soviet officials with enough authority to say "yes." In June 1989, both curator Cathy Lewis and Herken pleaded their case on separate research trips to Moscow.

On September 20 of that year, Senior Soviet Arms Control Negotiator Gennadyi Khromov visited NASM, and explained that the Soviet government viewed the trade as unequal since their SS-20 trainer was a real missile while the Pershing II trainer was a replica. The U.S. Army had removed all sensitive equipment from their Pershing without altering its exterior appearance. This option was extended to the Soviets, and seemed to satisfy them.

Official approval followed in November, and eventually Khromov invited Herken to witness the ongoing destruction of missiles. A total of 654 SS-20s, launchers, and trailers fell within the INF Treaty guidelines. Meanwhile, Soviet inspection teams were observing the scrapping of 234 Pershing II rockets and service equipment in the U.S.

And so, back from Kapustin Yar in April 1990, at Moscow's

Shremetyovo Airport, Herken, various Soviet and OSIA officials, U.S. Army personnel, and KGB Border Guards watched a U.S. Air Force Lockheed C-141 taxi up to the SS-20, which had been crated into several sections. But the crates wouldn't fit, so measurements were taken, and, as the missile was uncrated, it began to rain. The heavy loader provided by *Lufthansa* then broke down, and the tarp-covered weapon was stuck halfway on the transport jet. Finally, the Russians managed to push the missile in with a truck.

On June 20, 1990, the Smithsonian's National Air and Space Museum opened the *Trust But Verify* exhibit in the *Milestones of Flight* gallery. Today, inspectors from the U.S. and Russian governments continue to visit the Pershing II and repainted SS-20 occasionally to confirm that both are still inoperative.

Bryan Kennedy is an Associate Editor at Smithsonian Books.

PROFILE
DR. COMET

The schoolchildren gathered at the Smithsonian Astrophysical Observatory (SAO) in Cambridge, Massachusetts, for a lecture on Halley's comet responded enthusiastically, if not always correctly, to the pictures of famous astronomers. Edmund Halley, Sir Isaac Newton, and Sir John F.W. Herschel seemed vaguely familiar. But when a slide of Fred Lawrence Whipple, bespectacled, balding, and smiling, flashed on screen, one youngster shouted out, "That's Dr. Comet!"

For some science students and professional astronomers, Fred Whipple is, indeed, Dr. Comet, the scientist who first described comets as "dirty snowballs." His belief that they were hard-packed, frozen conglomerates of dust and ice that emitted plumes of water vapor when they neared the sun was confirmed in 1986 by spacecraft-flyby photos of Halley's comet. Whipple's comet-crowned head later appeared on different sets of postage stamps issued by Mauritania and St. Vincent and the Grenadines.

His colleagues at the SAO consider Whipple to be the director who rejuvenated a nearly moribund organization and set it on course toward becoming one of the world's preeminent centers of astrophysical research.

Born in Red Oak, Iowa, in 1906, Whipple grew up on a farm, where his father and mother raised cattle and horses. Sixteen years later, his family sold the farm and moved to Long Beach, California, where they opened a grocery store; young Fred helped out as a sales clerk. "To make an otherwise boring job interesting," Whipple later recalled, "I would add up the cost of items in my head. When customers were finished, I would tell them the total. They couldn't believe it. I then added it up on a piece of paper."

This obvious talent for numbers led Whipple to enroll as a math major at Occidental College, in Los Angeles. "I was also enthralled as a child with the stories of H.G. Wells, Jules Verne, Hugo Gernsback, and Edgar

Director of the Smithsonian Astrophysical Observatory from 1955 to 1973, Fred Lawrence Whipple receives the Distinguished Federal Civilian Service Award from President John F. Kennedy in 1963 for his leadership in developing an optical tracking system for the first artificial satellites.

Allen Poe." Perhaps it was the science-fiction promise of space flight that inspired him, but he left Occidental for the University of California at Los Angeles, and eventually earned a Ph.D. in astronomy at Berkeley in 1931. "Astronomy certainly seemed more exciting than mathematics."

In the fall of 1931, Whipple joined the Harvard College Observatory to take charge of a complete photographic survey of the sky. Again attempting to enliven a boring job that involved mainly checking negatives to ensure that the cameras were working properly, he began to look for any new comets that might have been captured on the films. Eventually he found six, all of which now bear his name, and in the process developed a passion for the small wanderers of our solar system: comets, meteoroids, and asteroids.

Like many scientists, Whipple joined the defense effort during World War II, working on so-called confusion reflectors designed to protect American bombers by jamming Nazi radar.

After the war, he rose steadily in the Harvard ranks—from lecturer to associate professor to professor to chairman of the department of astronomy, the position he held in 1955 when he was tapped to be director of the SAO.

The Smithsonian observatory had fallen on hard times during the war. Its solar observing stations abroad had closed down, and its presence on the Mall in Washington had been reduced to a small wooden building behind the Castle. Secretary Leonard Carmichael, as well as the Regents, felt that the SAO could be salvaged only by forging a strong relationship with a major university. A former president of Tufts University, Carmichael turned to his old friend Donald Menzel, director of the Harvard College Observatory, for advice. Menzel offered the SAO space in Cambridge, and, more importantly, suggested that Fred Whipple would be a good director.

Whipple accepted an offer and almost immediately took on an even greater challenge: In anticipation of possible space launches during the International Geophysical Year of 1957–58, he agreed to establish a worldwide network of 12 tracking cameras, maintained by a volunteer force of visual observers. He had never lost his childhood fascination with space—in 1946 he had invented a "meteor bumper" for spacecraft that was designed to protect them from collisions with micrometeoroids—and had already developed giant cameras to capture the brief flashes of meteors in Earth's atmosphere.

"I thought I could use the same photographic techniques to track artificial satellites," said Whipple. "And I was right." In fact, the SAO's network stood ready to track the first satellite, Sputnik 1, launched on October 4, 1957. Because the Smithsonian had no restrictions on the release of orbital information, overnight the observatory became the center of international attention.

The SAO itself grew and prospered under Whipple, reaching a staff of some 400 by the late 1960s. Excelling, naturally, in meteoritics and cometary studies, it also pioneered the development of orbiting observatories and the application of computer analysis to astrophysical problems.

However, the SAO needed a major ground-based observatory (something oddly lacking for the first 75 years of its existence), so Whipple found a site on Mt. Hopkins, in southern Arizona. In the early '70s, he and Aden Meinel, of the University of Arizona, joined forces to create—from the modest seeds of six surplus Air Force mirrors—the Multiple Mirror Telescope, literally the jewel on Mt. Hopkins' crown. (In 1982, recognizing Whipple's contributions to the Smithsonian and to astronomy, the Regents voted to rename the Arizona observatory in his honor.)

In 1973, after 18 years as director of the SAO, Whipple retired. At 89, an emeritus professor at Harvard and Smithsonian Senior Scientist, Whipple put in a full day at his office, usually arriving by bicycle from his home three miles away and working on theories of comets. He

maintained a busy speaking schedule, traveling across the country and overseas to address groups ranging from academic societies to amateur astronomers. Through it all, he also has maintained the humor and good spirits that have marked what one writer called his "long and steady orbit through science and life."

In 1992 this rotating oven at the University of Arizona was used to spin-cast a 6.5-meter replacement mirror for SAO's Multiple Mirror Telescope. The oven was loaded with 10 tons of borosilicate glass and spun at computer-controlled speeds until the molten glass took on the desired final shape of the mirror.

A WIND IN THE ATTIC

Looking behind the scenes in the Castle, right, a Richard Thompson cartoon. Below, Secretary S. Dillon Ripley at his desk.

"...Of what use are...proposed panaceas for the preservation of evolved civilization or the maintenance of cultures, if the majority of living people simply don't care?"

—S. DILLON RIPLEY
The Sacred Grove

His father's family name, Dillon, was associated with one of the great railroading empires, the Union Pacific, and sometimes with predatory capitalism. A portrait of his great-grandfather, Sidney Dillon, who helped to drive the line's last golden spike at Promontory, Utah, on May 10, 1869, hangs in the National Portrait Gallery today. In later life, Sidney Dillon Ripley made a point of relocating the replica of the spike brought back to New York by his great-grandfather because, as Ripley put it, "[I] was 'history-minded.' "

Born in 1913 in Manhattan and raised there and on the family property in Connecticut, Ripley's upbringing included foreign sojourns to Paris, where, at age 10, he wandered the Louvre, looking at the paintings by Rubens and Tintoretto and at models of ships in the fleet of Louis XIV. He played in the Tuileries Garden, intrigued by the puppet show and the carousel, amusement themes that would resurface in later life, in another place.

At the age of 13, Ripley took a walking tour of Tibet. He attended St. Paul's preparatory school, in New Hampshire, and then went on to Yale University, where some of his ancestors also had gone. The head-master of St. Paul's told Ripley: "I think you ought to go to Yale because there you'll surely learn how to slap people on the back." But Ripley was more interested in birds. A classmate at St. Paul's had first brought Ripley into the sphere of amateur ornithology, an interest augmented by Ripley's keen natural vision and the time he spent in rural New England.

In 1936 he joined a collecting voyage aboard a 59-foot schooner in the South Pacific, which he later characterized as "a 19th century voyage of exploration in the 20th century. Very romantic to…go down the wind slot in the Solomons in full moon, seeing the great, mysterious, brooding mountains." He had to explain at length where the Solomon Islands were, although, with the coming of World War II, this would soon be common knowledge in America. The trip reinforced his avian passion; he enrolled in a two-year program in zoology at Harvard University, and received his Ph.D.

In 1942 he traveled south from Cambridge to Washington, D.C., to work as an assistant curator of birds at the Smithsonian. His specialty was the birds of the islands off Sumatra, an area that had been visited by William Abbott half a century before. His work was routine—identification and storage. The antique quality of the Institution, including some older employees who actually lived in the Museum of Natural History, must have made a not altogether positive impression on the young ornithologist. (Jessie Beach, who worked in the paleontology division, was often seen wandering the halls at night in a dressing gown.) In any case, Ripley told Herbert Friedmann, "I don't think I'm cut out to be a civil servant."

WORLD WAR II TOOK RIPLEY AWAY FROM WASHington. Joining the ranks of the Office of Strategic Services (OSS), forerunner of the Central Intelligence Agency, under General William "Wild Bill" Donovan, he trained briefly in espionage near the capital, and then was sent to Southeast Asia. There he used his contacts, and to some degree his scientific knowledge, in the interest of the OSS.

In New Delhi, the tall, stooped, bookish extrovert worked to coordinate the intelligence efforts of the United States and Great Britain; in Ceylon—known

(Text continued on page 320)

In September 1965, the 200th anniversary of Smithsonian benefactor James Smithson's birth, Secretary Ripley (right) and the late Chief Justice and Smithsonian Chancellor Earl Warren lead a procession of scholars and dignitaries across the Mall. At right, the Smithsonian mace, created for the bicentennial, features the crest of Sir Hugh Percy, Smithson's father, and was designed with help from London's Worshipful Company of Goldsmiths.

MOVING MUSIC
by BILL YARDLEY

Mom always told me to keep my wallet in a front pocket when I walked down the streets of Manhattan. I grew up in North Carolina, and she was convinced that Northern city slickers were going to pick my Southern pockets clean. But Mom never told me how to behave on Fifth Avenue when I'm toting around multi-million-dollar cargo.

Not that I'm on foot much anymore in New York. Now, when I roll down Fifth Avenue, it's generally in a van, accompanied by armed guards.

The part of the Smithsonian's National Museum of American History where I work—the Division of Musical History—houses five stringed instruments made by Antonio Stradivari, who was born in Cremona, Italy, in 1644. Stradivari—who Latinized his name to Stradivarius on his labels—fashioned more than 1,100 instruments during his 93 years. About 650 are thought to remain in existence today; the Smithsonian has five of them.

One, the *Servais* cello—named after the celebrated 19th-century cellist Adrien-François Servais—came to the Smithsonian as an extraordinary surprise gift in 1981, and is now a permanent part of the collection. The other four—a cello named *Marylebone*, a viola called *Axelrod*, and two violins, *Ole Bull* and *Greffuhle*—are on loan to the museum from Herbert Axelrod, an ichthyologist and publisher with a passion for collecting antique instruments.

An amateur violinist himself, Axelrod believes his Stradivaris should be heard as well as seen, and we feel the same about our cello. Under the direction of Kenneth Slowik, the Smithsonian Chamber Music Society performs on the Stradivaris each season at the museum. The priceless strings are also in great demand around the country and around the world.

That's where I come in. Every now and then, under tighter security than even the President gets, we sneak the Stradivaris out of their exhibit display cases. Cutting through red tape to transport the "Strads" out of the museum isn't easy. Exit forms are filled out and documentary photographs taken. But once we get the instruments out the door, the van is waiting, as are the armed guards.

During the summer of 1994, our Strads traveled to Philadelphia and Saratoga so the American String Quartet could perform with them. And, each January for the past several years, the instruments have gone to Manhattan for recording sessions on the Sony Vivarte label. In New York, we pick them up from their secret storage site, wait while they're being used, and then return the instruments to storage at night. The work could be considered boring if the music weren't so beautiful!

The Strads also go by air sometimes. Since they've been at the Smithsonian, they've traveled once to Europe and several times to Japan. Japan sounds like harrowing duty for a transport crew, but it's not. Never ones to leave much to chance, the Japanese usually hire their own security staff—just to guard the Strads.

Kenneth Slowik, right, director of the Smithsonian Chamber Music Program, plays the *Servais* cello, the only permanent Stradivari in the National Museum of American History's collections. Above, under tight security, then museum specialist Bill Yardley loads the *Servais* onto a van for a trip.

Although we treat our Strads like gold, never let them out of our sight, and do everything we can to protect the delicate spruce-and-maple bodies from fluctuations in temperature and humidity, there is a certain irony in all this caution. After all, might not the great musicians who have their own Strads sometimes forget them in a restroom stall at Carnegie Hall or absent-mindedly leave them sitting next to a hot radiator?

I'd like to ask a great violinist like Isaac Stern about this, but he probably wouldn't understand. With nothing but a horsehair bow, Stern pulls life from a 300-year-old piece of dead wood, and makes it sing.

Me, I just haul the things around.

Bill Yardley, currently Art Coordinator for the America's Smithsonian *exhibition, was a Museum Specialist in the Division of Musical History from 1991 to 1994.*

today as Sri Lanka—Ripley trained and equipped agents heading for Siam (Thailand), Malaya, Java, Sumatra, and other areas of Japanese domination. He also fell under the sway of Ceylonese bird life, collected hundreds of specimens, which he sent back to the Smithsonian, and named a newly discovered species after General Donovan.

While in Ceylon, Ripley's passion for collecting may have caused him some momentary embarrassment. One evening, while shaving, he spied a rare green wood-pecker, *Picus chlorolophus wellsi*, that he wanted for his collection. Clad only in a towel, he rushed outside to shoot it, forgetting that Admiral Lord Louis Mountbatten, Supreme Allied Commander in Southeast Asia, was host-ing a cocktail party just a hundred yards away. The blast from the gun caused Ripley's towel to fall off. Lord Mount-batten was less than pleased with Ripley's unconven-tional behavior and lack of attire, but Ripley was unfazed.

After the war Ripley returned to the United States, and was appointed both assistant professor of zoology at Yale and associate curator of zoology at the university's Peabody Museum of Natural History. Having secured the time and the means to pursue his passion, he wrote about birds and published widely. His first book, *Trail of the Money Bird*, published in 1942, was a naturalistic work with a politically prescient title.

In 1949 he married Mary Livingston, who, while nurturing her own interests in photography, insects, and horticulture, shared his love of adventure. He later boasted of teaching her to skin birds and to preserve them. At their private aviary, "Paddling Ponds," on the Ripley country property in Litchfield, Connecticut, they collect-ed and bred rare species. Their joint ornithological expe-ditions to India and Nepal were often arduous, but were taken in stride by the independent Mary.

In 1959 Ripley became director of the Peabody. Soon thereafter, he set up an organization, the Peabody Associates, to raise money for the museum, and put into

At right, one of the horses from the Smithsonian's carousel. In 1977 the Secretary and special guests cele-brated the carousel's 10-year anniversary on the Mall in front of the Arts and Industries Building, where it remains today a popular attraction.

The collections of the National Postal Museum, which opened in 1993, include this inverted stamp and one honoring the Smithsonian, a romantic airmail portrait, mementos of a postal crime, and the package, far right (top), that brought the Hope diamond from New York to the Institution.

practice both a flamboyant style and a kind of practicality that would serve him well in times to come.

In 1964, when the Smithsonian's Regents chose Ripley to succeed Leonard Carmichael, they chose a scientist whose eclectic interests and considerable knowledge encompassed such diverse subjects as Oriental porcelains, early American silver, and railroad locomotives. More sophisticated than any of his predecessors, his declared allegiance, at least, was to research, which, he later told an interviewer, "is as much a goal for the Smithsonian today as it was in Henry's time." Yet the scope and audacity of his plans for the Smithsonian's "increase & diffusion of knowledge" would have amazed even that ever-collecting builder of the old National Museum, Spencer Baird.

Within a week of Ripley's arrival at the Castle that February, things began to change. According to William Warner, who became head of the Office of International Activities that Ripley created, the Secretary "laid out so many bold initiatives…that all of us with previous government experience were plunged into what can only be called a deep state of shock."

On only his second day on the job, Warner was sent to Congress to attend a hearing. The item to be discussed that interested Ripley was the proposed relocation of the giant monuments of King Rameses II and Queen Nefertiti at Abu Simbel, on the Nile River. "I thought to myself," Warner later recalled, "It's very nice that the Secretary takes an interest in such things. But how marginal, really."

The eventual outcome of Ripley's interest, however, and of his political élan—he had sent Warner on to the Senate to help save Abu Simbel—was a Congressional appropriation of funds and an agreement whereby the Smithsonian oversaw the archaeological grants associated with this colossal undertaking. Out of that victory would

(Text continued on page 326)

323

THE SAGA OF THE HEADSVILLE P.O.

by ELLEN RONEY HUGHES

During the mid to late 1960s, as part of a new social-history movement in museums, historians at the National Museum of American History (NMAH) sought to recreate an example of an American institution that had once served as the heart of communication and commerce in small-town America: the post office-general store. "The historical importance of such a typically rural American institution was obvious. And it was also obvious that for many decades the mails which welded the nation's people and commerce together reached virtually every community through small post offices," wrote then postal-history curator Carl H. Scheele.

Equipped with an 1890 *Postal Guide,* a camera, and camping gear, Scheele set out in 1969 to find a historic building to bring back to the museum and re-establish as a working post office. Practical restrictions narrowed the possibilities: The building had to be a 19th-century structure with little modernization; it had to fit into a modest floor area 14 feet high; it had to be available for acquisition; it had to be made of wood so that it could be reconstructed; and it had to be located within a 300-mile radius of Washington, D.C., a reasonable distance over which to move a building.

Scheele, usually accompanied by his wife, Joanne, and their two children, looped through small communities along rural roads, and photographed, measured, evaluated, and rejected more than 600 specimens. One year, 10,000 miles, and 13 states later, during a trip that wound through the Ohio Valley, Kentucky, and Tennessee, a casual chat with a highway flagman led to Headsville, West Virginia. At first sight of the boarded-up building, Scheele knew that the search had ended. A slat nailed over the letter chute proved that it had served the mails; old merchandise, including high-button shoes still on the shelves, told the rest.

Around 1860, proprietor Henry Head built the general store that served the little community of Sheetz's Mill, Virginia. Head acquired and lost the postmastership as the political situation changed, and the town switched its name to Headsville in 1863, when it became part of West Virginia. In 1932, the store closed, and the building was shuttered. It dozed undisturbed until 1971, when Head's descendants enthusiastically sold it to the Smithsonian for $7,000.

The structure was carefully diagramed, dismantled, numbered, fumigated, and transported to Washington by historic-restoration specialist Charles Rowell and other NMAH staff members, including the indefatigable Scheele. Just as carefully, it was reconstructed—minus about 20 feet—

Above, the old Headsville, West Virginia, general store and post office, which was built in 1860, closed in 1932, discovered by Smithsonian postal-history curator Carl Scheele in the late 1960s, and then painstakingly dismantled and transported to Washington. At right, the recreated building once again open for business as an official post office, circa 1910, at the National Museum of American History.

back at the museum to fit into a space near the Constitution Avenue entrance.

The interior was designed to look as it might have around 1910. Buggy whips, spice tins, shoes, patent medicines, buttons, and other goods originally found on the shelves were amply augmented with objects from the museum's H.K. Seybolt General Store Collection, as well as with new purchases from hardware stores. The U.S. Postal Service supplied the Smithsonian Station with its own postmark and a small staff to operate the

post office as a "living exhibit." On September 27, 1971, Daniel Boorstin, then director of the museum, and Carl Scheele proudly presided over the opening ceremonies.

Throughout the 1970s, the postal employees acted as historic interpreters while dispensing stamps and stamping mail; they wore the garb of an earlier era, and related the structure's history. Today the employees no longer interpret history, but they, as well as the preserved structure and the recreated exhibit, serve as a monument to the significant role the general store-post office played in 19th-century America, while still fulfilling its timeless postal function.

Ellen Roney Hughes is a Cultural Historian at the National Museum of American History.

At right, a World War I-era B & O Railroad factory in Baltimore employed a humming web of belts to power its machinery. Opposite, at the National Museum of American History, an 1850s Robbins & Lawrence metal lathe, with patented Howe tool-feed motion, holds the equipment of Harwinton, Connecticut, machinist Augustus Alfred.

grow the Foreign Currency Program, which, during Ripley's tenure, enabled the Institution to grant $53 million to more than 200 American universities for work on some 800 overseas projects and thus increase the general store of knowledge.

THE MONTH BEFORE RIPLEY WAS SWORN IN, THE new Museum of History and Technology (today's National Museum of American History) opened on Constitution Avenue. It may have owed its existence to former Secretary Carmichael, but its scope served as a symbol of Ripley's determination to expand both the Smithsonian's facilities and its staff.

Only a dozen or so of the 50 exhibition halls set up on three of the museum's five floors were ready for the public, but the impressive if utilitarian building included such crowd-pleasing attractions as a basement cafeteria next to a sunken garden and Southern Railway's resplendent green-and-gold 1401 locomotive, one of the most popular exhibits from the start.

Beginning with Colonial times, the museum would feature as many examples of American cultural and technological developments as possible, with exhibits including the first Secret Service mug book, the first American postal issue, and the first machine-made pocket watch. Within three years, the museum had received an average of 15,000 visitors a day, more than any other Smithsonian bureau.

IN ADDITION TO RIPLEY'S UNDERLYING PROFES-
sional interest in ornithology and history, he was also
deeply interested in art. When he saw an early opportunity to make his mark in this field, he acted: In June
1964, he wrote to Joseph H. Hirshhorn, who had made
millions in uranium mining, and expressed an interest
in Hirshhorn's unprecedented collection of modern art.

Among the approximately 4,000 paintings and
1,600 pieces of sculpture belonging to Hirshhorn were
works by Henry Moore, Willem de Kooning, Alberto
Giacometti, Edgar Degas, Henri Matisse, Honoré Daumier,
Auguste Rodin, Pablo Picasso, Thomas Eakins, Ben Shahn,
Stuart Davis, Andrew Wyeth, Jackson Pollock, and hundreds of other artists. Understandably, the governments
of Britain, Canada, and Israel, as well as museum groups
in Zurich, Baltimore, Los Angeles, and New York, all
were interested in acquiring Hirshhorn's collection. But
none of them could match Ripley's energy and persuasiveness once he had set his sights on these treasures.

The Secretary was not deterred by the fact that
the diminutive, energetic Hirshhorn had no connection
to the Washington art establishment. He told Hirshhorn
that the Smithsonian had a "lively interest" in establishing an American art museum like the Tate Gallery, in
London: "The National Gallery of Art, with its emphasis
on the arts of Europe and the past, leaves the capital and
the nation with no proper equivalent.... We would be
most happy to explore this concept with you."

In the fall of 1964, Ripley visited Hirshhorn in
Greenwich, Connecticut, to discuss with him the Smithsonian and its purpose. Although their backgrounds could
not have been more dissimilar, they got on; Ripley later
described Hirshhorn as "a wonderful man, in love with
his collection."

Ripley also arranged for Mr. and Mrs. Hirshhorn
to be invited to a White House luncheon that he was to

(Text continued on page 332)

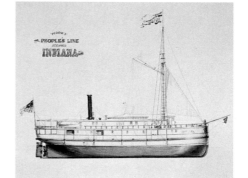

In 1979 the Smithsonian recovered
the 10-foot-in-diameter propeller of
the 1848 steamer *Indiana*, the oldest of its type known, from the bottom of Lake Superior. A yellow line
marks the place where, in 1858, the
blade broke off, causing the ship to
sink. The *Indiana* itself was called a
propeller in those days to distinguish it from the more common
paddle-wheelers.

STARING AT THE MIGHTY

by EDWARDS PARK

Ask your average queen, visiting Washington, where she wants to go, and instead of shouting "Disneyland!" she's apt to murmur, regally, "the Smithsonian." To a humble person like myself, that's a great fillip. I'm happy that queens—and kings, princesses, Princes of Wales, Emperors of Japan, Archbishops of Canterbury, Dalai Lamas, Grand Patriarchs, popes, prime ministers, presidents, and probably some others that I have inexcusably forgotten (all with spouses where applicable)—come to look us over. We certainly like to stare at them.

Soon after my employment at the Institution began in 1969, I started upon a career of outrageous rubbernecking. I thrilled at the roar of escorting motorcycles, the whisper of long limousines. I admired the discreet pinstripes worn by our Smithsonian greeters. I marveled at the tailoring of the male VIPs and the decorous hats of the ladies, and realized that Queen Elizabeth's royal wave with gently cupped hand was often simply her need to keep her hat from blowing off in an open car.

I stared at two of Queen Elizabeth's visits, amazed at her cool expertise at listening raptly to re-readings of James Smithson's will while her mind was on her demanding "shedule." I knew what she was thinking: "Only eight minutes for this lot. For goodness sake, let's get on with it!"

The Queen did, however, once look up at Secretary S. Dillon Ripley (about a yard taller than she) when he murmured some pleasantry, and favored him with a sudden delighted, little-girl grin. It was enough to make us Queen-watchers forgive every past transgression of the old Empire, and also to wonder what in the world the Secretary had said.

Queen Beatrix of the Netherlands proved to be so attractive that three mounted park policemen chose to clop alongside her limo when she whisked up to the Hirshhorn for an art show from her country. Her consort, Prince Claus, looked like actor Joel McCrea. Maybe…. Whatever happened to Joel McCrea, anyway?

Beautiful Queen Margrethe II of Denmark dashed through an exhibit at the National Portrait Gallery and was so delighted that she dubbed the museum's director a Knight of Dannebrog. Disappointingly, she failed to whack him on the back with a sword.

Hirohito, Emperor of Japan, was admitted to the bewildering innards of the National Museum of Natural History to check his private collection of hydroids with ours. He was heavily guarded. Standing outside, all agape, I glanced up at the roof and found two policemen staring coldly

Among the dignitaries greeted by Secretary Ripley during his tenure were England's Queen Elizabeth (with Vice President Nelson Rockefeller in the background), Pope John Paul II, and the exiled Dalai Lama of Tibet.

down at me, one watching through binoculars, the other holding a rifle.

We not only safeguarded Hirohito, but we also honored him with music from the giant orchestrion that used to entertain us in the old Arts and Industries Building. It played a selection from "The Mikado."

"Mikado" is a nice sounding name for man or musical. But the title "King of Spain" has a matchless ring to it. When Juan Carlos, looking the way the King of Spain ought to look, popped into the National Museum of American History, I watched avidly. Tall, handsome, charming, he strode from limo to pinstriped receiving line, turned toward us onlookers, and warmed us with a smile and a wave.

"Who is that?" asked a pretty stenographer.

"The King of Spain," I replied, letting the words roll out with their own blare of trumpets and roll of drums.

"Oh, wow!" she said. Everyone said that, back then, but this time it was exactly right.

"Prince of Wales" always sounds good to Americans, because they often visit us and like us. So when Charles showed up at Air and Space, I did, too, cordoned off well away from his arrival. It was raining, and I got soaked by the spray from a police car. I don't recall much about the Prince of Wales, except that he looked nice and dry. But my meticulous report of the event drew letters, all saying that never before in the field of journalism had so much been written about so little.

We rubberneckers all share a blessing that eludes our VIP visitors. Unlike them, we don't have to rush through our Smithsonian adventure. We have no strictures on what to see and learn, no lackeys reminding us that we're due at the President's Blue Room in 12 minutes. How lucky we are to partake of this feast on the Mall without a thought for our diet!

Edwards Park is one of the original Board of Editors for Smithsonian *magazine and for many years wrote the popular column "Around the Mall and beyond."*

attend with Roger L. Stevens, chairman of the John F. Kennedy Center for the Performing Arts—a titular arm of the Smithsonian—and Abe Fortas, a Washington lawyer who would soon become an Associate Justice of the Supreme Court. President Lyndon B. Johnson made a brief appearance, and Mrs. Johnson told Hirshhorn that she was interested in the prospect of a museum in Washington to house his collection.

In August 1965, the first lady and her older daughter, Lynda Bird, went to Greenwich to see Hirshhorn's art. Shortly thereafter, Hirshhorn suffered a heart attack. While he was recovering, he received a letter of condolence from President Johnson, prompted by "our friend Dillon Ripley." The President wrote that he had "a very considerable interest" in the prospect of a new museum, and hoped to "have the opportunity to see both you and your collection."

The course was now set for a new, thoroughly modern Smithsonian art bureau that would offer numerous contrasts with the staid National Gallery across the Mall. (In terms of appearance, the Hirshhorn's unusual, daring construction would inspire some to refer to it as "the doughnut.")

IN 1965 THE BICENTENNIAL ANNIVERSARY OF James Smithson's birth provided Ripley with his first opportunity to publicly display his vision of the Smithsonian's future. The idea for a celebration had arisen during Carmichael's administration, but it was Ripley who imbued it with excitement and institutional pride.

Staffing a bicentennial office next to his, he set up committees to deal with the many necessities, including the design of a Smithsonian mace and emblem, the construction of pavilions on the Mall, and the composition of music for this unprecedented event. To help accommodate the crowds that would be attending what Ripley envisioned as a public spectacle, arrangements were made

The Smithsonian's Anacostia Museum, which first opened in Southeast Washington's old Carver Theater in 1967, moved to a new building at nearby Fort Place, top, in 1989. Among its collections is this 1855 quilt made by Kissie Gary, who was a slave on the Owen Plantation in Columbia, South Carolina. In 1987 author Alex Haley made a public service announcement to encourage people to visit the Anacostia Museum.

with the National Park Service for water, lavatories, trash collection, and cleanup.

Advice was gleaned from the National Academy of Sciences, which had recently celebrated its centennial, and from Brown University, which had recently celebrated its bicentennial year. Some 800 room reservations were made at the Shoreham Hotel alone, and a block of rooms was reserved at the Willard Hotel. A dozen world-renowned scholars were asked to discourse on the state of knowledge in their respective fields. Eleven of them, including Arthur Koestler, George Evelyn Hutchinson, Sir Kenneth Clark, Lewis Mumford, Robert Oppenheimer, Claude Lévi-Strauss, and Fred L. Whipple, accepted. Invitations addressed by 20 secretaries went out to 3,500 special guests.

A grandstand was set up in front of the Natural History Museum, and the statue of Joseph Henry was turned so that it no longer faced the Castle but gazed out over a breadth of activities the first Secretary could not have imagined and probably would have deplored.

At 4 P.M., on September 16, a trumpet fanfare sounded from the rampart above the entryway of the Castle. A herald read aloud a Presidential proclamation commemorating the events, and a grand procession of dignitaries in bright academic robes—Ripley's had been specially designed—then crossed from the Castle toward the Museum of Natural History to strains of a Sousa march, under clear skies that former Secretary Abbot, using sunspot calculations, had predicted.

Included were the Institution's chancellor, the Regents, former Regents and Secretaries, university presidents, museum directors, foundation representatives, trustees of various art galleries, U.S. government dignitaries, and foreign ambassadors and other representatives from 90 countries.

The mace at the head of the procession had been

(Text continued on page 338)

ALL THAT JAZZ

by JOHN EDWARD HASSE

Electricity charged the air. Dozens of reporters, seven TV cameras, and scores of fans packed the Presidential Reception Suite at the National Museum of American History (NMAH). John Birks "Dizzy" Gillespie—one of the leading music innovators of the 20th century—had come to donate his trademark uptilted trumpet to the nation. After being introduced by then museum director Roger G. Kennedy, Gillespie held forth for nearly an hour, alternately serious and funny, always generous and endearing. Then, as if to summarize the presentation ceremonies, a British reporter spoke up. "Mr. Gillespie," he intoned, "what will that trumpet of yours say in 500 years?" "In 500 years," Gillespie deadpanned, "that trumpet ain't gonna say *nothing!*"

In 1985 my colleagues and I in NMAH's Division of Musical History began building a collection that would document one of the most significant musical genres America has produced—jazz. I had written Gillespie, asking that he donate his instrument to the museum, but months passed with no reply. The late critic Martin Williams, who had been producing acclaimed jazz record anthologies for the Institution, advised, "Get Lorraine [Dizzy's wife] involved." So I wrote her, asking if they'd agree to donate his trumpet. Four days later, a big box arrived in the mail, containing a well-traveled trumpet case with the prize inside!

A few months later, Duke Ellington's son, Mercer, notified a colleague in the division that the maestro's archives had not yet found a home. Here, within the Smithsonian's grasp, was a vast treasure trove that turned out to include 200,000 pages of materials—half of them original, unpublished music—along with publicity scrapbooks going back to 1930 and the Cotton Club era, business records, 2,000 photographs, and such memorabilia as the Presidential Medal of Freedom, which President Nixon awarded Ellington in 1969.

The museum began negotiations with the Ellington estate. Word of the collection reached Capitol Hill, and funds were earmarked for its acquisition, its transfer to Washington, and the daunting job of sorting, cataloging, preserving, and disseminating its contents to the public. In 1987, the U.S. Congress had passed a joint resolution that declared jazz "a rare and valuable American national treasure." Some members viewed the Institution's acquisition of the Ellington trove as the next logical step in the federal government's support of this music.

The Smithsonian jazz program has increasingly picked up steam

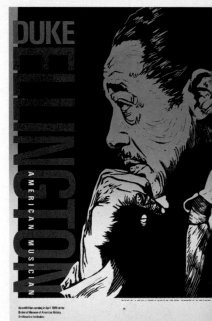

In 1985 jazz great Dizzy Gillespie, above, donated his trumpet, in its original case, to the National Museum of American History's Division of Musical History. Soon thereafter the Smithsonian acquired Duke Ellington's archive of more than 200,000 items, including this poster.

since 1988. The acquisition of the Ellington Collection, and of Gillespie's trumpet, has attracted other donations. These include 30 smaller collections of Ellington material, Benny Goodman's clarinet, Buddy Rich's drum set, Jimmie Lunceford's band music, and the Ernie Smith Collection of Jazz Films.

In addition, the Smithsonian Jazz Oral History Program—whose

Ellington's music and that of other big-band masters in free concerts for the American public. Under the direction of preeminent musicians David Baker and Gunther Schuller, the SJMO has become one of the most distinctive and acclaimed offerings of the Institution, taking jazz directly to the people. The 1995 season offered a series of concerts in Washington, a nationwide tour, and its own public-radio program called "Jazz Smithsonian."

Yet another program, Jazz Masterworks Editions (JME), operates in conjunction with the SJMO. JME has provided America's professional jazz bands and some 17,000 big bands at the high-school and college level the opportunity to perform the music of the masters—the same kind played by the SJMO. Because many pieces of classic jazz are still unpublished, JME has prepared and disseminated authentic transcriptions of jazz masterworks, including those of Ellington, Lunceford, Fletcher Henderson, and Count Basie. By making this music available, JME hopes to engage a new generation of players and audiences, and to inspire it to keep this music alive.

The Smithsonian jazz program took a quantum leap in 1991, when the Lila Wallace-Reader's Digest Fund established a $7-million, 10-year partnership with the Institution, called America's Jazz Heritage. This was the largest sum of money anyone had ever given to promote jazz, and the largest single grant the Smithsonian had received up to that time. The partnership provided for a series of traveling exhibitions, circulated by the Smithsonian Institution Traveling Exhibition Service. The first offerings were an Ellington exhibition, which will reach nearly 60 cities, and a show on Louis Armstrong.

Through generous outside donations and agency-wide cooperation, the Smithsonian has created the world's most comprehensive jazz program to document, preserve, and disseminate this important, lively, and enjoyable part of American culture.

mission is to preserve the life stories of leading musicians—has recorded more than 90 interviews with the likes of J.J. Johnson, Cab Calloway, and Artie Shaw.

In 1990 Congress authorized NMAH to establish the Smithsonian Jazz Masterworks Orchestra (SJMO), a 19-member ensemble, to perform

John Edward Hasse is Curator of American Music at the National Museum of American History, founder and executive director of the Smithsonian Jazz Masterworks Orchestra, and co-director of America's Jazz Heritage.

designed with the advice of the Worshipful Company of Goldsmiths in London, and enhanced with jewels from the Smithsonian's reserve stocks. The Institution's flag was emblazoned with a red demi-lion holding in its paws the sun "in splendor"—the crest of Smithson's father, Sir Hugh.

In addition, each Smithsonian bureau was represented by a blue flag bearing the sun symbol. The Marine Corps Band played the commissioned musical pieces (wincing at the atonal modern compositions). After remarks and speeches, a gala dinner was held at the Museum of History and Technology, followed by a reception at the White House.

The celebration, wrote Paul Oehser in his book *The Smithsonian Institution*, "lent a certain carnival air to the Mall that has never gone away. Band concerts, chamber music from the Smithsonian tower, carousels, kite-flying, balloon flights, barbershop quartet singing, and other divertissements, all in the open air, became the order of the day."

THE EFFECT OF THE BICENTENNIAL OF JAMES Smithson's birth, with its pomp and broad representation, was to reaffirm the Smithsonian as an essential part of the Washington establishment and a vital depository of national treasure, intellectual and otherwise. Still thought of as "the nation's attic," a notion that went back to the 1880s, the Smithsonian was in fact becoming a more open and popular Institution, with its various bureaus serving as part of the entirety rather than as independent agencies.

The bicentennial also boosted S. Dillon Ripley quickly and unequivocally into the limelight, where he was seen as a serious player in the politics of culture. According to David Challinor, a biologist who had worked with Ripley in New Haven and who took over the Smithsonian's Office of International Activities before being named Assistant Secretary for Science in 1971, Ripley's

style of operating "was to delegate authority, and set policy....He would have an idea, and say, 'See if it will work.' "

Ripley was not particularly collegial. He called meetings, told people what he wanted, and let them work out the details. If the project was of particular interest to him, attention was lavished on it. If a dinner he considered important was being planned, Ripley would ask the caterer to serve it to him and his advisers first, so it could be judged. Featured in these assessments were fine wines, a standard at the Ripley Smithsonian.

His inner circle of advisers included the Institution's general counsel, Peter Powers; Assistant Secretary James Bradley, who was credited by his associates as "the man who knew where the money was"; and the director of the Office of Education and Training, Charles Blitzer. Blitzer was hired to bring graduate students into the Smithsonian, and later became Assistant Secretary for History and Art.

Philip Ritterbush, an assistant to the Secretary who in 1968 was appointed director of academic programs, was the closest adviser to the Secretary. "I liked him to shock me into new ideas," Ripley later recalled about Ritterbush. "I wanted to revive the tradition of Baird, the ideal collector, who acted, as Ritterbush did to me, to spur Henry on."

With the help of these men, Ripley intended to broaden the Smithsonian's appeal while also enhancing its resources. Although Secretary Carmichael before him had softened Congress up, the Hill was still not particularly responsive to the Smithsonian's requests. And the first time Ripley appeared before the Bureau of the Budget, he later confided, "I felt I was up against a totally blank wall. I thought: 'What am I doing in Washington?' "

Yet in 1966, at a budget session on the Hill, members of Congress kept Ripley for more than two hours, asking broad-ranging questions. The Secretary conducted himself well, emphasizing the Smithsonian's research

Bow-tied philanthropist Joseph Hirshhorn inspects a model of the doughnut-shaped Hirshhorn Museum and Sculpture Garden with its first director, Abram Lerner. Hirshhorn's gift to the nation included Edward Hopper's *City Sunlight* (1954); Fernando Botero's *The Hunter* was acquired for the museum after 1980.

role, and received a budgetary increase from Congress of almost $4 million for fiscal year 1967.

RIPLEY DIDN'T WANT THE SMITHSONIAN BUREAUS to resemble the type of museum he had known as a child. As he described his early museum-going experiences, one closed oneself "away from the world and became very solemn-serious about it. You saw everywhere exhibits which were documented as precisely as the relics of the 'True Cross,' which, as everybody knows, were not real…. [I]t was essentially very dull. You did it on Sunday afternoon after a big lunch."

Ripley believed that he first had to get the attention of the public, and that he then had to develop a constituency large enough to command Congressional interest and support. One way to accomplish at least the first goal, he decided, was to stage camel races on the Mall, an idea he got while visiting Fez, Morocco. He put David Challinor in charge of finding the camels; when he learned that this plan was impractical, he urged that buses, to be pulled by camels, be provided instead, to transport tourists from museum to museum. This plan didn't materialize either.

Another idea, which he pursued more forcefully, was that of installing a carousel on the Mall. This again harkened back to Ripley's childhood days—those spent in the Tuileries in Paris—and would become a symbol of the Ripley era at the Smithsonian. He later described his vision: "I wanted to have Dutch music wagons and monkeys and hurdy-gurdies, and make the place a living experience…." Inside the museums, "We should take the objects out of the cases and make them sing…."

This vision led to the concept of a celebration of American folklife. As Ripley told the Regents in early 1967, "Although it has the world's largest collections of American folk artifacts, the Smithsonian, like all museums in our nation, fails to present folk culture fully and accurately."

Some members of Congress objected to what they saw as the potential violation of sacred ground. The Mall harbored the memories of Washington, Jefferson, and Lincoln—whose memorials were not far from the Castle, where Ripley wanted his carousel. Other politicians considered the Mall their private lawn, not a "midway."

Despite the criticism, the carousel arrived in April 1967, a fanciful but potent statement about the Ripley Smithsonian. The Secretary himself was seen riding the merry-go-round, his long legs wrapped around his wooden mount. That same spring, the first Festival of American Folklife took place, featuring such expressions of American folk art as fife-and-drum groups, gospel singers, Puerto Rican and Cajun music, King Island Eskimo dancers, and the crafts of basket makers, potters, and silversmiths.

SEEKING TO PLAY TO THE SENSES THROUGHOUT the Institution, Ripley suggested adding the aroma of chocolate to an exhibit of a 19th-century confectionary at the Museum of History and Technology and a recording of a trumpeting elephant in the rotunda at Natural History. (This latter innovation caused such a distraction that after a few weeks it was discontinued.)

The Secretary took responsibility for the actions of his assistants, and personally involved himself in promotional events. Many of the Regents were uncomfortable with all this activity, including Ripley's courtship of Joseph Hirshhorn. The Secretary, on the other hand, wanted to break what a colleague called the "WASP" glass ceiling—the transparent but seemingly impermeable barrier to anyone who was not white, Anglo-Saxon, and Protestant and aspired to positions of influence at the Smithsonian. "He had to be a WASP to do it," said Challinor. "He handled the board with kid gloves."

His combination of diplomacy and determination led to the appointment of Murray Gell-Mann, a Nobel

An 1879 photograph shows the original second-floor lobby of the Old Patent Office Building, which, restored to its former glory, joined the Smithsonian as the National Portrait Gallery in 1965. Here, prior to the gallery's opening, its first director, Charles Nagel, appears with a painting of Pocahantas by an unknown artist and George Peter Alexander Healy's 1887 portrait of President Abraham Lincoln.

Photographer Arnold Newman captured the essence of composer Igor Feodorovich Stravinsky in a portrait now in the National Portrait Gallery's collections. Artist Winold Reiss's son donated Reiss's pastel drawing of poet Langston Hughes to the National Portrait Gallery in his father's memory.

laureate, as the first Jewish person to serve on the Board of Regents. "Ripley was able to do something about elitism because he was socially and economically impeccable."

IN THE MID-1960S, RIPLEY UNDERTOOK A UNIQUE, controversial project a distance from the Mall in a poor Washington, D.C., neighborhood across the Anacostia River. He felt that, located as it was in a city whose population at the time was approximately 70 percent black, the Smithsonian should offer more that would be of interest to this community, as well as to minority visitors from other countries.

In his pursuit of a broader constituency for the Institution, Ripley realized that it was imperative to bring in people who might not otherwise be attracted to it and who were conspicuously absent from its museums and galleries. Consulting with advisers, he decided to create a special museum for Washington's black community in one of the most historic and stable black neighborhoods in Washington.

In 1966, Julian T. Euell, a community worker and jazz musician, served as a consultant on the idea of an Anacostia museum. In 1969 he was brought in as deputy and later Assistant Secretary for Public Service, and helped develop the Anacostia Neighborhood Museum, the first of its kind in the nation. Euell was the first African American to hold such a high-level position at the Smithsonian. On the day the museum opened— September 15, 1967—in a converted theater on what was to be named Martin Luther King Avenue, Ripley arrived for the ceremonies with such dignitaries as the city's Mayor-designate, Walter Washington.

Directed by prominent local minister John Kinard, the new museum featured six exhibits designed for visitor interaction: a reproduction of an 1890 neighborhood store, a full-scale mockup of the Mercury space capsule, a small zoo, natural-science objects, skeletons that could

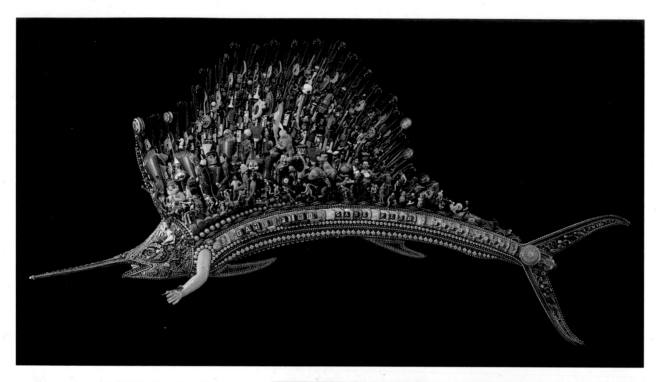

In 1962 First Lady Jacqueline Kennedy reviews plans for the restoration of Lafayette Square, including the Renwick Gallery, which opened in 1972. Larry Fuente's 1988 *Game Fish* is one of the Renwick's more fanciful pieces, while Dale Chihuly's spectacular vinyl, mylar, and plexiglass piece, a temporary installation at the Renwick, served as a backdrop for a production of Claude Debussy's opera Pelleus and Melisande.

The Renwick was designed by James Renwick, Jr., the architect of the Smithsonian Castle. Harvey Kline

Littleton's 1977 *Four Seasons*, opposite, is one of the Renwick's unusual glass pieces.

be disassembled, and a small theater for the viewing of closed-circuit television.

During its first year, the Anacostia museum attracted 80,000 visitors from all over the city.

IN 1968, DURING A MARCH IN WASHINGTON TO protest the Vietnam war, Ripley insisted that all the museums stay open, and that protestors be allowed to use the facilities. This shocked and dismayed many old-liners within the Institution, who predicted disaster for the collections. But no damage occurred, and Ripley's belief that the museums belonged to the people was once again vindicated.

Throughout these diversions, Ripley maintained the Smithsonian's momentum in the art field. In 1968 the National Portrait Gallery and the National Collection of Fine Arts opened in the refurbished Patent Office Building. In 1972 the Renwick Gallery became Ripley's first major acquisition for the Institution. Designed by James Renwick in 1859 as the original Corcoran Gallery, it had come into the Smithsonian's possession after the Secretary, over lunch at the White House, persuaded President Johnson to tour the building with him. They had walked across Pennsylvania Avenue to the corner of 17th Street to inspect the beautiful, historic structure—which would later take as its focus American design—and the President, impressed

with the Secretary's presentation, had declared it "Sold!"

Ripley knew that the best way to perform meaningful research in all fields was to provide funding that was not totally dependent upon the government. He set up additional trust funds for the Smithsonian, and hired professionals to manage them. He also courted donors. A trust fund offered by J. Seward Johnson led to the establishment in 1969 of the Smithsonian Marine Station at Link Port, a bureau for oceanographic research in Fort Pierce, Florida. Meanwhile, the government funded the Museum Support Center, in Suitland, Maryland, for the storage and maintenance of the Smithsonian's vast natural-history and technology collections.

The Secretary had helped raise private funds for the Renwick, but he also recognized the importance of the Institution's making money. He hired a business manager to expand the museum shops; the shop at the Museum of Natural History soon proved so popular that it had to be expanded to accommodate the crowds. A mail-order catalog was introduced, and additional cafeterias—providing food once available from local shops and vendors—opened. But Ripley needed a steadier, greater source of income for the realization of his grand design.

In 1965 the old *Annual Report* was replaced by the more accessible *Smithsonian Year*, which offered less detailed information about the Institution's growing bureaus and more about current events and future projects. Advance planning for *Smithsonian* magazine, the real revolution in publishing at the Institution, would start in late 1968.

RIPLEY NEEDED A SPECIFIC VEHICLE FOR HIS expansion. Just as he had sought to open up the Board of Regents, and broaden the Smithsonian's appeal through the Resident and National Associates programs—part of a drive, started in 1965 and 1970 respectively, to raise money for the Institution and to increase its visibility—he now fought for the creation of a bright, lively maga-

zine that would entertain as well as inform. Some Regents did not like the idea of a magazine, but among them were prominent business leaders who made the Secretary justify his proposals and then backed him up.

In 1968 Ripley hired a former managing editor of *Life* magazine, Edward K. Thompson, who brought in six other editors to develop the project. They were given various, sometimes inconvenient, offices in the Arts and Industries Building, easily accessible to Ripley, whose office in the east wing of the Castle gave him a view of both the museum and the Capitol in the distance. Edwards Park, one of the original board of editors, recalled Ripley dropping by to determine what articles were being planned and generally to urge the project along. "Because he was tall he was constantly bumping his head on the exposed steam pipes. He would say brightly, of our cramped quarters, 'This will bring out the best in you.' "

During the 18 months it took to plan and execute the magazine, the editorial staff determined that *Smithsonian* would present "soft" science, history, and art through photographs and good reporting and writing. And it would exercise some independence from the rest of the Institution. One of the editors, the late Ralph Backlund, characterized the magazine's field of inquiry as "everything the Smithsonian is interested in, will be interested in, or ought to be interested in"—or, in general, the world, with emphasis on the specific theme of "man and his environment." The magazine would be offered to members of the Smithsonian Associates.

Many at the Smithsonian remained skeptical about the magazine. Some felt it offered the unnecessary popularization, even trivialization, of the Institution's work and mandate. The new editors were shunned for many years by professional staffers, particularly those at Natural History, who considered them mere "publicists."

If the magazine did not succeed, Ripley's advisers agreed, the Regents would fire him.

Luis Jiménez's 1980 Vaquero, a 16-and-1/2-foot fiberglass-and-acrylic-urethane sculpture, greets visitors at the entrance to the National Museum of American Art.

PROFILE
WINGS

The National Air and Space Museum was one of many buildings that spread their wings on the Mall during S. Dillon Ripley's administration. It had been in the planning for decades—first as collections, then as the official National Air Museum. Now it was the grand culmination of everything related to flight.

While tolerant of the aeronautical collections, former Secretaries had been more interested in their own specialties. Even Carl W. Mitman, who had served as Assistant to the Secretary for the National Air Museum and had believed in the development of airplanes as an important part of American progress, had resisted some acquisitions on grounds that they were not "aeronautic." These included the NC-4, the U.S. Navy's flying boat, which had made the first transatlantic flight in 1919, and Goddard's rocketry artifacts. Eventually, of course, these were included in the collections.

In 1919 the U.S. Army had turned over to the Smithsonian a temporary Aircraft Building (located next to the Arts and Industries museum) that had housed the Signal Corps during World War I. After the building's opening in 1920, the public had been mesmerized by the exhibits, which over the years included the swept-wing Bell X-1, astronaut John H. Glenn, Jr.'s *Friendship 7* spacecraft, and Wiley Post's *Winnie Mae*.

Secretary Alexander Wetmore had persuaded Congress to formally create the National Air Museum against the wishes of some in the military who, backed by the Bureau of the Budget, had wanted to make a proposed National Military Museum the stage for this material. But Air Museum curator Paul Garber and Senator Jennings Randolph of West Virginia played active roles in promoting a grander air museum. Secretary Leonard Carmichael obtained funds for an architectural study, and a government search committee, which included Smithsonian representatives, began looking for an appropriate location.

In 1958, after rejecting various sites around

In 1961, one month after the successful launch of Soviet Cosmonaut Yuri Gagarin, Alan Shepard became the first American to rocket into space. Today Shepard's *Freedom 7* spacecraft is on display in the National Air and Space Museum's Milestones of Flight hall. Earlier, James Doolittle earned this Medal of Honor for the 1942 Tokyo bombing raid he led during World War II.

Washington, an expanse of green on the Mall between Arts and Industries and the Capitol was chosen. Philip S. Hopkins, head of the department of aeronautics at Norwich University in Northfield, Vermont, became the new museum's first director. Prefiguring a struggle between two often competing realms, the National Air Museum's name was amended to include the words "and Space" in 1966.

Six years later, Congress approved $40 million for construction of a building designed by architect Gyo Obata. Over the next few years it rose on Independence Avenue, a broad, towering structure that could accommodate huge aircraft and spacecraft and leave lasting impressions of flight. Secretary S. Dillon Ripley announced, "The museum will be a 'window on the world,' showing America's excellence in productivity, in creativity, and in technological ingenuity."

In June 1975, the first craft arrived—a Douglas World Cruiser, ushered in through a specially constructed 30-foot-by-20-foot door. The installation of the Skylab Orbital Workshop in the Space Hall required the lifting of the craft's upper two segments so that the third segment could be put into place; in the end, the 52-foot Skylab cleared the ceiling by a mere quarter of an inch.

A massive Saturn 5 F-1 engine was hoisted to the new museum's second floor and installed in the Apollo to the Moon Gallery. The most famous artifact, the Wright brothers' Kitty Hawk *Flyer*, made a decidedly anthropomorphic groan as it was lifted to its place of honor in the foyer. In June 1976, the last large artifact— a V-2 rocket—was hoisted into place by cranes that were then removed. (Meanwhile, in interesting juxtaposition, Arts and Industries became the site of a replication of the 1876 Centennial Exposition that had been held in Philadelphia and that had reflected the material progress in America during the country's first 100 years.)

The energetic leadership of former astronaut

The National Air and Space Museum's Milestones of Flight hall glows through one of the museum's giant walls of glass. In the hall's balcony hangs the Wright Model EX *Vin Fiz*, which, named for its grape-drink sponsor, made the first flight across the U.S. in 1911.

Michael Collins, who became director of the National Air and Space Museum in 1971, contributed substantially to the completion of the building and its exhibits ahead of schedule and $2 million under budget, a particularly extraordinary feat for the city of Washington.

On July 1, 1976, during the national bicentennial celebrations, the opening ceremony at the National Air and Space Museum brought together President Gerald Ford, Chief Justice Warren Burger, and a number of other dignitaries. Ripley suggested that the museum was a

"fitting expression of our collective interests…. The frontier shaped and molded our society and our people. Three and a half centuries later, our wilderness has been transformed…. Today millions around the world can hear—and see—the highlights of history as they are happening."

After a signal radioed back from the Viking spacecraft then near Mars burned through the opening-ceremony ribbon, the museum was thrown open to an eager crowd on the Mall. Inside, 23 different display areas offered visitors emblems of aeronautical progress:

a Gallery of Sea-Air Operations, a "touchable" moon rock, a "Spacearium," and films.

As many as 50,000 people a day were expected to visit the museum. Each person, according to C.D.B. Bryan, author of *The National Air and Space Museum*, was "affected personally by the sudden, unexpected intimacy of his contact with history,… so recent that it is not surprising when a Museum visitor is seen reaching hesitantly upward toward a spacecraft's heat shield, as if it might be still warm to the touch."

NOON OVER THE MALL

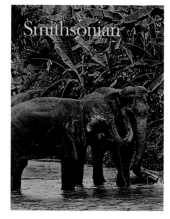

"An overcrowded museum is a healthy museum."

—S. DILLON RIPLEY
The Sacred Grove

Books, photographs, and artifacts in Secretary Emeritus S. Dillon Ripley's office in the National Museum of Natural History recall his life as an ornithologist. Above, the first issue of *Smithsonian* magazine, April 1970.

The first issue of Smithsonian magazine appeared in April 1970, emblazoned with a photograph of two elephants in Ceylon (Sri Lanka). The editors had decided that an animal would appear on every cover, although this decision wouldn't last. In any case, the magazine was an immediate success.

Early editions carried stories on such subjects as regulars in the U.S. Army, Paul Revere's horse, and the disastrous 1903 launching of Secretary Langley's plane, still a sore subject for some at the Smithsonian. This last article included lesser-known facts about the pilot, Charles Manly, such as that he had downed a shot of whiskey after being pulled from the Potomac and had used foul language—not the sort of information the public associated with the Smithsonian.

The magazine's initial circulation of 185,000 soon was augmented by a flood of new subscriptions, which, over the next five years, would approach the million mark. An ever increasing number of Smithsonian National Associates received the magazine automatically—an idea Ripley had gotten from the National Geographic Society—and the magazine's popularity continued to grow. As editor Edwards Park later recalled, "Nothing we did could fail. The science was interesting and appropriate. The staff had fun. It was a glorious time."

Ripley's energy and enthusiasm affected people in every bureau. He embodied the best of the era that had just past, symbolized by slain President John F. Kennedy. But the world had changed, and the

Smithsonian's need to keep abreast of it had aroused some resentment of what had become known as "the Ripley style."

His manner did not help to appease his critics: He could be pushy, and was often as much as an hour late for appointments. But he remained an astute judge of people, with an extraordinary memory for faces and names. He sometimes met with certain new employees in his Castle parlor, which was furnished with a blue-and-gold, Renaissance-revival settee; a 1690 Dutch cabinet used to exhibit insects; and a sculpture of a dodo—its feathers made of barnacles—under glass.

"[W]hether you were a scientist or an art historian or an expert on Americana," Edwards Park later wrote, "when you went through this ritual meeting, one-on-one with the Secretary, he would often ask one seemingly innocuous little question. This would neatly sum up all the fundamental problems…of your discipline."

Ripley could be forbidding. During staff meetings he would seem to be barely listening to some proposals, and suddenly announce, "No!" He did not necessarily compliment people who expected such recognition, nor did he remonstrate when a mistake was made, but maintained instead a glacial silence. He did not slap backs, and yet could write the most appreciative letters for services rendered.

Congress remained wary of Ripley's dynamism and independence, despite the fact that he went to considerable lengths to charm its members. These efforts included taking a pair of pistols—silver six-shooters—to the Hill for Congressional amusement and arranging for a baby orangutan, swaddled in a diaper, to be brought from the National Zoo to the Senate.

Some members of Congress had criticized the acquisition of the Hirshhorn collection; some now disagreed with the Smithsonian's decision to take over the almost bankrupt Cooper-Hewitt Museum of Decorative

Secretary Ripley (right) and the late Chief Justice and Smithsonian Chancellor Warren Burger arrive in a coach-in-four at the Arts and Industries Building on May 10, 1976, for the opening of "1876: A Centennial Celebration." At right, an antique insect cabinet (c. 1700) in Ripley's National Museum of Natural History office reflects the style of naturalist painter Jan van Kessel (1626–79). Ornithologist Ripley was often caricatured as a bird, top.

Arts and Design in New York City, a private endeavor that became the first Smithsonian museum located outside Washington.

The Cooper-Hewitt acquisition had been undertaken without any formal consultation with the Regents, or with Capitol Hill, and many in Congress resented this, particularly after bills for considerable amounts—for staff, building maintenance, guard service, heat, and light in the donated Carnegie Mansion where the museum was housed—came due.

THE SMITHSONIAN HAD PUBLISHED ITS FIRST BOOK in 1848; in 1966 its publishing division became known as Smithsonian Institution Press and developed into a fine university press that continued to put out scholarly works and research efforts, eventually joining forces with Smithsonian Books, a more popular, direct-mail publishing enterprise; the Smithsonian Collection of Recordings;

and Smithsonian Video. More recently, in 1986, the National Air and Space Museum began publishing its *AIR&SPACE/Smithsonian* magazine.

Meanwhile, money poured into the Smithsonian endowment. In the first 10 years of Ripley's administration, the Institution's operating expenses went from $17 million to $71 million, but a balance of sorts did prevail: 20 percent of the budgetary increase for 1975, for instance, went to science, 33 percent to administration, and 39 percent to the arts, perhaps the area of greatest expansion under Ripley.

The Secretary's high visibility—or lack thereof—proved risky, and, with the attention, brought more criticism. Despite the longstanding tradition of Secretaries' taking summers off to do research, some complained that Ripley frequently left the country when contentious issues arose concerning the Smithsonian. Congress and the press began to question his expeditions, although Ripley donated to the Institution more than 2,500 bird skins he himself had collected in Southeast Asia and the South Pacific.

In 1970, a Washington newspaper columnist took issue with the Secretary for chartering a 110-foot luxury yacht for $480 a day to sail the Aegean Sea in search of the Audouin's gull and for spending some $2,800 on "fine drink" and Palaiokastritsa lobsters. Ripley pointed out that the trip had been financed by a private donation, not tax money, and that he not only had found an Audouin's gull but also had spotted a rare Eleonora's falcon. Three years later, Ripley was again criticized by the same columnist for being away on expeditions for 28 weeks in one year and for spending $15,000.

A perception problem had arisen, and some people, including politicians and journalists, resented Ripley's patrician manner and apparently charmed stewardship. There were gathering signs that the eighth Secretary had been too successful.

Below left, philanthropist and inventor Peter Cooper with his granddaughter Eleanor Hewitt about 1870. After his death, granddaughters Eleanor and Sarah founded the Cooper Union Museum, where art students, left, copy paintings about 1915. Eventually transferred to the Smithsonian, the museum is today the Cooper-Hewitt National Design Museum. Here, part of an embroidered waistcoat in the Cooper-Hewitt's textile collection.

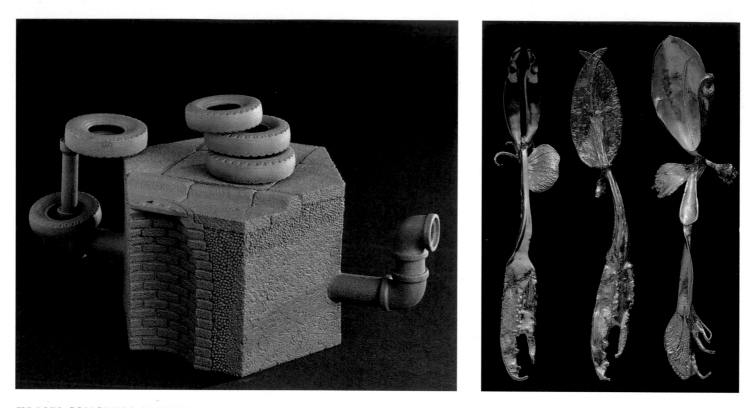

IN 1978 CONGRESS AUTHORIZED LEGISLATION TO merge the Museum of African Art with the Smithsonian. Launched back in 1964 by Warren Robbins, who had spent 10 years in Europe as a cultural attaché in the U.S. Foreign Service, the museum was originally located in the Capitol Hill row house in which abolitionist Frederick Douglass had once lived.

Robbins had initially approached Gordon Gibson, a curator of ethnology in the Museum of Natural History, in an attempt to launch a formal relationship between the museum and the Smithsonian's Department of Anthropology. However, the Institution did not have the funding at that time to support such an endeavor.

Meanwhile, the museum's acquisitions had grown to include some 5,000 African art objects and a collection of paintings by 19th-century African-American artists. The one row house had become nine, with 12 galleries, a small auditorium, and a library, and operating expenses continued to mount. Finally, with the support of Senator

Hubert Humphrey, who, as Vice President under Lyndon B. Johnson, had served as a Smithsonian Regent, proposed to Ripley that the Museum of African Art become part of the Smithsonian.

Growing awareness of African-American heritage and growing political clout now made the prospect of adding the museum to the Smithsonian's other bureaus a real one. A proposal, signed by more than 30 Senators and 100 members of the House of Representatives, was made to the Chancellor of the Smithsonian, Chief Justice Warren Burger. Burger and Ripley were in favor of acquiring the museum, if federal funds could be obtained for its maintenance and for future acquisitions.

In addition to its science, history, and art museums—the Smithsonian had grown to include tropical research stations and astrophysical observatories; the Woodrow Wilson International Center for Scholars, established in 1969 as an independent agency but housed in the Castle; and the John F. Kennedy Center for the

From the decorative-arts collection at the Cooper-Hewitt National Museum of Design: Richard Notkin's unconventional stoneware teapot; part of a silver cutlery set cast from seashells, leaves, and insect carapaces by Claude Lalanne; and Tone Vigeland's necklace of flattened nails.

Off the coast of Belize, Carrie Bow Cay houses a Smithsonian research facility where scientists conduct long-term studies of the region's marine flora and fauna. Below, biologist Sara Lewis uses a grid system laid out over the sea floor to study algal populations.

Performing Arts, which opened in 1970 with its own board of trustees.

In 1973 the National Zoo established a Conservation and Research Center on 3,150 acres in Front Royal, Virginia, where such animals as zebras, Asian barking deer, oryx, and Bactrian camels could roam in spacious pastures. A bird hatchery, equipped with large brooding cages that the Washington facility could not accommodate, is located here, as well as other facilities for breeding and caring for endangered animals. The center also grows great quantities of hay, much of which is transported 75 miles back to the District to feed hungry residents of the Zoo itself.

Another new bureau, the Smithsonian Environmental Research Center (SERC), formerly the Chesapeake Bay Center for Environmental Studies, was opened on 2,600 acres of watershed on the Rhode River, an estuary of the bay. Here scientists undertake projects involving general ecosystem research, land use, and forest ecology. Some of the land has never been disturbed, enabling researchers to conduct comparative analyses of species and to study forest succession in a unique environment. SERC offers broad educational programs—including special courses for children—to the public.

Also created during this era were the Belmont Conference Center; the Office of Fellowships and Grants, which encouraged students and visiting scholars to pursue their research at the Institution; the Oceanographic Sorting Center, with facilities in Washington and Tunisia; and myriad related activities and affiliations around the world, from Belize to Nepal.

IN 1976 THE SMITHSONIAN RECALLED THE NATION'S 1876 Centennial Exposition. On May 10, an exhibit opened in Arts and Industries with characteristic Ripley flair, "complete with carriages, prayers, the Hallelujah Chorus, release of pigeons, and the John Philip Sousa music composed for the occasion. Each of these great exhibits… creates an atmosphere of excitement, of sheer pleasure, and of enthusiasm which is contagious," the Secretary himself intoned.

As was most readily apparent in the largest, most colorful, and most varied celebration yet of the Festival of American Folklife, that summer was the Institution's apex. With the assistance of the American Revolutionary Bicentennial Administration, the Smithsonian brought in people from all over the United States, including many Native Americans, and from 35 other nations. "Working Americans," "Old Ways in the New World," and "African Diaspora" were among the main themes in a universal celebration of grassroots culture on a scale not seen before in Washington.

The festival lasted 12 weeks, during which the Mall was crowded with a living demonstration of American cultural wealth and more than four million eager spectators from all over the country who presented the National Park Service with the formidable challenge of preserving the grass. But, as Richard Kurin, a cultural anthropologist and director of the Center for Folklife Programs and Cultural Studies, said later, the celebration avoided becoming a "massive state spectacle." Instead it "retained its intimate presentational modes…small performance stages, narrative workshops, intimate crafts and foodways…children's participation areas, and the like…. The Bicentennial Festival illustrated in the strongest terms the living nature of folk culture throughout the United States and the world."

The folklife festival also represented the cooperation of thousands of people, from national and international scholars to community activists, and was established in the Office of Folklife Programs as a permanent part of the Smithsonian. The late folklorist Ralph Rinzler was appointed the office's first director, and soon extended

(Text continued on page 369)

Smithsonian art galleries line the south side of the Mall. Above, a view of the entrance to the S. Dillon Ripley International Center from the Enid A. Haupt Garden.

THE MAKING OF A MUSEUM
by SONIA REECE

Asked how he came to establish the National Museum of African Art, its founder, Warren Robbins, replied, only half facetiously, "It began [in 1962] when a political appointee bumped me from my parking space in the State Department garage, and I resigned in protest from the U.S. Foreign Service." Just before doing so, however, Robbins was asked by then Assistant Secretary of State for African Affairs Mennen Williams to give a talk for the wives of African ambassadors stationed in Washington. Subsequently published as "Tradition and Transition in African Art" and then as a Peace Corps training paper, his lecture soon developed into an idea for an exhibition that in turn evolved into a permanent museum.

Unlike Charles Freer, Joseph Hirshhorn, Arthur Sackler, or, indeed, James Smithson himself, Robbins was not a wealthy patron who provided funds to build a museum to house his collection. Nor was he an Africanist by training; in fact, he had never even been to Africa. But he had acquired African art while serving as a diplomat in Europe, and he recognized that it represented one of humankind's great creative traditions. He was convinced that if the general public—beyond the world of specialists and art lovers—could be made aware of that greatness, it might help break down the walls of prejudice that often separate black and white people.

On June 7, 1964, the museum opened in the Capitol Hill home of the 19th-century African-American abolitionist Frederick Douglass. By 1979 it had grown to include a new wing and a block of Victorian houses.

Writing and lecturing extensively, Robbins conducted an innovative public-education program, and mounted some 50 exhibitions, using objects lent by other museums and major private collectors of African art. Gradually, he won the attention of educators, artists, the media, government officials, and the African diplomatic corps.

As a result, substantial financial support was forthcoming: To the list of great American foundations such as Ford, Rockefeller, Mellon, and Kress was added the support of such philanthropists as George Brown, of Texas; Joseph Akston, of Florida; Lee Bronson, of California; Mrs. Vera List, of Connecticut, and David Kreeger, of the District of Columbia. But it was the National Endowment for the Humanities that was most directly responsible for African Art's growth to national-museum status in only 15 years.

By the time the museum merged with the Smithsonian in 1979, thousands of public-school, university, and church groups had visited it, and civil-rights groups, cabinet officials, and members of Congress had

The Capitol Hill residence of African-American abolitionist Frederick Douglass was the original home of the Museum of African Art, founded by diplomat Warren Robbins, above, in 1964. Fifteen years later the Smithsonian acquired the museum, and, in 1987, relocated it in the new Quadrangle complex on Independence Avenue.

used it as a venue for social functions, swearing-in ceremonies, and fundraisers. It had also become a stopping place for visiting African heads of state, and two American Presidents and their Vice Presidents were among its strongest advocates.

"Possibilities at the original museum were limited, however," Robbins pointed out, "not only by space but by the lack of permanent funding, and our collection—composed entirely of donations from collectors— was not uniformly of the aesthetic standards that would befit a national

museum. The Smithsonian affiliation provided the necessary added dimensions for us."

Spurred on by his sister Frances Howard, Senator Hubert Humphrey, of Minnesota, who had served as Vice President under Lyndon Johnson, sponsored the legislation that brought the museum into the Smithsonian's fold. Indeed, Humphrey was its most active public proponent: On the very day before he died, he telephoned his colleague from Minnesota, Senator Wendell Anderson, asking him to introduce the legislation.

Having brought to fruition the National Museum of African Art, Robbins understandably reflects that "warm glow of a proud parent of modest means whose child married into a large and prominent family."

Sonia Reece is an Associate Editor at Smithsonian Books.

From the Smithsonian's National Museum of African Art's Eliot Elisofon Photographic Archives: a 1970 photograph of a Bozo woman near Mopti, Mali; a wooden, double-sided female figure called *akua'ba*, from the Asante people in Ghana; and a 1959 image of masqueraders during a yam festival, *Onwasato*, held by the Ibo peoples in Ugwuoba village, Nigeria.

the range of fieldwork and education. For example, the Smithsonian Folklife Studies Series, launched that bicentennial year, published information about American and other cultural traditions, and produced documentary films to accompany these works.

The festival's scholarly and community-service extensions provided a thoroughly contemporary approach to the increase and diffusion of knowledge that inspired two other national programs for the preservation of folk traditions: the American Folklife Center at the Library of Congress and the National Endowment for the Arts Program in the Folk Arts.

IN THE TWO YEARS AFTER THE JULY 1976 OPENING of the National Air and Space Museum (NASM), the building received 20 million visitors. Behind the scenes in this, the most popular museum in the world, research facilities—like the Center for Earth and Planetary Studies, which conducts research in lunar and planetary photography and on terrestrial deserts, building an extensive collection of photographs and images from space—pushed ever outward the limits of human knowledge, one of James Smithson's original mandates.

In 1980, the Museum of History and Technology (which had been renamed the National Museum of History and Technology in 1969) became the National Museum of American History, signifying a significant shift of emphasis from the old engineering and industry themes to those of culture and American studies. It soon appealed to the public as a repository of wildly varying Americana, some of the exhibits complete with scents—such as those of chocolate in a 19th-century confectionary or of a Southern sharecropper's barnyard. One year's gifts included a pair of Muhammad Ali's boxing gloves, an "Impeach Nixon" T-shirt, and Rosalynn Carter's inaugural gown. But out of view of the general public, curators and other staff delved into historical theory and the

infinitely intriguing aspects of American history, from the country's early intellectual and political leadership to the privations of modern-day inner-city life.

During this time, Ripley's wife, Mary Livingston Ripley, created the Smithsonian Women's Committee, which continues to raise funds through craft shows and other functions and whose members play an important role in the Institution's programs and activities. In 1977, Corinne C. (Lindy) Boggs, of Louisiana, a member of the House Committee on Appropriations, was appointed the first woman Regent, replacing Sidney Yates, of Illinois. Her appointment was another milestone in Ripley's tenure.

Meanwhile, however, accusations against Ripley, ranging from the trivial to the substantive, continued. It had been suggested in Congress, for instance, that Ripley had improperly transferred from the Zoo to his preserve in Connecticut five ruddy ducks—the expressed purpose being to induce breeding—an indication that no detail of the Smithsonian's business would pass unnoticed. The

Secretary also was criticized for giving himself $100,000 worth of grants for studying birds.

While the Institution enjoyed unprecedented public approval, in 1977 the General Accounting Office charged that the Smithsonian had attempted to conceal its financial dealings from Congress. Then the Institution was accused by a House subcommittee of mismanagement of its world-renowned gem collection. The Smithsonian parried the charges with announcements of policy changes, but recrimination was in the air.

Some of this bad press was indirectly the fault of Ripley. "In some ways he is not personally well suited for a political and bureaucratic town like Washington," Larry van Dyne wrote in The Washingtonian. "His interests, while perfectly admirable, do not match those of political and media insiders…. Ripley is more likely to be spending his weekend organizing to save some endangered variety of parrot or rhinoceros."

(Text continued on page 374)

Zairian artist Pilipili Mulongoy's *Pintades* ("Guineafowls"), painted about 1950, offers a brilliant example of early modern African art. At left, glass beads and cowrie shells decorate a rare, late-19th-century, life-size figure from the Bamum peoples of Cameroon, in western Africa. The figure may portray a high-ranking Bamum man in a posture of constraint and subservience to his king.

FESTIVAL OF AMERICAN FOLKLIFE

by DIANA PARKER

Directing the Festival of American Folklife must be the best job in the world. One of its many rewards is the late, late night sessions when festival staff, too exhausted to move, finally sit down, and one of the old-timers says, "Remember the time that…," and the stories begin. For all the years that the festival has been presenting folklore, it has also been generating its own.

The repertoire of festival stories evokes a range of emotions—funny, sad, poignant, profound. Like all folklore, the importance of these stories lies not in whether the details are factual, but in what the story conveys. Most festival workers' stories share one element: the lessons staff have learned from the festival participants, who have given us elegant solutions to immediate problems and profound insights into more global ones. When you bring together from three to four hundred of the world's most talented and interesting people, amazing things happen. Take the runaway calf in 1975, for instance.

Late one Friday afternoon in July, a rambunctious calf jumped the corral fence on the festival site on the Mall and headed down Independence Avenue to freedom. U.S. Park Police in patrol cars, festival staff in golf carts, and helpful bystanders on foot all took off in hot pursuit. As the Keystone Cops atmosphere intensified, an extraordinary horse handler from the Northern Plains, who was participating in the festival that week, rode up, hat in hand, and asked, "Would you like me to fetch him, Ma'am?" I told him that would certainly be helpful, and off he went, down the middle of Independence Avenue, lasso flying overhead. As rush-hour motorists sat staring in astonishment, the calf, cowboy close behind, made it all the way to the underground parking lot of the John F. Kennedy Center for the Performing Arts. There the cowboy lassoed the calf, calmly laid it over his horse's neck, rode back to the Mall, and released it, unharmed, into the corral from which it had escaped. A Washington *Post* reporter, who was at the Kennedy Center covering a performance, witnessed the lassoing, and the story made the next day's front page.

The cowboy never really quite understood what all the fuss was about. Out where he's from, calves get away and are returned to the corral all the time. I think he thought we were all a little silly. He was happy to have been able to do something helpful, and delighted with the photo of him and his horse that he got in return, but it was just all in a day's work. And frankly, he told me, he was a little embarrassed by all the attention.

Another often told story involves the juxtaposition in the 1991 Family Farm program of the participants from Indonesia and the farmers from the American Midwest. By the second week, interpreters had gotten several conversations started at the hotel in the evenings, and the groups had been surprised at how much they had in common. A woman in her late 60s from the island of Borneo and a U.S. farmer some 10 years her junior had been sharing ideas about when in a season one should plant, how to know when it would rain, and so forth, and they had forged a strong mutual respect. On the last night of the festival they began to say their good-byes. The woman, emboldened, said there was one question she would like to ask before she left. Why, she wondered, was the farmer always in a wheelchair. He explained that a farm accident had taken away the use of his legs. She smiled a warm smile, gave him a hug, and said, "You are such a lucky man. I know many people who have lost pieces of their soul. You only lost a piece of your body; your soul is complete."

As the festival continues, the stock of stories that staff share late at night grows. It is our hope that members of the audience are also talking to participants and acquiring their own new chapters of festival folklore.

Diana Parker is the Director of the Festival of American Folklife.

A musician at the 1974 festival plays a copper washboard; below, Pete Seeger entertains in 1982; dancers and musicians from India, far left, perform at the 1985 festival as part of a collaboration with the National Museum of Natural History's exhibition *Aditi—A Celebration of Life*, in which the balladeers, left, participated.

Ripley himself believed that "if you stick your toe out of the door in Washington, you have to be prepared for someone to beat on it. It was a calculated risk to bring the Smithsonian out into the light of day, but we took that risk to get things that were good for Americans."

NOT YET THROUGH TAKING RISKS, RIPLEY HAD IN mind a scheme that was to be the capstone of his administration, although he didn't have an obvious place to put his new enterprise. The last available plot on the Mall, east of the Air and Space Museum, had been eyed by backers of proposals for several new museums. Marvin Sadik, at the time director of the National Portrait Gallery, had proposed a museum of the American Indian. Sadik and others saw Native American culture as a rich source of both art and history beyond the scope of their bureaus.

Sadik's elegant Portrait Gallery, housed in the Old Patent Office Building—described by poet Walt Whitman as "that noblest of Washington buildings"—already had some 10,000 art objects and a clear mandate going back to the times of Charles Wilkes. Since opening to the public in 1968, the gallery had attempted to present a coherent reflection of the American experience through portraiture. Located five blocks north of the Mall on 8th and F streets, Northwest, the Portrait Gallery steadily pursued accessions for a collection that grew to include a 1616 engraving of Pocahontas, an etching of Benedict Arnold, a bronze bust of civil-rights leader Rosa Parks, and a portrait of the artist Mary Cassatt by Edgar Degas.

The National Collection of Fine Arts (renamed in 1980 the National Museum of American Art), the oldest federal art collection in the country, was also located in the Old Patent Office Building and likewise had expanded, in its case to reflect two centuries of the visual arts. The museum's portraiture (including the paintings of Indians by Charles Bird King), landscapes, impressionistic and realistic paintings, photography, crafts, and graphic

Painted in Tabriz, Iran, about 1530, this illustration of a reclining prince is one of a number of Islamic manuscript pages acquired in 1913 by Parisian jeweler and art collector Henri Vever. Another noted collector, psychiatrist and medical publisher Arthur M. Sackler, above, donated to the Smithsonian some 1,000 pieces of Asian art and $4 million to found the Arthur M. Sackler Gallery, which opened in 1987. The gallery purchased the Vever collection in 1985.

design by largely self-trained artists constituted an impressive compendium of American achievement.

Searching for space for yet more art, Ripley turned to the Castle's own back yard. He had long been frustrated by the no-lending restriction placed on the Freer collection by its donor, Charles Freer, and by other restrictions regarding the Freer Gallery itself. Next to the gallery, however, lay an opportunity: the parking lot once occupied by the tin shed that had housed part of the National Air Museum's collections. Here Ripley envisioned something grand and audacious: an underground museum complex. Since the District of Columbia's Council for the Arts opposed any new construction on the Mall, Ripley saw this concept as a novel way to create space by revamping part of the Smithsonian grounds that had been largely ignored for 130 years.

By 1980, the project was underway. Ripley commissioned Japanese architect Junzo Yoshimura to produce a design for a three-level, underground development that became known as "the Quadrangle" and was also to include handsome gardens and an impressive entrance gate off Independence Avenue. At different times, the Quadrangle was seen as a new home for the Smithsonian Institution Traveling Exhibition Service (SITES), for the Institution's 30,000 rare books, for African and American Indian art, and for the cars of visitors and staff.

The concept that finally prevailed was for a museum of African art, politically the most viable proposal, and another for a second collection of Eastern art to augment and complement the Freer's. (Congress had approved the acquisition of the already existing Museum of African Art, including its bronzes from the Guinea coast, jewelry and ceremonial robes, masks, fetishes, headdresses, and an extensive collection of musical instruments, with Senator Claiborne Pell, chairman of the Senate Rules Committee, insisting upon the condition that the Smithsonian find a more suitable location for the museum than the Capitol Hill row houses.) The Quadrangle's remaining space would house the Institution's public-program offices and its Directorate of International Affairs.

Ripley secured from Congress an agreement to appropriate half the funds required for the project and set about personally raising the other half—some $36.5 million—from the Japanese government and corporations, from the Korean government and wealthy Saudis, and from private American citizens. A generous contribution from Enid Haupt, the sister of publishing baron Walter Annenburg, would build the beautiful Victorian Haupt garden.

Ripley persuaded Dr. Arthur M. Sackler, a psychiatrist and wealthy medical publisher, to donate 1,000 pieces of Asian art valued at close to $75 million and $4 million for the construction of a Far Eastern gallery within the Quadrangle. After Yoshimura suffered a stroke, the architectural details were taken over by Jean Paul Carlhian, a principal in the Boston architectural firm of Shepley, Bulfinch, Richardson and Abbott.

IN *SMITHSONIAN YEAR* 1982, THE SECRETARY, IN reference to the Quadrangle, wrote what amounted to a summation of his final vision for the Smithsonian: "For perhaps the first time in our history, we are embarking in a spirit of social responsibility on a creative effort to increase understanding and respect for our neighbors. One of our mandates, the diffusion of knowledge...works both ways, within and without. We can, for example, tell Americans about their history, but how can we extend that to...the rest of the world? Traditions and cultures alien to the massive onslaughts of mechanistic technology are fragile indeed. They are being eroded every day just as the forests of the tropics disappear. Cultures drift away like the dust that follows the draft of a lifting jet plane on a far-away runway...."

Displays of African, Near Eastern, and Asian art,

Chinese child prodigy Wang Yani creates a work of art at the Sackler gallery in 1989. By the age of 6, Yani, the youngest artist ever to have a one-person show at the Smithsonian, had painted 4,000 pictures. Her spontaneous style of painting, called *xieyi*, or "idea writing," can be traced back to the late-19th century.

it was hoped, would foster global understanding while helping to preserve distant civilizations and, Ripley implied, an awareness of the diminishing physical world. At the same time, there was no reference to the world of science, once the foremost concern of the Smithsonian but now eclipsed in the Quad by art.

Some aspects of the Quadrangle—aside from those concerning the amount of money required—proved controversial. For instance, people questioned the advisability of including an Islamic center that might become a focus for activities beyond those inherent in a museum. "Are you the Ripley of 'Believe it or Not' fame?" asked one correspondent outraged by Ripley's solicitation of money from the Saudis. "This is a political-religeous [sic] activity…and entirely out of keeping with what the Smithsonian stands for."

Nonetheless, a vast hole opened up south of the Castle. Into it eventually would go some of the most daring architecture in the nation's capital, art treasures, and, ironically, the final aspirations of an ornithologist who had transcended the cultural and political limitations of former Smithsonian Secretaries but not his own institutional mortality.

RIGHTLY OR WRONGLY, MEMBERS OF CONGRESS perceived that Ripley was no longer in control of the Smithsonian's large bureaucracy, which had become perhaps too concerned with pomp, circumstance, and buildings. He was given credit for considerable diffusion of knowledge, but its increase under his stewardship was questioned; some thought the Institution, its annual appropriation now grown to about $100 million, out of touch with modern times, particularly with regard to minority hiring.

Ripley's detractors were not limited to Congress. Chief Justice Warren Burger, head of the Smithsonian Board of Regents, was also critical of the Secretary's autonomy and of what some viewed as high-handedness.

As of 1972, the Institution was no longer run on a daily basis by Under Secretary James Bradley, who retired that year. Ripley's initial choice of a classical scholar to replace Bradley did not please the Regents. Finally, in 1980, Ripley hired Phillip Samuel Hughes, a long-time and consummate public servant whom he knew the Regents respected.

Despite the fact that the new Under Secretary involved himself in policy as well as management, Hughes got along well with Ripley. In 1982, Hughes asked Edward Rivinus, at the time Acting Assistant Secretary for Public Service, to form the Committee for a Wider Audience (CWA).

Once the CWA was established, its members sought to assure that, in Smithsonian programs and exhibits, proportionate recognition was given to all the varied communities that had participated in the development of American culture and society—an issue that would take on greater weight in the years ahead. (In 1990 the Smithsonian Office of Wider Audience Development was established.)

AT THIS POINT, RIPLEY HAD BEEN SECRETARY FOR almost 20 years, during which time the number of items in the Smithsonian's charge had grown from 74 million to more than 100 million. A possible replacement for Ripley began to be discussed in earnest: another era was ending.

But Ripley's vision, and his aura of a personal mission, still pervaded the Smithsonian. "He had nerve, as well as charm, wit and great intelligence," recalled Charles Blitzer, director of the Woodrow Wilson International Center for Scholars, in discussing Dillon Ripley. "How he imposed his will on such a large place remains a mystery."

The most flamboyant and perhaps most successful Secretary in the Institution's history would leave a tremendous challenge to the person chosen to follow him.

Donated to the Smithsonian by Arthur M. Sackler, this intricately carved lacquer tray is from China's Southern Song dynasty (1127–1279). Its red lacquer, or *t'i-hung*, was achieved by using cinnabar (red mercuric sulfide).

PROFILE
BIOPARK

Since a procession led by the two elephants Dunk and Gold Dust made its way through downtown Washington, D.C., on April 30, 1891, en route to the site of the new National Zoological Park on land overlooking Rock Creek, the Zoo has grown into a unique and commanding bureau of the Smithsonian. It has added to and sustained its population of exotic animals for generations, filling the capital's nights with vocalizations more familiar to distant lands.

In 1916, after the departure of the Zoo's first superintendent, Frank Baker, who had been appointed by Secretary Langley in 1893, Ned Hollister, former assistant curator of mammals in the National Museum, became superintendent. Hollister died in 1924, and was succeeded the following year by William M. Mann, an internationally known entomologist and avid circus fan, who, like all the Zoo's directors to follow, would leave a distinct, lasting imprint on the Smithsonian's animal world.

By 1934 the Zoo had received more than 2.4 million visitors, many drawn by the animals Mann had collected himself. He had traveled widely—Palestine, North Africa, the South Pacific—and was not only an expert on ants and termites but a determined collector of animals of all sorts. In 1926 Mann convinced American automobile manufacturer Walter P. Chrysler to finance a Smithsonian-Chrysler expedition to Tanganyika (Tanzania), where no fewer than 584 birds, 393 tortoises, 158 mammals, 56 snakes, 12 lizards, and a frog were collected. Included were two young giraffes and five impalas—these last the only members of that species to be exhibited at a zoo at that time.

In 1927 the Zoo received an appropriation for a new bird house, and in 1929 the Reptile House went up. During the Depression, the Public Works Administration allocated $680,000 for new construction, which helped build both a Small Mammal and Great Ape House, a Pachyderm House, and an addition to the Bird House.

Crates of live animals collected in 1926 by National Zoo director William M. Mann, right (wearing helmet), await shipment from Tanganyika (now Tanzania). Giraffe, top, was caught during a 1937 National Geographic trip. Loss of habitat pointed up the importance of captive-breeding programs. The successful hatching of 13 Komodo dragons at the National Zoo in October 1992 was a first outside their native Indonesia.

The Zoo used more New Deal artists to decorate its grounds than any other local agency, and the palatial new buildings were constantly welcoming new arrivals.

A Smithsonian-National Geographic Society expedition to the Dutch East Indies in 1937 yielded 115 crates of birds, 74 crates of mammals, and 30 creates of reptiles, a bounty that stocked not only the National Zoo but other zoos across the nation. Then, in 1940, Harvey Firestone, Jr., financed what would be the last big collecting expedition before World War II. This one would go to Liberia, and would supply the Zoo with, among other animals, a female pygmy hippopotamus (Matilda) for the male (Billy) already in residence.

During the war, the Zoo's venomous reptiles were traded out of fear that they could escape if their building were damaged in an air raid. But for the most part animals were added to the collection, often in unlikely circumstances. For instance, a retired military man brought in some animals he had collected in the Philippines—tree shrews, Mindanao tarsiers, and bushy-tailed cloud rats—which Mann promptly added to the Zoo's ranks.

By 1956, when Mann retired, the Zoo's operating budget was becoming inadequate to support its collections. Mann's successor, Zoo veterinarian Theodore H. Reed, became director in 1958, the same year a two-and-a-half-year-old girl climbed over a safety fence and was killed by a lion. The accident occasioned hearings on safety issues, and resulted in increased appropriations for improvements in the Zoo's safety measures.

As human encroachment began to take a toll on animal populations in the wild, Reed saw the necessity of breeding rather than collecting exotic animals. In setting up captive-breeding programs, however, he had to work with antiquated equipment in decaying facilities. The Zoo's budget was so tight that often Reed bought drugs for the animals with his own money.

Reed was vocal about the Zoo's needs, and in 1958 his calls for help were answered by a group of concerned citizens, who formed the Friends of the National Zoo (FONZ). Soon FONZ began to operate some concession stands at the Zoo, and it quickly developed into a network of influential people whose support for Zoo programs proved crucial. In 1960 the Zoo's budget exceeded the $1 million mark for the first time.

When S. Dillon Ripley took over as Secretary, all but one of the keepers at the Zoo were men ("solitary males," according to one observer), although many women, including William Mann's wife, had worked

Zoo world. They belonged to a living giant-panda population of only about 1,000, and therefore served as potent reminders of dwindling wild-animal populations and habitat destruction everywhere.

Nearly as popular as the pandas were the white tigers and Smokey Bear, the living symbol of the importance of forest-fire prevention. Meanwhile, Reed's breeding programs—particularly those involving the lesser pandas and gorillas—steadily gained credence. However, the project that merged both public appreciation and species propagation was that of successfully breeding the golden lion tamarin, a tiny South American monkey threatened with extinction.

During Reed's 28-year tenure the Zoo bloomed: the Great Flight Cage, the Giant Panda House, the renovated Great Ape House—which housed Ham, the first chimpanzee to travel into space—the Mann Lion/Tiger Exhibit, and Monkey Island all embroidered a landscape that was representative of the best in the zoological world. One of Reed's major contributions was to expand the Zoo's mandate from that of simply serving as a public exhibition of animals to one of building a vital research center in veterinary science, genetics, and ethology—the study of animal behavior.

In 1984 Reed stepped down. The subsequent appointment of Michael Robinson, former Deputy Director of the Smithsonian Tropical Research Institute in Panama, brought to the Zoo a biologist with 20 years of experience in the field. Ripley proclaimed Robinson "a devotee of zoos and a keen, industrious field biologist."

Conservation thenceforth was to be as integral a part of the Zoo's mission as animal physiology, pathology, and genetics; indeed, the very idea of a zoo itself would be reappraised under Robinson's leadership, for he believed the overall concept of a biological park should replace that of a zoological one. "In the real world," he said, "plants, animals, and people are all intertwined."

diligently in the animals' interests. The Zoo's first woman keeper, Brenda Hall, worked in the reptile division. To emphasize the Zoo's needs, Reed hired another woman to carry a diapered baby orangutan, Melati, to budget hearings on Capitol Hill.

In 1972 the Zoo became the center of international attention when it received two giant pandas from the People's Republic of China as a gift to the people of the United States in recognition of the new political accommodation between the countries. Visitors mobbed the Zoo to see Hsing-Hsing, the male, and Ling-Ling, as they instantly became the most popular animals in the

CONTINUUM

The Regents' task in choosing a successor to S. Dillon Ripley, now 70, was complicated by the long shadow the Secretary cast. Ripley had been in charge of the Smithsonian for close to 20 years—a length of time at the Institution's helm matched only by Secretary Charles D. Walcott. Ripley had been spectacularly successful at empire building and at practicing his own particular brand of diffusion, but he was perceived as less successful in promoting research and effective management and at opening the Institution to all strata of American society. Members of Congress and the Board of Regents wanted a new kind of leadership.

Many felt that museology should be moving away from the storing and displaying of artifacts to using them as a means for teaching science, history, art, and other subjects. People were not simply to be attracted by exhibits; they were to be instructed. This mission demanded someone— as had been said in the past—to bring the Smithsonian into modern times, someone who would again re-interpret the words of James Smithson and re-balance the administration of Smithson's legacy.

The man the Regents favored to be the ninth Secretary contrasted strongly with the eighth, and not just in training. Archaeologist Robert McCormick Adams, provost of the University of Chicago, had been born and raised in Chicago. An egalitarian, tall and physically imposing—he moved many tons of sandstone to build his summer house in Basalt, Colorado—Adams was an expert on patterns of settlement in ancient Mesopotamia, and a determined university man.

"Museums are, in the last analysis, our major repositories of highly charged cultural symbols."
—ROBERT McCORMICK ADAMS

This figure of a king made of clay is from ancient Mesopotamia, part of modern-day Iraq and an area in which archaeologist Robert McCormick Adams, the Smithsonian's ninth Secretary, has done much field research.

Adams distrusted Washington, although he recognized the Smithsonian's importance and its unique position as an institution of learning. In an interview held in a conference room of the Supreme Court with the Regents' Search Committee, he expressed concerns about appropriation battles on the Hill, lack of time to do his own research and writing, and the frustrations of running a large bureaucracy. He refused the Regents' initial offer.

Although distinct from the federal government, the Smithsonian was dependent upon federal appropriations, and the Secretary of the Smithsonian traditionally had been involved in helping obtain this money. As it turned out, Adams's original concerns, including those concerning administrative life in Washington, were well grounded. As a member of the Search Committee later commented, "No one anticipated how political things would get, or how tight the budgets."

But, out of some 300 people considered, Adams was the Search Committee's unanimous choice. Despite personal reservations about the political and economic pressures Washington brought to bear on an Institution dependent upon federal support, Adams agreed to reconsider the offer, and, in January 1984, finally accepted.

AN INTELLECTUAL OF BROAD RANGING INTERESTS, Adams was well acquainted with the real world. He had enrolled as a physics major at the Massachusetts Institute of Technology in 1943, at age 17, but soon lost interest in this field. Enlisting in the Navy as an engineering officer candidate, he was transferred to boot camp as an apprentice seaman, and, at the end of World War II, having completed training as a radio technician, he was sent to Shanghai, where his duties included serving as a shore patrolman. In 1946 he enrolled in the University of Chicago, took courses in history and political science, and toyed with the idea of becoming a journalist. He dropped

out in 1949 to work first on a Ford assembly line and then in a U.S. Steel mill.

In 1950 Adams re-enrolled in the University of Chicago, and joined an expedition to Iraqi Kurdistan that led to extensive studies of water courses and settlement patterns in Iraq, studies that were frequently interrupted by political developments in the Mideast. Still, Adams, his wife, Ruth Salzman Skinner, and their children spent a lot of time in the country around Baghdad.

In 1975 Adams completed a monumental work, *Heartland of Cities: Surveys of Ancient Settlement and Land Use on the Central Floodplain of the Euphrates*, which covered population dynamics over a period of 6,000 years. He was hampered in furthering the study by his limited access to the region. "Iraq is like a wonderful laboratory whose door is out of my control," he said.

The newly chosen Secretary had also done field work in Mexico, Syria, and Saudi Arabia, and had accompanied scientific missions to Europe, China, and the Soviet Union. At the University of Chicago, he had served as director of the Oriental Institute, dean of the Division of Social Sciences, and then as provost.

Adams spent his summers in the inter-mountain West, reading, writing poetry, and working with his hands. No stranger to Washington, he had for years been active in the National Academy of Sciences and its National Research Council. But his academic past had not fully prepared him for the unique problems of the Smithsonian that descended upon him from the moment he arrived in town.

ADAMS MOVED INTO THE SECRETARY'S OFFICE IN the East Wing of Castle in the autumn of 1984, and took over responsibility for what he described as "a shining constellation of museums spanning the arts, natural sciences, and technology, with the responsibility to use these resources for the cultural enrichment and education of the nation."

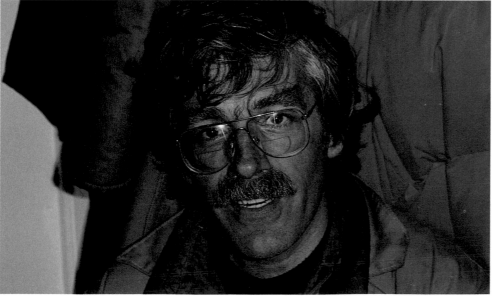

In July 1991, a team of U.S. and Canadian scientists led by Smithsonian archaeologist William Fitzhugh, left, excavated Inuit house sites on Kodlunarn Island in the Canadian Arctic, where between 1576 and 1578 Elizabethan explorer Martin Frobisher made the first known English contact with the New World. At the Kuyait site, above, scientists excavate one of the houses occupied by Inuit shortly after their contact with Frobisher's party.

In one of his first acts as Secretary, he gave the museum directors the freedom to follow their own initiatives. Adams saw this primarily as an attempt at decentralizing what he liked least, the bureaucracy. He would later characterize his style as "acephalous" (headless) leadership—decision-making by consensus. This was hailed as overdue reform by some within the Smithsonian, and criticized by others for diluting the Secretary's leadership role.

Adams further shook things up by changing the duties of some assistant secretaries, making one responsible for research instead of science, and the other for museums instead of history and art. Since all museums had research functions, this caused some confusion about administrative authority.

As the successor to Sam Hughes, the long-standing and effective Under Secretary, he chose Dean Anderson, a young man with comparatively little administrative experience. The Smithsonian was changing quickly from an almost regal Institution to one of more modest material ambitions that was facing demands for social equality and in need of ever larger appropriations to meet a rapidly expanding payroll.

The challenge was to keep the Smithsonian focused on its original mandate—the increase and diffusion of knowledge—at a time when traditional roles of all sorts were being re-examined in academia and when what was seen as the dominant culture was being called into question. These concerns would affect research and exhibits and cause contentious debate both within the Institution and without.

In Adams's first public statement as Secretary he expressed the view that Joseph Henry's intention "to enlarge the bounds of human thought by assisting men of science to make original investigations in all branches of knowledge" was no longer within the capability of museums or of the Smithsonian. That role, he

Smithsonian photographer Carl Hansen took these photographs of Canela Indians, in Brazil's savannah region, during a 1993 expedition. Children of the village, right, gathered around Hansen's portable television to watch their relatives during a ceremony that he had videotaped earlier that day; an elder, above, walked from dwelling to dwelling in the village while singing.

said, had passed to universities and special institutes.

The value of the Smithsonian and other museums, he felt, lay in maintaining collections for systematic research, and in educating the public. He praised the breadth and depth of the Institution's collections, which seemed to put him more in the camp of former Secretary Spencer Baird than in that of Joseph Henry.

In 1986 the Smithsonian's new Arthur M. Sackler Gallery, an elegant, underground museum within the Quadrangle that was connected to the Freer by a tunnel, purchased the stunning collection of Henri Vever, a

Parisian jeweler and art-nouveau-movement leader who had died in 1942. Included in the collection were 160 works of Persian and Indian art from the 11th to the 19th centuries—paintings, manuscripts, calligraphy, and book bindings. "The acquisition," Adams said during the official opening of the Quadrangle in 1987, "makes the Smithsonian Institution, with the Freer-Sackler combined, a major world center for the study and exhibition of Islamic manuscripts."

In addition to the art museums—the other being the National Museum of African Art—the Quadrangle housed the Directorate of International Activities, the Smithsonian Institution Traveling Exhibition Service, and the National and Resident Associates programs. The ribbon-cutting ceremonies lacked the pomp of past openings, but in its first year the graceful, imaginative, and expensive Quadrangle attracted 1.6 million visitors.

MEANWHILE, THE OFFICE FOR A WIDER AUDIENCE, the outgrowth of an ad hoc committee formed in 1983 to broaden the Smithsonian's appeal to minorities, called for revamping exhibits that reflected outmoded or unpopular views of natural science. The Office of Equal Employment and Minority Affairs continued to work for broader representation in hiring, but the Regents criticized it for lack of progress in solving the problem of equal employment—a problem older than Adams's regime.

In the 1989 *Smithsonian Year*, Adams asked, "What does the Smithsonian stand for *today*?" In answering, he pointed out that it could not claim a "comprehensiveness of knowledge increased and communicated," but could claim to be a "living institution, actively engaged on many fronts, and committed to public service and public dialogue." In other words, the Smithsonian was squarely in the world, not above it.

In addition to praising the Institution's collections and the independence of its staff, Adams expressed *"an overarching concern for preserving and articulating our cultural and natural heritage."* This was the Smithsonian's greatest responsibility, he said, as well as a clear indication of Adams's own priorities.

He stressed the need to monitor, understand, and try to stop "deterioration of the global environment." His choice of botanist and conservationist Thomas E. Lovejoy as Assistant Secretary for External Affairs indicated that he took the Institution's environmental role seriously.

The Regents kept the pressure on Smithsonian management to broaden its ethnic appeal. Adams rearranged the areas of responsibility of some Assistant Secretaries, and in 1990 appointed as his new Under Secretary an African-American woman, Carmen Turner, who had formerly served as general manager of the Washington Metro Area Transit Authority. Yet various ethnic groups continued to seek representation.

Adams narrowed what he considered the Smithsonian's proper focus. In addition to maintaining the collections "while deepening the public's appreciation," he wrote, it was also "to advance research in those areas

(Text continued on page 394)

A detail of the painted hide shirt, part of the National Museum of the American Indian collection, that belonged to Crazy Horse, a member of the Oglala Sioux "shirtwearers," or councilors. First displayed during the Centennial Exposition in Philadelphia and again during the bicentennial exhibition at the Arts and Industries Building, this prehistoric Mississippian-culture head pot, A.D. 1350–1400, is in the collections of the National Museum of Natural History's Department of Anthropology.

SONGS MADE VISIBLE
by RICHARD WEST, JR.

Jacki Rand, an insightful woman (sometimes wickedly so) of Choctaw descent who has contributed a great deal to the conception of the National Museum of the American Indian (NMAI), described to me an early meeting of one of the committees charged with the museum's creation. A roomful of serious, sympathetic people asked her how she thought they should begin. "You should go to Indian Country," she said, "and speak to people there about what they'd like the museum to be." "Yes...," they said thoughtfully. "Go to Indian Country.... What do you mean by that?" They thought she was evoking a cryptic metaphor.

Jacki's committee went to Oklahoma, and one of the things they learned there, besides the fact that Indian Country is a real place, is that Indians want the museum to be, among other things, a meeting ground, where they can sit down with non-Natives and talk about who they are.

In creating a new museum, we are rethinking how the interpretations of American culture we present reflect and address the cultural diversity of this country. We are not interested in merely saying the same things museums have always said to a more diverse audience. Far more fundamentally, we are searching for ways to bring the diverse elements of American cultural life into museums and to allow them to speak for themselves in these institutions, which have such a powerful role in describing, shaping, and defining American culture.

As a Southern Cheyenne, I've known, from my own childhood, that the intellectual and spiritual realities Native peoples bring to their cultural patrimony differ, often profoundly, from the ways others may see the same objects. The 1994 inauguration of the George Gustav Heye Center in New York provided us with our first major opportunity to affirm these distinctions through the use of the unfiltered Native voice on the exhibition floor, in our public programming, and in new, more inclusive and collaborative approaches to scholarship.

In the catalog for *Creation's Journey,* one of the Heye Center's inaugural exhibitions, my colleague Rick Hill tells a story that I hope illustrates the sometimes elusive point I am trying to make. It is about a northern California Indian named Mrs. Matt, who was hired to teach basket making at a local university. After three weeks, her students complained that all they had done was sing songs. "When," they asked, "were they going to learn to make baskets?" Mrs. Matt replied that they were learning to make baskets. She explained that the process starts with songs that are sung so

as not to insult the plants when the materials for the baskets are picked. So her students learned the songs and went to pick the grasses and other plants to make their baskets.

Upon their return to the classroom, the students were dismayed when Mrs. Matt began to teach them yet more songs, this time songs that must be sung as they softened the materials in their mouths before starting to weave. Exasperated, they protested that what they wanted to learn was how to make baskets. "You're missing the point," Mrs. Matt told them. "A basket is a song made visible."

I don't know whether Mrs. Matt's students went on to become

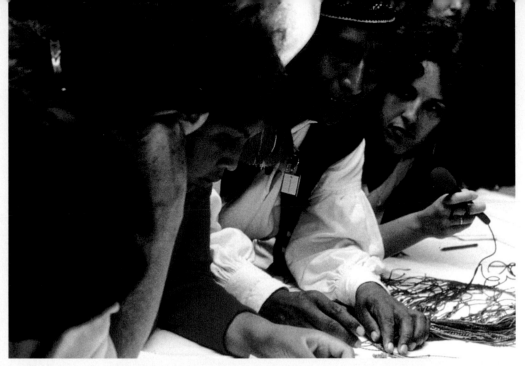

Moccasins and other footwear, left, and an early-20th-century Bamtush-weave basket were among the objects displayed at the 1994

·BOWLING GREEN ELEVATION·
SCALE ¼ FOR FOOT

V·S·CVSTOM HOVSE·NEW YORK

CASS GILBERT · ARCHITECT

opening of the National Museum of the American Indian George Gustav Heye Center in New York City. Alejandro Flores Huatta, of Taquile, Peru, confers with NMAI staff members, and, at right, a lithograph of the old U.S. Custom House, in which the center is located.

exemplary basket makers. I do know that perspectives like Mrs. Matt's, which embody a whole philosophy of Native life and culture, merit inclusion in our cultural institutions. However, the absence of her eloquent and revealing voice from the galleries of many museums deprives their audiences of a singularly authentic perspective on the meaning of what they see.

Museums continue to represent valuable aggregations of human and material resources that contain substantial stores of information, potential knowledge, and educational impact. Their capacities to educate most effectively, however, depend in large part on the degree to which they encompass this society they are attempting to represent and interpret.

Looking toward the next millennium, I remain hopeful and, indeed, optimistic that if museums can accomplish cultural inclusion, they have the historic opportunity to become, on a far broader basis, vital centers for the exchange of ideas. More important, they can become not only forums for debate but genuinely creative instruments of the cultural reconciliation that society appears so desperately to need.

W. Richard West, Jr., is the Director of the Smithsonian's National Museum of the American Indian.

where the Institution has a special position of leadership and responsibility." These areas included the Smithsonian Astrophysical Observatory in Cambridge and the Smithsonian Tropical Research Institute in Panama, both of which operated on the fringes of the Smithsonian bureaucracy. He broke up the old Radiation Biology Laboratory, reassigning most of its scholarly staff.

Finally, Adams opined, the Smithsonian had "to respect and justify the national support on which we depend by effectively reaching out to increasingly diverse, geographically dispersed audiences." He felt that, with regard to the arrangement of its programs, the greatest need was for "a broadening and strengthening of the Institution's outreach to all the varied cultural and ethnic groups making up this nation." Clearly, cultural as well as biological diversity was important to Adams, and gradually the face of the Institution began to change.

THOSE ACCUSTOMED TO THE URBANE RIPLEY holding forth in the rarified climate he had created in the Castle and at Smithsonian functions found Adams aloof by comparison, even abrupt. His fundraising abilities and rapport with members of Congress also contrasted with Ripley's. Amassing money from contributors and stroking members of Congress was part of the job, but Adams was not particularly adept at either. Because congressmen were adversely affected by budget restraints, they were far less likely to go along with Smithsonian requests than they had in the past, and that was no fault of the Secretary's.

Many who worked with Adams considered him refreshingly straightforward and easily approachable in a professional capacity. The consummate professor, he ran meetings as he would a graduate seminar, and his speeches were often esoteric and profound. "He doesn't like crowds or tuxedos," said a colleague who often witnessed

(Text continued on page 403)

Top, the renovated rotunda of the Custom House, designed between 1899 and 1905 by architect Cass Gilbert. From the National Museum of the American Indian collections: an early-20th-century photograph of a native Alaskan woman and a Pomo cooking basket (1900–30).

BRAVE NEW WORLD

by AMY DONOVAN

Most of us who live near urban population centers are used to seeing tower cranes, great, elongated, right-angled machines that lift steel beams and other heavy objects and assist in the construction of modern buildings. We might, however, be somewhat surprised to encounter one in the veritable sea of tropical vegetation that is the Republic of Panama's Parque Natural Metropolitano, just outside Panama City. But we needn't be, for a tower crane has been here since late 1990, engaged not in construction—well, not of buildings, anyway—but in providing scientists with a unique method of accessing the canopy of the tropical forest.

It is the brainchild of the late Alan P. Smith, former assistant director for terrestrial research at the Smithsonian Tropical Research Institute (STRI), which is based in Panama City and which owns and operates the crane. The only one of its kind so far in the tropics, the crane represents an amazing breakthrough in canopy research for perhaps the simplest of reasons: it's *taller* than the forest. Every other way of getting into the canopy or into the forest—*any* forest, not just tropical forest—whether by ropes, pulleys, walkways, or other means—requires having the tree support one's weight. One can get only as far as the load-bearing limb, and this is generally not where the plants and organisms that are of most interest to scientists are found.

Riding in the specially adapted gondola suspended from the tower crane's 50-meter arm, or jib, one can be lowered down *on top* of the forest, and gain access to the tips of even the most delicate branches and to previously unreachable plants and animals. Controlled by the crane operator, the gondola can move horizontally as well as up and down, providing scientists great versatility and freedom of movement. Additional advantages include the crane's minimal impact on the vegetation and its capacity to transport scientific equipment into the canopy.

The forest's uppermost layer, the canopy is home to more than 50 percent of tropical-forest-dwelling species. Much of this vast reservoir of life remains undocumented, although scientists are becoming increasingly aware of its abundant biodiversity. In 1982 Terry Erwin, of the Smithsonian's National Museum of Natural History, estimated that as many as 30 million species of arthropods—mainly insects, spiders, and mites—inhabit tropical-forest canopies, a large proportion of all the organisms on the planet.

As rich a species pool as is the entire tropical canopy, it is its uppermost layer—where Earth's biosphere meets the atmosphere—which,

Suspended from a 100-foot-high tower crane above Panama's Parque National Metropolitano, right, Smithsonian Tropical Research Institute (STRI) scientists Alan P. Smith, above (left), and Geoffrey Parker measure temperature and humidity at varying levels of the canopy. Smith's brainchild, the crane, or Tropical Canopy Access System, allows safe, rapid access to canopy species and their habitats and is at present the only one of its kind in the tropics.

because of its exposure to direct sunlight and the increased photosynthesis, plant reproduction, and insect life that result, fairly teems with biological activity, and which had remained for the most part tantalizingly out of reach.

So far at least 20 different countries have sent scientists to work on the crane. The international thrust of this research is important, for the United Nations Environment Programme (UNEP), with financial support from the Smithsonian National Associates and the governments of Norway, Finland, and Germany, played a key role in providing funding for the crane's purchase. Demand for the crane is such that scientists must request research time with it years in advance; projects involving the crane currently are planned for the next two years. Several other organizations may soon install similar construction cranes to access other forest canopies, from the Pacific Northwest to coniferous forest in Norway to lowland tropical forest in Venezuela, and STRI hopes to install a second crane in a contrasting everwet tropical-forest environment.

The three main areas of canopy-crane research—insect biodiversity, plant-animal interactions, and plant life—support a host of ongoing studies. The crane operates seven days a week, its schedule dictated by the biology of each day's experiments. But whether one rides the gondola into the canopy before dawn, during daylight, at dusk, or at night, one enters a world of more than 50 tree species and 20 species of liana; of epiphytic plants, such as orchids and bromeliads; of diverse communities of microorganisms and myriad insects and other arthropods; and of spectacular vertebrates, including green iguanas and other lizards, tamarin monkeys, and hundreds of species of birds. And one enters as well a brave new world of biological research. The crane, which makes all this possible, is busy constructing after all.

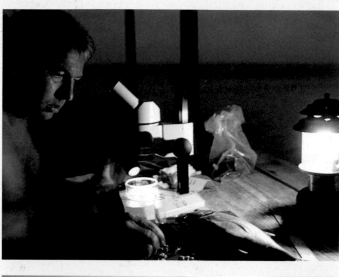

A major focus of STRI research since the 1920s has been the complex behavior of tropical animals, such as the *Cenprolenella spinosa,* or "glass frog," right. At STRI's San Blas Field Station, research associate Ken Clifton, top, dissects a yellow jack; above, with his computer, he records data on the coral reefs and fish around the San Blas Archipelago.

Amy Donovan is Editor at Smithsonian Books.

Opposite, National Museum of Natural History technician Fred Grady excavates fossil remains of *Arctodus simus*, or greater short-faced bear, perhaps the most powerful predator in Pleistocene North America, from a cave in Virginia. Back at the NMNH laboratory, Grady examines portions of the bear's skull and jaw fragment.

THE SHORT-FACED BEAR

by BRYAN KENNEDY

National Museum of Natural History staffer Fred Grady first saw the pelvic fragments in 1993. After a little research, he decided they were from some sort of large bear, but he couldn't tell much else. A large bear? From a Virginia cave? He compared the fragments to bear pelvises in the Smithsonian collections, but he couldn't find any nearly as big.

Grady works in the Natural History Museum's paleobiology prep lab, but his real passion is underground exploration. He went on his first cave trip in 1966; two years later, he happened upon some fossil bones in a cave in Pennsylvania. By 1978, Grady was actively searching below ground for Pleistocene fossil sites. West Virginia was a favorite spot. There, he and his adventurous colleagues located the remains of a jaguar, a cheetah-like cat, and several Ice Age saber-toothed cats—the first ever found in that state.

The Virginia bear fossils came to him by way of some fellow cavers, who had acquired them from a group of high-school students in Alleghany County. Intrigued, Grady decided to investigate for himself. After talking with one of the students, Grady located the cave's owner, and, with the owner's permission, secured an excavation permit. As is often the case with cave exploration, it was slow going; the passage to the bear site was about 50 degrees F, muddy, and very constricted. Most of the time Grady worked with his arms pinned above his head. He used a screwdriver to gently pick at what turned out to be the bear's skull, which was bonded to the cave wall. His patience paid off: In four trips, he located 40 percent of *Arctodus simus,* a greater short-faced bear. It's the first of its kind from Virginia, and, although it hasn't been dated yet, it may have lived between 12,000 and 30,000 years ago.

First described by paleontologist Edward Drinker Cope in 1879, *Arctodus simus* was strangely long-legged and short-bodied for a bear, with a distinctive broad, stubby muzzle. The positioning of the toes is unlike that in living bears. The animal appears to have been built for speed—the "cheetah bear," it's been called—and yet it could reach the size of a grizzly, measuring as much as eight feet in length and weighing 800 pounds. As short-faced bears go, Grady's bear is on the small end of the scale, and may have been a female. *Arctodus simus* has been described as "the most powerful predator in Pleistocene North America." Like many other species of North American megafauna, these bears seem to have died out sometime near the end of the last Ice Age.

Fearing vandals, Grady is reluctant to reveal the whereabouts of

the bear cave. He hopes soon to have located the bear's hind limbs, if in fact the rest of the bear is there. Of course, it may not be the only skeleton in that location. Potter Creek Cave, in Northern California, has offered up the remains of eight short-faced bears over the years, which suggests the animals had favorite caves. Either way, Fred Grady's childhood interest in natural history has yielded an intriguing addition to the Smithsonian's paleobiology collections.

Bryan Kennedy is an Associate Editor at Smithsonian Books.

On September 19, 1994, I. Michael Heyman, above, became the Smithsonian's 10th Secretary. A few of the more than 6,000 employees he now oversees appear at right, engaged in activities that reflect the Institution's wide spectrum of disciplines.

the Secretary pursuing his daily agenda at the Castle, "but he was accessible, and absolutely honest. You could engage with him."

THE SMITHSONIAN TROPICAL RESEARCH INSTITUTE (STRI), one of the bureaus of which Adams was proudest, had been the Canal Zone Biological Area until 1966. Far from Washington and the emphasis on diffusion of knowledge, STRI had continued to work for its increase.

A land bridge separating two continents and two oceans, Panama enjoys unprecedented biological diversity, including some 900 species of birds, and affords an increasing number of scientists from the Smithsonian and from other institutions both in the U.S. and abroad a unique opportunity to do research in an area that has remained relatively undisturbed for more than half a century. A small plot on Barro Colorado Island in Gatun Lake, for instance, contains some 300 species of trees and is a bonanza for tropical biologists.

As appropriations from Congress increased, STRI achieved broader recognition as a research center. It also played an important role in the growing appreciation of tropical forests and seas as crucial to the health of the planet. Knowledge attained at STRI has implications extending far beyond the isthmus.

In 1973 STRI's operations expanded to include a new mainland headquarters on the site of the old Tivoli Hotel in the Ancon section of Panama City. STRI's facilities continued to expand, taking in a network of marine and terrestrial field stations, various laboratories, and, with funds provided by the family of Tupperware fame, the Earl S. Tupper Research and Conference Center, an extensive tropical-sciences library. In 1985 the government of Panama bestowed upon STRI the recognition and benefits of an international mission that caters to hundreds of scientists from all over the world.

STRI scientists pursue studies on global warming,

ocean circulation, tropical ecosystems, and species extinction, as well as on animal behavior, evolution, physiology, genetics, systematics, anthropology, archaeology, and paleontology. At such sites as the Punta Galeta Marine Laboratory, on the Atlantic Coast near the city of Colon, researchers collect data for STRI's marine environmental monitoring program. At the institute's largest marine facility, the Naos Island Laboratories, which are near the Pacific entrance of the Panama Canal and are connected to the mainland by a causeway, researchers investigate adjacent intertidal shores, cobble and sand beaches, and estuarine habitats. STRI scientists detected early effects of the 1983 "El Niño" meteorological disturbance by recording unusually high sea-surface temperatures and subsequent damage to coral reefs, fish, and sea-urchin populations; they gained further international recognition by demonstrating the potential dangers that would be posed by construction of a sea-level canal, which would allow passage of such noxious organisms as poisonous sea snakes from the colder Pacific to the Atlantic.

On Barro Colorado Island, STRI's main site for the study of lowland moist tropical forest, scientists like James Zetek and Thomas Barbour once lived in huts. Today researchers enjoy modern living quarters, a cafeteria, and air-conditioned lab facilities, and are engaged in projects ranging from fitting bats with radio-transmission devices to tagging some 240,000 plants in the 124-acre Tropical Forests Dynamics Plot.

At various sites throughout the isthmus, paleoecologists probe the region's three-million-year history to study the effects of climatic and sea-level fluctuations and to find evidence of human settlement over the last 11,000 years. In the ultraviolet light of STRI's molecular biology lab, scientists isolate genetic material into fluorescent flashes of DNA that may prove crucial to the perpetuation of Earth's biodiversity.

Ongoing research in the raising of tropical food

sources explains the presence of large rodents called pacas in cages at the Tupper center and of green iguanas on Barro Colorado, where game wardens patrol to prevent poaching. Drawn by STRI's international fellowship and by intern programs that train 50 young people a year, half of them from Latin America, students move continuously between these facilities.

MEANWHILE, PLANS FOR THE NATIONAL MUSEUM of the American Indian (NMAI) moved ahead. The idea of a hemispheric museum dedicated to Indians, the continent's first inhabitants, had been around for some time and enjoyed Adams's unqualified support: He considered it both intellectually appropriate and in keeping with the Smithsonian's mandate and history, the latter so wrapped up in westward expansion and the collection and preservation of Native American artifacts.

The Smithsonian had been negotiating for years with the custodians of the Museum of the American Indian in New York to secure the collections of George Gustav Heye, who had died in 1957. Heye had been a wealthy friend of David Rockefeller, the brother of Nelson Rockefeller, who, in 1976, as Vice President of the United States and a Smithsonian Regent, had pushed for transferring the collection to Washington to be housed in a new museum. The unprecedented number of artifacts—more than one million—that Heye had voraciously collected were stored at the time in unsatisfactory conditions in the Bronx, essentially unavailable to scholars. Interpretations of Heye's will by authorities in New York seemed to preclude the collection's leaving the city. The Smithsonian remained in "a watchful posture rather than an active one," in Adams's words, waiting for the courts to resolve the issue.

For two years, negotiations—and wrangling—over what would be the final resting place of the collection involved state officials, Indian spokespersons, and

Smithsonian Astrophysical Observatory astronomer Margaret Geller stands before a three-dimensional map of part of the universe she and her colleagues first charted. The map's boundary is 400 million light-years from Earth. Each point represents a galaxy similar to the Milky Way. SAO scientists have mapped some 20,000 galaxies thus far. To explain this process to a broad audience, Geller collaborated with a filmmaker to produce *So Many Galaxies…So Little Time*.

various members of Congress, among them Senators Patrick Moynihan, a New York Democrat and Smithsonian Regent who in the end supported the collection's transferal, and Daniel Inouye, a Democrat from Hawaii. Inouye wanted the museum in Washington, but advocated the return of all identifiable Indian remains to the tribes requesting them.

Finally, in 1989, legislation establishing the National Museum of the American Indian (NMAI) was passed by Congress and signed by President George Bush. The new museum was to be located on the last open space on the Mall, east of the Air and Space Museum. Congress agreed to meet the Smithsonian's obligations by appropriating federal funds for the restoration of the Alexander Hamilton U.S. Custom House in lower Manhattan, where some of the Heye artifacts would be exhibited; for construction of a storage facility at Suitland, Maryland; and ultimately for two-thirds of the cost of the museum on the Mall.

The controversy surrounding the return of ancestral Indian bones came to involve the Smithsonian's collections in the Museum of Natural History, and developed into one of the most significant public issues affecting the museum. Originating with those Indians who wanted the remains of relatives and tribal elders returned, the controversy eventually involved native groups worldwide, which now sought to prevent the exhumation and scientific examination of human remains.

Some anthropologists at the Smithsonian felt that all artifacts should be retained as part of the Institution's irreplaceable, scientifically invaluable collections; others thought that religious considerations and moral responsibility required restitution of materials that had been collected over the years without regard for the beliefs, or the feelings, of indigenous peoples.

In 1990 legislation was passed requiring repatriation of identifiable remains, upon request, to descendants or tribal groups that can demonstrate entitlement to the property in question. The NMAI policy provides an even broader mandate for the repatriation of sacred objects, and the Smithsonian returned all identifiable human remains, including an extensive collection of bones in the Museum of Natural History that had been taken from burial sites in Alaska by the late Aleš Hrdlička.

TO MEET ITS FINANCIAL RESPONSIBILITIES FOR THE NMAI, the Smithsonian had to raise one third of the estimated $105 million cost for the design and construction of a museum on the Mall. In addition to this facility—which was scheduled to open in 2001—the George Gustav Heye Center, a cultural resource center located in the old Custom House in New York, opened in 1994.

There would also be built at the Institution's Museum Support Center, in Suitland, Maryland, a unique facility that merged collections with related research, display, and community services; this was scheduled to open in 1997. Such unprecedented custodial capacity was conceived to encourage the performance of Indian religious ceremonies and to make artifacts and cultural objects available to the Indian community at large.

Extensive meetings were held with Indian groups around the country to determine how the facility's objectives might best be accomplished and how it could be opened up to diverse tribes and activities. In part as a reflection of Adams's desire for the dispersal of knowledge, a fourth, traveling museum had been envisioned to take artifacts and related activities into the field.

The Secretary selected W. Richard West, of the Cheyenne-Arapaho tribes of Oklahoma, as director of the NMAI. It was agreed that the Indian artifacts still housed in the Natural History Museum would remain there, along with the files and records of the old Bureau of American Ethnology. Related material in the Museum of American History would also remain separate.

West set about trying to raise $35 million for the new museum. A strong attraction for potential donors was the breadth and magnificence of the Heye collection, which represented all great American Indian civilizations. Its treasures ranged from feather work by remote forest tribes of the Amazon to carved masks by Arctic Inuit, fine stone carvings from the Northwest Coast, Kachina dance masks from the Southwest, gold work from Peru, and Olmec and Mayan jade, and included a vast array of tools, weapons, clothing, ornaments and ceremonial objects.

Plans for an African-American museum also had begun. Initially, feeling that museums should not be dedicated to every ethnic group in America, Adams expressed doubts about its appropriateness. However, he eventually supported the concept, which the Regents endorsed in February of 1992, and it was proposed that the museum occupy part of the Arts and Industries Building, next to the Castle. In June 1993 the House of Representatives unanimously passed legislation authorizing the creation of a National African American Museum at the Smithsonian, but the legislation died in the Senate the following year. Efforts to make this museum a reality continue under the auspices of the African American Museum Project.

DURING THIS TIME, CONTROVERSIES AROSE OVER the content of exhibits, and, more specifically, over labels in the National Museum of Natural History, many of which were branded as elitist or out-of-touch with current social realities. Among those offered as examples were John Smith's first encounter with the Indians along the James River and the African lion exhibit featuring animals shot by Theodore Roosevelt. Labels were altered to reflect changing attitudes about suitable content and interpretation, but their replacements were sometimes dismissed by those with a more traditional view as revisionist or "politically correct."

Three generations of tenant farmers lived in this Maryland farmhouse. It now appears, with furnishings from the Smithsonian's collections, in the National Museum of American History's exhibit *Field to Factory: Afro-American Migration, 1915–1940.*

The Smithsonian's first photographer, Thomas W. Smillie, captured this wax Japanese warrior figure in the Castle about 1873. At right, the National Museum of Natural History's Japanese armor collection at the Museum Support Center.

These so-called dilemma labels, which highlighted what were considered the inaccuracies or prejudices of the past, caused dissension both within the Smithsonian and without. Experts and commentators who saw the value of an exhibit's original components and interpretations clashed with those who wanted a more fashionable, up-to-date approach; this again raised questions of objective truth that first had been addressed at the Smithsonian by George Brown Goode more than a century before.

Other critics pointed to the Smithsonian's new practice of soliciting from institutional or corporate donors monetary contributions that were earmarked for particular programs, and then publicly attributing the program or exhibit to the donor. This, the critics felt, smacked of commercialism. Nevertheless, the Natural History Museum decided to name its popular insect zoo after the founder of a corporation that used vast amounts of insecticide in pest control. Also, in 1989, admission was charged for access to an exhibit of mechanical, "living" dinosaurs, the first time such a fee was ever required at the Smithsonian.

In another experiment, officials placed collection boxes in two museums, two galleries, and at the Zoo to encourage voluntary contributions from visitors. The Smithsonian had been financially strapped before, but nothing of this kind had ever been attempted. The experiment continues to be only a modest success.

Increasingly Adams found himself caught between camps, between proponents of an activist Smithsonian and those favoring the museum's traditional role and between champions of revisionist American history and detractors of this approach.

As a case in point, in 1991 a number of people took issue with the National Museum of American Art's exhibit "The West As America," which portrayed the opening of the West and employed some unusually didactic labels suggesting that the enduring view of Western expansion was overly rosy and ignored the morally dubious subjugation of Indians and the despoliation of the land. The exhibit brought harsh criticism from influential members of Congress, and more charges of political correctness by newspaper commentators. As a result, some labels were altered to present a less polemical view. But this affair was only a warm-up for what would soon erupt into perhaps the largest controversy ever over a Smithsonian exhibit.

Also in 1991, Congress authorized an annex to the Air and Space Museum. It was to be built at Dulles International Airport outside Washington for the exhibition of such acquisitions as the supersonic SR-71 spy plane, a 747 airliner, and a space shuttle. Adams enthusiastically supported this idea; he felt it important that some of the Smithsonian's functions be dispersed to other parts of the country in order that Americans elsewhere might gain access to Smithsonian treasures and that certain exhibits escape the proximity of official Washington.

In 1992, Adams warned that the Smithsonian's funds for exhibition, research, and services were being cut. He predicted layoffs among the 6,600 staffers. The Institution was receiving some 26 million visitors a year and an annual appropriation of more than $350 million—a substantial increase over the $203 million it was allotted at the time Adams took office. The endowment approached $400 million, but $229 millon of that was needed just for maintenance on Smithsonian buildings.

As time went on, Adams could cite as an accomplishment an increase in minority staff. Sylvia Williams, head of the Museum of African Art, was the first African-

(Text continued on page 414)

A chair said to have been used by Abraham Lincoln during cabinet meetings was donated to the Smithsonian by Elwood Middleton, whose great-grandfather, Charles Middleton, reportedly accompanied Lincoln to the Mall for shooting practice. It now resides in the National Museum of American History's political-history collection, with Lincoln's hat and shawl.

GOOD BREEDING
by AMY DONOVAN

Stormy, left, a Masai giraffe, was born at the National Zoological Park in 1993. In training for possible return to its native Brazil, a golden lion tamarin eats in the trees above the Zoo's Valley Trail. The monkeys roam free, but stay in the area for food and shelter.

If William Hornaday championed the founding of the National Zoo in great part to save the American bison from disappearing from the face of the earth, he would no doubt be astounded at the importance accorded conservation at the Zoo today. The staff of the National Zoo works with colleagues around the country and around the world in developing species-preservation strategies. Of key importance among these strategies are captive-breeding programs, and the Zoo has had notable success in this arena.

The Golden Lion Tamarin Conservation Project represents what could be considered the flagship of the Zoo's captive-breeding program. Tiny, lion-maned, fiery-orange-furred monkeys, golden lion tamarins faced the prospect of imminent extinction when the Zoo began to study them intensely in the early 1970s. Captive populations bred poorly, and the tamarins' native rainforest habitat of coastal Brazil was disappearing rapidly. Gradually, Zoo personnel gained an understanding of the animals' social structure, and developed improvements to the monkeys' diet, environment, and veterinary care, with dramatic results: The Zoo's breeding pairs of golden lion tamarins began to enjoy unprecedented reproductive success, and the colony grew as never before. Sharing its information with other zoos that had been trying to breed these beautiful animals, as well as with Brazilian colleagues, Zoo scientists monitored the now increasing populations of captive-bred tamarins, and began to consider what only a few years earlier had been unthinkable: the reintroduction of zoo-bred animals to the Poço das Antas reserve, where nearly all of the remaining wild golden lion tamarins survived, about two hours from Rio de Janeiro.

After setting up a "basic-training" program to teach the animals to find food, watch for predators, and otherwise fend for themselves, the first group of tamarins was flown to Brazil, acclimated to their new Atlantic coastal forest home, and set free in Poço das Antas. A program to reintroduce and support zoo-born tamarins continues today; summer visitors to the National Zoo are often treated to sights of brilliant, orange-gold tamarins living and cavorting freely in the trees along the Valley Trail in preparation for possible release in Brazil. Meanwhile, offers by Brazilian landowners to set aside forested tracts for use in the golden-lion-tamarin-conservation effort represent yet another hopeful sign for the recovery and continued existence of this species.

The international breeding program pioneered for the golden lion tamarins, with its painstaking attention to genetic management, served as a model for the American Zoo and Aquarium Association (AZA), which began setting up captive-breeding programs called species-survival plans, or SSPs, for other endangered or threatened species. Today the National Zoo participates in nearly half of the 70 SSPs that have been established. Some of these SSP species, along with other rare animals, are found at the Zoo's Conservation and Research Center (CRC), in Front Royal, Virginia. Here, at this 3,150-acre site 75 miles west of Washington, live Père David's deer, Eld's deer, Przewalski's horses, Guam rails, Micronesian kingfishers, and black-footed ferrets, all of which are extinct or all but extinct in their native habitat. (There is hope, however: Successful captive-propagation efforts have enabled the Zoo to participate in reintroduction programs involving Eld's deer, Guam rails, and black-footed ferrets, among others at CRC.) Off-limits to the public so that the staff can concentrate on the animals, the Center's spacious pastures and enclosures and specially outfitted buildings provide an ideal setting for research into animal behavior and social organization, and Front Royal, not surprisingly, has produced a significant number of Zoo births.

But one needn't travel to the foothills of the Blue Ridge Mountains to see some of the Zoo's endangered species, nor to celebrate significant births. On December 14, 1993, the National Zoological Park, in Washington, welcomed Kumari, its first elephant calf ever, a 264-pound baby Indian elephant delivered by mother Shanthi. The delight of all who saw her and witnessed her amusing antics, Kumari died suddenly and tragically in April 1995; she will not soon be forgotten. On Memorial Day, 1994, Mandara, a lowland gorilla, gave birth to her second infant in three years, which she is raising successfully, along with a baby born to another gorilla in 1992 and subsequently abandoned by its mother.

Also of prime importance—and enjoyment—are the two broods of baby Komodo dragons produced at the Zoo, the first—a clutch of 13 that hatched in September/October 1992, the offspring of the Zoo's two dragons, which were a gift from the people of Indonesia; and the second—14 new dragons the following August/September—resulting from the union of the Zoo's female with a male Komodo at the Cincinnati Zoo, at the time the only other zoo in the country where dragons were kept. The dragon hatchings ushered in a new era on several fronts: The first was the first ever produced of the highly endangered Komodos outside of their native Indonesia; the second added invaluable genetic diversity to the species' North American

Adoptive mother Mandara, a lowland gorilla, cares for her own offspring, Kejana, and another young gorilla, Baraka, in 1992. Strangely, Mandara traded babies with Baraka's mother, Haloko. Careful study of gorilla social structure in the wild, as well as the exchange of gorillas with other zoos, has led to a healthy, growing captive population of these endangered animals.

gene pool. The Zoo then sent a number of young dragons to other zoos in the United States. This arrangement represented a dramatic departure from the protocol of olden days, some 50 years ago, say, when a North American zoo might have tried to sell highly sought after offspring from

rare or endangered animals to the highest bidder. Instead, the zoos receiving komodos will donate funds to the National Zoo to support a field biologist's study of the ecology of these great lizards in Indonesia.

There are so many other stories to tell, efforts to praise, successes to share. Suffice it to say that we all stand to benefit from the new covenant between zoos to work together to try to safeguard the future of rare and endangered animals.

Amy Donovan is Editor at Smithsonian Books.

American director on the Mall; Spencer Crew, officially appointed to replace Roger Kennedy as director of the Museum of American History in January 1994, was the second. Constance Berry Newman, also African American and formerly director of the U.S. Office of Personnel Management, replaced the late Carmen Turner as Under Secretary.

Smithsonian divisions continued in their pursuit of knowledge, often with spectacular results. In addition to STRI's accomplishments and the bold initiatives at the National Zoological Park, including the re-introduction of the golden lion tamarin to Brazil, the Astrophysical Observatory discovered the brightest exploding star seen in 400 years, and the Office of Fellowships and Grants made hundreds of grants every year.

As further signs of progress, new East Wing facilities were constructed at the Museum of Natural History, and the Great Hall of the Castle was at last transformed into an effective visitor information center. The Smithsonian organizational chart grew to include, among other bureaus, the Biological Diversity Program, an Office of Human Resources, an Office of Environmental Management and Safety, and the National Sciences Resources Center.

Impressed with the ability of children to learn from exhibits, particularly in the Museum of Natural History, Adams was convinced that an educational role was one of the most important and enduring the Smithsonian could foster.

But he had tired of the endless struggles, and of what he now referred to as Washington's "poisonous" atmosphere. In 1993, after nine years as Secretary, Adams decided to step down on the 10th anniversary of his installation. The Smithsonian, he maintained, continued to embody "some of our nation's most important aspirations and values"; serving as its Secretary, he added, had provided him with—appropriately—"an education."

ON RECEIVING ADAMS'S RESIGNATION, CHIEF Justice William H. Rehnquist, Chancellor of the Smithsonian, praised the Secretary for his work in "sustaining the excellence of the Smithsonian's scholarly research, on enhancing the quality of its exhibitions and on expanding its educational programs."

Again, a Search Committee was appointed to find a successor to Adams. Never before—not even in the time of Joseph Henry—had assertive, inspired leadership been more in demand. The committee was headed by Ira Michael Heyman, a lawyer and a scholar and former chancellor of the University of California at Berkeley. He and his colleagues began the evaluation of some 300 prospective Secretaries, an arduous task that would have an unexpected, and unprecedented, outcome.

Meanwhile, a controversy arose over a planned exhibit of the *Enola Gay*, the B-29 bomber that dropped the first atomic bomb on Hiroshima in 1945. The written material accompanying the exhibit tended to portray the Japanese as victims and to characterize the American objective as the destruction of Japanese culture rather than the winning of the war and the avoidance of the enormous human casualties that would have resulted from an invasion.

Martin Harwit, then director of the National Air and Space Museum, had to defend his exhibit against irate critics in the United States Air Force and other military veterans groups, in various patriotic organizations, and in much of the national press. The controversy represented the culmination of the trend that had become prevalent during Adams's tenure to re-examine history from the perspective of the sufferer, a trend that reflected the forces at play in academia that cast into doubt previous views of American culture.

The *Enola Gay* exhibit brought a new, more damaging notoriety to the Smithsonian. In the past, whatever its difficulties and perceived shortcomings, the

National Museum of Natural History cephalopod specialist Clyde Roper photographed this octopus minutes after it hatched. It may reach a length of three feet. In 1993 NMNH marine-snail specialist M.G. Harasewych used the Johnson Sealink submersible, above, to collect samples of deep-sea mollusks in the Bahamas for analyses of their DNA.

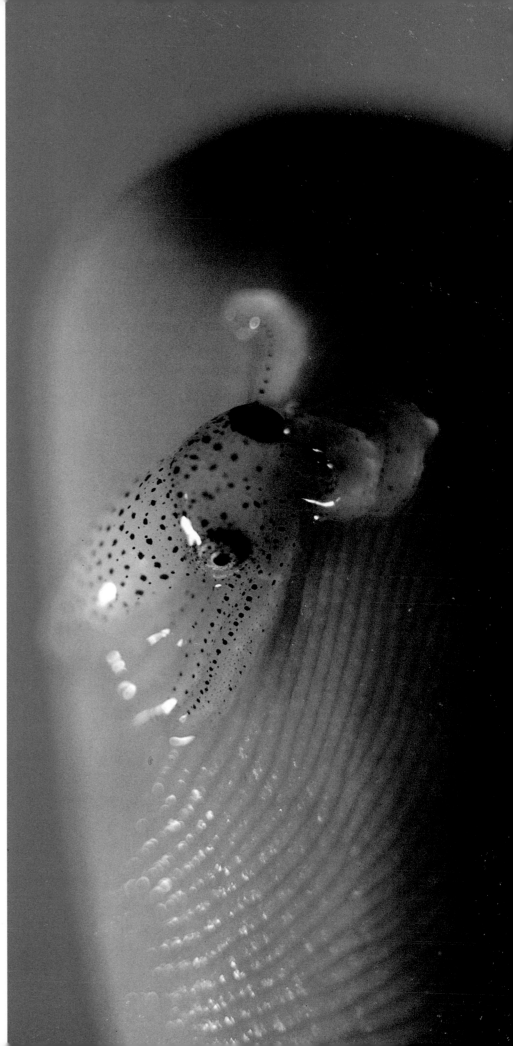

Institution had always been seen as the quintessentially American repository of sacrosanct national icons, champion of national accomplishment and national ideals. Now, for the first time, Americans began to question these assumptions, as well as the Smithsonian's motives and direction.

Military veterans demanded, and received, access to revised exhibit descriptions and labels about the *Enola Gay*, an unprecedented development that threatened the independence of all curators. The Institution consequently found itself under attack from all sides, and riven from within by the continuing discontent of traditionalists and the demands of those with broader social objectives. Once again the Smithsonian reflected powerful forces stressing and shading the American fabric.

ONLY WEEKS BEFORE THE SEARCH COMMITTEE made its selection of Adams's successor, Michael Heyman removed himself from its ranks so that he, too, might be considered for the position of Secretary, but not before insisting that the merits of the other finalists be carefully weighed and an impartial decision reached.

Serving as chancellor in California during the contentious '80s, Heyman had established a reputation of firmness but fairness, and had protected the ideal of impartial higher education while dramatically increasing the university's endowment. Tall and amiable, his habitual bow tie and suspenders suggesting a sense of style and tradition as well as a certain jauntiness in the face of difficulty, Heyman soon ascended to the top of the Regents' list.

Then, after final deliberations, the Search Committee chose Heyman, the only non-scientist in the Smithsonian's 148-year history to serve as Secretary. In making the announcement in May 1994, Regent Barber Conable described Heyman as "a generalist whose range of skills meshes with the Smithsonian's interests. As chan-

National Museum of Natural History exhibits specialist Sally Love poses with insects, above, from NMNH's Insect Zoo, including, from top, a New Guinea walking stick, a Madagascar hissing cockroach, a unicorn beetle, and an Australian walking stick. Samples of *Dillenia indica*, left—a tropical tree that sprouts grapefruit-size fruit—are in the Botany Department herbarium, which contains a total of 4.5 million specimens.

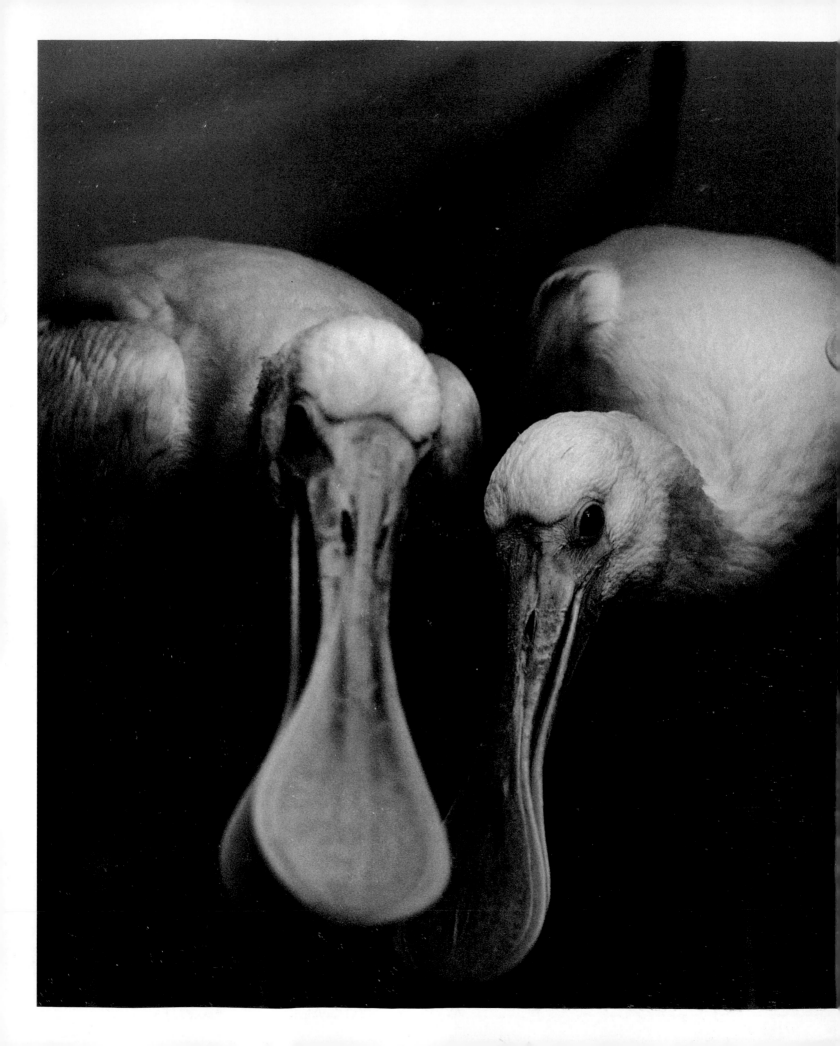

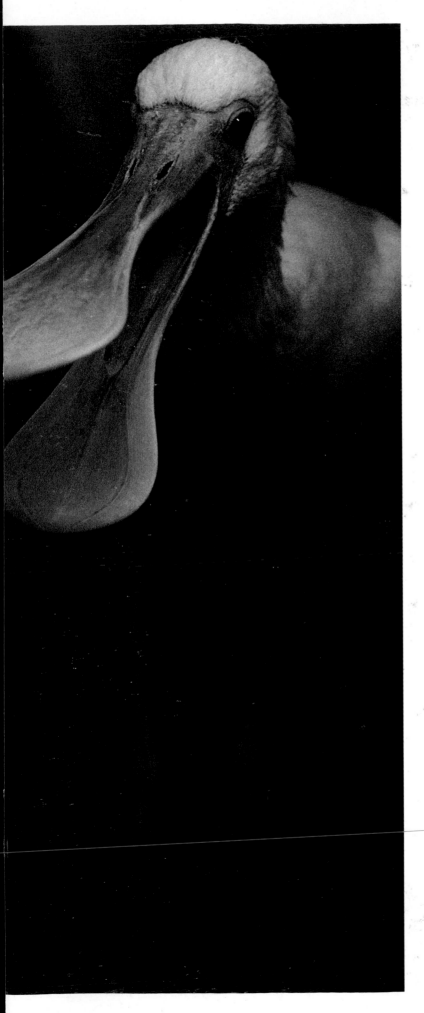

A trio of roseate spoonbills, left, from the National Zoological Park; a collection of birds' eggs, right; and, below, an illustration of the resplendent quetzal, of Central America, hint at the extraordinary adaptability, diversity, and beauty of the world of birds.

cellor of Berkeley, he saved the biosciences departments and sustained the university's strong reputation in physics. But in addition, he is accomplished in fundraising."

Like Dillon Ripley, Heyman was a Yale man. A former editor of the *Yale Law Journal*, he had served as chief law clerk to Chief Justice Earl Warren in 1958, and had begun his university career as a law professor at Berkeley the following year. He also had taught at Yale and Stanford universities. Widely published, he had served as the Selvin professor of law at Berkeley and as a Smithsonian Regent since 1990. He came to Washington in 1993 with his wife, Theresa Thau Heyman, senior curator of art on leave from the Oakland Museum, to serve as special counselor to the Secretary of the Department of the Interior.

ON A BRILLIANTLY CLEAR SEPTEMBER DAY IN 1994, Smithsonian employees spilled out of the museums and gathered on the Mall with the many visitors and dignitaries. On a dias set up in front of the Castle and the statue of Joseph Henry sat the Heymans, the Adamses, and Chief Justice William Rehnquist. The U.S. Navy Ceremonial Band played the national anthem, and the colors were presented by the Joint Armed Forces Color Guard. Rehnquist spoke of "the infrequent succession of great scholarly leaders, rooted in the rhythms of academe more than politics." During the Smithsonian's long history, he said, there had been no fewer than 12 Chief Justices, 30 Presidents, and 33 Speakers of the House of Representatives. He then presented Heyman with the Smithsonian symbol of succession, a five-inch brass key to the Castle.

Standing under the bronze eyes of the first Secretary, the 10th Secretary spoke of the awe engendered by the surroundings, and of the sight of the Capitol to the east. "Every Secretarial era," he said, "reflects unique circumstances and poses its own opportunities and prob-

lems." Heyman wished to increase the awareness of the Smithsonian in the minds of all Americans by increasing its resources, maintaining a strong relationship with Congress, and greatly enhancing fundraising efforts.

Heyman wanted to provide greater access to the Smithsonian's treasures through electronic links to exhibits, collections, and research, and he soon announced the appointment of Thomas Lovejoy, formerly Assistant Secretary for External Affairs, as a special counselor to the Secretary on environmental matters, a reflection of Heyman's and the Smithsonian's long-standing concerns.

Heyman then addressed the Enola Gay controversy. The earlier perspective of the bombing of Japan had lacked balance, he said, suggesting that this element of balance would be restored not just to the controversial exhibit at the National Air and Space Museum, but to all Smithsonian endeavors.

And, of course, he had other ideas about how the Institution should be run and about what its priorities should be (they should, he felt, include reducing the Institution's size without damaging its effectiveness and returning control of many functions to the bureaus). He wanted to assess the research then under way at the Smithsonian to assure that it compared favorably with research being done elsewhere; he wanted to encourage diversity and the fulfillment of projects that dealt with the history and culture of America's ethnic groups, although not necessarily to the extent of building new edifices or creating new museums to accommodate such projects.

Ultimately, the new Secretary sought to maintain the Institution as an incandescent reflection of the Smithson bequest that was of special relevance to Americans. "I want people all over the United States to cherish the Smithsonian," Heyman said, "not simply because they came to Washington and visited it once, but because it plays some role in their lives."

ACKNOWLEDGMENTS

Many people assisted me in the writing of this book, but none more than E.F. Rivinus, himself an accomplished writer and historian. Ted's research proved invaluable, his general enlightenment on the intricacies of "the increase & diffusion of knowledge" stimulating and enjoyable. I am immensely grateful to him, and to Ellis Yochelson, who provided me with materials, advice, and oversight I could have gotten nowhere else.

I am also indebted to Alexis "Dusty" Doster for his fine editing, to Pat Gallagher for shepherding this project, and to Felix Lowe for his backing. Everyone at Smithsonian Books dealt thoroughly and imaginatively with a mere manuscript that in their hands became a great deal more, and I thank them all.

Tom Lovejoy endorsed the idea of the book early on, and Marc Pachter offered assistance along the way. Others in the Castle who helped and encouraged me include James Hobbins and Peter Powers. Both Secretaries during the period of my research—Robert McC. Adams and I. Michael Heyman—were supportive and generous with their time and insight, and Dillon Ripley was most cordial. Insight into his years as Secretary was provided by many people, among them David Challinor and Charles Blitzer.

Scholars who helped me shape the Smithsonian's historical cast include Wilcomb Washburn, Nathan Reingold, Bob Post, Art Molella, and Tom Crouch. The staff at the Smithsonian Archives was very responsive. I am particularly indebted to Bill Deiss and Pam Henson.

People at the various bureaus who kindly assisted me are too numerous to name. I particularly want to thank Edwards Park at *Smithsonian* magazine, Roslyn Walker at African Art, Mike Morgan at the Zoo, Tom Harney at Natural History, Jim Demetrion at the Hirshhorn, Ira Rubinoff and Georgina De Alba at Smithsonian Tropical Research Institute, Alan Fern at the Portrait Gallery, Mary Rice at Link Port, and Jim Cornell at Smithsonian Astrophysical Observatory.

I remain grateful to everyone within the Smithsonian who responded so well to all inquiries.

James Conaway

The Editors of Smithsonian Books are particularly grateful for the assistance of James M. Hobbins, Peter G. Powers, Edward F. Rivinus, and Ellis L. Yochelson, who read the manuscript of *The Smithsonian* in its entirety, and for Marc J. Pachter's constant enthusiasm and encouragement. Thanks also are due the following people:

Smithsonian Archives/ Architectural History and Historic Preservation:
Bill Cox, Cynthia Field, Terrica Gibson, Susan Glenn, Bruce Kirby, Jay Orr, Kathleen Robertson, Richard Stamm, Paul Theerman, Lynn Wojcik, Ashley Wyant

Anacostia Museum:
Harold Dorwin, Zora Felton, Lauri Hinksman, Portia James, Sharon Reinckens

Conservation Analytical Lab:
Martha Goodway, Pamela B. Vandiver

Center for Folklife Programs and Cultural Studies:
Richard Kurin, Diana Parker

Cooper-Hewitt National Design Museum:
David McFadden, Milton Sonday, Marilyn Symmes, Joanne Warner

Freer Gallery of Art/Arthur M. Sackler Gallery:
Susan Bliss, W. Thomas Chase, Elizabeth Duley, Laveta Emory, Ann Gunter, Linda Merrill, Marianna Shreve Simpson, Jenny So, Jan Stuart, John G. Tsantes, Ann Yonemura

Hirshhorn Museum and Sculpture Garden:
Neal Benezra, Teresia Bush, Valerie Fletcher, Sidney Lawrence, Ann Steter

Museum Support Center:
Kerry Button, Harold Dougherty, Vincent Wilcox

National Air and Space Museum:
Mark Avino, Alfred Bachmeier, Paul Ceruzzi, Tim Cronen, Linda Ezell, John Clendening, Jeffrey Goldstein, Matt Greenhouse, Greg Herkin, Peter Jakab, Susan Lawson-Bell, Ed Marshall, Lars McLamore, Dominick Pisano, William Reese, Carolyn Russo, Howard Smith, Alex Spencer, Zabih Zadighian

National Museum of American Art:
Courtney De Angelis, Marianne Gurley, Kelly Johannes, Michael Monroe, Joan Stahl

National Museum of African Art:
Christraud Geary, Amy Staples

National Museum of American History:
Richard Ahlborn, David Allison, Carlene Barnard, Larry Bird, Stephanie Burnett, Betsy Burstein, Nancy Card, Michael Carrigan, Debbie Carter Griggs, Shirley Cherkasky, Richard Day, Michelle DeLaney, Odette Diaz, Jon Eklund, Kelly Fennell, Bernard Finn, John Fleckner, Susan Foster, Robert Harding, John Hasse, Kate Henderson, Barbara Janssen, David Jellama, Michael Jo, Paula Johnson, Paul Johnston, Ken Jordan, Kimberley Kelly, Peggy Kidwell, Harold Langley, Peter Liebhold, Jennifer Locke, Elizabeth McCullough, Densic Marshall, Denise Meringolo, Douglas Mudd, Craig Orr, Heather Paisley-Jones, Dina Rosenthal, Harry Rubinstein, Scott Schwartz, Chris Shaffer, Wendy Shay, David Shayt, Vanessa Simmons, Kenneth Slowik, Elvira Stefanelli, Carlene Stephens, John Stine, Gary Sturm, Susan Tolbert, Margaret Vining, Lynn Vosloh, Deborah Warner, James Weaver, Roger White, Polly Wilman, William Withhun, William Worthington, Jon Zackman

National Museum of the American Indian:
Laura Nash, Lou Stancari, Holly Stewart

National Museum of Natural History:
Cindy Ahearn, Michael Brett-Surman, Judy Cash, Jennifer Clark, Chip Clark, Roy Clarke, William Crocker, William Fitzhugh, Paula Fleming, Mark Florence, Fred Grady, M.G. Harasewych, Gary Hevel, John Homiak, Francis Hueber, Deborah Hull-Walsky, Adrian Jones, Rafael Lemaitre, Sally Love, James Luhr, Vichai Malikul, Ray Manning, Edward McCoy, Laura McKie, Joan Nowicke, Mary Pacaro, Mary Parrish, Felicia Pickering, Paul Pohwat, Richard Potts, Bob Purdy, Karen Reed, Clyde Roper, Raymond Rye, Marilyn Schotte, Gail Solomon, Dennis Stanford, Linda Stevens, Vyrtis Thomas, Jann Thompson, Douglas Ubelaker, Gus Van Beek, George Venable, Jane Walsh

National Portrait Gallery:
Joanna Britto, Cecilia Chin, Jean Fitzgerald

National Postal Museum:
Jim Bruns, Timothy Carr, Joe Geraci, Nancy Pope, Daisy Ridgway, Jack Vaughn

National Zoological Park:
Jessie Cohen, Robert Hoage, Suzi Hoffman, Kay Kenyon, Christen Wemmer

Office of Development:
Laura Russell

Office of Public Affairs:
Dan Agent, John Barratt,
Michelle Carr

Office of Plants Services:
Barbara Faust, Sung Kim

*Office of Printing and
Photographic Services*:
Lorie H. Aceto, David
Burgevin, Mary Ellen
McCaffery, Joyce
Goulait, Joe Goulait,
Donna Greene, Carl
Hansen, Eric Long, Terry
McCrea, Laurie Minor-
Penland, Diane Nordeck,
Nick Parrella, Dane
Penland, Terri Spruell,
Richard Strauss, Jeff
Tinsley, Ricardo Vargas,
James Wallace

Office of Protection Services:
Joanne Conatser, Willie
Kemp

*Smithsonian Astrophysical
Observatory*:
Julie Corliss

*Smithsonian Collection of
Recordings*:
Dennis Britton

*Smithsonian Environmental
Research Center*:
David Correll

*Smithsonian Institution
Libraries*:
Silvio Bedini, Timothy
Carr, Nancy Gwinn,
Nancy Matthews, Leslie
Overstreet, Barbara
Smith

*Smithsonian Institution
Traveling Exhibit Service*:
Liz Hill

Smithsonian Magazine:
Ruth Ravenel

*Smithsonian Tropical
Research Institute*:
Debra Casana, Mary Ann
Lindgren, Antonio
Montaner, Ann Rand, Ira
Rubinoff, Joseph Wright

ALSO:

Ross Chapple

Chicago Academy of Sciences:
Ron Vasile

Robert Elwood

Folk Masters:
Leslie Spitz-Edson

Foxes Music Company:
Kevin Landis

Library of Congress:
Sally Livingston

Crimilda Pontes

Mrs. Mary Livingston
Ripley

Warren M. Robbins

*U.S. Holocaust
Memorial Museum*:
Jeffrey LaRiche

U.S. Patent Office:
Jim Bradley, Jim Davie

Michael Ventura

Bill Yardley

*PRODUCTION
ASSISTANCE:*

Ecological Fibers, Inc.:
George Hall

*RR Donnelley & Sons
Company.:*
Ron Heyman, Cliff
Mears, Gary Ryman,
Shirley Schulz

Holliston
Rick Busick

The Lanman Companies
Stan Boone, Bob Crooks,
T. Halter Cunningham,
Bill Dingle, Carole Gates,
John Rosquist, Steve
Schwacke, Dick Sheats,
David Sterling, Michael
Wight

*Reiner Design Consultants,
Inc.*
Roger Gorman,
Hannah Leider

ResourceNet International
Jerry Benitez

The Editors extend their
apologies to anyone
whose name has been
inadvertently omitted.

PICTURE CREDITS

Legend: B Bottom; C Center; L Left; R Right; T Top

The following are abbreviations used to identify Smithsonian Institution museums and bureaus. Negative numbers appear between parentheses.

SI Smithsonian Institution

AAA Archives of American Art

A&I Arts & Industries

AMSG Arthur M. Sackler Gallery

C-H Cooper-Hewitt National Design Museum

FGA Freer Gallery of Art

HMSG Hirshhorn Museum & Sculpture Garden

NAA National Anthropological Archives

NASM National Air & Space Museum

NMAfA National Museum of African Art

NMAA National Museum of American Art

NMAH National Museum of American History

NMAI National Museum of the American Indian

NMNH National Museum of Natural History

NPM National Postal Museum

NPG National Portrait Gallery

NZP National Zoological Park

SAO Smithsonian Astrophysical Observatory

SIA Smithsonian Institution Archives

SIL Smithsonian Institution Libraries

Front Matter: p.1 Chip Clark, NMNH/SI; 2 Carl Hansen/SI [89-11008]; 3 FGA/SI [74.21]; 4 Dane Penland, NMAH/SI [78.1385]; 5 *Eye of a Lady* c. 1800 NMAA/SI, gift of John Gellatly; 6–7 Jeff Tinsley/SI [93-3910F]; 7 Joe Goulait/SI [89-5784]; 8 Richard Strauss, NMAH/SI [89-6756]; 9 Mark Avino, NASM/SI.

Introduction: pp.10–11 Clyde Roper, NMNH/SI; 12T Chip Clark, NMNH/SI [77-10004]; 12B Rembrandt Peale, *George Washington*, NPG/SI [NPG.75.4]; 13 Dane Penland, NMNH/SI [78-3986].

I Bright Lamps, Bold Adventure: 1846–1878:
pp.14–15 Library of Congress; 16 Chip Clark, NMNH/SI; 17 Aquatint, from a sketch by Cornelius B. Hulsart, Peabody Museum of Salem.

A Gift: pp. 18 SI [79-11648]; 19 Jeff Ploskonka/SI [82-14343]; 21L Alfred Harrell/SI [72-3961A]; 21R Erich Lessing/Art Resource, NY; 22 Johns, *Smithson, James*, NPG/SI [S/NPG.85-44]; 22–23 Erich Lessing/Art Resource, NY; 24–25 Jean Baptiste Genillion, *Eruption of Vesuvius*, Musee des Beaux-Arts, Lille, France, photo by Giraudon/Art Resource, NY; 27 SIL/SI, photo by Mark Gulezian/QuickSilver; 28,29 Chip Clark, NMNH/SI; 30 NMNH/SI, photo by Ross Chapple; 31T Larry Gates SIL/SI [90-15791]; 31B Larry Gates SIL/SI [94-13485]; 32 White House Historical Association; 33 Library of Congress; 34 Background Alfred Harrell/SI [72-3960]; insert Richard Strauss/SI [95-3469]; 35T SI [73-10118]; 35B SI [19645]; 37 Richard Strauss/SI [95-3573-E]; 38 Gift of Mrs. Joseph Harrison, Jr., NMAA/SI [1985.66.129]; 39 George Catlin, *George Catlin from Catlin Sketchbook*, The Thomas Gilcrease Institute of American History and Art, Tulsa; 40 SI [3667]; 41 Victor Krantz/SI [93-2188].

A Hole in the Floor: pp.42 SI; 43 SI; 44–45 Richard K. Hofmeister, NMAH/SI [74-4488]; 45 Alfred Harrell/SI [72-3962]; 46 SI [19072]; 47T NMAH/SI, Pat Lanza; 47BL Terry McCrea/SI [90-15620]; 47BR SIL/SI, photo by Mark Gulezian/Quicksilver; 48,49 NMNH/SI, photos by Michael Ventura; 50 Richard Strauss, NMAH/SI [95-3566]; 51T Diane Nordeck/SI [91-7345]; 51B Steve Lubar *Engines of Change: An Exhibition on the American Industrial Revolution* NMAH/SI; 52–53 Library of Congress [LC-B8 184 BH33]; 53 SI [75629]; 54 Terry McCrea/SI [93-2053]; 54–55 Richard Strauss/SI [95-2250-4]; 56T SI [82-3228]; 56B SI [3251]; 58 Titus Lucretius Carus. *De rerum natura liber* [Book on the nature of things]. Verona, 1486. Gift of the Burndy Library. photo by Terry McCrea SIL/SI; 59L Jeff Tinsley/SI [93-116-14]; 59TR John Coakley Lettsom. *The naturalist's and traveller's companion, containing instructions for collecting & preserving objects of natural history*. 2nd edition, corrected and enlarged. London, 1774. From the Charles W. Richmond collection. Photo by Rick Vargas SIL/SI [95-1614]; 59BR SIL/SI [SA 841]; 60 Willy Ley. *Die Möglichkeit der Weltraum-Fahrt* [The feasibility of interplanetary travel]. Leipzig, 1928. SIL, NASM/SI; 61 Sears, Roebuck & Co. *Honor-bilt modern homes*. [Chicago], 1930. photo by Terry McCrea SIL/SI [93-691]; 62 SIA/SI photo by Michael Ventura; 62–63 SI [6085]; 64 SI [56814]; 64–65 From *Reports of Explorations and Surveys*, v. 11, Washington DC, 1855. SIL/SI, photo by Ed Castle; 66 Courtesy, Peabody Essex Museum, Salem, Mass.; 67 Eric Long /SI [94-5982]; 68 Richard Strauss/SI [90-5495-18]; 69T SIL/SI, photo by Michael Ventura; 69B Terry McCrea, NMAH/SI [91-2965]; 70 Rick Vargas, NMAH/SI [95-3558]; 71 NMNH/SI, photo by Ed Castle.

To the Territories: pp. 72 NMNH/SI, photo by Michael Ventura; 73 NMNH/SI, photo by Ross Chapple; 74–75 Art by Albert Herter, photo by Carol Highsmith, Courtesy of National Academy of Sciences Press; 76T SI; 76B SIA/SI, photo by Michael Ventura; 77 Detail, Bequest of Henry Ward Ranger through the National Academy of Design, NMAA/SI [1936.12.4]; 78T Burroughs Collection, The Bostonian Society; 78B Larry Gates/SI [95-1933]; 78–79T Eric Long/SI [95-1155-10]; 78–79B Robert Myers/SI [75-298]; 80T J.J. Young from a sketch by H.B. Mollhausen, *Chimney Peak*, photo by Ed Castle/SI; 80B J. Hudson Snowden, *Bugcatching*, photo by Ed Castle, National Archives; 81 John Mix Stanley, *Buffalo Hunt on the Southwestern Prairie*, NMAA/SI [1985.66.248,932] Gift of the Misses Henry (daughters of Joseph Henry), 1908; 82T Library of Congress; 82B NMAA/SI, lent by the US Dept. of the Interior; 83 NMNH/SI, photo by Ed Castle; 85T SI [1237]; 85B SI [71-988]; 86 Chip Clark, NMNH/SI; 87L SI [43604]; 87R Joe A. Goulait/SI [82-13315]; 88-89T Joe A. Goulait/SI [88-1654]; 88-89B Eric Long/SI [92-16888]; 89B Larry Gates/SI [94-523]; 90 National Archives; 91 NPG/SI [NPG.68.51]; 92,93 NMAH/SI, photos by Mark Gulezian/QuickSilver; 94,95 SI, photo by Michael Ventura; 96 Kim Nielsen NMAH/SI [83-3047]; 97 Richard Strauss/SI [94-12479]; 98 Alfred Harrell/SI [74-11031]; 99 Alexander Gardner, NPG/SI [NPG.81.M1]; 100–101 Transfer from the National Gallery of Art; gift of Andrew W. Mellon, 1942, NPG/SI [NPG.65.60]; 102 SIA/SI, photo by Michael Ventura; 103 Illustration by George Venable, NMNH/SI; 105T SIA/SI [58765]; 105B Richard Strauss/SI [95-3572-A];

107 Joe A. Goulait/SI [88-1608]; 108–109 NAA/SI [1591]; 110T Thomas Moran, *View from Powell's Plateau*, 1873, Gift of Thomas Moran, photo by Ken Pelka, C-H/SI/Art Resource, NY; 110B Larry Gates/SI [94-2019]; 111 SI [56-331].

Centennial: pp. 112 John Steiner/SI [86-930]; 113 A&I/SI, photo by Robert C. Lautman; 114 Diane Nordeck/SI [91-7356]; 115 Larry Gates/SI [94-5808]; 116 SI [72-2375]; 116–117 SI [76-4464]; 118–119 Michael Lawton/Grafica; 119T SI [81-11824]; 119B John Frazee papers, Archives of American Art/SI; 120 Michael Lawton/Grafica; 121 SI [81-11817]; 123T Alfred Harrell/SI [76-2655]; 123BL SI; 123BR Rick Vargas/SI [95-3552]; 124T A.J. Russell, The Oakland Museum (History Department) of California; 124B SI [76-2962-25A]; 125L Joe A. Goulait/SI [91-13665]; 125R Michael Lawton/Grafica; 126 Richard Strauss NMAH/SI [91-6511]; 127 Richard Strauss NMAH/SI [91-6524]; 128T Robert C. Lautman; 128B SI, photo by Andy Russetti [92-6610]; 128–129 Charles H. Phillips; 130 NMNH/SI [72-9313]; 131 insert, Eugene Mantie NPG/SI [76-6997]; 131 background, University Microfilms International; 132–133 Joe A. Goulait [89-08911]; 35T Paul Takacs; 135B SI [4995]; 136 A&I/SI, photo by Robert C. Lautman; 137 A&I/SI, photo by Charles H. Phillips; 138L SIA/SI, photo by Michael Ventura; 138R NMAA, NMNH/SI; 138–139 *Smithsonian Butte* by William Henry Holmes. From Clarence E. Dutton *Tertiary History of the Grand Cañon and Atlas* 1882. Monograph of the U.S. Geological Survey, v.11. SIL/SI, photo by Ed Castle; 139 SIL/SI, photo by Ed Castle.

II Universe: 1879–1949: pp.140–141 illustration by Montgomery Meigs/SI; 142–143 Painting by Robert Sivard, gift of the Robert Sivard family, photo by Larry Gates/SI [95-3262].

The Americans: pp. 144 Lelia/FOLIO; 145 SI [75-3338];

146 NMNH/SI [54857]; 146–147 NAA/NMNH/SI [64-A]; 149T NMNH/SI, photo by Ed Castle; 149BL NAA/NMNH/SI [55755]; 149BR Larry Gates/SI [93-7501]; 150 NAA/NMNH/SI [22-G]; 150–151 NAA/NMNH/SI [22-A]; 152 SI [78165]; 153 SI [9307]; 154 NMNH/SI, photo by Charles H. Phillips; 155 Chip Clark NMNH/SI; 156 Office of Architectural History/SI; 157 SI [75-15856]; 158L Terry McCrea/SI [91-13224]; 158TR Eric Long/SI [92-1467]; 158BR Diane Nordeck/SI [91-4147]; 159 SI [78-5099]; 160–161 SI [11805]; 162T Dane Penland/SI [86-15283]; 162B Charles H. Phillips; 163L Richard Strauss/SI [91-6526]; 163R SI [SA-747]; 164–165 SI [16238]; 166 SIA/SI, photo by Michael Ventura; 166–167 SIA/SI [10715]; 167 SIA/SI, photo by Michael Ventura; 168 NAA/NMNH/SI [18041]; 169 NAA/NMNH/SI.

Icarus on the Mall: pp. 170 NMAH/SI, photo by Ross Chapple; 171 Richard Farrar/SI [76-5925]; 172 SI [A-3590]; 172–173 NMAH/SI, photo by Ed Castle; 174–175 SIA/SI, photo by Michael Ventura; 175T NASM/SI; 175B NASM/SI [72-8385]; 176–177T NZP/SI; 176–177B SI [75-1755]; 177 SIA/SI, photo by Michael Ventura; 178T,178C SIA/SI, photos by Michael Ventura; 178B Library of Congress; 179L From *Alaska; History, Geography, Resources, v. II*, by William H. Dall, New York, Doubleday, Page & Company, 1902, SIL/SI, photo by Michael Ventura; 179R SIA/SI, photo by Michael Ventura; 180–181 Diane Norbeck/SI [MISC-9]; 181 Sagamore Hill National Historic Site, National Park Service; 182L NMNH/SI, photo by Ross Chapple; 182R Laurie Minor-Penland/SI; 183L Dane Penland/SI; 183R From *Annual Report of the Board of Regents of the Smithsonian Institution*, 1901; Washington Government Printing Office, 1902, SI, photo by Michael Ventura; 185 Rick Vargas/SI [91-9808]; 186 NASM/SI [A18887]; 187L Charles H. Phillips; 187R Mark Avino, NASM/SI [94-8252]; 189L NASM/SI [A18824]; 189T

NASM/SI [A18861]; 189B NASM/SI [A30162]; 190 NASM/SI [A44046A]; 191 Carolyn Russo/SI [92-2946]; 192–193T Dane Penland, NASM/SI [79-5758]; 192–193B Carolyn Russo, NASM/SI; 193BL SIA/SI, photo by Michael Ventura; 193BR SI; 195TL Mark Avino/SI [85-9004]; 195BL SI [1130-11A]; 195TR,CR,BR Peter Jakab, NASM/SI; 196 SIA/SI, photo by Michael Ventura; 197 NMNH/SI, photo by Ed Castle; 198L NAA/NMNH/SI [55375]; 198,199 From *Twenty-second Annual Report of the Bureau of American Ethnology*, 1900–1901, J.W. Powell, Director, Washington Government Printing Office, 1904, SIL/SI, photos by Michael Ventura.

Voice from the Cambrian: pp. 200 SI [82-3144]; 201 ©John Sibbick, reproduced courtesy of Boxtree Limited, UK; 202 Joe A. Goulait/SI; 203 Chip Clark/SI; 204 Chip Clark/SI; 205 Lorie H. Aceto NMNH/SI [85-4049]; 206L Chip Clark NMNH/SI; 206T SI [82-3231]; 206B Chip Clark NMNH/SI; 207 NMNH/SI, photo by Dennis Brack/Black Star; 208 Eric Long/SI [90-2509]; 209T Eric Long/SI [92-15252-16]; 209BL Richard Strauss/SI [95-1914]; 209BR SI, photo by Michael Ventura; 210 Joe A. Goulait/SI [84-6676]; 211T Insert Joe A. Goulait/SI [84-6677]; 211B Background Dane Penland/SI [82-12235]; 213T Mark Avino NASM/SI [89-22371]; 213BL SI, photo by Charles H. Phillips; 213BR SI; 214 Robert Meyers/SI [74-9415]; 214–215 Terry McCrea/SI [92-2913]; 215T Robert Meyers/SI [74-9438]; 215B Eric Long/SI [91-9496]; 216–217 NAA/NMNH/SI, photo by Michael Ventura; 218 Mark Avino, NASM/SI [92-13510]; 219T NASM/SI, photo by Ross Chapple; 219B NASM/SI [A33465-A]; 220 SI [79-317]; 221 Chip Clark/SI; 222–223 Hugh Talman NAA/NMNH/SI [93-14067]; 224L Courtesy of Robert Purdy; 224TR Alfred Eisenstaedt, *LIFE* magazine, ©Time Inc.; 224CR SI [78-8853]; 224BR Chip Clark NMNH/SI; 225TL Lucerne Robert *Bern Dibner*, c.1957, David Dibner Collection, Jeff Tinsley SIL/SI [93-12977];

225BL SIL/SI, photo by Mark Gulezian/Quicksilver; 225TR Foto Olaf St. Moritz; 225BR Lynn Vosloh NMAH/SI; 226TL Mary Vaux Walcott, *Yellow Dryad (Dryas Drummondii)*, NMAA/SI Transfer from Smithsonian Institution Archives, [1970.355.702]; 226BL SI [88-7391]; 226–227 SIA/SI, photo by Michael Ventura; 228 SI, photo by Charles Phillips; 229T National Aeronautics and Space Administration, photo courtesy of Mrs. Esther C. Goddard [74-H-1215]; 229B NASM/SI [A624-B]; 230 The Goddard Library, Clark University; 231 The Goddard Collection, Clark University.

Celestial, Terrestrial: pp. 232 SI [32227]; 233 Mark Avino, SIL/SI [85-12214]; 234–235 SI [33668A]; 237L Dwight Bowman/SI [80-4951]; 237R Richard Strauss/SI [94-4039]; 238 NMNH/SI, photo by Michael Anderson; 239 Doug Ubelaker, NMNH/SI; 240 FGA/SI; 241 FGA/SI; 242TL Bella Landauer Sheet Music Collection, SIL NASM/SI; 242BL NASM/SI, photo by Ed Castle; 242TR NASM/SI [A746-C]; 242CR Mark Avino, NASM/SI [93-5867]; 242BR Mark Avino, NASM/SI [93-5869]; 243 SI, photo by Ed Castle; 244–245 *Superman* is a trademark of DC Comics ©1987; 244L Mark Avino, NASM/SI [93-1078]; 244C Dane Penland/SI [86-11313]; 244R Mark Avino, NASM/SI [93-15839]; 245T SI [73-8062]; 245B Mark Avino, NASM/SI [93-5404]; 246 Alfred Harrell/SI [74-797]; 247T Jeff Ploskonka/SI [81-5294A] ©Turner Broadcasting Inc.; 247BL Richard Smart/SI [94-10175]; 247BR Rick Vargas/SI [94-13679] Gift of the Walt Disney Company; 248 Kim Nielsen/SI [86-878]; 249T Kim Nielsen/SI [83-7967]; 249BL Eric Long and Jeff Tinsley/SI [95-3545]; 249BR Terry McCrea/SI [93-1773]; 250–251 NMAH/SI, photos by Ross Chapple; 252 Jeff Tinsley/SI [82-13467]; 253T Eric Long/SI [95-3340]; 253B Eric Long/SI [95-3341]; 254 Diane Nordeck/SI [91-7421]; 254–255 C-H/SI [1969-137-3]; 256 NMAH/SI [66677]; 257 FDR

Library, National Archives, SI [88-5339]; 258 SI; 258–259 Mark Avino, NASM/SI; 260–261 Keith Ferris, NASM/SI [92-6535]; 261 NASM/SI, photo by Ross Chapple; 262 NASM/SI, photo by Michael Ventura; 263 NASM/SI, photos by Ross Chapple; 265 Mark Avino, NASM/SI; 266 Eric Long/SI [93-10496]; 267T Jeff Goldstein, NASM/SI; 267B Matt Greenhouse, NASM/SI; 268 Richard Strauss/SI [95-3575-A #2]; 268–269 NMAH/SI, photo by Ross Chapple; 271T SIA/SI, photo by Michael Ventura; 271BL NMNH/SI, photo by Carl Fries; 271BR SIA/SI, photo by Michael Ventura.

III The Living Museum: 1950–1966: pp. 272–273 Fred Maroon/FOLIO; 274 Jeff Tinsley/SI; 275 SI, photo by Chip Clark.

Stirrings: pp. 276 SI [79-7800]; 277 SI [17021]; 278T SIA/SI, photo by Michael Ventura; 278B Chip Clark, NMNH/SI; 279 Art by George Venable, NMNH/SI; 280 Chip Clark, NMNH/SI; 281L John Steiner/SI; 281R Arthur Rackham, *Little Miss Muffet, Mother Goose*, photo by Terry McCrea/SI [90-1562]; 282 NMNH/SI, photo by Ross Chapple; 282–283 SI [49366-A]; 284–285 Eric Long/SI [89-5015]; 286T Terry McCrea/SI [90-5314]; 286B Terry McCrea/SI [93-2778]; 286–287 Alan Hart/SI [77-14863]; 287 Eric Long/SI [94-11176]; 288T Terry McCrea/SI [91-11800]; 288BR Terry McCrea/SI [90-16298]; 289 Terry McCrea/SI [93-2501]; 290–291 SI [79-11047]; 291TC Hugh Talman/SI [95-3584]; 291BC Larry Gates/SI [95-3397]; 291R Jeff Tinsley/SI [87-8780]; 292T Laurie Minor-Penland/SI [92-14915]; 292–293 NMAA/SI [NC-276]; 293 Eric Long/SI [93-975]; 294 National Geographic Society Image Collection; 296 Chip Clark NMNH/SI; 296–297 Jenny Clark NMNH/SI; 298T Chip Clark NMNH/SI; 298B Diane Nordeck/SI [90-6151]; 299 Art by John Gurche, photo by Chip Clark NMNH/SI; 300T Laurie Minor/SI [89-19699]; 300B

Richard K. Hofmeister/SI [77-3569]; 301 Dane Penland/SI [92-13642]; 302 Mark Avino, NASM/SI; 302–303 Dale E. Hrabak/SI [91-16258]; 304–305T Dane Penland, SAO/SI [85-2563 x24A25]; 304C SAO/SI; 304B SAO, photo by Lori Stiles; 304–305B SAO/SI [82-1110]; 305 SAO/SI [85-1158]; 307TL NASM/SI [66-HC-714]; 307BL C-H/SI Gift of Ludmilla Shapiro; 307R Suzanne Bono/SI [88-11917]; 308,309 Greg Herken, NASM/SI; 310 SAO/SI, Harvard College Observatory [7604.30D]; 311,313 SAO/SI.

A Wind in the Attic: pp. 314 Richard Howard; 315 Illustration by Richard Thompson ©1985, photo by Larry Gates/SI; 316 SI; 317 Jeff Ploskonka/SI; 318,319 photo by Ross Chapple; 320–321 Lynn Sahaydak; 321 SI [77-4393-32]; 322 NPM/SI; 323T Larry Gates NPM/SI [94-8362/4]; 323C NASM/SI, photo by Ed Castle; 323B,324 NPM/SI; 324–325 Alfred Harrell/SI [74-4921]; 326 NMAH/SI, photo by Pat Lanza; 327 NMAH/SI, photo by Ross Chapple; 328 Larry Gates/SI [94-5241]; 328–329 Eric Long/SI [90-7407]; 330–331T,B SI, copy photo by Michael Ventura, 331 FGA-AMSG/SI [5790912 #3-1]; 332T SI [87-17335]; 332B Dane Penland/SI [87-17335]; 333 Harold Dorwin, Anacostia Museum/SI; 334–335 John N. Robinson, *Here, Look at Mine*, 1980, Anacostia Museum/SI, photo by Harold Dorwin; 336–337 Tim Motion; 336B Linoleum print by Peter Bodge, *Meditation*, 1987, NMAH/SI; 337B Jeff Polonska/SI [86-11768]; 339TL ©Arnold Newman; 339TR Fernando Botero, *The Hunter*, 1980, photo by Lee Stalsworth, HMSG/SI [80.111]; 339B Edward Hopper, *City Sunlight*, 1954, photo by Lee Stalsworth, HMSG/SI [66.2505]; 341T SIA/SI; 341B James P. Blair/National Geographic Society Image Collection; 342–343 Arnold Newman, *Igor Feodorovich Stravinsky*, ©1974, NPG/SI; 343 Winold Reiss *Langston Hughes*, c.1925, NPG/SI Gift of W. Tjarh Reiss in memory of his father, Winold Reiss; 344T Larry Fuente, *Game Fish*,

1988, NMAA/SI, photo by Bruce Miller, gift of the James Renwick Alliance; 344B John F. Kennedy Library; 344–345 Dale Chihuly, *Dale Chihuly Installation at the Renwick Gallery*, May 1994, photo by Mildred Baldwin, Renwick, NMAA/SI; 346 Ferdinand Petrie, gift of Mrs. Milton Turner, courtesy of the Office of Architectural History and Historic Preservation; Castle Collection/SI; 347 Harvey Kline Littleton, *Four Seasons*, 1977, NMAA/SI; 349 Luis Jimenez, *Vaquero*, 1980, NMAA/SI gift of Judith and Wilbur L. Ross, Jr., Anne and Ronald Abramson, Thelma and Melvin Lenkin; 350 Mark Avino NASM/SI [92-14517]; 350–351 NASM/SI, photo by Ross Chapple; 352 Fred Maroon/FOLIO; 353 NASM/SI, photo by Ross Chapple.

Noon Over the Mall: pp. 354 John Eisenberg photo, *Smithsonian* magazine, April 1970, copy photo by Michael Ventura; 355 NMNH/SI, photo by Ross Chapple, (foreground) John C. Anderton's illustrations for the forthcoming book *A Field Guide to the Birds of South Asia*, to be published by the University of Texas Press, 1997; 356T Illustration by G.B. Crockett ©1968, photo by Michael Ventura; 356CL Richard Hofmeister/SI [76-6222-14A]; 356–357 NMNH/SI, photo by Ross Chapple; 358 Bequest of the Reverend Alfred Duane Pell, by transfer from the NMAH, C-H/SI, photo by Dennis Cowley, Art Resource, NY; 359TL Wurts Brothers, NYC ©1915, C-H/SI; 359BL C-H/SI; 359R Steve Tague, C-H/SI [S0054107]; 360L Richard Notkin, *Hexagonal Landform Teapot*, 20th c., C-H/SI [1985-59-1]; 360R Claude Lalanne, *Place Setting*, 1966, The Decorative Arts Association Acquisition Fund in honor of John L. Marion, C-H/SI photo by John White; 361 Tone Vigeland, *Necklace, 1983*, C-H/SI, photo by John White; 362–363 Kjell B. Sandved/SI; 363 Chip Clark/SI; 364 Jeff Tinsley/SI; 365 Robert Llewellyn; 366 Dennis Brack/Black Star; 367 NMAfA/SI; 368,369 Eliot Elisofon, Eliot Elisofon Photographic Archives,

NMAfA/SI; 369 Franko Khoury, NMAfA/SI; 370 Pilipili Mulongoy, *Pintades*, c. 1950, photo by Franko Khoury, NMAfA/SI; 371 Gift of Evelyn A. J. Hall and John Friede, photo by Franko Khoury, NMAfA/SI; 372 John Neubauer; 373L Daphne Shuttleworth, from: *Aditi: The Living Arts of India*, Smithsonian Institution ©1985; 373TR Jeff Tinsley/SI [82-9372]; 374–375 Reed & Susan Erskine/Lightworks; 375 AMSG/SI; 376–377 Chick Harrity/*U.S. News and World Report*; 378–379 AMSG/SI; 380T National Geographic Society Collection; 380B Jessie Cohen, NZP/SI; 381 NZP/SI [1390]; 382 Jessie Cohen, NZP/SI; 383 Margaret Thomas.

Continuum: pp. 384 Jeff Ploskonka/SI [85-430]; 385 Kim Nielsen/SI [78-8743]; 387T William Fitzhugh; 387B Arctic Studies Center, Department of Anthropology, NMNH/SI; 388,389 Carl Hansen/SI; 390 Joe Goodwin/SI; 391,392,393L NMAI/SI, photos by David Heald; 393TR NMAI/SI, photo by Karen Furth; 393BR SI [78-18834]; 394 NMAI/SI, photos by David Heald; 395 NMAI/SI [36101]; 396 Carl Hansen/SI; 397 STRI/SI, photo by Tetsuya Sato, Think Bit Corporation; 398 STRI/SI, photos by George Steinmetz; 399 Carl Hansen/SI; 400 Chip Clark NMNH/SI; 401 Mary Sue Socky; 402L Robert Strauss/SI [95-1380-2]; 402C Michael Ventura; 402RB Jessie Cohen NZP/SI; 402 other Chip Clark; 404–405 ©1994 Roger Ressmeyer/Starlight; 407 NMAH/SI, photo by Ross Chapple; 408L SI; 408R Harold "Doc" Dougherty/SI; 409 Kim Nielsen/SI; 410,411 Jessie Cohen, NZP/SI; 412–413 NZP/SI, photo by Gary Jacob; 415L Chip Clark, NMNH/SI; 415R Clyde Roper/SI; 416–417 ©Kjell B. Sandved; 417 Laurie Minor-Penland/SI; 418–419, 419T photos by Pat Vosburgh; 419B Illustration by Elizabeth Gould. From *A Monograph of the Trogonidae, or family of trogons*, 1835–1838, by John Gould, SIL/SI, photo by Mark Gulezian/Quicksilver; 420–421 NMAH/SI, ©Henson Associates, Inc. 1980.

INDEX

The Smithsonian was designed by Roger Gorman with the assistance of Hannah Leider at Reiner Design Consultants, Inc., New York, NY. Digital-type composition and page layout were originated on an Apple Macintosh Quadra 650 utilizing QuarkXPress. The text type is 10pt Latin 725 BT with 8pt Trade Gothic Bold Condensed captions. Color separation and film output were provided by The Lanman Companies, Washington, D.C. Five-color web printing and Smythe-sewn binding were done at RR Donnelley & Sons Company, Willard, OH, on 80# Warren Web Gloss. The endsheets are Ecological Fibers 80# Rainbow Antique, and the book cloth is Holliston Kingston. Jackets and onlays were printed by Phoenix Color, Hagerstown, MD.